Pages 59/60 mi

297-041

D0494622

WITHDRAWN

'9 JUN 2022

140691

SECTARIAN INFLUENCES
WITHIN ISLAM IN BRITAIN
with reference to the concepts of
'ummah' and 'community'

Ron Geaves

Monograph Series
Community Religions Project

Department of Theology and Religious Studies
University of Leeds

1996

This is the fifth in a series of monographs produced by the Community Religions Project in the Department of Theology and Religious Studies at the University of Leeds.

The Community Religions Project is a research group committed to working on contemporary issues related to religions in Britain, particularly those of relevance to ethnic communities. In addition to the production of monographs, it publishes a series of research papers. A list of titles appears at the back of this volume. For further information on the work of the Community Religions Project, contact Dr. Kim Knott, Community Religions Project, Department of Theology and Religious Studies, University of Leeds, LS2 9JT.

Series editor: Kim Knott
Project Secretary: Jill Killington

This monograph is based on a PhD thesis submitted to the University of Leeds in 1994

Contents

ACKNOWLEDGEMENTS

CHAPTER I INTRODUCTION

Aims and Objectives   1
Methodology: Research Strategies and Fieldwork   2
Transcription and Technical Terms   5
Title and Contents   7
Endnotes   8

CHAPTER II THE CONCEPT OF COMMUNITY IN ISLAM

Introduction   10
The Qur'an   11
Mecca and Medina   14
The Umayyad and Abbasid Dynasties   16
The Caliphate   18
Islah and Tajdid   21
The Impact of Europe   23
Conclusion   26
Endnotes   28

CHAPTER III A SOCIOLOGICAL ANALYSIS OF UMMAH

Introduction   41
Sociological Analysis of Ummah   41
The Rural and Urban Divide   42
Muslim Minority Communities   43
Sociological Analysis of Community   44
Conclusion   47
Endnotes   48

CHAPTER IV ISLAM IN BRITAIN

Introduction   52
First Generation Migrants v. Later British-Born
Generations   57
Women v. Patriarchal Structures of Asian Society   59
Secular Education v. Religious Education   61
Integration v. Assimilation   64
Sufism v. Reform Islam   65
Status within Migrant Community v. Class Position
in British Society   66
Regional Languages v. English   68
Majority v. Minority (Racism)   69
Dar al-Islam v. Dar al-Harb   70
Ethnicity v. Islam   71
Individual v. Community   74
Tradition v. Modernity   75

Fundamentalism v. Secularisation   76
Conclusion   78
Endnotes   80

CHAPTER V BARELWIS IN THE SUBCONTINENT

Introduction   91
Sufis and Shrines   91
Local Customs   93
The Barelwis   95
Conclusion   96
Endnotes   98

CHAPTER VI BARELWIS IN BRITAIN

Introduction   100
The Barelwi Imam   106
The Living Pir   109
The History of the Tariqa   110
Personal Impressions of Sufi Abdullah   112
The Special features of Worship (Adab)   113
Other Features of the Dar ul Uloom Islamia   115
Sajjada Nashin   118
Biography of Sultan Bahu   119
The Sultan Bahu Trust in Birmingham   119
The Religious Practices Unique to Sultan Bahu   121
Conclusion   122
Endnotes   126

CHAPTER VII THE RISE OF THE ISLAMIC REFORM
MOVEMENTS IN INDIA AND THEIR ROLE
FOR MUSLIMS IN BRITAIN

Introduction   130
The Origins of the Reform Movement: Akbar and Sirhindi   130
Shah Wali-allah (1702-1763)   131
The Issuing of Fatwas   133
Sayyid Ahmad of Rae Bareilly   134
Strategies Towards the British   135
The Relevance of the Reformers in Britain   137
Conclusion   138
Endnotes   140

CHAPTER VIII NINETEETH CENTURY REFORM MOVEMENTS

Introduction   145
Development in the Subcontinent Reform Movement Prior
to the Establishment of Deoband   145
Delhi College   146
Deoband   147
Tabligh-i Jamaat   152
Conclusion   154
Endnotes   156

CHAPTER IX THE REFORM MOVEMENT IN BRITAIN

Deobandis in Britain	159
Deobandi Dar al Ulums in Britain	164
The Problem of Deobandi Isolationism	166
Deoband and Tabligh-i Jamaat	168
Conclusion	172
Endnotes	174

CHAPTER X *JAMAAT-I ISLAMI* - INDIA AND PAKISTAN

Introduction	180
Pakistan	180
Maulana Mawdudi - A Brief Biography	182
The Ideas of Maulana Mawdudi	183
Jamaat-i Islami - A Vehicle for Mawdudi's Ideas	185
The Organisational Structure of Jamaat-i Islami	186
Islami Jami'at-i Talaba	188
Jamaat-i Islami Hind	189
Jamaat-i Islami in Pakistan Today	190
Endnotes	193

CHAPTER XI *JAMAAT-I ISLAMI* IN BRITAIN

Introduction	198
The UK Islamic Mission	199
The Islamic Foundation	202
Young Muslims UK	206
The Muslim Educational Trust	208
Conclusion	208
Endnotes	210

CHAPTER XII CONCLUSION

CHAPTER XII CONCLUSION	214
Endnotes	226
APPENDIX A *The Occurrence of Ummah in the Qur'an*	227
APPENDIX B *The Constitution of Medina*	229
APPENDIX C *Salaam*	232
APPENDIX D *The Spiritual Genealogy of the Naqshbandi Sufi Order of Ghamkol Sharif, Kohat, Pakistan*	235
APPENDIX E The Genealogy of the Reform Movements tracing their origins to Shah Wali-allah	240
APPENDIX F *The Curriculum of Dar al-Ulum Deoband*	241
APPENDIX G *The Constitution of the Islami Jamiat-e Talaba Pakistan*	247
APPENDIX H *The Constitution of the UK Islamic Mission*	273
APPENDIX I *The Constitution of Islamic Society of Britain*	286
GLOSSARY	293
BIBLIOGRAPHY	302

Acknowledgements

I would like to acknowledge the financial assistance of the *British Academy* which enabled me to carry out research in Britain and the subcontinent. I thank my two supervisors, Kim Knott and Neal Robinson. The former for her patience in dealing with the occasional physical and emotional crises I experienced in the duration of this thesis as well as her invaluable academic assistance. The latter I thank for his instruction in Islamic Studies. I am also indebted to Tony St.Quintin who came to my aid to resolve severe computer problems and to Jane Sand for her help in proof-reading. She also picked up the pieces when things went wrong. Further invaluable proof-reading services were provided by Catherine Barnes at the time of producing this Monograph. Special thanks must go to Neil North for sharing with me his contacts within the Muslim community in Birmingham and providing a taxi service.

Finally, I would like to acknowledge the co-operation and hospitality of all the Muslims I interviewed in Britain, Pakistan and India. In this context, I am especially grateful to Shaikh Niyamatullah, *Shaikh al-Hadith* of *Deoband dar al-Ulum*; Muhammad Aslam Saleemi, Secretary-General of *Jamaat-i Islami Pakistan*; Ishtiaq Gondal of the *Islami Jamiat-i Talaba Pakistan*; Ejaz Ahmed Aslam, Secretary-General *Jamaat-i Islami Hind*; S.M. Tanzeem Wasti, Secretary-General of the *UK Islamic Mission*; Dr.Manozir Ahsan, President of the *Islamic Foundation*; Wasim Yaqub and Rukhsar Shafiq of *Young Muslims UK*; Abid Hussein of the *Dar ul-Uloom Islamia*; Muhammad Saleem Akhtar, President of the *Configuration of Sunni Mosques Midlands*; Imam Pirzade of the *Sultan Bahu Trust*; Yousef Kamaur, Director of the *Asian Advisory Centre*, Birmingham;Maulana Noor Ul Aqtab Siddiqi of the *International Muslim Organisation*; Sher Azam of the *Bradford Council of Mosques*; Maulana Shahid Raza Khan, Executive-Secretary of the *Shari'ah Council*; and Dr.Zaki Badawi. There are many more I could mention whose names are not acknowledged for reasons of space. I apologise for their omission but hope that they are aware of my gratitude.

1 Introduction

Aims and Objectives

This thesis was written as a contribution to the Community Religions Project (CRP) as based in the Department of Theology and Religious Studies at the University of Leeds. The CRP studies contemporary minority faith communities in Britain and publishes a series of monographs and research papers.[1] I chose to do my M.A. in Religious Studies at the University of Leeds (1988) specifically because of the presence of the CRP. It was while researching an essay submitted in partial fulfilment for that degree, entitled 'An attempt to isolate a uniquely religious dimension in the choices facing the Islamic minority as it comes to terms with living in Britain', that I first began to be interested in the themes explored in this thesis.

My initial premise for that essay was that Muslim migrants of subcontinent origin would not necessarily follow the same pattern of development as the other minority faith communities originating from the same region. This is because Islam is neither a religion that began in the sub-continent nor is it centred in that region. It is a world religion in the widest sense of the term, practised by many diverse ethnic groups and nationalities around the globe. Subcontinent Muslim migrants, although heavily influenced by the culture of their original communities, also feel themselves to be a part of the worldwide Muslim *ummah*. Consequently, they will be affected by changes and developments within Islam over a wide arena.

It was in the context of exploring this idea that I became aware that some young British Muslims were asserting a religious identity as a self-conscious choice in order to cope with their situation in Britain. The majority of first generation migrants came from rural areas of the subcontinent. One of the problems involved in analysing the meaning of Islam in their lives is that it is very difficult, and sometimes impossible, to separate religion from ethnicity in the context of subcontinent village life. I agree with Eric Butterworth's comment in an early study that 'life and belief are linked in an all-embracing way'[2] in the traditional village background of many of the Muslim migrants. It is also undoubtedly true that many of the customs and beliefs of the subcontinent Muslim village have been imported into Britain, and are used to reinforce the ethnic distinctiveness of the various communities in reaction to an often hostile receiving community. It is my contention, however, that despite the difficulties in separating religion from culture, it is precisely this process of separation that is beginning to take place. This is giving a uniquely religious dimension to the experience of many young British-born Muslims of subcontinent origin. This attempt to embrace Islam as a religious experience rather than as cultural heritage is providing increasing numbers of young Muslims with an alternative both to pressure to assimilate into the indigenous culture and to their parents' persuasion to conform to the various brands of imported ethnicity.

This takes the thesis into an area of study of interest to some social scientists and, increasingly, scholars of Religious Studies, namely, the relationship between religion and ethnicity. Social scientists working in the field have tended to study religion as a constituent reinforcing ethnic identity[3]. Knott has stated that 'there are times when religion plays a more active role in the definition of an ethnic group's identity and behaviour'.[4] The relevance of this statement is borne out when the role of Islam is examined amongst Muslim migrants. The debate concerning the relationship between ethnicity and religion is not only of interest to social scientists and Religious Studies scholars, it is also an historically ongoing and emotionally charged issue within Islam itself. Throughout the Muslim world there have been attempts to rediscover the pristine faith of Islam by uprooting and destroying local cultural accretions which are deemed to be unIslamic. This old debate within the faith has taken on new meaning for some British-born Muslims as they attempt to establish a community whose basis is faith rather than ethnic identity. Other Muslim migrants have sought to retain local expressions of their faith imported from the place of origin, and may well use their religious practices to reinforce their various ethnic identities.

Various Islamic movements have been transferred from the subcontinent during the process of migration, and all of these groups have been historically engaged in the above debate. Membership of such groups will engage Muslim migrants not only in the historical debate within the context of the subcontinent but also in its new expression within the context of the development of Islam in Britain. It is my contention that this debate will become of increasing importance between British-born Muslims and first-generation migrants. The future of Islam in Britain obviously lies with the present and future British-born generations. They will need to resolve the problem of citizenship as negotiated between nationality, ethnicity, sectarian membership and identification with the worldwide Muslim *ummah*. This thesis seeks to clarify the above issue by assessing the probable impact of the key Islamic groups imported from the subcontinent upon Islam in Britain, with a particular emphasis on community. My contention is that the formation of a community seeking its identity in religion will be shaped by various other real and symbolic communities existing within the total population of Muslims in Britain. A community based on Islamic identity will need to resolve issues generated from a complex relationship between the particular ideologies of various Islamic groups, the persistence of cultural/religious customs pertaining to ethnic identity, the identification with the historic *ummah* and its contemporary expressions and, finally, expressions of identity arising out of other forms of social organisation created by the migration process, not necessarily unique to Muslims, which have been studied and defined by sociologists.

Methodology: Research Strategies and Fieldwork

This thesis utilises the Religious Studies approach to examine processes through which subcontinent Muslims have transplanted Islam to Britain, and the consequent ongoing formation of Islam as a major minority faith community in this country. It acknowledges that many Muslims may seek ways of life outside of religious commitment, but leaves this area of study to social scientists working in the field of migrant communities. As a Religious Studies scholar my concern is with the shape and form of the community developed by those to whom faith is central.

It is essential that religion is studied both as an historical process and as a contemporary mode of living which interacts with other areas of human concern.[5] In this context Knott observes that religion must be studied both diachronically and synchronically.[6] This is particularly important when studying the religions of ethnic minorities where there is a crucial interplay between historical developments in the country of origin and the new forms that the faith takes to express the often traumatic and dramatic process of settlement. To facilitate an understanding of these processes, Religious Studies utilises a multidiscipliary approach. This draws upon research undertaken in the fields of History, Islamic Studies, Sociology, Anthropology, Politics, Psychology, Theology, and Philosophy, to name only the main areas where I have searched for texts. The other important element of Religious Studies is that it is a non-confessional approach to the study of religion. In this respect it acknowledges the phenomenological ideal that the researcher should suspend judgement concerning the truth claims of the data under investigation. I agree with Philip Lewis that this is difficult when some of the topics under scrutiny are highly emotive, both amongst Muslims themselves and within the wider community.[7] I have had to acknowledge my own deeply-held convictions on matters such as gender, colonialism, expressions of personal freedom, and religious belief.

In order to achieve the above goals I have had to make a considerable study of the texts relating to the history of Islam in the subcontinent as well as those drawn from Islamic Studies. I have examined the substantial body of ethnographic material created by anthropologists researching localised expressions of Islam both in the subcontinent and in Britain, and my own fieldwork draws heavily on this approach.

There are many studies which examine Muslim communities within individual towns and cities throughout Britain and I acknowledge my debt to them. I decided, however, to seek a more overall British perspective. This was essential in order to determine if there was such an entity as the 'Muslim community', and if so, what forms it was taking. There are obviously as many dangers here as there are in generalising from local studies. I can more easily analyse national trends, but need to avoid overlooking the significance of local expressions of Islam. In order to establish both a national perspective and an awareness of the diversity of local expression I decided to spend periods (between two weeks and a month) undertaking fieldwork in key areas of Muslim settlement. I chose London, Leicester, Birmingham and the area around Leeds which includes large populations at Bradford, Batley and Dewsbury. My focus of attention was on members of the religious groups that I was investigating, but I also interviewed many Muslims who were not particularly affiliated with any groups plus members of other Islamic groups who are not studied here. This was done to ascertain the degree to which the concerns of the groups upon which I have focussed are of central significance to other Muslims outside of their membership.

I chose Leicester and Birmingham as sites for in-depth participant observation study. Leicester has been a centre of activity for *Jamaat-i Islami*-inspired organisations and is close to the Markfield conference centre which contains the *Islamic Foundation* and the national headquarters of *Young Muslims UK*. The concentrated presence of Muslims in the Alum Rock and Sparkbrook districts of Birmingham provided a unique opportunity to observe the activities of all the groups I was interested in within a relatively small geographical space. I was especially interested in the various Sufi-inspired *Barelwi* groups that were prominent in these two districts. Sparkbrook also contained a Yemeni community living alongside the Muslims originating from the subcontinent. This provided the environment to examine the reality of claims for an Islamic identity which transcended ethnic origins put forward by activists of *Young Muslims UK*. In each of these locations I lived amongst Muslims, attending the mosques daily and spent considerable time enjoying the hospitality of my Muslim hosts in their own homes. I intentionally avoided the habits and contacts of my own lifestyle in order to experience the ambience of the Muslim communities. I believe that this was a successful strategy as the vast majority of contacts I made took me into their confidence and welcomed me. I thank them for this. Their hospitality was all the more remarkable as I took a deliberate decision not to make any advance arrangements for my arrival. I chose this spontaneous approach as a way of avoiding any animosity towards interrogative outsiders in the wake of the Rushdie affair. I felt confident that my familarity and affection with the culture of the subcontinent gained by my considerable periods of time spent in Pakistan and India would be acknowledged and overcome any doubts concerning my motives. However, this strategy did not meet with success everywhere. Both in Britain and in the subcontinent, some organisations and institutions were deeply suspicious of my interest in them, notably those where there was a strong *Deobandi/Tabligh-i Jamaat* interconnection.

I carried out many interviews both of a formal and informal nature. Although I prepared some necessary questions in advance, I allowed the interviews to be flexible, and was always prepared to explore unexpected avenues of interest. Many of the formal interviews were with leaders of the groups under study. I was aware that this could heavily bias my findings on two accounts: I was receiving the official view, and most of the leaders were first-generation migrants. I also needed to find out the views of the younger generation who were not usually in the position of leadership. I considered the idea of questionaires but dropped it for practical and methodological reasons. I decided, finally, to conduct a series of informal interviews with the younger generation and rank-and-file members. These interviews were undertaken after formal meetings with the leaders. They often took place over meals, in cafés, in homes, or sitting on the floor of the mosque. The discussions were lively and allowed me to check the information provided in formal meetings with community leaders.

Before undertaking research in Britain I spent six weeks in Pakistan and India in order to observe those movements which I was studying, in their place of origin. I was particularly interested to discover changes that had taken place in transporting the movements to Britain. I spent time at Mansurah in Lahore, the national headquarters of *Jamaat-i Islami* in Pakistan. I visited the tombs of several prominent Sufi saints, and also travelled to Mirpur, the place of origin of so many Muslims in Britain. I then moved on to India, and stayed in the Deoband *dar al-Ulum* before visiting the *Barelwi dar al-Ulum* in Bareilly, *Nadwah* in Lucknow, the national headquarters of *Jamaat-i Islami Hind* and the world headquarters of *Tabligh-i Jamaat* in Nizzamuddin, the last two of which are both situated in Delhi. In general, I observed the same methodological practices as described above for research undertaken in Britain.

Like Barton, I am acutely aware of the problem of gender when undertaking research projects amongst subcontinent Muslim populations.[8] All male researchers are confronted by the restrictions imposed by the varying degrees of *purdah* existing in Muslim society. Wherever possible I have attempted to determine the position of women on the various issues under discussion. This was achieved by interviewing Muslim women themselves in such groups as *Young Muslims UK* or the equivalent youth organisations in India and Pakistan. I was also able to meet with some older women in Birmingham who were involved with education in the Central Mosque. I was aware that all these women were highly educated and middle class. They all worked in professions such as teaching and medicine. It was impossible to gain access to the vast majority of Muslim women, especially those involved with the *Deobandi* or *Barelwi* school of thought. In order to find out anything about their involvement in those groups I had to rely on the accounts of men, and the evidence of my own eyes.

My other limitation was language. I am not a linguist or a scholar of Islamic Studies. Although I attempted to correct this by studying Arabic with first-year B.A. students in the Arabic department of the University of Leeds, my efforts were doomed to failure because of the demands created by the workload. My lack of knowledge of Arabic and my very limited knowledge of Urdu denied me access to considerable information. This was particularly true during my stay in the subcontinent. My interviews were either with those who spoke English or were limited to the vagaries of well-meaning translators. I am aware that this confined my investigations to the more educated sections of the community. I was unable to gain information from the kind of informal conversations that were going on around me. Considerable data could also have been collected on the subject of *ummah* and other central themes by listening to the Friday sermons of *imams* in the mosques of Britain.

Transcription and Technical Terms

As I am not a scholar of Arabic and Urdu, transliteration from those languages was problematic. In arriving at the following solution I acknowledge my debt to Neil North at the Centre for the Study of Islam and Christian-Muslim Relations and to the advice of one of my two supervisors, Dr. Neal Robinson.[9]

My first problem before even considering how to transliterate was when to use Arabic or Urdu variations for Islamic religious or cultural terms. In my textual-based study, most of the terms I needed to use were transliterated from Arabic but there was still considerable variety of spelling as utilised by different authors. Once I began my fieldwork I discovered that most of the Arabic terms had Urdu variations which were more often used by subcontinent Muslims. As Neil North has pointed out, 'Urdu has a special prestige as a language for religious affairs and is common in most mosques and *madrasahs*'.[10] The problem here is that there is no common transliteration system used for Urdu by Muslims in Britain. After considerable thought I decided to keep it as simple as possible. Essentially I use the transliteration of Arabic according to the *Encyclopaedia of Islam*, and maintain that spelling throughout the thesis unless I need to use an Urdu variation for proper names. Thus *'madrasa'* remains *'madrasa'* unless the Urdu variations of *'madrasah'* or *'madrassah'* are used in the names of actual schools. The same applies to *'Dar al-Ulum'*. I acknowledge the Urdu variations of *'Ramadan'* to *'Ramazan'*, *'Adhan'* to *'Azan'*, *'Dhikr* to *Zikr'*, but choose to maintain the Arabic transliteration throughout unless quoting from sources using the Urdu variation. There are some exceptions to this rule in deference to the main area of study in this thesis, and so, in a few cases, I follow the customary Urdu variation. I therefore prefer to use *'shaikh'* rather *'sheikh'*, a 'q' for 'k', and a final 'h' for the Arabic 'ha' and *'te marbuta'*. Occasionally I have had to use Urdu terms spoken locally which have no Arabic equivalent. Where this is the case, as in *'namaz'* or *'julus'*, I maintain the Urdu and do not provide an Arabic equivalent in the glossary. Generally, in order to respect the high regard of subcontinent Muslims for Urdu, the glossary of terms will contain both the Arabic and Urdu variation. The

Urdu transliteration will follow the *Ferozson's Urdu English Dictionary*.[11]

In accordance with Neil North's advice, wherever possible I pluralise Islamic terms by adding an 's'. Where this is clumsy in pronounciation as in '*hadith*' or '*hafiz*', the same form is used for both singular and plural. I do, however, distinguish between the singular '*alim*' and the plural '*ulema*'. There are no changes to reflect Arabic grammatical constructions. Consequently, there are no subscript dots or diacritical marks and no superscripts to denote long and short vowels. The '*hamzah*' and '*ain*' are indicated by apostrophes. This simplification should not cause undue distress to Arabic readers who, I hope, will be tolerant of my lack of knowledge of the language and the difficulties involved with computer keyboards.

Translations of the Qur'an follow Abdullah Yusef Ali[12] unless I have quoted from a source which utilises a different translation. In such cases, the endnote will indicate the source from which I have quoted rather than which version of the Qur'an was used.

There are two terms used which are controversial to many Muslims and could cause offense. These are 'sectarian' and 'fundamentalism'. I acknowledge Muslim objections to both terms. I have used 'sectarian influences' in my title to describe what Philip Lewis more accurately and diplomatically calls 'the development of distinct *maslak*, discrete schools of Islamic thought and practice'.[13] I am aware that this is a sensitive issue as there are *Hadith* in which the Prophet warns that the *ummah* will be divided by sects. Obviously, no Islamic organisation would define itself as a sect or wish to be defined as a sect. However, I maintain that there are tendencies in those schools of thought which are sectarian, even while I acknowledge that the *maslaks* are not sects within Islam. This is argued throughout the thesis and is central to acknowledging the impact of these groups upon the ideal of *ummah*. It is not my intention to cause offense, but I cannot shy away from sensitive issues which are central to the question under scrutiny.

I am even more sympathetic to the Muslim objection to the term 'fundamentalism', a term used frequently by the media to describe any attempt by devout Muslims to practice their faith that does not conform to the secular philosophy. This loose and derogatory use of the term could be applied to all the Muslims involved in the groups studied in this thesis since Islam occupied the central place in their world-view. This is obviously nonsense. After considerable thought I decided to keep the term. Where it occurs, it is used in a specialised sociological sense and therefore has to be defined. I have drawn upon the work of Hadden and Shupe[14] and also that of Lawrence.[15] Hadden and Shupe define 'global fundamentalism' as a 'pattern of many contemporary socio-political movements that share certain characteristics in their responses to a common globalisation process which may be described as secularisation'.[16] Secularisation is defined as the process whereby religion is increasingly 'compartmentalised from other institutionalised spheres'.[17] Hadden and Shupe define the common characteristics of these groups as resistance to secularisation, a refutation of both the sacred and the secular spheres that have evolved with modernisation, and a coherent ideology which seeks to bring religion back to the centre stage in public as well as private life. In order to achieve this, the fundamentalist groups need to claim authority over a sacred tradition 'which is to be reinstated as the antidote for a society which has strayed from its cultural moorings'.[18] Lawrence adds an important contribution to this definition by stating that there is a 'peculiar tension' which exists in fundamentalist organisations. This tension is generated by the fact that they accept the benefits of modernity, particularly through the use of technology, whilst rejecting modernism as a ideological framework. Thus fundamentalism is a modern phenomenon which attacks the ideology of modernism.[19]

Title and Contents

I have already defended the use of the term 'sectarian influences' in the title of the thesis. This term defines the impact of the *maslaks* transplanted from the subcontinent on the Muslim *ummah* as expressed in Britain. I have used 'Islam within Britain' rather than 'British Islam' although the latter term was often used by some of my interviewees; this is because other Muslims have pointed out that there can be no such thing as 'British Islam' as Islam is a universal faith. Finally, I have used both *'ummah'* and 'community' throughout because I believe that Muslim migrant expressions of Islam will be influenced not only by concepts arising out of the ideal of *ummah*, but also by other types of community originating from their Muslim past, ethnic origin, and unique status as migrants.

This differentiation between *'ummah'* and 'community' is acknowledged in the opening chapters. Chapter II attempts to analyse the origins of the term *'ummah'* in the Qur'an and the historical development of the *ummah* as a cultural/symbolic phenomenon with obvious political overtones. Stresses and strains upon the ideal unity of the *ummah* are explored along with pragmatic Muslim solutions. Chapter III explores some sociological ideas about community and also offers a sociological interpretation of *ummah*. This was necessary in order to demonstrate that Muslim migrants are not only members of the *ummah* but also belong to other types of community which have arisen through the migration process. I wanted to show that the formation of the Muslim community in Britain would be influenced by both the ideal of *ummah* and the reality of other types of community as have been investigated by social scientists. Having provided this frame of reference, in Chapter IV I examine the situation of Muslims in Britain. I have tried to analyse the tensions existing in the transplantation of Islam from the subcontinent by setting up a series of dichotomies as observed within the Muslim community. The intention of this approach is that each of the groups studied may be examined to see whether or not they resolve these conflicts. Thus their impact on the future of Islam in Britain may be ascertained. Chapters V to XI focus on the particular Islamic groups or movements under examination. Each group has a chapter which explores its origins in the subcontinent and another chapter which examines its development in Britain. Chapters V and VI look at the *Barelwi* strand of Islam. I begin with this movement as it can be argued that the type of Islam represented by the *Barelwi* tradition is the norm in the rural areas of the subcontinent (although I acknowledge that Ahmad Riza Khan Barelwi organised the beliefs of this strand of Islam into a coherent movement responding to the success of the *Deobandi* critique). The various movements studied in the following chapters represent historical attempts to reform that tradition. Chapters VII and VIII examine the origins and development of the reform movement through to its institutional expression in the nineteenth century under the name *'Deobandi'*. Chapter IX focusses on the main expressions of *Deobandi* tradition in Britain. Finally Chapters X and XI study the twentieth century ideological expression of the reform ideal, the socio-political/religious group called *Jamaat-i Islami*, in its subcontinent manifestation. Chapter XII concludes the thesis.

Endnotes

[1] For a full account of the aims and objectives of the Community Religions Project refer to Knott, Kim, 1992, 'The Role of Religious Studies in understanding the Ethnic Experience' *Community Religions Project*, Research Paper 7, Department of Theology and Religious Studies, University of Leeds, pp. 6-9.

[2] Butterworth, Eric, 1969, 'Muslims in Britain', *A Sociological Yearbook of Religion in Britain 2*, ed. Martin D. & Hill M., London.

[3] Examples of this approach are as follows: Gordon, M., 1964, *Assimilation in American Life*, Oxford University Press, New York; Dashefsky, Arnold, 1972, 'And the Search goes on: Religio-ethnic Identity and Identification', *Sociological Analysis 33:4*, 239-245; Francis, E.K., 1976, *Interethnic Relations*, Elsevier, New York; Lewins, Frank, 1978, 'Religion and Ethnic Identity', *Identity and Religion: International Cross-Cultural Approaches*, ed. Mol, Hans, Sage, Los Angeles.

[4] Knott, op.cit., p.12.

[5] Knott, op.cit., p.9.

[6] ibid.,p.10.

[7] Lewis, Philip, 1993, *Bradford's Muslim Communities and the Reproduction of Islam*, PhD, Department of Theology and Religious Studies, University of Leeds, p.4.

[8] Barton, Stephen, 1986, *The Bengali Muslims of Bradford*, Community Religions Project, Monograph Series, University of Leeds, p.11-12.

[9] North, Neil, 1986, *Mosques and Madrasahs in Birmingham*, M.Phil., Centre for the Study of Islam and Christian-Muslim Relations, Selly Oak, Birmingham.

[10] ibid, p.5.

[11] *Ferozson's Urdu-English Dictionary*, Revised Edition, Ferozsons (Pvt) Ltd., Lahore, Pakistan.

[12] Ali, Abdullah, Yusef (trs.),*The Holy Qur'an*, revised and edited by The Presidency of Islamic Researches, IFTA, *Mushaf Al-Madinah An-Nabawiyah*, King Fahd Holy Qur'an Printing Complex, Saudi Arabia.

[13] Lewis, op.cit., abstract.

[14] Hadden, Jeffery & Shupe, Anson, 1989, *Secularisation and Fundamentalism Reconsidered - Religion and the Political Order, Vol.VIII*, New Era Books, New York.

[15] Lawrence, Bruce, 1990, *Defenders of God - The Fundamentalist Revolt Against the Modern Age*, I.B.Tauris, London.

[16] ibid, p.111.

[17] ibid.

[18] ibid.

[19] Lawrence, op.cit., p.17.

2 Ummah: the concept of community in Islam

Nu'man Ibn Bashir said, 'I heard the Messenger of God, may God bless him and give him peace, say "the Muslims in their mutual affection and mercy should be as a single body; if one member is affected, the other members suffer fever and sleeplessness"'.[1]

Millions of Muslims and some prominent orientalists[2] portray Islam as a transnational community that transcends ethnic, racial, linguistic and national identities. It is argued that membership of the Islamic *ummah* confers on the individual, be they male or female, rich or poor, black or white, a belonging which is based on the equality of all believers before Allah. To be a member of this community of faith, all that is necessary is a confession of the *Shahadah*.[3] The Islamic perspective of community, unlike that of many western sociologists,[4] does not have a spatial limitation; the *ummah* incorporates the totality of all Muslims regardless of where they live. A Muslim may be living in a non-Muslim state, but that does not nullify membership of the worldwide *ummah*. It is the only community to which a Muslim belongs simply by virtue of being a Muslim. For millions of human beings, membership of the *ummah* happened through the fact of being born.

The ideal of the *ummah*, then, is that of a community bound together by its belief in one God, Allah, and in the message conveyed to mankind by His prophet Muhammad. The purpose of the *ummah* is to act as a witness for Allah to mankind through the example of obedient worship and through the relation of its members to each other. The *ummah* is an indivisible organisation which is responsible for upholding the true faith and for instructing mankind in the revealed way of God as contained in the Qur'an and the *Sunna* of the Prophet.

At the beginning of Islam's history, membership of the *ummah* supplanted the powerful communal tribal solidarity of the Arabs as the strongest identity of the individual in relation to society.[5] Once Islam was established, it carried out a major change in the area of law and order. Islamic law, which was based on the injunctions of the Qur'an, remodelled and often replaced customary tribal laws.[6] The *ummah* can be described as a community which grew out of the process of obedience to Islamic law. The *ummah* is ruled by Allah. His sovereignty is real and immediate. He controls the *ummah* through His commands as revealed to Muhammad and written in the Qur'an.[7] These commands are the Law and Constitution of the *ummah*.[8] Consequently, the concept of the *ummah* has had in the past and still maintains in the present a profound effect upon the political dimension of Islam. Guided by the word of God and the actions of His Prophet, the *ummah* has a moral mission to create a new social order based on faith and obedience. Muhammad and the early Muslim community are seen as exemplifying this ideal, creating from the tribes of Mecca and Medina a socially just society that was free from exploitation. This ideal has supplied a rationale for political and moral activism.[9] It is reasonable to argue that it is the ideal of the solidarity of the *ummah*, or threats to its apparent unity, which have been Islam's major contribution to the political sphere.

The *ummah* is held together not by any formal organisation but by a collective act of will, inspired by personal conviction and embodied in the ritual duty of daily prayer, the month-long fast of *Ramadan* and the annual pilgrimage to Mecca. Five times a day; millions of Muslims face Mecca, all at the same time, to observe the same ritual prayers. This core of shared ritual practices combined with observance of the *Shari'ah* is integral to Muslim life, and creates the bonds that tie together the *ummah*.

Despite the ideal held by many Muslims of a single, divinely revealed and united Islam, there have been and continue to be diverse interpretations of Islam. It is an historical fact that the community was already torn by dissent and split into factions within the lifetime of the first generation of believers. The initial division occurred over the issue of the leadership of the *ummah*.[10] As will be seen, the Qur'an offers no single definition of *ummah*, and so other divisions were created concerning the nature and shape of the community itself. Major stress was also placed on the *ummah* by the spread of the Arab empire and its attendant rapid incorporation of older, more sophisticated cultures into the fold of Islam.[11] In recent history, Muslims have had to face the challenge of European culture and values. In particular, the ideologies of nationalism and secularism have provoked a strong reaction from many segments of the Muslim world. The ideal of the *ummah* as a united, indivisible, transnational community has been developed by some modern Islamic thinkers to resist the pervasive influence of these two western concepts. In spite of the attempts of Muslim scholars and theologians to deal with these historical crises by claiming the political and social unity of the *ummah* in Islam's history,[12] it is debatable whether the *ummah* ever actually existed in this form after the Prophet's death except as a symbol of cohesion in the psyche of the faithful.

The Qur'an

It is necessary to begin the search for the Islamic concept of community in the Qur'an. It is not the intention here, however, to enter into an etymological analysis of the Arabic word '*ummah*' or to examine how it is used in the poetry of pre-Islamic Arab culture, but rather to demonstrate how the concept of *ummah* is developed in the Qur'an. Whatever the origins of the word, the term was taken up by Muhammad and acquired a specific Islamic meaning. The term '*ummah*' occurs sixty-four times in the Qur'an (see Appendix A), and its plural form '*umam*' is used thirteen times.[13] The passages in the Qur'an where the terms '*ummah*' or its plural '*umam*' actually occur are so varied that it is often difficult to define the precise meaning implied. Regardless of the variety of ways in which the term is used, however, it seems always to apply to an ethical or religious body of people with whom God works in history to fulfil the divine plan for salvation.[14] With three exceptions,[15] it always refers to a group of people who constitute a religious/moral community.

The variety of ways in which the term '*ummah*' is used in the Qur'an would suggest that the revelations were addressed to those who were perplexed by the problem of religious disunity amongst mankind (*Yunus* 10:19; *Al-Anbiyaa* 21:92,93; *Al-Muminun* 23: 52,53), and developing towards the Islamic concept of community as Muhammad's mission proceeded through setbacks to success (*Al-Imran* 3.110). Frederick Denny[16] argues that there is a progression from Mecca to Medina towards the full-blown concept of the *ummah* as representing the Muslim community.

Fazlur Rahman[17] agrees that the theological problem was not resolved until the Medinan period when the Muslim community was formally established as the ideal community, but argues that even in Mecca, the Prophet wished to unite the various communities of the *Ahl al-Kitab* into one single religious community which acknowledged his prophethood. It would appear that as Muhammad gradually came to understand the strength of the differences between the adherents of the earlier monotheistic faiths and the degree of their divisions into various sects, he realised that this would not occur.

Initially in the period of Muhammad's preaching to the Meccans, the Qur'an does not mention separate or exclusive communities.[18] *Al-An'am* 6:38, *Al-A'raf* 7.38 and *Al-Ahqaf* 46.18 suggest that all living creatures (even the *jinn*) constitute *ummahs*, but always there is an implication of salvation and judgement. *Al-An'am* 6:108 and *Al-A'raf* 7:34 state that every *ummah* is brought to judgement.

More specifically, the term is used to describe a community to whom God has revealed his presence and purpose in order to guide them to the right path. Some members of that community will have obeyed and some will have disobeyed, but all will be judged on the basis of their response to the revelation. In *Al An'am* 6:42, *Yunus* 10:47 and *Ar-Ra'd* 13:30 the Qur'an warns of the fate awaiting those communities which do not heed the message. In these verses it is also possible to trace a connection that is being made between an *ummah* and a Messenger. *An-Nahl* 16:36, 16:63 and *Al- Muminun* 23:44 appear to define *ummah* as a people to whom a Messenger has been sent, and often rejected.

In the above,[19] there is no suggestion that *ummah* means those who have accepted Muhammad and embraced Islam. The term *ummah* is still being used to describe complete communities or peoples who have been specially chosen to receive God's message. Within the *ummah*, some will choose to reject the message and some will choose to accept it *(Fatir* 35:32).The Qur'an states that every community has received a Messenger to remind them of their obligation to God and to warn them of the consequences of forgetfulness and disobedience. Every community which ignored God's message and His Messenger, we are told, was replaced by a succeeding community *(An-Nahl* 23:44). The arrival of each new prophet then began a new *ummah*, and marked the end of the previous one. On the Day of Judgement, God will call His Messengers to be witnesses against those who denied the truth in their respective *ummahs (Al Muminun* 23:44).

In this *Sura* the Qur'an indicates that some *ummahs* are sent a book as well as a prophet. Islamic theology differentiates between the Messengers of Allah on the basis of whether or not they are given a book to reveal. Those who were given a book are called *rasul* (messenger); those who were not are called *nadhir* (warner). The communities which received both a messenger and a book are seen as a definitive communities; they are known as the *Ahl al-Kitab* (the people of the book). Primarily these are the Jews and the Christians.

In Medina the term '*ummah*' seems to be used exclusively to describe the 'people of the Book'. The Qur'an uses the term '*ummah*' in a modified sense when referring to these communities. Instead of calling the totality of the Jews and Christians an *ummah*, only the righteous and obedient amongst them are described as such. Here *ummah* is used to describe smaller groups within larger communities *(Al-Imran* 3:113, *Al-Ma'idah* 5:66, *Al-A'raf* 7:159).

Just as God has sent a messenger to every community, so he has established a rite for each community as well. In the above passages the Jews and Christians who constitute an *ummah* are seen as those who follow their given rites. The *ummah* is more than religious identity; set forms of worship are the outward and visible expressions of submission and obedience. The rituals of prayer, fasting, and pilgrimage ensure that an *ummah* is kept upon the straight path. Thus a true *ummah* is one which steadfastly and regularly, by day and by night, worships God through the required rites (*Al-Baqarah* 2:128, *Al-Hajj* 22:67, 22:34, *Al-Ma'idah* 5:48). The revelations of the Qur'an appear to be working their way towards developing the concept of the *ummah* as follows: a community of believers united in their common worship of God in the prescribed form as revealed through the Messenger, who in this case is Muhammad (*At-Tauba* 9:71).

Having used the term '*ummah*' to separate out the righteous amongst the *Ahl al-Kitab* (*Al-Imran* 3:113), the Qur'an accuses these communities of dividing themselves into sects and warns the Muslims to avoid the same error. It is clear that God does not tolerate the fragmentation of the *ummah*, and commands unity of cult and faith (*Al-Muminun* 23;52,53). Here already the Muslims are being described as an *ummah* in their own right.[20] By the Medinan period, the Qur'an is using the term to describe the Muslims as the latest recipients of revelation (Al-Imran 3:110). It is not until the late Meccan or early Medinan period that Muhammad begins to define the *ummah* as the Muslim community. It is probably not until Medina that the concept of *ummah* as a religious community reaches its most developed stage. In the Meccan *suras* the term *ummah* can be used to describe a people that rejected God's Messenger who was sent to them, but in Medina the term is used exclusively to describe the Muslims as 'the *ummah* par excellence'.[21] Those who follow the message of the Qur'an, carrying out its commandments and worshipping according to its prescribed rites, living by its code of life and obeying the last and final Prophet, Muhammad, constitute a model *ummah* (*Ummah Wusta*). This *Ummah Wusta* or *Ummah Muslimah* is defined as a model for all mankind. It is a witness to mankind just as Muhammad is the witness to the Muslims themselves of God's manifest will (*Al-Baqarah* 2:143). This *ummah* replaces all the *ummahs* which preceded it. It is the recipient of the last and final revelation, the final form of *ummah*.

This fully formed and Godly *ummah*, then, is a moral community which not only hears the Law but upholds and enforces it (*Al-Imran* 3:110). A Godly *ummah* is obedient and faithful, and according to the Qur'an it is bound to be successful (*Al-Imran* 3:179). The righteous *ummah* is the saved *ummah*. As far back as the early Meccan period, however, the Qur'an warns that even within the *ummah* of believers there will be varying reactions to the message. There will be those who will fall away; there will be those who are half-hearted (*Fatir* 35:32).

One verse of the Qur'an highlights this problem and appears to offer the solution to it when it uses '*ummah*' in a specialised sense. Although usually the term '*ummah*' applies to the totality of the Muslims, it is also used to mean a righteous group of believers who have been selected from the wider community and who are charged with the duty of inviting other Muslims to obedience. This righteous and faithful *ummah* within the wider *ummah* functions as a guide and arbiter (*Al-Imran* 3.104). This particular passage could be used as a justification for sectarianism in Islam. A self-defined righteous group within the wider community could draw upon this passage to make the claim that they were the true '*ummah*'.[22]

Mecca and Medina

The above analysis of *ummah* in the Qur'an demonstrates how the concept changed and developed throughout the Meccan and Medinan periods. It would appear that in the beginning, Muhammad saw the *ummah* as a people to whom the prophet or messenger was sent. The Qur'an defines *ummah* as a community of believers, and the Meccan *suras* as recited before the *Hijra* already use the term in this way. This conception of the *ummah* developed at the foundation of Islam in Mecca, and was then fully developed in Medina.

In Mecca, Muhammad's first followers forsook kith and kin out of loyalty to Islam and its Prophet. This came about as their increasing faith in the oneness of God and the prophethood of Muhammad began to transcend their loyalty to tribe and clan when opposed by them. The transformation to a separate community was probably gradual, occurring slowly and organically as those who were attracted to Muhammad's message and ideas began to join him in worship. Montgomery Watt suggests that in the early stages these people would not have been distinct from the rest of the Meccan population. As opposition developed against them, however, the first Muslims would have become increasingly isolated, and they would have been forced to fall back on each others' resources.[23] In this way a separate community identity grew, and a bond of unity was forged that was welded together by persecution, a common faith, and a shared moral outlook. The introduction of common ritual prayers would have cemented this union. The early converts thus came to see their companions in the faith as belonging to one family under the sovereignty of Allah, regardless of their worldly status.

It is not surprising that the *ummah* took on a political dimension. The Arab tribes were a cohesive social unit, and there was a marked degree of communal solidarity based on tribal membership. Prior to the commencement of Muhammad's preaching, this solidarity was beginning to break up under the pressures of commercial prosperity.[24] The Meccan merchants were adopting a more individualistic mode of life based on personal wealth and competition.[25] Right from the beginning, Islam's message was relevant to the social and political organisation of the community; economic injustices and unethical commercial practices were strongly denounced.[26] Muhammad preached a redistribution of wealth as based on spending money for the communal good, explaining that this was a way to please Allah.[27] He stressed the need to feed the poor and to protect the weak in the community from oppression. Once the system of *Zakat* was introduced in Medina, it would have helped to reinforce fraternal feelings of mutual affection.[28] Thus Islam restored the feeling of communal solidarity that was beginning to break down in Mecca, but attached it to the growing community of believers rather than to the tribe. This momentum towards unity was reinforced by injunctions in the Qur'anic revelation. In this way did the *ummah* begin in Mecca.

In Medina the *ummah* developed into a community which incorporated an organised political life; a society based on tribal loyalty, laws and customs was replaced by a religiously bonded community that was governed by God's law. In an extraordinary document named 'The Constitution of Medina' (see Appendix B), the term '*ummah*' appears for the first time in Muslim history outside of the *suras* of the Qur'an. It begins:

This is the writing of the Muhammad the Prophet between the believers and Muslims of the *Quraysh* and the *Yathrib*, and those who follow them and are attached to them and crusade along with them. They are a single *UMMAH* distinct from other people.[29]

The document was drawn up to establish and confirm Muhammad's legal and political position in Medina;[30] Muhammad himself is unequivocally described as the Prophet.[31] It establishes the relationship between the Muslims and the tribes of the city, including the Jewish claims.[32] '*Ummah*' is used to describe a people sharing the same features and agreeing to the same conditions. These features are outlined and they define the membership of the *ummah* in terms of belief in Allah.[33] This shared attitude regulates their relationship with each other and to the rest of Medinan society.

The *Hijra* had already fractured loyalty to blood ties as it removed the Muslims physically from their kinfolk. The most important aspect of the *Constitution* is that it completely negates that sovereign concept of blood ties which lies so much at the root of all pre-Muslim Arabian values. It prepares the way for a theocratic, supratribal community which will become a universal community of believers and which will include non-Arabs in its ranks. This process would have been spurred on by the victory at Badr and the split with the Jews.

The revolutionary aspect of the *Constitution* was its insistence that from henceforth, faith should be the criteria for community membership. In Medina, Muhammad was able to consolidate his position and to insist upon his dictum that Islam must take precedence over all other loyalties. Once Islam began to grow in strength, the key division in society became that of believer and unbeliever rather than inter-tribal conflict.[34] The document demonstrates, however, that Muhammad did not attempt to abolish the old tribal constitutions, but rather that he expanded and reformed them in order to make them relevant to the larger community of Islam.[35] Ultimate authority was now no longer seen as resting with the tribal leaders and the collective voice of the people, but rather with Allah and Muhammad.[36] There was to be no division of church and state, and Muhammad was to be recognised as deriving his political and religious power from his office as Prophet of Allah.[37]

The period in Medina was the turning point in Muhammad's life. No longer the despised irritator of the Meccan merchants, he was now accepted as an honoured statesman and a Prophet of God. Islam developed from a religious belief amongst the Arab tribes into initially a community that governed all aspects of life, and finally into the state itself. The Medinan *suras* of the Qur'an are noticeable for their length and their emphasis on laws controlling the operation of society. There are religious laws regulating fasting, almsgiving, prayer and the pilgrimage to Mecca.[38] There are also social and political rules which deal with marriage, divorce, inheritance, rights of women, and the treatment of slaves and prisoners of war.[39] In Medina Muhammad finally broke with Judaism and Christianity, defining them as older *ummahs* which had already received their revelation but which had gone astray from it.[40] The Muslim *ummah* was now declared by Qur'anic revelation to be the recipient of the latest, best and final revelation from Allah.[41] It is in Medina that the uniquely Muslim religious customs of Friday congregational worship, fasting during the month of *Ramadan*, the *Hajj*, and facing Mecca in prayer are all established.[42] It is impossible to over-emphasise the importance of these customs in the cementing of the new community, from the beginning right down to the present day.

Out of the religious community of Medina grew the larger state of Islam. It was the first attempt in Arabian history to form a social organisation that was based upon religion. Everyone accepting Islam, regardless of their tribal affiliation, was now seen as brother and sister in the faith, at least in principal. This state of unity was doubtless true of the first converts of Mecca and Medina, but problems were to arise with Islam's rapid success. In the beginning individuals or even tribes embraced Islam out of genuine conviction, but success would have encouraged whole tribes to join for reasons of convenience or political expediency. As the Arab empire spread this problem became more acute, with conquered nations and civilisations having to be incorporated into the Islamic fold. Muhammad had succeeded, however, in creating a community which would grip the imagination of generations of devout Muslims. It is said that even at the end of his life, Muhammad's last concern was for the solidarity of the *ummah*.[43]

The Umayyad and Abbasid Dynasties

As far as is known, there was unity within the community during Muhammad's lifetime. In the rare occasions when conflict occurred, Muhammad was able to use his authority and status to resolve it. After his death, however, tension was generated amongst the Muslims over the issue of leadership. Out of this issue there eventually arose the major split in the Islamic community: the *Shi'a* and *Sunni* division. There will be no attempt to explore the development of the *Shi'a* here. Instead I will concentrate on the developments that took place in the main branch of *Sunni* Islam. It is sufficient to note that although most Sunni Muslims acknowledge the period of the rule of the four Caliphs that followed immediately after Muhammad's death as the continuation of his ideal Muslim community, major rifts did in fact occur over who had the right to lead the *ummah*.[44] From very early on we find the leaders of the Islamic state having to use force to repress sectarian tendencies and inter-tribal conflict.[45] The rulers of the *Umayyads* relied on Islam for legitimacy,[46] and Islamic beliefs and values became the official code for personal and public life throughout the empire. The *Umayyad* caliphs appointed themselves defenders of the faith.[47] As the *Umayyad* empire expanded it underwent the process of centralisation and militarisation; this process alienated many groups in Muslim society.[48]

Although in theory all Muslims were equal before God, Watt argues that until the end of the *Umayyad* dynasty the *ummah* was perceived as a federation of Arab tribes.[49] Goldziher had earlier argued in a similar vein that the *Umayyads'* view of Islam was political in that 'it had united the Arabs and led them to rule a world empire'.[50] In reality the empire was divided into four separate classes. The first two comprised the *ummah*. The social elite of the *ummah* were the Arabs, particularly those who had been companions of the Prophet.[51] After this came the non-Arab converts to Islam. Initially these were attached to an Arab tribe as clients (*Mawali*), and until the end of the *Umayyad* dynasty this seems to have been the only way in which they could be received as full citizens of the Islamic state.[52] They were apparently treated as second class members of the *ummah*, and were expected to continue paying taxes that were not levied on the Arab Muslims.[53] The last two classes were the *dhimmi* and the slaves.[54] The admission of increasing numbers of non-Arabs into the *ummah* created considerable tension; they objected to the preferential treatment received by the Arab Muslims and regarded their lesser status as a denial of their rights in Islam.[55]

The non-Arab Muslims were not the only discontented section of society. Many Arab nomadic tribes objected to the increasing bureaucratisation and centralisation of the *Umayyad* dynasty. To the east of the empire, a distinctively Persian political structure had combined the culture of that ancient civilisation with Islamic doctrines.[56] To the west, the empire was expanding into Egypt and North Africa. Those on these outer frontiers also began to object to tight central control.[57] Pious Muslims also viewed with deep suspicion the opulent and luxurious lifestyle of their rulers, seeing this as a grave departure from the Islamic way of life.[58]

Because of the religious basis of the Islamic community, any divisions have always tended to be justified at the theological level, and the leaders of the community have looked to religious solutions to restore unity. Besides the major division between *Sunni* and *Shi'a*, the other important sectarian group of the time was the *Kharijites*.[59] In common with the other major schools of though, the *Kharijites'* central concern was with the make-up of the community. They had a radically different concept of the nature of the *ummah*.[60] Observing the unIslamic lifestyle of the rulers, the *Kharijites* espoused a rigorous and committed asceticism that was lived in the spirit of egalitarianism.[61] They were pious believers who interpreted the Qur'an literally.[62] They believed in the principle of demonstrating faith with action, and they detested hypocrisy.[63] They decided that a Muslim's public actions must conform with Islamic principles if he was to' be included in the *ummah*.[64] Sinners, i.e. those who are disobedient to the teachings of the Qur'an, should either repent or be regarded as apostates guilty of treason against the *ummah*.[65] This treason was punishable by death,[66] and all true believers were obliged to fight against these nominal or self-styled Muslims.[67] The *Kharijites* withdrew from the wider Muslim society and lived together in a community which was supposed to be modelled on the life of the Prophet and the first Muslims in Medina.[68] From their armed encampments they waged *jihad* against the *jahiliyya* of the *Umayyads*.[69]

The *Murji'ites* countered the *Kharijite* position. They argued that the decision as to whether a Muslim belonged to 'the people of paradise' or 'the people of hell' could only be made at the Day of Judgement by Allah himself.[70] Lawbreakers could be punished, but they could not be excluded from the *ummah*.[71] The Prophet would eventually intercede on behalf of even those Muslims who were in hell; they would eventually be forgiven and enter paradise.[72] All Muslims would in the end reach paradise simply because they were members of the Islamic *ummah*.[73] Although the *Murji'ite* conception of the *ummah* is the traditional one found in Islam to the present day, the *Kharijite* ideal of the righteous minority that forms the true *ummah* is still influential amongst many Islamic reform and revivalist groups.

The *Umayyad* and *Abbasid* dynasties represent a period of exciting developments in Islam that arose partly out of questions concerning the nature of the *ummah* and who should have control over it. Dabashi argues that this period marks the beginning of the process of institutionalisation of Muhammad's original charismatic leadership.[74] There was intensive analysis of the relationship between religion and politics. Obviously control of the *ummah* was a political issue, but many different groups of the devout were not prepared to leave the moral and religious guidance of Muslims to the whims of often irreligious rulers. *Sunni* scholars were concerned to establish a theory of the Caliphate which clarified the relationship of the Caliph to the *ummah*. The Arab concept of the *Sunna*, which had become one of the central concepts of Islamic law, was under intense scholastic scrutiny towards the end of the *Umayyad* period.[75] The scholars were concerned to know whether or not the customary laws conformed to the Qur'an. Many of these scholars were the same pious Muslims who objected to the lifestyle of the *Umayyad* rulers.[76] It was their interest in religion that led them to define the law in such a way that the Islamic ideal could permeate all aspects of life. They subjected the existing law to a thorough Islamic over-haul, injecting into it the ethics, mores and religious ideas derived from the Qur'an.[77]

Incorporated into the law was the body of duties to which every Muslim was bound. This foundation of the *Shari'ah* was to have profound effects upon the *ummah*. By the beginning of the *Abbasid* dynasty, the *Hadith* were collected and placed into a chain of transmission to determine authenticity. This was an attempt to remove all eccentric opinions, to reinforce the *Shari'ah*, and to give authority to the values and ideals accepted by the main body of the *Sunni* community and their *ulema*.[78]

By the time of the decline of the *Abbasid* Caliphs, the religious authorities were winning their struggle to make themselves independent of the domination of political rulers.[79] This separation of religion and politics, however, did not cause as much damage to the unity of the *ummah* as it might have done. The development of the *Shari'ah* ensured that the oneness of the faith was maintained throughout the turbulent times that were to come. By the thirteenth century, the *Abbasid* empire was a fragmented, deteriorating commonwealth of self-governing states ruled by military commanders.[80] Political unity existed only in theory, with this fictional unity of the *ummah* being embodied in the powerless Caliph in Baghdad.[81] The final end came with the invasion of the Mongols. After the fall of Baghdad in 1258, for the first time since its inception, the Muslim world was without a Caliph whose name could be remembered at the Friday prayers[82]. For two and a half centuries, the ideal of the Caliphate was kept alive by the Mamluks. The Sultan, Baybars (1260-1277) inaugurated a new series of Abbasid caliphs in order to secure legitimacy for his reign in Egypt. They carried the title but none of the earlier authority of the of-fice[83]. The Caliphate was finally abolished and replaced by independent Sultanates at the conclusion of the fifteenth century.[84] Muslim power peaked under the Ottomans in the next century, only to decline under the threat of the advancing European powers. Throughout these dramatic changes in circumstances and fortune, the Islamic faith provided an underlying unity, a source of identity and a direction to Muslims. In order to see how this came about in the *Umayyad* and *Abbasid* Dynasties it is necessary to explore the issue of the Caliphate and the development of the *Shari'ah* in more detail.

The Caliphate

An examination of the historical debate on the theory of the Caliphate reveals a pragmatic atti-tude amongst the scholars and jurists of Islam. They are acutely aware of the political develop-ments of their period, and they are above all determined to preserve the underlying unity of the people. This often manifests as a fear of anarchy and disorder in society. The original charis-matic community of Islam had developed into a highly sophisticated civilisation spanning a large part of the world. Consequently, even the greatest religious scholars were more concerned with maintaining order in society than with reinforcing the traditional ideal relationship between Caliph and *ummah* with its basis in religion.

For the Muslim, this life is a preparation for a fuller life after death. The ideal state is one that would provide the maximum means for all its citizens to perform their religious and ethical duties according to the ordinances of the *Shari'ah*, so that they would be best prepared for the life hereafter. The Caliphate would maintain society with the interest of the people uppermost both in this life and the next. It would prepare them to enter paradise. Muhammad had formed the 'people of Paradise' under Allah's guidance; it was the duty of the Caliph to protect the people from anything, whether outside or inside the community, that could threaten their position in this context. The Caliphs were considered the rightful successors to the Prophet, even though they did not have his prophetic authority. It is essential in a community governed by revealed law to bring the people into conformity with its regulations and dictates. This is the role of the Caliph; he is the defender of the faith. The Caliphs's task is to preserve the *ummah*, keeping it free from disunity, strife or heresy. The Caliph as the actual, and later symbolic, leader of all Muslims was the head of the community. He represented in his person the unity of the *Dar Al-Islam*, the Muslims *ummah*. Al Mawardi (d.1058) expressed this very succinctly:

> There is no religion in which his power has disappeared without its institutions being changed... because with power is guardianship of religion and its defence..... it is incumbent to appoint an *imam* to be the sultan of his time and the leader of the *ummah*, so that religion may be guarded by his power.[85]

Al Mawardi stresses the indivisible, universal and divine nature of the *ummah* by maintaining that the Caliphate was a canonical rather than rational requirement, and that therefore there could not be more than one Caliph at a time.[86] Individuals who ruled over sections of Islamic territory only had legitimate power if they accepted the overall authority of the Caliph.

Both *Sunni* and *Shi'a* scholars were forced to compromise with this orthodox position and political reality as the *Abbasid* Caliphate went into decline and finally collapsed. They appealed to the principles of necessity and public interest in order to justify their accommodation.[87] To *Sunni* jurists like Al-Baghdadi (d.1037) and even Al-Ghazali (d.1111), the idea of political disintegration and its inevitable attendant anarchy was a horror to be resisted at all costs.[88] They compromised accordingly in order to maintain the myth of legal and political unity. It was essential that there should be a strong ruler to maintain law and order. Al-Ghazali quoted an *Hadith* to express this opinion: 'Sovereignty endures even when there is unbelief, but will not endure where there is injustice'.[89]

Many considered that any kind of stable government was preferable to civil unrest, even if the ruler had usurped his position by military force and had remained in power through tyrannical means. Ibn Hanbal, the great jurist and creator of one of Islam's four schools of law, legitimised this attitude:

> Whoever overruns the people by sword becomes Caliph, and is addressed as *Amir al-Mu'minin*, it is not permitted for anyone who believes in God and the hereafter to spend a night without recognising him as the *Imam*, whether he be pious or evil-doing.[90]

The above quotation indicates the degree to which the scholars of Islam were prepared to go in order to preserve the unity of all Muslims.

Al-Mawardi attempted to redefine the role of the Caliph in his work *The Ordinances of Government*.[91] He needed to compromise his traditional view on the Caliphate with the realities of the situation as the *Abbasid* dynasty declined. Increasingly the empire was breaking up into separate kingdoms or sultanates that had been grabbed by military strength. He discussed the relationship between the '*de jure*' authority of the Caliph in Baghdad and the '*de facto*' rule of the sultans. He suggested that the Caliph should authorise the rule of the sultans by investing his authority in them. They would then rule as deputies, with the Caliph as their symbolic head.[92] The problem with this solution was that many of the sultans had taken their territories from the Caliphate by force. Al Mawardi suggested that the Caliph should accept the rule of the sultan on condition that the latter in turn acknowledged the status of the Caliph and gave him religious loyalty,[93] and this in fact became the political reality as the empire declined. Since the Caliph had no power to enforce his will on the sultans, the Caliphate took on a symbolic role that expressed the unity of the *ummah*. Al-Ghazali acknowledged this change in the role of the Caliph arguing that 'whosoever he may be to whom the holder of the military power professes his allegiance, that person is the Caliph'.[94]

Al-Ghazali's argument is that even if the Caliphate has lost its political functions, yet it still remains as the representative of the supremacy of the *Shari'ah*. As long as the sultans guaranteed to maintain the *Shari'ah* in their symbolic oath of allegiance to the Caliph, then the community was still living within the law of Islam. Al-Ghazali suggests that the sultan would require a jurist to help him manage human affairs in accordance with the *Shari'ah*.[95]

Ibn Taymiyya (1263-1328) argued that there is no obligation on Muslims to acknowledge a single Caliphate.[96] The political leaders of the *Umayyad* and *Abbasid* dynasties were, according to him, only temporal rulers anyway;[97] their authority to be the *Imam* was given them by the *ummah*. The *ummah* was perceived to be 'a spiritual unity of all Muslims though they might live in different places and have a number of difficult rulers'.[98] The function of the rulers was to cooperate with the *ulema* in order to ensure that the *Shari'ah* was correctly followed in the state, and to carry out their religious and political duties as the *Shari'ah* directed. Generally, the only requirement for membership of the *ummah* is the confession of the *Shahadah*.[99] That requires complete obedience to Allah and His messenger, but does not limit the number of leaders who can rule through implementing the *Shari'ah*. It is the supreme authority, the divinely revealed law, the exclusive and complete guide of the *ummah*.[100] He acknowledges the practicalities of obedience to temporal authority but ignores the issue of the Caliphate altogether. Ibn Taymiyya says simply that the head of state and his government should be ruled by the Qur'an and the *Sunna*, and that in religious matters he should rely upon consultation with the *ulema*.

Despite the compromises of the scholars with political reality, the struggle confirmed the victory of the *ulema*, or religious institution of Islam, over the Caliphate, or over for that matter any other political institution. This source of authority could not be controlled by governments, but was possessed by the *ummah* itself. The *Sunni* jurists and *ulema* had established that the *ummah* was to be based upon the *Shari'ah*. The historical development of the *Shari'ah* could not be at fault, for Muhammad himself had said: 'My *ummah* will never agree upon an error'.[101]

On these bases the community could not have strayed into sin, and therefore all its religious and judicial activities were valid. The Caliphate was ignored and the bond between the *Shari'ah* and the *ummah* was emphasised. The essential reality was that the vitality and unity of Islam depended upon a community that was held together by *Shari'ah* law. This had been facilitated by the work of Nizam al-Mulk (d.1092), the vizier of the Seljuks who ruled over the *Abbasid* empire in the 11th century. He can be credited with developing a system which allowed for the preservation of the unified *ummah* even when political circumstances threatened to tear it apart. Nizam al-Mulk established *madrasas* throughout the lands of the Caliphate.[102] He even managed to open the famous college of *Madrasa Nizamiya* in Baghdad itself, the seat of the Caliph. In 1091, he appointed Al-Ghazali to the chair of *Shafi'i* Law in the college.[103] In these numerous small colleges, students were taught the four schools of jurisprudence. Some famous *madrasas* even taught all four as in the case of the *Mustansiriyya Madrasa* in Baghdad.[104] The teachers moved across the empire from one school to another. In this way, in spite of the fragmentation into various sultanates, a cohesive and unified theological outlook was maintained throughout the Caliphate. The colleges would have supplied *Qadis* for the legal system and clerks for the bureaucracy. It is perhaps even more important that they provided a uniformly trained *ulema*, which in turn helped to maintain a unified Islamic outlook as based on the *Shari'ah* while the empire collapsed.

The *Shari'ah* provides the Muslims with a sense of continuity and tradition. The key position of the *Shari'ah* in the *ummah*, together with the degree of uniformity in its application through the development of a *madrasa*-trained *ulema*, helped to ensure the unity of doctrine and belief. By virtue of its being an expression of God's will and by the common acceptance of its prescriptions by the majority of Muslims, it provided the morality, authority and sanctions which ensured the survival of the *ummah* after the collapse of the Caliphate. The following quotation from Abu Abdullah Muhammad al-Shafi'i (d. 820) encapsulated that relationship of the *Shari'ah* to the *ummah* which has lasted to the present day and survived further massive crises as Islam's civilisation had to bow to the superior might of Europe.

> The Questioner asked, 'What is the meaning of the Prophet's command to cleave to the Collectivity?' I said 'There is but one meaning to it.' He said,'How may it only have one meaning?' I replied, 'When the Collectivity of Muslims was dispersed in various countries, one could not cleave to a Collectivity whose members were scattered, and besides, they were found together with Muslims and unbelievers, with pious men and profligates. Thus it could not mean a physical 'cleaving' because that was not possible, and because physical nearness would in itself effect nothing, so that there is no meaning in cleaving to the Collectivity except in agreeing with them in what they make lawful and forbidden, obedience in both these matters'.[105]

Islah and Tajdid

Under the *Abbasids* the *ulema* developed into a religious elite within Muslim society. Their authority was derived from their knowledge of the Qur'an, the *Hadith* and the *Shari'ah*. They became the theologians, jurists and teachers within Muslim society and the official protectors of orthodox interpretation of the law and the traditions.[106] We have seen how they attempted to create cohesion by unifying the expanding empire via the *Shari'ah*; they were only partially successful in this. Not all rulers were prepared to follow the *Shari'ah* if it conflicted with their personal desires and ambitions. Amongst the educated minority there may have been a degree of integration from the tenth and eleventh centuries onwards, but the gap between the *ulema* and the populace almost certainly widened. This can be seen in the success of the Sufi brotherhoods and in the degree of cultural and ethnic variation in the religion of the common people.

Various individuals and religious groups attempted to counter this. They saw any political, military or economic decline of the *ummah* as caused by spiritual and moral decay, a wandering away from the straight path of Islam. The revitalisation of the *ummah* could only come about through a return to the original principles of Islam as embodied in the Qur'an and the *Sunna* of the Prophet. Once the Qur'an and *Sunna* became established canon it became possible to use them as a standard by which to judge contemporary Muslim society. Even when various dynasties were flourishing, there were those who were critical of the moral standards of the prevailing regime. Reformers could call for a change on the basis of scriptural interpretation. From the ninth century onwards, various individuals and groups had called for a return to the strict obedience of Qur'an and *Sunna* in order to renew the Muslim *ummah* and to bring it back to the pristine faith of the Prophet and his companions.[107] In the eighteenth and nineteenth centuries there was a marked decline in the political fortunes of the Muslim world. This was caused by the internal collapse of Muslim empires and the increasing ascendancy of European power. This period is characterised by a religious revival brought about by several revivalist groups from various parts of the Muslim world.[108] They all preached religious reform in order to combat political decline.

The concepts of *tajdid* (renewal) and *islah* (reform) were central to these revivalists.[109] *Islah* called upon Muslims to realign their lives to the fundamental tenets of Islam. It is a term used in the Qur'an[110] to describe the preaching of the prophets when they warned their respective communities of the need to return to God's ways by obedience to His law.[111] Voll states that '*islah* is the effort to increase the righteousness of the people'.[112]

Esposito provides four central ideas that are implicit in the concept of *tajdid*:[113]

(a) The belief that the righteous community as established and guided by the Prophet at Medina represented the norm that should be sought by all Muslims, both individually and communally.

(b) A purging from the community of all foreign or cultural accretions which were not Islamic. These were seen as '*bida*' or forbidden innovation. This included an attack on the Sufis, whose *tariqas* offered an alternative sense of community for the common people.

(c) A criticism of the establishment, both rulers and *ulema*.

(d) The belief that a renewer (*mujaddid*) of the faith will be sent at the beginning of each century to restore Islam and to regenerate a community which tends to drift from the straight path as laid down for it at the beginning of Islam's history. This is based on a *Hadith*: 'God will send to his *ummah* at the head of each century those will renew its faith for it'.[114]

Many of these groups viewed as unbelievers those Muslims who resisted their message.[115] There are obvious parallels here between this position and the beliefs of the *Kharijites*. Like them, these groups tended to establish their own integrated charismatic communities and then to divide into sects. Consequently, these attempts to unite the *ummah* often resulted in further fragmentation along theological lines.

The Impact of Europe

Throughout the eighteenth and nineteenth centuries the impact of European expansion began to be felt throughout most Islamic territory. Economic control in the eighteenth century gradually became political and military domination in the nineteenth.[116] Muslims increasingly found themselves living under the dominion of Christian or even secular rulers whose customs and beliefs were alien to them. This had a profound effect upon the Muslim psyche. The *ulema* were inadequate to deal with the new situation. They were increasingly confronted by a superior European technology and military might that was founded upon economic power and the discoveries of science. In addition to this, they had to deal with a radically different world view. This world view was based on a philosophical and political history that had given rise to ideas on statecraft which in turn had their roots in democracy, nationalism, and secularism.[117] The *ulema's* inadequacy arose from the fact that the European powers were consistently successful in taking over the territory of Islam. This provoked a crisis within the faith which the rigidly traditional ulema were not equipped to resolve. Foreign domination by non-Muslims raised questions concerning the health of Islam and reasons for why divine guidance apparently no longer provided success to the *ummah* as it had in the past.

The problem of inner decay had already been prominent in the minds of Muslim thinkers and reformers, but now they had to consider the possibility of Muslim civilisation being unable to survive this new external threat.[118] Most of them agreed upon the necessity of Islamic revival in order to restore the past glories of the Muslim *ummah*, but there was disagreement over how this could be achieved. Jamal al-Din al-Afghani (1838-1897), Muhammad Abduh (1849-1905) and others attempted to show that Islam and modern Western civilisation were not irreconcilable. They believed that the Muslims could rediscover their power by rejuvenating the morality and ethics of Islam and learning from Europe the developments that had been made in science and technology.[119] The important thing was to know what was essential in the faith and what was not. Once the essentials were established, Muslims could safely go on to reform their legal, administrative and educational institutions and to compete with European nations.[120] This required an re-examination of *ijtihad*.

The *ulema* believed the door of *ijtihad* to be closed, and that by the tenth century the codification of Islamic law was essentially complete. The majority of the *ulema* decided that independent interpretation of the law was no longer required. Muslims were simply to follow past precedent as elaborated by the early jurists; new problems were to be resolved by studying the established legal texts. This decision established the existing law as sacrosanct and made Muslim society very inflexible to changing situations.[121] Prominent revivalists like Al-Ghazali, Ibn Taymiyya, Shah Wali-allah and Abd al-Wahhab on the other hand, had claimed the right to practice *ijtihad* themselves in order to revitalise Islam. They believed that Muslim scholars should go direct to the Qur'an and the *Sunna* to provide a renewed vision rather than studying the legal texts. In contrast to both these views, the modernist reformers of the nineteenth and twentieth centuries believed that *ijtihad* was open to all Muslims to discover the way to adapt Islam to the changing conditions of modern society. This allowed for legal and social reform.[122] The reformers accused the *ulema* of holding back progress by being out of touch with the modern world. The *ulema* retaliated by accusing the reformers of introducing innovations (*bida*) from the Christian West which corrupt Islam.[123]

A new intellectual class of Muslims, educated to western standards, taking on the values of the conquerors and lacking the Islamic outlook of the reformers, gradually developed to challenge the authority of the traditional *ulema*. They stressed loyalty to the nation rather than to the *ummah*. Rifa'a Badawi Rafi al-Tahtawi (1801-1873), an Egyptian writer resident in France for five years as Imam to the student mission, and influenced by French ideas, appears to be the first of these to have introduced the idea of fatherland (*watan*) and patriotism (*wataniyyah*) into Arabic.[124] He said that 'the sons of the *watan* be united always by their language, by their allegiance to one king and by their obedience to one divine law and political administration'.[125] In the collapsing Ottoman Empire, the sociologist Ziya Gokalp (1876-1924) propounded the theory of Turkism. He saw Islam as a source of ethics which could be adapted to the needs of the time, but religion and nation had to be separated for the common good of both. He argued that it was possible to retain Islam's fundamental values and principles and to develop a modern Turkish national culture in which religious law would be replaced by secular law. Islam would function as a national religion to supplement Turkish culture. It could be used to develop connections with the wider Muslim world, but the interests of the Turkish nation must always be paramount. The nation was a natural integrated unit which through its language expressed a distinctive folk-culture.[126] This debate on the nature of the state and the question of loyalty took place throughout the Muslim world at this time. Each Muslim nation arrived at its own individual solution. In this respect the concept of the *ummah* took on a different symbolic meaning amongst Muslim minority communities from that in the Arabic speaking heartlands. For the Arabic-speaking nations '*ummah*' was a term used in everyday language to denote various types of community. Where Arabic was not spoken as an everyday language '*ummah*' existed only as a very powerful cultural/religious symbol which could be drawn upon to promote Muslim identity against the majority population.

The situation was further complicated by the success of the Western-educated elites in seizing control of the newly emerging independent Muslim nation-states after the end of World War II. The new governments embraced the ideals of secularism and nationalism as learnt from their former rulers. Secularism, the separation of the spiritual from the temporal, affirms that an individual's religious life is a private matter; this tended to divide the community's political life from its religious heritage. Both this ideal and the phenomenon of separate nation states was in opposition with the classical Islamic ideal of the united community of believers, even though it should be remembered that many Muslims had previously given their loyalty to states perceived as Islamic which were often in conflict with other Muslims (e.g. The Ottoman Empire v. Safavid Iran). Throughout the nineteenth and twentieth centuries the *Shari'ah* has been modernised in most Muslim nations by the replacement of traditional Islamic codes with those derived from European legal systems. Even family law, which was the heart of the *Shari'ah* and involved the laws of inheritance, divorce and marriage, laws which had remained intact as the major force to govern the lives of Muslims throughout the Islamic world, now began to be tampered with. An Islamic rationale was provided by governments wishing to reform their legal codes. They proclaimed their right to practice *ijtihad*. The *ulema* either cooperated with this process by working for the government or felt themselves powerless to stop the process even while they viewed it as profoundly unIslamic.

The new nation states have inherited all these divisions as generated by the rise of European power. So far, they have not been able to create a society which claims the allegiance of all their people, nor have they established themselves as the primary locus of Muslim identity. The state sought to appropriate to itself those loyalties which Muslims traditionally gave to the universal community as established by Muhammad. This is further complicated by the rise of different ethnic identity awareness which existed within the frontiers of individual nations. The emergence of separate Muslim states, each one jealously protecting its independence, created serious divisions within the religious camp.

Besides the conflict between the Western-influenced ruling classes and the *ulema*, there was a third major division. The massive injection of European ideas gave impetus to the revivalist groups whose central tenets included the idea of removing foreign cultural accretions. New revivalist organisations appeared; the members of these tightly-knit groups did not belong to the *ulema*. Unlike the earlier revivalists, they were not formed around the teachings of a prominent *madrasa*-trained member of the *ulema*.[127] Instead, they rejected all forms of nationalism and the hidebound, ineffective traditionalism of the *ulema*. They fought against the idea of loyalty to the nation-state by asserting that the only homeland for Muslims was the global community of Islam.[128] They declared that the only real choice lay between Islam and *jahiliyya*. The latter pervades the whole of mankind, including those societies which normally call themselves Muslim but in practice violate the *Shari'ah*.[129] The *Shari'ah* had maintained Islamic unity since the decline of the Caliphate, and was essential to the survival of the *ummah*. They demanded that Muslim nations establish themselves firmly on the *Shari'ah* and become Islamic states.[130]

Twentieth century revivalists insisted that the *Shari'ah* must be accepted in its entirety.[131] The revivalists were not prepared to be apologists for Islam; they condemned the West and its values and asserted the self-sufficiency and superiority of Islam.[132] They did not condemn Western technology and scientific knowledge, but encouraged Muslims to learn it and to integrate it into an Islamic life. They attacked both the ethos of personal piety and the rise of ethnic or national consciousness.[133] Islam, they urged, had to be a comprehensive ideology for personal and public life. It had to be the only foundation upon which Muslim society and state could be built. They combined their religious ideas with social and political activism; true believers were distinguished from their fellow Muslims and were to be totally committed to the struggle to transform society along Islamic lines.[134]

These groups developed into ideological structures with a well-knit, socio-religious organisation that is often divided up into a network of branches and cells. Their members are carefully selected, and trained to ensure an ideological conformity that is based on religious conviction and a personal moral code.[135] These *jamaats*, for example *Jamaat al-Ikhwan al-Muslimin* and the *Jamaat-i Islami*, function as a group of like-minded and totally committed Muslims whose aim is to transform their societies from within.[136] Maulana Mawdudi, the founder of *Jamaat-i Islami*, states that when the *ummah* is not functioning as it should, the Qur'an itself (Al-Imran 3.104) insists that there must be one group within the wider community that takes upon itself the task of preserving Islam.[137] The work of these *jamaats* is backed up by a programme of religious instruction, youth work, schools, hospitals, religious publications, and social welfare projects. These groups reinterpreted Islamic history and tradition to enable their members to respond to the circumstances of the twentieth century. They insisted upon the union of religion and society, the relevance of Islam to every area of life, and the sovereignty of Allah over mankind as embodied in the all-comprehensive nature of the *Shari'ah*. They have presented a powerful challenge to the governments of many Islamic nations throughout the Muslim world. Their challenge to the established authorities is usually built around the conviction that an Islamic state is essential for the renaissance of the *ummah* and the true practice of the faith.[138] These tightly-knit organisations function independently of each other but recognise a common ideological allegiance which they refer to as the Islamic Movement.

The revivalist movements are an attempt to recreate the *ummah* as based upon the integrated community of the Prophet in Medina, but there are huge difficulties in the way of transferring this vision to the entire Muslim world. The Muslim nations differ on how their societies should be ruled; the *ulema* are divided into many different theological camps and the revivalists, despite common features,[139] are split into several movements each of which demand primary loyalty to their own community.

Conclusion

It can be argued that the integrated community of believers submissive to the will of Allah as proclaimed by the Qur'an has not existed since the death of the Prophet. Sectarian divisions over the question of authority split the community, and the various aspects of the Prophet's charismatic authority were passed on to several different institutions. The *ummah* was maintained by the political institution of the Caliphate and by the *ulema* who codified and preserved correct doctrine. The Umayyads transformed the *ummah* into an Arab dynasty. Under the *Abbasids* the *ulema* and the Caliphate had separated from each other, and eventually the Caliphate itself had ceased to exist in all but name. Independent Muslims kingdoms came into being, but the *ulema* managed to hold the Muslim world together through the *Shari'ah*. However, the *ulema* were split by differences of belief and were unable to maintain their hold under the challenge of European civilisation.

Throughout their history, devout Muslims have been concerned with the question of what constitutes the true *ummah* and how it should be maintained. A following *Hadith* demonstrates this concern:

> When the Prophet once said: 'The saved group among the religious group is one', the Companions asked , 'Oh, Messenger of God, which one?' He said, 'The people of the *Sunna* and the followers of the community.' They asked, 'Who are the people of the *Sunna* and the followers of the community?' He said, 'Those who follow what I and my Companions abide by'.[140]

Exactly who constitutes this group has been a source of argument ever since the Prophet's death. This debate has been exacerbated by the conflict between the respective values of Islam and the West. The result has been the division of the *ummah* into many factions, each justifying their position by various interpretations of the message of Islam.

Gibb argues that 'the first lesson learned by them was that the community must not be identified with or confused with political regimes. Political division in no way impaired the unity of the *ummah*'.[141] He argues that the doctrine of *tawhid* justifies Islamic totality and universalism. The aim has always been to establish a highly integrated and united *ummah*. In fact, Islamic sectarianism has its roots in the political division of the *ummah* and in various attempts to restore unity. These factional differences in the community are in direct opposition to the ideal of universalism which they themselves preach to Muslims everywhere. An *Hadith* demonstrates that Muslims were aware of and gravely concerned with this tendency to divide into factions:

> Ibn Idris al-Khawtani said: 'I said to the Messenger of God, what do you order me to do if I shall live until the time of the troubles?' He said, 'Cleave to Collectivity of the Muslims and their *Imam*.' I said 'And what if they have neither Collectivity nor leader?' He said, 'Then withdraw from the factions altogether, even if you must gnaw the roots of trees until you die'.[142]

Despite all this, ordinary Muslims can look to the wider Islamic community and feel that they belong to it even though it is divided into various competing groups. In particular, there is a sense of belonging which is maintained through the unity of Islam's ritual or cultic practices. The *salat*, *Hajj* and *Ramadan* provide Muslims with a strong sense of religious communion. There are, however, powerful groups of Muslims who insist that this is not enough. They say that Islam has to be a fully comprehensive way of life taking its inspiration from the life of the Prophet and his companions. Their definition of the *ummah* is far more exclusive.

Endnotes

[1] Al-Ghazali, Muhammad Ibn Muhammad, *Revivification of the Sciences of Religion*, Book 15, Ch.3 quoted by John Alden Williams, 1971, *The Themes of Islamic Civilisation*, University of Berkeley Press, California, p.17.

[2] Several orientalists describe the *ummah* in such terms. The following examples are typical:

> Beyond all these considerations it remained a fact that the ordinary Muslim could look at the great Islamic society or community and feel that he belonged to it and that it was in a sense his - that it did not belong to one or more ruling groups however great their powers might be. In other words, the Islamic state had gone a long way towards being a genuine community.

Watt, W.Montgomery, 1961, *Islam and the Integration of Society*, Routledge and Kegan Paul, London, p.174.

> The Islamic society is held together by ideological harmony, composed of individuals with various ethnic-linguistic and racial backgrounds. What distinguishes individuals in such a socially diverse society is not their ethno-linguistic and racial characters, rather, it is in their identification with the Islamic ideology.

Adams, Charles, 1983, 'Mawdudi and the Islamic State', *Voices of Resurgent Islam*, ed Esposito, John, Oxford University Press, New York, p.120.

> It consists of the totality of individuals bound to one another by ties, not of kinship or race, but of religion in that all its members profess their belief in one God, and in the mission of the Prophet Muhammad. Before God and in their relation to Him, all are equal, without distinction of rank, class or race.

Gibb, Hamilton, 1963, 'The Community in Islamic History', *The American Philosophical Society Proceedings*, Vol.107, No.2, April, p.173.

[3] Confession of the *Shahadah* has been the only requirement to become a Muslim from very early on. Ibn Taymiyya (1263-1328) tightened up the procedure by formalising the process and insisting that only the *Ahl al-Sunna* were members. (Al Braik, Nasser, Ahmed M., 1986, *Islam and World Order: Foundation and Values*, PhD, The American University, Washington, p.46.). Ibn Taymiyya, however, seems to advocate that *Shahadah* is not sufficient as the requirement of membership of the *ummah* unless religious duties are performed and the *Shari'ah* obeyed.

[4] See Chapter III.

[5] Dabashi, Hamid, 1989, *Authority in Islam*, Transactions Publishers, New Jersey states that 'the establishment of the *ummah* as the Islamic community was the most significant expression of Islamic solidarity against the traditional tribal structure' (p.76). Dabashi argues, however, that the Arab tribal authority reasserted itself in the institutionalisation of the Prophet's charismatic authority which took place immediately after his death. This phenomenon manifested itself initially as the Sunni line of succession through the Caliphate (p3).

[6] Watt, op.cit., 1961, pp. 185ff.

[7] Dabashi states that 'the authority of Muhammad is thus legitimated because of its being "authorised by Him unto Whom belongeth the sovereignty of the heavens and the earth" (op.cit.,

p.43). According to the *Constitution of Medina* drafted by Muhammad (Watt W. Montgomery, 1968, *Islamic Political Thought*, Islamic Surveys 6, Edinburgh, p.130) the *ummah* was a religious community, that is, 'a community whose reason for existence was constituted in a belief in religious brotherhood and a universal recognition of Allah's sovereignty and Muhammad's prophethood'. This concept of Allah's sovereignty was developed into a comprehensive political philosophy by Maulana Sayyid Abul A'la Mawdudi (1903-1980). According to Mawdudi, *Tawhid* is the central issue. Power, politics and state cannot be left out of any discussion of Allah's sovereignty. Mawdudi argues that no-one can exercise power, or demand obedience, independent of God without becoming a god (Mawdudi, 1984, *The Islamic Movement - Dynamics of Values, Power and Change*, ed. Murad, Khurram, Islamic Foundation, Leicester). *Tawhid*, therefore, requires that political authority must be administered according to God's will.

[8] Rahman states that 'the Qur'an, the most consummate and final revelation of God to man, must be made the primary and indeed the sole direction of human life and the source of the law' (Rahman, Fazlur, 1966, *Islam*, Holt, Rheinehart and Winston, New York, p.69). He admits, however, that the actual legislation of the Qur'an acknowledged existing Arab society as the framework for its instructions. He states that 'this clearly means that the actual legislation of the Qur'an cannot have been meant to be literally eternal by the Qur'an itself'. He argues that Muslim lawyers and theologians confused the issue with the doctrine of the eternity of the Qur'an and attempted to fit the legal injunctions of the Qur'an to any human society regardless of its social structure (ibid.,p.39).

[9] Hodgson argues that the *ummah* manifested the Qur'anic mandate 'to transform the world itself through action in the world' (Hodgson, Marshall. S., 1974, *The Venture of Islam*, Vol. I, University of Chicago Press, Chicago, p.185). Esposito supports this view. He argues that based on the Qur'an's message to strive to realise God's Will in history, the Prophet and the first Muslims established the community in Medina which then became the inspiration for the mission to spread Islam throughout the world (Esposito, John L., 1982, *Islam in Transition*, ed. Donohue, John and Esposito, John L., Oxford University Press, New York, p.6). Esposito agrees that the Medinan community became the aspiration and ideal for millions of Muslims throughout the history of Islam (Esposito, John L., 1988, *Islam - The Straight Path*, Oxford University Press, New York, p.37).

[10] When Muhammad died in 632, he made no provision for a successor to lead the Muslim community. After consultation all agreed to accept Abu Bakr as Caliph. Abu Bakr only lived for another two years. He was succeeded in turn by the other three 'rightly guided Caliphs': Umar (634-644), Uthman (644-656) and Ali (656-661). The fact that both Uthman and Ali were murdered indicates the degree of upheaval in the community after the Prophet's death. The three principal divisions to develop in the community at this time were the *Kharijites*, and those that were later to be called *Sunnis* and *Shi'as*. Dabashi argues that in the *Sunni* tradition there was a tendency towards the institutionalisation of the Prophet's charisma which manifested itself through the reassertion of pre-Islamic Arab traditions and culture. The *Shi'a*, on the other hand, attempted to preserve charismatic religious leadership through the *Imamate*; whilst the *Kharijites* tried to maintain the revolutionary spontaneity of Muhammad's lifetime (Dabashi,op.cit., pp.5-7).

[11] In 661, Mu'awiya made Damascus the new capital of what became the *Umayyad* dynasty. From this centre, the *Umayyads* succeeded in conquering Persia and half the Byzantine empire. Even prior to Mu'awiya's seizure of power, Islam had already spread to Egypt, Libya, Syria, Iraq, and into Persia (Esposito op.cit., p.46).

[12] The ideal is that the primary loyalty should be to the *ummah*, not the ruler or the state. Mawdudi argues that prior to European colonialism 'a Muslim from any part of the world could go to any Muslim land without any restrictions, move freely in that country, stay there as long as he wished, engage in any trade, secure the highest government post in that country, get married without any difficulty' (Mawdudi, Sayyid Abul A'la, 1967, *Unity of the Muslim World*, ed. Ahmad, Khurshid, Islamic Publications, Lahore, pp.14-15). Lewis suggests that though 'Muslim protocol usually despised territorial limitations, regarding them as something to be applied to others rather than to their own rulers, they were nevertheless aware of the existence of territorially defined kingdoms' (Lewis , Bernard, 1988, *The Political Language of Islam*, The University of Chicago Press, Chicago, p.39). Al-Ahsan argues that Muslims adopted the idea of nationalism from the Europeans as a part of their struggle against colonialism (al-Ahsan, Abdullah, 1992, *Ummah or Nation?*, The Islamic Foundation, Leicester, p.27).

[13] Aasi, Ghulam, Haider, 1986,'The Qur'an and Other Religious Traditions', *Hamard Islamicus*, Vol. IX, no.2, p.73.

[14] Paret, R., 1987, 'Umma', *First Encyclopaedia of Islam 1913-1936*, 2nd Edition, Vol.VIII, ed. Houtsma, Wensinck, et al., A.J. Brill, Leiden, P.1015.

[15] In *Sura* 11:8 and 12:45 *Ummah* is used to denote 'a time', or a period of time. Here the Qur'an asserts that for every people a period of time or a term has been decreed. They will then suffer destruction. Thus *ummah* denotes an age. In Sura 16:120, *ummah* is used to describe Abraham by himself as an *ummah* of one. Al-Ahsan argues that according to commentaries by Al-Razi, Vol. 20, p.134, and Al-Zamakhshari, Vol 2, p.433, Abraham is being used as an ideal model of the *ummah* itself, as he combined within himself all the qualities of the God-given beliefs of a God-conscious community (Al-Ahsan, Abdullah, op.cit., p.13).

[16] Denny, Frederick, 1974, *Community and Salvation: The Meaning of Ummah in the Qur'an*, PhD, the University of Chicago, Chicago, p.55.

[17] Rahman, Fazlur, 1980, *Major themes in the Qur'an*, Bibliotheca Islamica, Chicago, p.138.

[18] There is some dispute over this. According to the Noldeke-Schwally chronology there are no references to *ummah* in the first Meccan period (Denny,op.cit., p.43). Both Richard Bell (ibid) and Muslim sources (taken from 'Tables of Names of *Suras* showing the Makkan and the Madinah ones', *The Holy Qur'an*, tr. Ali, Abdullah Yusef, Al-Madinah Al-Munawarah, Medina), however, argues that *Fatir* 35:24 and 42 are early Meccan. Nöldeke-Schwally disagree and date them as Third Meccan period (ibid). Both these *ayats* seem to use the term '*ummah*' to refer to communities or peoples in a general sense with no specific religious or moral context, although it is indicated that a Messenger is sent to all human societies.

[19] All the *ayats* quoted here are from the Third Meccan period according to Noldeke-Schwally (ibid). Richard Bell generally agrees but considers *Al-Ahqaf* 46:18 to be Medinan. Muslim sources (*The Holy Qur'an*) agree with the Nöldeke-Schwally chronology and place them all as late Meccan.

[20] The Nöldeke-Schwally chronology dates this *ayat* as Second Meccan (ibid.) but Richard Bell regards it as early Medinan (ibid). Muslim sources say it is late Meccan (The *Holy Qur'an*).

[21] Denny, op.cit., p.54.

[22] Khurram Murad uses this *ayat* in precisely this way to justify Maulana Mawdudi establishing the *Jamaat-i Islami* (Mawdudi, 1986, *Witness Unto Mankind*, ed. Murad, Khurram, The Islamic Foundation, Leicester).

[23] Watt, W. Montgomery, op.cit.,1961, p.46.

[24] ibid., pp. 7-8; Esposito, op.cit.,1988, p.7; Watt, Montgomery W., 1968a, *What is Islam?*, Longmans, London, p.45.

[25] ibid., p14.

[26] The Qur'an perceived the cause of the social tensions in Mecca to be the belief of the great merchants in 'omnicompetence, indeed the omnipotence, of human planning and human wealth'. It demanded that they acknowledged the existence of a superior power and to behave in a manner that would bring approval from that power. They were asked 'to be generous, not niggardly with their wealth and to use some of it to relieve the needs of unfortunate members of the community' (ibid, pp.96-97). *The Holy Qur'an*, *Al-Lail* 92:18-21, *Al-Balad* 90:5-20.

[27] ibid., *Az-Zariyat* 51:19. In Mecca almsgiving, although emphasised remained a voluntary action to support the poorer sections of the community. In Medina the *Zakat* was established on a formal basis (Rahman, op.cit., 1966, pp. 36-37).

[28] Watt, op.cit.,1968a, p.146-147.

[29] *The Constitution of Medina*, Appendix B, opening paragraph and Paragraph 1. (taken from Watt, Montgomery W., 1972, *Muhammad at Medina*, Clarendon Press, Oxford, pp.221-225).

[30] There is a sense in which the new alliance is not only political but religious. Membership of the alliance was open only to those who accepted Muhammad as the Messenger of God. See ibid., opening Paragraph and Paragraphs 1, 15, 16, 23.

[31] ibid., Appendix B, Paragraph 42.

[32] ibid., Appendix B, Paragraphs 16, 25.

[33] ibid, Appendix B.

[34] Dabashi, op.cit., p.3, p.49.

[35] *The Constitution of Medina*, op.cit., Appendix B, Paragraphs 1-10; Dabashi, op.cit., p.54, p.57.

[36] *The Constitution of Medina*, op.cit., Appendix B, Paragraph 23.

[37] Dabashi, op.cit., p.60. The Qur'an describes the relationship between Allah, Muhammad and the Community in *Al-Araf* 7;158

> Say: O men! I am sent
> Unto you all, as the Messenger
> of Allah, to Whom belongeth
> the domination of the heavens
> and the earth: there is no god
> but He: it is He that giveth
> Both life and death. So believe
> in Allah and His Messenger.
> The unlettered Prophet,
> Who believeth in Allah
> And His Words: follow him
> That ye may be guided.

[38] Many of these laws and prescriptions are found in *Sura 2 Al-Baqarah* revealed at the time of the breaking with the Jews. E.g. fasting (2:183-185); almsgiving (2:43,277); prayer (2:125,238-239); pilgrimage (2:196-197,199,189).

[39] These are mainly found in the first five *suras*: There are references to marriage (*Al Baqarah* 2:221,223,234; *An-Nisaa* 4:3,4:22; *Al-Ma'idah* 5:5); divorce (2:228-32, 236-7, 241-2); inheritance (2:180-182; *An-Nisaa* 4:11-12; 19); rights of women (4:15-42,127).

[40] *The Holy Qur'an*, Al-Baqarah 2:135-141.

[41] ibid., *Al-Ma'idah* 5:3.

[42] The Medinan *suras* lay down ordinances for the religious life of the community. *Ramadan* (2:183-185); *Hajj* (2:196-203); the *Qibla* (2:144); the setting aside of Friday (62:9); dietary requirements (5:3) are all detailed.

[43] O ye men! Hearken unto my words
> and take ye them to heart!
> Know ye that every Muslim is a brother
> unto every other Muslim,
> and that ye are now of one brotherhood.
> It is not legitimate for any one of you
> therefore, to appropriate unto himself anything
> that belongs to his brother unless it is
> willingly given him by that brother.

According to Ibn Hisham, as quoted by Hitti, Philip, 1970, *The History of the Arabs*, Macmillan, London, p.120, this was uttered by the Prophet at the Farewell Pilgrimage.

[44] Dabashi argues that the issue of the leadership after Muhammad's death was left to the community (op.cit, p.57). He states that the appointment of Abu Bakr was a successful attempt by the *Quraysh* to reaffirm their traditional status among the Arabs (ibid., pp. 65-66). Dabashi believes the Abu Bakr argued for his case by maintaining that the unity of the Islamic community and its survival in the future depended upon Muslims only having one leader and that he should belong to the Prophet's tribe. The *Shi'a* line of succession, in contrast, was an attempt to keep the line of succession and the leadership of the community within the family of Muhammad (ibid., p.99).

[45] Abu Bakr was involved in suppressing several tribes who rebelled against the central authority of Medina (Watt, op.cit., 1968a, p.113). Two civil wars were fought from 656-661, and again from 680-692 (ibid., p.114) over the question of leadership.

[46] Watt, W.Montgomery, 1973, *The Formative Period of Islamic Thought*, University of Edinburgh, Edinburgh, pp.83-84.

[47] ibid.

[48] Watt argues that *Kharijite* groups in particular were protesting against the strictures of the organisational structure in which they were caught up (ibid., p.20). Also Watt, op.cit., 1961, p.95.

[49] ibid., p.108.

[50] Goldziher, Ignaz, 1981, *Introduction to Islamic Theology and Law*, Princeton University Press, Princeton, p.71.

[51] Dabashi, op.cit., 1988, pp.79-80.

[52] Watt, op.cit., 1961, p.108.

[53] Esposito, op.cit., 1988, p.45 & p.47. Omar II's fiscal reforms brought equality in taxation between the Arabs and the *Mawali* (Vida, G. Levi Della, 1987, 'Umaiyads', *First Encyclopaedia of Islam 1913-1936*, 2nd Edition, eds. Houtsma, Wensinck et al., A.J.Brill, Leiden, p.1002).

[54] Esposito, op.cit., p.45.

[55] Watt maintains that the *Abbasids* were supported by the *Mawali* (op.cit., 1968a, p.123). The *Abbasids* were able to argue that they were following Islamic principles as opposed to the *Umayyads* who were maintaining old Arab ideas (ibid). This brought them the support of many with a genuine religious interest (ibid.,p.123). A part of the programme of the *Abbasids* against the *Umayyads* was to secure the full Islamic rights of the *Mawali* (ibid., p.121).

[56] ibid., p.124; Esposito, op.cit., p.58.

[57] ibid., p.55.

[58] ibid., p.56.

[59] The *Kharijites* were not one unified group. Dabashi claims that there were at least twenty different *Kharijite* communities of which the principle ones were the *Azraqites*, the *Najdites*, and the *Waqifites* (Dabashi, op.cit., p.131).

[60] The *Kharijites* argued that authority was vested in the *ummah*. Their leaders were selected by the majority of the community and could be removed in the same way. They also stressed that the only prerogative for leadership was religious piety. None of their leaders were from the *Quraysh*, nor were they believed to be divinely ordered to command (ibid., p.137).

[61] The *Kharijites* insisted upon the equality of all believers (Von Grunebaum, G.E., 1970, *Classical Islam: A History, 600AD-1258AD*, Aldine, Chicago, p.62). They challenged the *Umayyads* and the *Shi'a* by declaring that they would create a society in which even a 'black slave could become the leader of the *ummah* through popular consent' (Dabashi, op.cit. p.124). Dabashi states that 'election and radical puritanism' were the only criteria for membership of the community (ibid.). He argues that the absence of the institutional authority to regulate the leadership of the *Kharijite* communities made them unstable. Leaders were constantly challenged on their degree of piety (ibid.,p.128) and divisions within the *Kharijite* groups were usually over the question of what constitutes a sinful act (ibid.).

[62] Dabashi argues that it was the *Kharijites* who were the first to insist that the community be established strictly according to Qur'anic principles (ibid.,p.140).

[63] ibid., p.124.

[64] Watt, op.cit., 1973, p.22; Dabashi, op.cit., p.131.

[65] ibid. The *Azraqites* believed that it was not sufficient to merely hold correct beliefs. To remain at home and not join them was considered a mark of unbelief (Watt, op.cit., 1961, p.100) and punishable by death. Other groups were not always as extreme. The *Najdites* came to control most of Arabia until defeated by the *Umayyads*. Watt argues that this led them to modify their position concerning expulsion from the community (ibid.). Dabashi suggests that this was because they had to institutionalise their attitude regarding authority in order to rule over territory (op.cit., pp.132-133).

[66] The *Kharijites* made *jihad* the sixth pillar of the faith (ibid.p.129). Lambton states that 'they allowed assassination for religious reasons' (Lambton, A.K.S., 1981, *State and Government in Mediaeval Islam: An Introduction to the Study of Islamic Political Theory: The Jurists*, Oxford University Press, Oxford, p.24.) Hitti says that 'in endeavouring to maintain the primitive, charismatic principles of Islam, the puritanical *Kharijites* caused rivers of blood to flow in the

first three Muslim centuries' (Hitti, Philip.K, 1970, *The History of the Arabs*, Macmillan, London, p.247).

[67] Dabashi states that the *Kharijites* considered their own communities as *Dar al-Islam* and everyone else as *Dar al-Harb* (op.cit., p.131). This permitted the use of *jihad* against everyone that had not made the *Hijra* to *Dar al-Islam* (ibid).

[68] Esposito, 1988, p.48.

[69] ibid.

[70] ibid., p.70.

[71] ibid.

[72] Guillaume, Alfred, 1963, *Islam*, Cassell, London, p.115.

[73] ibid., p.114.

[74] Dabashi, op.cit., pp.152-153.

[75] Esposito, op.cit., p.76.

[76] ibid.

[77] The great legal scholars, such as Abu Hanifa (d.767), Malik ibn Annas (d.796), Muhammad al-Shafi'i (d.819) and Muhammad ibn Hanbal (d.855), the founders of the four schools of law, were overhauling *Umayyad* laws and customs in the light of Qur'anic teaching (ibid., p.76).

[78] Watt states that by the late ninth century the *Sunna* of the Prophet was established by sound traditions and accepted by the majority of *Sunni* Muslims (op.cit., 1973, p.266). The six most authoritative collections of *Hadith* all appeared in this century. They are (1) Al-Bukhari (d.870); (2) Muslim (d.875); (3) Abu Dawud (d.888); (4) Al-Tirmidhi (d.892); (5) Al-Nasai (d.915) (6) Ibn Madja (d.886) (Juynboll, The.W., 1987, 'Hadith', *Encyclopaedia of Islam*, Vol. III, p.194).

[79] Esposito, op.cit., pp.58-59.

[80] ibid., p.65.

[81] Hitti, op.cit., pp.676-677.

[82] Ibid., p.489.

[83] Ibid., pp.676-677.

[84] Esposito, op.cit., p.65.

[85] Mawardi, Adab al-Din wa'l, *Dunya*, p.115 quoted in Abdullah, h. Kh. A. Hamed, 1988, *Some Aspects of Arabic/Islamic Political Thought in Iraq (4th - 8th c. A.H./ 10th-14th centuries AD*, PhD, University of Manchester, p.50.

[86] ibid., p.115-116.

[87] Lewis, Bernard, op.cit., p.99; Najjar, Fauzi, 1984, 'Islamic Political Philosophy', *Islamic Theology and Philosophy*, ed. Marmura, Midail, State University of the New York Press, Albany, p.95.

[88] Al-Braik, op.cit., p.38.

[89] Bagley, F.R.C. (trs.), 1964, *Ghazali's Book of Counsel for Kings*, al-Ghazali, Muhammad Ibn Muhammad, Oxford University Press, London, p.46.

[90] *Abu - Ya ha Muhammad Ibn al-Husayn al Ahkam al-Sultaniyya*, ed. M.H. al-Faqi, Cairo, 1938, quoted in Abdullah, op.cit., p.192.

[91] Al-Braik, op.cit., p.39.

[92] Najjar, op.cit., p.97.

[93] ibid., p.94.

[94] Al Ghazali, Muhammad Ibn Muhammad, *Ihya 'Ulum Al-Din,*, p.124 quoted in *Law in the Middle East*, Vol.I,1955, ed.Khadduri, Majid & Liebesny J., The Middle East Institute, Washington DC, p.13.

[95] Najjar, op.cit., pp.98-99.

[96] Ibn Taymiyya only acknowledges the first four *Rashidun* as Caliphs (ibid.,p.99).

[97] Al-Braik, op.cit., p.46.

[98] Najjar, op.cit., p.100.

[99] See endnote 3.

[100] ibid.

[101] *Ibn Maja*, book 36, Bab 8 quoted in Williams, op.cit., p.9.

[102] Makdisi, George, 1981, *The Rise of Colleges*, Edinburgh University Press, Edinburgh, p.22.

103 ibid., p.155.

104 ibid., p.299.

105 Al-Shafi'i, Muhammad, ibn Idris, *Al-Risala*, Shakir Edition, Cairo, 1940, p.476.

106 Esposito, op.cit., pp.58-59.

107 There are examples of this throughout Muslim history. The first group manifestation was the *Kharijites*. Ahmad Ibn Hanbal (780-855) and Ibn Taymiyya (d.1328) both called for strict obedience to the Qur'an and *Sunna*. The latter opposed popular practices which the people considered Islamic but which had no justification according the Qur'an or *Sunna*. Popular Sufism, Greek philosophy, and later Western influences were all opposed by men who asserted a revival or reform based on the canon of scripture (Voll, John, 1983, 'Renewal and Reform In Islamic History', *Voices of Resurgent Islam*, ed. Esposito, John L., Oxford University Press, Oxford, P.38).

108 Examples of such groups are the *Wahhabis* in Arabia, founded by Muhammad ibn Abd al-Wahhab; the *Sanusiyyah tariqa* established in North Africa by Muhammad ibn Ali al-Sanusi; and the *Deobandi* movement in India (see Chapter VI and VII).

109 Voll, op.cit., p.32.

110 *The Holy Qur'an*, Al-A'raf 7:170; Hud 11:116; Al-Qasas 28:19.

111 Esposito, op.cit., p.118.

112 Voll, op.cit., p.33.

113 Esposito, op.cit., p.118.

114 Voll, op.cit, p.33.

115 The *Deobandi* school has issued several *fatwas* declaring that those who opposed their message are *kafirs* or *mushriqs* (see Chapter VI and VII).

116 Donohue, John J. & Esposito, John L, (eds), 1982, *Islam in Transition*, Oxford University Press, Oxford, p.5.

117 ibid.

118 Hourani, Albert, 1962, *Arabic Thought in the Liberal Age*, Oxford University Press, London, p.104.

119 ibid., p.151.

[120] ibid.

[121] Esposito, op.cit., p.85.

[122] ibid., p.146.

[123] ibid.

[124] Donohue & Esposito, op.cit., p.11.

[125] ibid.

[126] Geaves, Ronald, 1988, 'Islam and Nationalism: Turkey and Saudi Arabia', M.A. paper, University of Leeds, Leeds, p.14.

[127] Prominent examples of this phenomenon are the *Jamaat-i Islami* founded by Maulana Mawdudi and the *Jamaat al-Ikhwan al-Muslimin* founded by Hassan Al Banna.

[128] Haddad, Yvonne Y., 1983, 'Sayyid Qutb: Ideologue of Islamic Revival', *Voices of Resurgent Islam*, ed. Esposito, John L., Oxford University Press, Oxford, p.79.

[129] ibid., p.85.

[130] Adams, op.cit., pp.113-114.

[131] ibid.

[132] Haddad, op.cit., pp.79-80.

[133] Mawdudi, Sayyid, 1986, *The Islamic Way of Life*, ed. Ahmed Khurshid, The Islamic Foundation, Leicester, pp.54-55; Donohue & Esposito, op.cit., pp.94-97.

[134] Haddad, op.cit., pp.87-88.

[135] *Jamaat-i Islami*, founded in India by Maulana Mawdudi, is a group which typifies this kind of structure. It has offshoots in Britain and will be examined in detail in Chapters X and XI.

[136] Esposito, op.cit., p.154.

[137] Mawdudi,op.cit., 1986, p.21.

[138] Esposito, op.cit., p.157.

[139] The common ideological framework of Islamic Revivalism has been analysed by John L. Esposito (1988). He lists seven features common to the ideological outlook of the earlier revivalists. They are as follows:

1)   The process of renewal required a reenactment of the first and paradigmatic Islamic revolution or reformation of the Prophet.

2)   Religion is integral to state and society.

3)   Departure from the norm leads to the fragmentation of the community and a decline in its fortunes.

4)   Only a purging of unIslamic behaviour and a return to the straight path of Islam, a life governed by Islamic law, can restore the community to its rightful place of ascendancy and power.

5)   Major causes of Muslim decline are the unchecked cultural syncretism of popular Sufism and the uncritical acceptance of *taqlid*.

6)   True believers, like the early Muslims, may need to separate themselves to preserve their faith and form a righteous society or brotherhood.

7)   Those Muslims who resist are no longer to be regarded as Muslim but numbered amongst the enemies of God (1988, pp.126-127).

Esposito goes on to list the common features of the modern revivalists emphasising the distinguishing factors belonging to the activist groups:

1)   A crusader mentality - Western and Eastern neocolonialism, and the power of Zionism pit the West against the Islamic world.

2)   Establishment of an Islamic system of government is not simply an alternative but an Islamic imperative, based on God's command or will. Therefore, all Muslims must obey and follow this divine mandate by struggling to implement and follow God's law.

3)   Since the legitimacy of Muslim governments is based on the *Shari'ah*, those governments that do not follow Islamic law, government and individuals are guilty of unbelief. They are no longer Muslim, but are atheists whose unbelief demands holy war.

4)   Opposition to legitimate governments extends to the official *ulema*, the religious establishment, and state supported mosques and preachers who are considered to have been co-opted by the government.

5)   *Jihad* against unbelief and unbelievers is a religious duty. Therefore, all true believers are obliged to combat such governments and their supporters, whether individuals or foreign governments. Like the *Kharijites* in early Islam, radicals demand total commitment and obedience. One is either a true believer or an infidel, saved or damned, a friend or an enemy of God. The army of Allah is locked in holy war with the followers of Satan.

6)   Christians and Jews are generally regarded as unbelievers rather than 'People of the Book' because of their connections with Western Christianity (colonialism) and Zionism. They are seen as partners in a Judeo-Christian conspiracy against Islam and the Muslim world. Thus, non-Muslim minorities are often subjected to persecution (ibid.,pp.170-172).

[140] Othman, Ali, Issa, 1960, *The Concept of Man in Islam in the Writings of Al-Ghazali*, Dar

al-Maaref, Cairo, p.213.

[141] Gibb, op.cit., pp.174-175.

[142] Bukhari, Book 92, Bab 11, quoted in Williams, op.cit., p.10.

3 A sociological analysis of 'ummah'

Introduction

The previous Chapter has examined the Muslim concept of community which   is rooted in revelations concerning '*ummah*' contained in the Qur'an and further developed by various *Hadith*. This approach to the *ummah* is not, however, sufficient in itself to fully understand developments in the Muslim world. The following overview of various sociological analyses provides alternative ways of regarding developments that have taken place in the *ummah* which have to be combined with the Muslim perspective to ascertain the possibilities that could occur in Britain. Before the following chapter focuses on the situation of Muslims in Britain it is necessary to balance the Muslim perspective of community with insights drawn from sociological studies. It is also important to realise that the Muslims in Britain are a minority migrant community and therefore form other kinds of community more amenable to analysis through sociological study than solely by reference to the Islamic concept of *ummah*.

Sociological Analysis of *Ummah*

McWilliams, in spite of his use of androcentric language, provides a concept which throws light on the situation of the Islamic world.[1] He speaks of 'fraternity,' which he defines as a relation of brotherhood or as an organisation based on fraternal relations between members.[2] The fraternity is a common bond based on a a common creator who has established the relationship of brotherhood amongst mankind.[3] McWilliams states that the initiate brother is incorporated into a new community which breaks away or replaces an older community. In fact, membership is based upon accepting a set of values and beliefs which are considered higher than those of the older community.[4] This bond of companions linked by a common vision resembles but is superior to the community that is based on familial relations. McWilliams argues that the fraternity always contains the seed of its own destruction.[5] The ultimate conclusion of the fraternity's beliefs is to suggest that they should be incorporated into a universal community. All men should be united under the common creator. If this conviction is pursued with any degree of success, it creates a vast state in which the original fraternal relationship breaks down since the members can only know each other as abstractions. McWilliam's analysis can be usefully applied to the history of Islam and the concept of *ummah*. The rapid growth of the Muslim empire would have placed massive stress on the ideal of community as based on the close-knit companionship of the early followers of Islam.

The usual Islamic conception of *ummah* is an historical one developed during the mediaeval period. The idea of the *ummah* as a theoretical construct is one thing, but its application within a dramatically changing world is quite another. Karl Mannheim argues that in a world in constant upheaval where new belief systems are constantly being introduced and old ones fundamentally challenged, the conflict of ideas will go so far as to attempt to destroy the actual foundations upon which the old beliefs and values rest. This collapse of intellectual unity comes about when the belief systems of different groups are diametrically opposed.[6] The Muslim nations contain such opposing ideologies, and unless a solution can be found which satisfies all groups, any inherited unity based on Islam is in profound danger. The other solution is that one group becomes strong enough to impose its will on the others by force. Something of this has already been seen in Iran.

Chapter II has demonstrated that there have been various creative responses to political and social change in order to maintain the integrity of the *ummah*. Arnold Toynbee suggests that civilisations break down when they are no longer able to respond creatively to new situations. He argues that this breakdown occurs not because of any physical circumstances, but because of false attitudes leading to a failure of the inner spirit which embodies the civilisation's values. The civilisation tends to rest on its laurels, idolising either the whole society at the moment of success or else some special institution to which success was due.[7] Interestingly, Toynbee posits that this kind of breakdown occurs quite early in a civilisation's history. It is followed by a series of rallies and relapses, but once the initial breakdown has occurred, death is inevitable.[8] The *Umayyad* and *Abbasid* dynasties could be viewed as the loss of the original values of Muhammad's community. Since that time, the civilisation founded on Islam has sometimes rallied and sometimes relapsed. It has often been guilty of idolising a vision of community which it has not been able historically to maintain. Toynbee, however, suggests that if the community is a religious one, breakdown need not inevitably be followed by death; it can alternatively be followed by renewal.[9] If Toynbee is correct, the revivalist solution may well be the only one that can revitalise the charismatic community initially conceived by Muhammad. The problem here, though, is that the revivalist groups, like the early *Kharijites*, hold a more exclusive definition of *ummah* than that generally held by most Muslims who feel that simply to be born a Muslim is sufficient qualification for membership. Consequently, the revivalists create elite groups within the wider *ummah* which often create division and conflict within Muslim societies. There are also many different groups based on ideological thinking. Toynbee argues that ideological thinking inflates the ego-consciousness: individuals exaggerate their own significance. A similar phenomenon takes place with groups; there is an inflation of group consciousness bound up with a strong awareness of separation from others based on a feeling of moral superiority.[10] This will make it difficult for the various Islamic groups to resolve their differences and recreate the utopian united community they aspire to.

The Rural and Urban Divide

In addition to the above stresses on the Islamic ideal of *ummah* there is also a major divide caused by the diverse forms of religion which develop in the cities and the countryside respectively. Gellner has established two sets of characteristics which he claims distinguish urban Islam from that of rural areas. The characteristics of the former are strict monotheism; puritanism; stress on scriptural revelation and therefore on literacy; egalitarianism amongst the believers and consequently an absence of human mediation and its accompanying hierarchy; a minimisation of elaborate ritual or mysticism and a focus on sobriety and moderation instead; and finally a stress on the observance of rules rather than emotional states. The latter set is comprised of a tendency towards this-world and other-world hierarchies; a reliance on human intermediaries in this world and a hierarchy of spirits in the other; the development of perceptual symbols or images rather than the abstract word which leads to a multiplicity of ritual and mystical practices; and finally loyalty towards personalities rather than a formal set of rules.[11]

Gellner argues that the urban, literate, egalitarian Islam represented by the *madrasa*-trained *ulema* is to some degree identical throughout the Islamic world and can be defined as orthodox.[12] He goes on to suggest that the 'hierarchical, less puritanical, emotionally and sensually indulgent Islam of the saints, holy men etc' is more fragmented.[13] It is 'discontinuous in its organisation, which undergoes fairly frequent and fundamental transformations'.[14]

Gellner bases his observations on the argument that the rural Muslims whether from tribe or village require spiritual intermediaries between themselves and a remote deity because illiteracy renders the abstract reasoning of theologians and trained *ulema* and even the revealed voice of the deity itself beyond them.[15] He suggests, however, that rural Muslims require the sacred for settling disputes and defining the norms of village or tribal life.[16] For this reason hierarchical, charismatic religious personnel are essential. He concludes that the relationship of this religious elite with their followers is one of intense personal loyalty rather than obedience to a set of principles or rules and that this is liable to expose the villagers or tribesmen to accusations of heterodoxy.[17] On the other hand, the city-dweller is more likely to be literate and therefore the literate *ulema* can best function as mediators of scripture.[18] This manifests as a division between the orthodox *ulema* and the Sufi *shaikhs* or pirs.

Gellner acknowledges that in the city both forms of Islam can be found but he suggests that the followers of a personal saint are recruited in a different way than in rural areas. He argues that in the city a saint's following is individual and elective, whereas in the villages and tribes it is by group and ascribed.[19] This urban/rural divide in the *ummah* may contain aspects of what is known as *Gemeinschaft/Gesellschaft* relations.[20] Some urban Muslims, especially those that have migrated from villages may seek the closer ties and enhanced status of affiliation to revivalist groups or orthodoxy to replace the *Gemeinschaft* relations of the village or tribe which they may have lost in the more impersonal and individual life of the city-dweller.

Muslim Minority Communities

A further complicating factor occurs when a minority community of Muslims lives within a larger community of unbelievers, either as a result of conquest, migration, or assimilation. Minority communities tend to organise themselves on an ethnic basis maintaining their original languages, very often living in close-knit inner-city enclaves to protect themselves from assimilation into or hostility from the majority culture. This creates a different kind of community formed around kin networks and place of origin which may use religion to reinforce ethnic identity. In the case of Muslims this may conflict with the religious definition of the *ummah* which insists upon universal Islamic identity being primary. This situation will prove a strong breeding ground in which revivalist groups can flourish. Divisions are likely to occur between religious and ethnic loyalties. This will be further complicated by pressures to assimilate into the mainstream culture. The receiving culture will insist that the new migrants obey the political authority and observe the laws of the country in which they find themselves. The dominant non-Muslim government, particularly in contemporary liberal secular societies, will try to distinguish the religious from the political by tolerating the former but curbing the latter. For many Muslims, it may not always be easy to distinguish between the two. It is inevitable that the non-Muslim state will demand the political loyalty and allegiance of all its minorities. In the case of Muslims, where the *Shari'ah* bridges the divisions between politics and religion, this could create conflict. The various Muslim responses to this situation will create further divisions within their community. The Muslims will have no choice but to uphold their position in order to protect themselves. It is, however, almost impossible to ascertain whether this would lead to unity or to factions along the lines of divisions already historically existing within the community in their countries of origin. In the case of Muslim migrants who originate from the subcontinent, the impact of western colonialism and the consequent introduction of secular values has already led to a crisis of identity in the countries of origin which has affected the survival of the community, the self-awareness of Muslims, and their relationship to non-Muslims.

Sociological Analysis of Community

It is essential, then, to balance the Islamic ideal of the *ummah* as the universal brotherhood of believers, with some sociological definitions of community. This is especially so in the context of Muslim migrant minority communities. Generally sociologists make the distinction between a social system and a community on the basis of space. A social system is a set of inter-related social institutions covering all aspects of social life, familial, religious, judicial, etc., and the associated belief systems belonging to each. A community is usually defined as a local social system where such a.set of inter-relations exists in a geographically defined area.[21] On the basis of this type of definition, the area of the globe covered by Islam is far too diverse to be described as a community. It could, however, certainly be viewed as a social system containing many different kinds of communities.

Colin Bell and Howard Newby argue that the study of community should be undertaken by 'locality' studies; in other words, it should be the study of the interrelationship of social institutions within a territorially-defined area.[22] A limited geographical space combined with some elements of Tonnies's *Gemeinschaft* seems to be the common denominator of most modern sociological definitions.[23] Stein's definition is typical: a community is 'an organised system standing in a determinate relation to its environment which has a local basis but not necessarily a rigid boundary'.[24] So many human groups have been studied by sociologists that it is an impossible task to pin down a single definition of a community. Poplin attempts to clarify this by dividing the sociological use of the term into three categories :

(a)   As a synonym for religious organisations, prisons, mental hospitals, and minority groups.

(b)   As moral or spiritual phenomena where community is seen as some kind of ideal in the post-industrial revolution world. This is particularly expressed in phrases like 'a sense of community'.

(c)   As units of social and territorial organisation such as hamlets, villages, towns, or districts of cities; that is to say, places where people maintain their homes, earn their livings, rear their children, carry on life's activities.   Here there are three common factors: a geographic area, social interaction and a common tie or ties.[25]

Amongst studies based on the latter definition there are many of migrant communities in inner city 'ghettos' or urban villages.   These fit comfortably into most definitions that sociologists have arrived at, and may be termed 'par excellence communities'.[26]   In this respect community is referred to as a condition in which human beings find themselves enmeshed in a tight-knit web of meaningful relationships with their fellow human beings.[27] This kind of community has been of particular interest to sociologists engaged in the urban studies. In an early study of urban life, Louis Wirth defined the city as 'a relatively large, dense and permanent settlement of socially heterogeneous individuals'.[28] He perceived the city-dweller to be 'anonymous, isolated, secular, relativistic, rational and sophisticated'.[29] Wirth concludes that the social system of the city is similar to Tonnies's *Gesellschaft*.[30] Wirth's study was undertaken in 1938 prior to suburbanisation. Gans argues that Wirth's analysis is now possibly only valid in the inner-city whose populations are typically heterogeneous and transient.[31] The presence of migrant communities in the inner-city challenge Wirth's analysis. They demonstrate that a significant proportion of the inhabitants live within social structures and cultural patterns which they brought with them from elsewhere and develop to fit the new situation.[32] These populations, which include large numbers of Muslims, form relatively homogeneous groupings protected from the attributes of city life as defined by Wirth. Rex and Josephides suggest 'it is still true that the springs of *Gemeinschaft* are far more evident amongst ethnic minority immigrants in industrial society than they are in the host community'.[33]   These migrant communities are likely to use religion as one of several means to reinforce their ethnic identity as a wall against the perceived threat of the *Gesellschaft* aspects of the alien city which they have to establish as their new home.

MacIver makes the distinction between community and association.[34]   He argues that a community is merely a 'common living of human beings', whereas 'an association is an organisation of social life, definitely established for the pursuit of one or more common interest'.[35]   The association is a consciously formed group of people who come together to attain a specific goal which is easier to obtain when all unite to achieve it.   Within a community there may be many associations.   Rex argues that the distinction between community and association needs to be made more subtle to fit the reality of migrant communities within inner cities. This is based upon his own research in Sparkbrook, Birmingham.[36] He draws a distinction between 'primary communities' and associations. He states:

> In primary communities men reveal more of themselves. They turn to their fellow-members in times of emergency. They tell secrets about themselves. They share excitements and joys. They feel able to relax and 'to let their hair down'. In ordinary life outside they measure themselves against what they think other members of the primary community might think is proper behaviour.[37]

Most individuals find their primary community amidst their immediate family. This would certainly apply amongst the Muslim minority in Britain especially once the South Asian migrants moved out of the all-male stage of community development. Rex argues that the membership of a primary community is not sufficient to fulfil all the interests that people have in a complex economic and social urban environment.[38] He suggests that structured interaction begins to take place in the form of associations. The membership of an association presupposes a shared world-view.[39] In the case of migrants, Rex argues that the associations they form will be concerned with the morality of the younger generation; the maintenance of food taboos and religious observance, and keeping contact with the culture of origin. He suggests that the concern with religion will be bound up with the problem of conserving culture in the new environment.[40]

> Faced with the welter of conflicting cultural meanings of the city, the immigrant, at least, until he knows his way round, needs a cultural retreat, where he knows the rules, and knows that other people accept the rules. For a while, therefore, he must live 'in a colony'. The colony may grow around a church or mosque.[41]

Rex argues that migrant associations will not only be concerned with spiritual well-being but also the practical problems and difficulties of immigrants. They will be called upon to deal with employment problems, passport difficulties, legal concerns, housing, and all the other problematic areas which arise in dealing with living in an unfamiliar environment. He suggests that individual immigrants need to know that there is one of their own kind, sharing their own world-view, who can assist them through the maze of problems and concerns.[42]

Many of the religious groups in Islam, especially those formed in the twentieth century, could fit into MacIver's definition of association. All the mosques in Britain, however, are affiliated to a particular strand of Islam, the majority having loyalty either to the *Barelwi* or *Deobandi* groups whose origins are further back in subcontinent history. Each mosque functions as a centre to reinforce a particular world-view and finds itself not merely a place of worship but an association which fulfils the needs put forward by Rex. Joly points out that the earlier Muslim associations in Britain were concerned with immigration issues and return to Pakistan,[43] and that they were rarely British-wide or international organisations.[44] She goes on to demonstrate that later associations are more concerned with the maintenance and reproduction of the community in Britain. In this context the central concern has become the preservation of Islam and the promotion of Islamic identity, particularly in regard to the British-born generations.[45] These groups are more likely to be associated with international Islamic movements. In Britain they are national organisations established around a particular programme or ideology. Joly argues that they all 'share the firm intention of securing a place for Muslims and Islam in Britain, outside the *Dar al Islam*'.[46]

There are two other conceptual types of community which can be useful to understand this latter development of Muslim associations in Britain identified by Joly. These are the 'moral community' and the 'intentional community'. Poplin defines the moral community as having the following qualities: the members have a deep sense of belonging to a significant meaningful group in which they have a sense of pursuing common goals and feel a oneness with other community members; they are submerged in various groups and feel a compelling need to participate in these groups where they are regarded as whole persons who are of intrinsic significance and worth.[47]

The intentional community overlaps with the moral community. Shenkar defines the intentional community as one which is founded as a conscious and purposive act and where membership is voluntary and also based on a conscious act (even if the member is born in the community). He goes on to say that the group sees itself as separate from and different to its environment and relates as a group to its environment. This includes withdrawal from the environment. This means that the community is relatively self-contained and most of its members can potentially live their entire lives in it. Sharing is part of the community's ideology and it has collective goals and needs and expects members to work towards their satisfaction. The ideology expounded claims that the goals of the community, even if orientated to the benefit of the individual, can only be obtained in a collective framework as it is not the individual that constitutes the source of authority, but the community or people appointed by the community. The general way of life of the community is considered to be inherently good, i.e. it is seen as an end in itself over and above its instrumental value and the community's existence has a moral value and purpose which transcends the time-span of individual membership.[48]

Muhammad's original *ummah* in Mecca and Medina, so often the inspiration of Islamic revivalist groups, could be defined as both a moral and an intentional community. The present-day *ummah*, based as it is simply on being born a Muslim, is far too large and diverse to be defined as this kind of community. Within it there exist groups of Muslims who have formed organisations with specific Islamic goals to recreate the conditions of Muhammad's original *ummah*. These too are both moral and intentional communities. These groups have been imported into Britain through the process of migration and will have a profound impact in their interaction with other forms of community organisation which exist amongst the Muslim migrants.

Conclusion

This overview of various sociological analyses provides alternative ways of regarding developments that have taken place in the *ummah* which have to be combined with the Muslim perspective to ascertain the possibilities that could occur in Britain. The urban village comprised of a migrant community living within its own socially, linguistically and ethnically defined borders, and interacting in a selective way with the broader non-Muslim society around it may either function with the ideal of the *ummah* to reinforce Muslim identity or it may conflict with the Islamic vision of a universal, egalitarian society based on the revelation of the Qur'an and the *sunna* of the Prophet. Various Islamic groups operating in Britain utilising a revivalist ideology received from the wider Islamic world which incorporates the ideal of the *ummah* may find themselves in open opposition to the ethnic-based urban village community. Before going on to examine some of the most important of these groups which have established themselves in Britain, it is essential to look in more detail at some of the issues facing the Muslims in Britain as they attempt to establish themselves with a viable communal identity based on Islam.

Endnotes

[1] McWilliams, Wilson Carey, 1974, *The Idea of Fraternity in America*, University of California Press, Berkeley.

[2] ibid.,p.2.

[3] ibid.,p.4.

[4] ibid.,p.23.

[5] ibid.,p29.

[6] Mannheim, Karl., 1948, *Ideology and Utopia*, Routledge and Kegan Paul, London, p.57.

[7] Somervell, D.C., *A Study of History - Abridgement of Vol.I-VI* by Arnold Toynbee, Issued under the auspices of the Royal Institute of International Affairs, Oxford University Press, London,pp.253-256.

[8] ibid.,p.253.

[9] ibid.

[10] ibid., p.256.

[11] Gellner, E., 1968, 'The Pendulum Swing Theory of Islam', *Sociology of Religion*, ed. Robertson, Roland, Penguin, London, p.130.

[12] ibid.

[13] ibid.

[14] ibid., p.133.

[15] ibid.

[16] ibid., p.134.

[17] ibid.,p.135.

[18] ibid.

[19] ibid.,p.136.

[20] One of the earliest and most influential sociological insights concerning community is Ferdinand Tönnies' concept of *Gemeinschaft* and *Gesellschaft*. Despite its age and the fact that it is

heavily value-laden, Tönnies' ideas are still being used as a tool by sociologists to examine different types of community. Tonnies describes the *Gemeinschaft* as the original, organic and natural community (Tönnies, Ferdinand, 1963, *Community and Society*, trs. & ed. Loomis, Charles, Harper & Row, New York, p.33). It is based on mutual aid, mutual interdependence and bound together by sentiment. Authority in the *Gemeinschaft* is based upon age, wisdom and benevolent force. The members of the *Gemeinschaft* share sacred traditions and a spirit of brotherhood which grows out of blood ties, a common locality and a common mind. The laws of the *Gemeinschaft* are based on folk mores and communal customs passed down through the generations. These laws are seen to possess eternal truths and never lose their binding force (ibid.,pp.33-34). Tönnies states that shared norms and values are defined as friendship, and common ancestors are venerated and recalled in memory. He defines village and tribal societies as examples of *Gemeinschaft* (ibid., pp.33-44).

The *Gesellschaft*, on the other hand, is a society where everyone is concerned only for them selves. Individuals are concerned only for their advantage, and only affirm the action of others if they themselves are able thereby to benefit. This concern for self-betterment and self-importance demonstrates itself in competition, which then becomes the norm in human communication. The exchange of commodities becomes the model activity of the *Gesellschaft*. The demonstration of wealth and rampant materialism becomes a key value in society, and we increasingly find isolated individuals living in a constant state of tension with all other members. Tönnies argues that merchants are the natural denizens of the *Gesellschaft* because they acquire the liquid assets through which they purchase the power to control the society (ibid.,pp.76-78).

It is possible to argue that the *Gemeinschaft* culture of the Arab tribes was under pressure from *Gesellschaft* traits manifesting themselves in Mecca. The revelation of Islam and the vision of Muhammad restored the *Gemeinschaft* in a new form that was well able to either overcome or integrate the *Gesellschaft* aspects of Meccan society. The history of Islam could be viewed as a constant repetition of the pattern to integrate the *Gemeinschaft* and *Gesellschaft* elements in the social system that was so successfully achieved by Muhammad. The temptation to create a new *Gemeinschaft* based on the principles of the first one is always liable to divide the Muslims into sectarian movements which attempt to revive the *ummah*.

21 Poplin, Dennis E., 1972, *Communities - A Study of Theories and Methods of Research*, The MacMillan Company, New York, p.26.

22 Bell, Colin and Newby, Howard (eds), 1974, 'Introduction', *The Sociology of Community*, Frank Cass & Co, London, p.xliv.

23 The following sociologists are typical of this approach: MacIver,1931; Hillary,1955; Stein,1961; Martingdale,1969; Greer,1970; .

24 Stein,Maurice, Robert, 1961, *The Eclipse of Community: An Interpretation of American Studies*, Princeton University Press, Princeton, pp.100-101.

25 Poplin, op.cit.,pp.1-4.

26 McIver, R.M., 1970, *Community: A Sociological Study*, Frank Cass & Co., London, p.23.

[27] ibid.

[28] Wirth, Louis, 1938, 'Urbanism as a Way of Life', *American Journal of Sociology*,44 (July), reprinted in Hatt, Paul and Reiss, Albert (eds), 1957, *Cities and Society*, The Free Press, Illinois, p.56.

[29] Gans, Herbert J., 1985, 'Urbanism and Suburbanism as Ways of Life', *An Introduction to Sociology*, eds.Bocock,R., Hamilton,P., Thompson, K., Waton, A., Open University Press, Milton Keynes, p.397.

[30] ibid., p.399.

[31] ibid.,p.398.

[32] ibid., p.400.

[33] Rex, John and Josephides, Sasha, 1987, 'Asian and Greek Cypriot Associations and Identity', *Immigrant Associations in Europe*, eds. Rex, John; Joly, Daniele; Wilpert, Czarina, Gower, Aldershot, p.19.

[34] McIver, op.cit.,p.23.

[35] ibid., p.24.

[36] Rex, John, 1973, *Race, Colonialism and the City*, Routledge and Kegan Paul, London, p.15.

[37] ibid.

[38] ibid., pp.15-16.

[39] ibid., p.19.

[40] ibid., p.27.

[41] ibid.

[42] ibid.,p.26.

[43] Joly, Daniele, 1987, 'Associations Amongst the Pakistani Population in Britain', *Immigrant Associations in Europe*, eds. Rex, John; Joly, Daniele; Wilpert, Czarina, Gower, Aldershot, p.69.

[44] ibid.,p.66.

[45] ibid.,p.69.

[46] ibid.

[47] Poplin, op.cit.,p.6.

[48] Shenkar, Barry, 1986, *Intentional Communities - Ideology and Alienation in Communal Societies*, Routledge and Kegan Paul, London, p10.

4 Islam in Britain

Introduction

Any attempt at research in the mosques, which are still growing in number in many British cities, will reveal that nearly all of them are aligned to various movements originating in the subcontinent. Although their relative influence will vary considerably from city to city, there can be no doubt of the importance of these groups imported from the subcontinent in the struggle for the hearts and minds of British Muslims. Both the historical relationship between these groups and their various strategies developed to deal with the decline of Muslim power in India have been transported via the migration process to Britain, and will influence the development of Islam in this country.

Before proceeding to focus on the four prominent strands of Islam represented by the *Barelwis*, the *Deobandis*, *Tabligh-i Jamaat* and *Jamaat-i Islami*, it is essential to look more generally at the situation of Muslims in Britain and to pinpoint some of the dilemmas and challenges which they face. Only then is it possible to say something about the role of the above religious movements in shaping the community as it attempts to respond to these problems. Although the major issues have been isolated and looked at as dichotomies, it is necessary to remember that this is an academic exercise. In reality, these isolated dilemmas are intertwined and interconnected in a very complex manner to form a single whole. The tensions between these dichotomies will function as the dynamics to determine the direction of change in the Muslim community. Muslims living in Britain, particularly those born and educated here, confront these dilemmas as their unique inheritance, and finding a solution to them is crucial in the process of carving out their own identity both as individuals and as a community.

It is not the intention to dwell on the origins and the early development of the Muslim community in Britain. This has been covered thoroughly by others in several comprehensive studies.[1] This chapter will only draw on material from this well-ploughed ground insofar as it is relevant to the analysis of certain problems discussed herein.

Since the 1950s Britain has received tens of thousands of Muslim immigrants from the subcontinent. They came in response to the host nation's demand for cheap labour and to join with their family members already here. They risked leaving their countries of origin to find work with higher wages, often intending to return home eventually. Most, however, have remained in Britain and formed themselves into communities established around their religion, places of origin and kin networks. John Rex succinctly sums up this process:

> The presence of major Islamic communities in the British Isles in the 1980s is to a large extent the result of a late imperial process, common to all of Western Europe - the migration of people into Britain seeking work from former British colonies.[2]

As with the other migrant communities, the first notable Pakistani presence appeared in the 1951 census. With the arrival of dependants beginning in the 1960s, the population of sub-continent Muslim migrants substantially increased.[3] It is difficult to determine exactly how many Muslims there are in Britain today as the Census does not have a category to distinguish people by religion. Even should one take the trouble to sift arduously through the categories of ethnic origin in the 1991 census in search of Muslim surnames, the results are likely to be highly inaccurate.[4] Many will refuse to identify themselves by ethnic origin as they strongly identify themselves with a common Islamic identity. Others may not reveal their presence on the Census as they are in Britain illegally. The significant figure, however, is not so much the total estimate but the ever-increasing proportion of Muslims born and educated in Britain as compared to the proportion of migrants born in the subcontinent.[5] If the immigration laws continue to make it increasingly difficult for subcontinent migrants to enter the country, this figure will increase to almost 100% within the duration of one generation's lifespan as first-generation migrants die.

The other significant statistic amongst those who were born in the subcontinent is the diversity of regional place of origin.[6] Although often defined by the receiving culture as an homogenous minority (Pakistani), the self-definition of the immigrants has tended to revolve around the customs and beliefs inherited from localised extended family groupings confined to small areas of rural Pakistan, Bangladesh and, to a lesser extent, India. It is becoming increasingly difficult to pass on the values and traditions of these villages of origin to a generation born and educated in Britain who identify themselves as British. This cultural clash of values that manifests itself across the generations is central to the various dichotomies that Muslims in Britain need to resolve in order to form a communal self-identity within which individual self-esteem can be enhanced.

Striking examples of common unity and fellowship arising from membership of the Muslim *ummah* can be found within this diversity of ethnic groupings, where regional and tribal divisions can still further divide a single national grouping. The *salat*, *Ramadan*, the *Hajj*, and the respect and status given to the Qur'an still provide powerful reinforcement to the awareness of shared identity. The principle of *tawhid*, the unity and uniqueness of God, binds Muslims together in a common faith which can be the basis of unity. This strong shared faith enables the individuals concerned to cope with the difficult experience of living as a minority in Britain despite the loss of living under *Shari'ah* law. It could be argued that these symbols of Islam become even more powerful in what is perceived to be a hostile environment by many of the Muslim population.

Ethnicity,[7] which embraces all the symbols of religion in order to affirm itself, becomes an important factor for minority groups. There is no doubt that the Muslim migrants passed through a stage of extreme entrenchment in which ethnic identity was reinforced.[8] Nielson states that the growth of mosques in Britain is linked to the immigration process.[9] The arrival of wives and families brought a dramatic increase in religious practices, and a new awareness of religious life which is reflected in the increase in the number of mosques. The mosques function, however, not only as places of worship, but also as centres to maintain and reinforce shared memories, values and goals located in the place of origin. Barton noted in his study of Bengalis in Bradford that the mosque is used as a refuge from British society, and as a 'focal point for the recollection of a personal and corporate identity that is rooted in Sylhet'.[10] This process of ethnic consolidation helped to establish the boundaries of the communities.[11]

In some ways this appeared to be a religious revival as symbols of religion were utilised to re-inforce group identity, but is more likely that the phenomena of religion manifested to reinforce ethnic identity.[12] Certainly it can be observed that this gathering around Islamic symbols which was used by the first generation migrants to sanctify the customs of their cultures of origin,[13] does not sit easy with the younger generation of British-born Muslims. Many of them have utilised religion to attack the ethnic customs of their parents as unIslamic.[14] They often seek a different kind of Islam, an Islam freed from South Asian cultural accretion. Regardless, however, of the divisions, and the fact that the majority of the Muslim migrants are British citizens, there is no doubt that membership of a universal community - the Muslim *ummah* - is an important aspect of self-awareness and understanding. The *ummah* has always drawn its membership from a variety of ethnic, national, and linguistic groups; ideally it should override them. Religious identity should be the first loyalty and common fealty of the Muslim. The *ummah* transcends these boundaries, and helps to unite Muslims by providing a shared world view based on common belief, values and norms.

In fact, while they have much in common, Muslims in Britain do not form an entirely homogenous community. Peter Clarke sums up the situation:

> The encounter for the first time with different cultural and religious forms and even with different Muslim traditions, as well as British society, and the emergence of second generation of British born and British educated Muslims has made the creation of an Islamic community that is not seen to be too closely linked to any particular cultural tradition a top priority.[15]

Central to the problems of the Muslim is the distinction between the ideals and values of Islam on the one hand and the cultural mores of a particular time-space milieu on the other. Muhammad Mushaq Ibn Ally argues that the emergence of an Islamic community that is integrated in British society depends upon Muslims separating out the universals of Islam as revealed in the Qur'an from the accretions added by culture, custom, and history. He states:

> One important need of the Islamic *ummah* in Britain and every sub-group within it, is to distinguish that which is essential to the faith, and that which is transitory, cultural, historical, or national expression. There needs to be a turning away from the customs of the ancestors. Muslims must be prepared to be permanently rooted both psychologically and spiritually in Britain.[16]

For most Muslims in Britain, this is not a simple transformation. It is extremely hard for them to find, in the midst of ethnic differences, a religious/cultural consensus which is simultaneously based on Islamic principles and capable of encompassing full participation in the cultural resources of the receiving culture. It is a balancing act which, if not successful, can divide the community on religious as well as ethnic grounds. Failure can lead either to extreme fundamentalism with the community alienated from both the indigenous and the migrant cultures; or else to assimilation into Britain's secular society, thus reducing Islamic belief and practice to the private sphere. This latter possibility is problematic. John Rex points out that in principle Islam is not able to accept the distinction which our society has made between the public and the private sphere. It is a central tenet of Muslim belief to maintain that Islam is a whole way of life. Consequently, it affects attitudes not only in private moral and cultural matters, but also in the social, political, and the economic sphere.[17] It is debatable whether Islam could in fact lose this dimension without losing something fundamental to its identity as a faith.

Despite the problems involved in dealing not only with major ethnic and geographical divisions but also with important regional, linguistic, social, and political differences within the major groupings, there are signs that Islam is becoming the mark of identity for Muslim minorities all over Europe. Three important strands can be distinguished which contribute to this phenomenon:

(a) Various studies have shown that when Muslims from rural areas migrate to the cities, a transformation takes place in their religious life. In the village, the beliefs and practices of Islam are part of an inherited total way of life reinforced by the close-knit nature of a small community. The move to the more impersonal, individualistic, urban culture leads to a questioning of the village values, and a conscious redefinition of Islamic identity.[18] The move from the villages of the subcontinent to the major urban/industrial centres of Western Europe is an extreme version of this phenomenon. It is resulting in a shift of focus of religious identity from the subcontinent to the inner cities of Britain. It can be argued that this is counteracted by the immediate and personal experience of stress caused by the movement of the migrant from one social world to another. Verity Saifullah Khan argues that the traditional institutions of village life re-emerge in modified form to help the migrants cope. She suggests that there is an idealisation of the village life-world.[19]

(b) Most Muslim migrants find themselves to be a minority. However, in the case of subcontinent Muslims they are psychologically and sociologically used to being part of a minority through their long history in India even though they may have migrated from the Muslim nations of Pakistan and Bangladesh. For these Muslim minority groups the ideal of the *ummah* can become even more important than the place of origin as a marker of identity.

(c) Interconnected with the previous two strands is the world-wide resurgence of Islam. Priorities being decided at an international level become hard to ignore. Choices and perspectives being developed at this level may have little bearing on the Muslims' experience in their new host cultures.

Badr Dahya suggests that Pakistanis in Britain are feeling alienated not only from the receiving culture but also from their culture of origin. This is particularly acute for the younger generation born in Britain, but at least they are more able to identify with the receiving culture which is their land of birth. He argues that first-generation Pakistani migrants are starting to reject the traditional expectation on the part of kinfolk and fellow villagers back home that they should distribute expensive gifts when they revisit. They are also alienated by the treatment given to them by custom officials, taxi drivers, hoteliers, and shop keepers. Supposedly returning home, they are received with rudeness and dishonesty and exploited as foreign tourists. He suggests that the alienation felt from both cultures is leading to a change of image. 'Such changes suggest that the migrants are now discovering the ethical and moral values of Islam, or rather reinterpreting their conception of what Islam is about'.[20]

Certainly all of this indicates that religious identity in the Muslim community is becoming the sharpest focus for establishing a sense of selfhood. The framework transferred from the Muslim majority societies is no longer relevant. The early migrants experienced a sense of loss, but the second generation feels a sense of denial of self. Its members need to discover, or at least to redefine, both a spiritual and a social self. Alienated, disorganised and floating, many young Muslims in Britain have begun to refuse the classification of 'black' or 'Asian'. They have found a strategy for self-rehabilitation by claiming their identity as 'Muslim'. Clifford Longley succinctly sums up this social phenomenon stating that it has the potential 'to fuse into something extraordinary - British Islam'.[21]

In contrast to this, it must be remembered that no single view of Islam is held by all members of the community. The process of organising the Muslim community on a national basis is as old as its presence in Britain. The pattern of chain migration reinforced by *biradari* networks[22] has significantly strengthened ties to extended families that originated in small locales of Pakistan and Bangladesh. This is reflected in the way the communities have been organised in Britain. Pnina Werbner has observed that, by now, virtually all the religious divisions prominent in Pakistan have their local institutional expression in Britain.[23] Mosques and welfare organisations proliferated throughout the 1970s and 1980s, each representing small sub-groups within the community.[24] Any attempts to create umbrella organisations to represent the community on a national level were relatively unsuccessful.[25] There is a large number of Muslim organisations in Britain. In 1986 it was estimated that there were over four thousand, mostly concerned with local welfare.[26] Tensions between the universal and the particular are ever-present. Any move towards establishing the kind of national organisation based on the universals of Islam which would represent the whole community is likely to be seen as a critique of those values and traditions which many Muslim immigrants still hold dear.

Very often the ideal of the *ummah* is seen to be betrayed by any degree of integration with the host community. Many Muslims go as far as to question whether a truly Islamic life is even possible in the West where Muslims are in a minority.[27] Up until now the mosques have not responded positively to the challenge of modernity. This has resulted in the mosques' inability to attract young people and a neglect of a public participation of women in religious activities. It is amongst these two groups that the search for common identity is most acute.

In regard to the minority question, it must be remembered that prior to the creation of Pakistan in 1947, Muslims had always been a minority in the subcontinent. Muslims in India long regarded themselves as separate and distinct from other religious and social groupings. They developed strategies to deal with living alongside a Hindu majority, and later to deal with being ruled by the British. Essential to these strategies was the message of return to the basics of Islam in order to revitalise the community, which had found itself in danger of being relegated to a minor position. In the 19th and early 20th century several theological/political groups emerged in the subcontinent in response to the decline of the Muslim community and the successful spread of European culture.[28] The central tenet of their message was a return to the fundamentals of Islam based on the Qur'an and *Sunna*, and a stripping away of anything that was seen to be cultural accretion. The influence of some groups has increased recently as a result of the general resurgence of Islam throughout the Muslim world.

It is not surprising that these theological/political movements have become much more influential in Britain than have the locally organised welfare organisations. The apparent emphasis on the universals of Islam, the history of Islamic revival, and the fact that many first-generation Muslims would have existing loyalties to one or the other of them transferred from the subcontinent has enabled them to flourish in Britain. The twentieth century ideological movements are more likely to be attractive to young Muslims and Muslim women born in Britain. Perhaps even more attractive is the fact that these groups were formed partly in opposition to British colonialism and Western values. Muhammad Anwar points out that the relationship between Muslims and the indigenous population can best be understood against the background of the colonial encounter, and the unequal economic and political power relationships generated by colonialism both in British India and now in Britain.[29] If this is true, then the success of these groups must be attributed to the fact they have developed historical strategies to cope with Muslims being a minority ruled over by the British. The confrontation with British colonialism and Western values has been transplanted to Britain from the subcontinent by the economic processes of capitalism. The Muslim minority of the subcontinent, once ruled by a British colonial minority, now finds a part of itself to be an economically and socially deprived minority in the land of its old rulers. The major difference here in the new situation is that the old rulers are now the majority population.

It has to be ascertained whether these revivalist organisations[30] can really fulfil the expectations of British-born Muslims. One has to examine critically their proclamations of a culturally-free emphasis on the universals of Islam. This may have been true at the time, within the context of their creation but they may now be too caught up in the history of subcontinent Muslim sectarian conflict to be of any use in helping to create a unified British Muslim community. A history of mutual recrimination and even excommunication has characterised their relationship with each other in the subcontinent, and is seen to have spilled over into Britain.[31] This has resulted in dividing some small communities and has led to power struggles for control of some mosques. The different groups are intensely suspicious of each other and do very little to integrate amongst themselves. They all retain strong links with their parent organisations in the subcontinent. There is the strong possibility that they are in danger of imparting divisions which developed in the history of subcontinent Islam which could seriously undermine any efforts they might make towards developing a truly native version of Islam in Britain.

A number of major dilemmas, which I will look at as dichotomies, need to be resolved by Muslims in Britain before a community can be established that exhibits a minimum basic degree of unity. It is essential to examine these closely in order to appreciate the difficulties involved. This exercise will also facilitate a deeper understanding of the role of sectarian movements in the formation and shaping of the community in Britain.

First generation migrants v. Later British-born generations

The third generation which are now coming up are calling themselves Muslims, not Pakistanis or Asians. They are speaking English, their culture is British, and they are Muslims. What it means, of course, is that we have decided to stay here in Britain. We have to be able to discuss the common issues facing the whole British Muslim community. Now people have no intention of returning to Pakistan.[32]

The greater divisions will not be between Britain and the Muslims, but between the two factions within the faith. This will not be entirely generation-defined, yet it will be the younger people who will decide. They see their parents besieged. They are more rigid in their religion than they would have been even in their old homeland, and they see that they cling to the conservatism from comfort, from fear.[33]

In the above quotation Sher Azam has pointed out a crucial change of self-identity amongst the British-born descendants of the original settlers. He is right when he suggests that they have no intention of returning to Pakistan, but he does not mention that this indicates a serious split in attitude between generations. The first generation migrants had used 'the Myth of Return' to legitimise continued adherence to the values of the homeland, and to condemn any assimilation of British cultural values as irrelevant and destructive. Most of the parents come from rural areas in the subcontinent and were not educated. They have tried to maintain a world outlook which is foreign to the values of the receiving culture. Very often this has resulted in a conservatism that even in the original homeland many would find rigid and old-fashioned. The countries of origin have undergone considerable changes since the departure of the original migrants to Britain, but they often continue an emotive attachment to the way things were at that time. This can become idealised and mythologised; the values brought over are not to be challenged. Many migrants find it difficult to understand their children who were brought up and educated in Britain. Sometimes attempts to question or break away from the parents' values is seen as corruption by the host nation's unIslamic values and as a move towards godlessness and the disintegration of the community. The children can find it equally difficult to understand the beliefs and lifestyle of their parents.

Despite their greater contact with the values of the indigenous culture through the medium of education, the family still remains tremendously important to the majority of young Muslims. Muhammad Anwar found that 94% of those whom he interviewed claimed they would not be prepared to do anything that would damage the prestige of their family.[34] The concept of *izzat* acts as a powerful agent of reinforcement for the passing down and maintenance within the family of the rules and customs of the community. There are powerful emotive inhibitions against disgracing the family or letting down the family honour. The most important part of the *Shari'ah* is Muslim family law, which insists that religious duty governs personal relations. Consequently, *izzat* is maintained and sanctified by a complicated pattern of behaviour evolved from Islam and the time-honoured customs of the family's place of origin and social status. To the older generation who find themselves struggling to maintain their ethnic/religious identity as a minority group, *izzat* becomes of great significance. Very often the particular and the universal have equal importance. Their Islam is not based on the study of Qur'an and *Hadith*, but has been formed by the rites and ceremonies of family and village life. Religion is indistinguishable from their way of life, and these traditions are zealously guarded in the alien and often hostile environment of Britain.

When Zaki Badawi speaks of 'two factions within the faith', he is accurately pinpointing a major ideological split over what constitutes Islam. He is right to suggest that this has a strong generational element. Muhammad Anwar suggests that the first generation are seen to be more committed to religious observance and therefore appear to be more orthodox in response to 'Western' values.[35] Dr. Farhan Nizami, the Director of the *Oxford Centre of Islamic Studies*, appears to contradict Muhammad Anwar's view. He argues that studies have shown that second generation followers of Islam are often more strict in their observance than their parents. Even those exposed to a modern Western education often feel a need to return to their Muslim roots.[36] This apparent contradiction of Muhammad Anwar's findings is reinforced by two comments from a newspaper cutting. Hannana Siddiqi observes, 'Over the years my parents have become less orthodox, but my brothers have become more religious'. Prajna Patel reinforces this, stating,

I confused Islam and Asian: they are not the same. I feel as if I have to fight all the way; people said to me, "sit back, you're a girl", and my parents told me not to go to school. If I hadn't discovered Islam, I would have become westernised.[52]

Many are discovering that the emancipation of women was apparently a matter of importance to the Prophet. They refer to his wives, particularly Khadijah who was a successful businesswoman, and Aisha who became a stateswoman in the early years of Islam's development. They claim that 1400 years ago women were liberated by the establishment of Islam. They were given inheritance rights, the right to keep their earnings, the right to divorce, and the right to maintain their own surnames. Subsequently, they argue, various cultures have superimposed their own variation of gender inequality onto Islam as it spread through Asia. Many claim that this is particularly the case in South Asia.

The whole issue of the rights of Muslim women born in Britain is beginning to centre upon the challenge Islam is posing to both ethnicity and westernisation. The opposition to uncritical acceptance of western values is central to the ideology of Islamic resurgency throughout the world. By incorporating this into their view of British life, many young Muslim women are able to feel both solidarity with the Islamic movement globally and to develop a critique towards the dominant culture's attitude towards them. At the same time they can utilise the revivalists' stance against cultural accretion entering into Islam to defend themselves against attitudes which often belong more to the subcontinent village than the teachings of the Qur'an. Knott and Khokher point out that this stategy enables young Muslim women born and educated in Britain to neither feel torn between two cultures or to switch back and forth between two opposed worlds, but to find a way forward utilising their religion.[53]

Secular education v. religious education

Having looked briefly at young people and women, it becomes apparent that the issue of education is very important amongst Muslims here in Britain. Moeen Yaseen of the Islamic Schools Trust has defined education as 'the major instrument of cultural engineering'.[54] Many Muslims feel uneasy about the presence of their children in British state schools. Dr. Haleh Afshar of the University of York has described this dilemma as a conflict between home and school, which she further elaborates as 'school at school' versus 'school at home'; the former is reinforced by television.[55] School is the place where Muslim society and British society most deeply interact. It is this interaction between values that leads Muhammad Anwar to state that young Muslims are 'caught between two cultures'. This argument is challenged by research which suggests that British-born Muslims are having 'the best of both worlds'.[56] The popular perceptions and sentiments expressed by Muslims themselves of all generations, however, agree with Anwar. Most of the young Muslims interviewed for this study were deeply involved with practising their faith. Many of them were active members of Islamic organisations. All expressed a feeling of identity crisis of the type identified by Anwar. They felt that only their allegiance to Islam could resolve this. It may well be that young Muslims who feel that they have 'the best of both worlds' are adopting a secular alternative and come from homes whose attitude to the British way of life and practice of Islam is more tolerant.

If education is viewed as a means of cultural engineering, then it will sometimes clash with an equally powerful form of socialisation that takes place within the family. Parents themselves are often torn between their loyalty to traditional value systems incorporating religious and social authority on the one hand, and a desire to see their children succeed in the educational system on the other. Distrustful of a Western secular society which is popularly viewed as corrupt and blatantly sexually promiscuous, they attempt to counteract this influence of school by nurturing their children into the overarching belief system of Islam. This last will include views of European culture, perceptions of education, the right behaviour between the sexes and between the generations, and codes of moral behaviour and appearance. All of these will be reinforced by the code of *izzat*. This is likely to be imposed more on the girls than the boys. Mirza argues that the girls are victims of double standards of morality in which actions deemed improper for a woman are accepted when performed by men.[57] She states that women are put under stricter surveillance after the onset of puberty as it is considered that too much freedom will ruin a girl's reputation.[58] Even British teaching methods based on enquiry and the development of freedom of thought could be highly suspect.

The Qur'an or mosque school is used to support this framework of the family and its values. Several nights a week the children will attend two-hour sessions. They will be taught by rote the Arabic of the Qur'an, basic religious instruction, and sometimes the mother-tongue of their parents. Usually the instruction is by the *imam*. Often he will be suspicious not only of the influence of British secular education on the children but also of the influence of their parents, whose knowledge of Islam he may not trust.

The main purpose of the mosque school is to inculcate into the children the awareness that they belong to a Muslim community. Stephen Barton points out that when the children are asked, 'Who are you?' the correct answer expected is, 'A Muslim'. He compares this with the beginning of the Anglican catechism[59] and concludes that the Muslim child's sense of identity in relation to itself and its faith lies not in individual identity nor even in relationships to family but membership of the household of Islam. In fact, the child's education at mosque school will ultimately depend on the calibre of the *imam* and the brand of Islam that he himself follows. Much of the teaching is very basic, simplistic and taught in what must be seen as a boring way. This deficiency is inherent in that system of part-time religious schools run alongside the English system of education which became the pattern under the British administration in colonial India. At the time it considerably disadvantaged Muslim youth, and it will continue to do so. At best it gives a very elementary knowledge of the faith; at worst it defeats its own object by turning the children against their own religion. The extra studying hours placed upon small children could well be to the detriment of their education at school. It could also create a clash of values.

Some Muslims believe the solution to be the establishment of Islamic schools which teach academic subjects alongside religious instruction in Islam. The major religious movements are increasingly establishing *dar al-ulums* which provide full-time religious education combined with a few core subjects from the British curriculum. Essentially these schools are based on the sub-continent Islamic curriculum which was established to train the *ulema*. The demand for places in the *dar al-ulums* is growing rapidly especially amongst Muslim parents with *Deobandi* sympathies. The major problem here is that there is hardly any agreement on which 'Islam' should be taught. An article in *Link International* identifies two dimensions here. First, it notes the divisions along sectarian lines that prevail in the community. Muslims with loyalties to

Deobandi, *Barelwi*, *Tabligh-i*, and *Jamaat-i Islami* brands of Islam each want to teach their children according to their own ideology, and consequently consolidate divisions within the community. Second, the article comments on 'Sufistic' interpretations of Islam incorporating all sorts of practices brought from home villages in the subcontinent, which can only be described as syncretistic. These reinforce the inward-looking maintenance of ethnic values.[60]

Sharif suggests that girls are more likely to be aware of the disparity between the values of home and and the values of school.[61] Many Muslims in Britain originate from the rural areas of the subcontinent and received little informal education themselves. The education of girls was not considered important as marriage is considered to be their destiny. Training in running a home is felt to be more important than formal education.[62] As a consequence the parents expect girls to concentrate on housework, cooking and looking after children, rather than schoolwork.[63] Sharif found that boys were given more encouragement with homework and that television was often censored for the girls.[64] Mirza argues that educated women were perceived as a threat by men who considered them too assertive. She also suggests that in-laws expect their sons' wives to be servile.[65] Many of the girls are sent to single sex schools to protect them from the perceived sexual promiscuity of British culture. Teachers are often asked to keep them closely supervised. Parents and brothers often chaperone them to and from school.[66] Despite this difference in attitude and closer control of girls, many find that school provides them with opportunities to be more critical in their thinking, and to develop the ability to differ with their parents.[67] Many parents are not able to sympathise or even be aware of the ethos of individual fulfilment and development offered to both sexes in school as it is not a part of their cultural background. This conflict of values has led many parents in Britain to become more repressive.[68] Higher education by girls is rarely achieved without struggle[69] and many religious parents see that the solution is to provide girls with a *dar al-ulum* education only. Yasmin Ali sums this up:

> The education of Muslim girls has less to do with schooling than with the exercise of control by Muslim men over the lives of women in the family and wider community. Generally, control is maintained by monitoring the level and amount of interaction with male relatives and the local community. But in the area of schooling, Muslim parents feel that their grip on their daughters' lives is weaker. Single sex education is preferred by Muslim parents, and nearly always for their daughters.[70]

In the meantime there is considerable evidence that Muslim children of subcontinent origin are not doing as well in school as they should be.[71] Young Pakistanis have a much higher unemployment rate than either the indigenous population, or indeed any other minority group.[72] Monica Taylor states that 'the schooling of a minority is dependent on how powerful they are'.[73] It is only since the Rushdie protest in 1989 that Muslims in Britain are beginning to realise that organised unity is powerful, and that their common Islamic identity is the banner behind which they need to unite.

Integration v. Assimilation

A great deal of sociological analyses of migrant communities, including Muslim communities, has focused on the alternative choices of either assimilation into the British 'way of life', or an assertive embracing of distinctive ethnic cultures based on the lifestyle, religion and customs of the place of origin.

Muhammad Anwar defines the concept of 'pluralistic integration' as that 'whereby a group maintains itself as a unit on its own, but is nevertheless accepted by the majority itself as part of the wider society'.[74] In this model the minority group maintains such distinguishing features as religion, family structures and language. The increase in the numbers of migrant Muslims has made this possible. Economic, social and emotive needs can be found amongst family, friends and ethnic services. Consequently, there is a decrease in the opportunities for contact with the indigenous population. As the contact lessens, so the acquisition of skills required for full participation in the advantages of the majority society are proportionately hindered. This independence and isolation from the indigenous population is reinforced by a fear of its 'corrupting' influence. The idea of assimilation is seen as betrayal; a loss of religion and cultural norms from the place of origin that results in the family losing face in the minority community. The burden of maintaining this ethnic purity falls on the younger generation; their opportunity for contact with the culture of the receiving society is perceived as considerably greater than the first generation migrants. This is often viewed with suspicion, and the family itself then becomes the place of inter-generational tensions as signs of assimilation are looked for.

Verity Saifullah Khan confirms this view. She argues that 'the climate of ethnic "cultural resistance" is thus as much an outcome of internal hegemonic struggles as it is a response to outside domination'.[75] Various religious organisations imported from the subcontinent help to maintain and preserve the cherished ethnic identity with a proselytising zeal. The mosque becomes the symbolic centre for this religio-cultural awareness, and very often the *imam* himself will come from the place of origin. He is still in touch with home village gossip and politics. He will preach in the local language, and sometimes will be unable to speak English. Isolated from British culture, he comes to represent uncontaminated ethnic identity. His religious function confirms the perceived bond between Islam and home culture.

Very often the community leaders who make up the mosque committees employing the *imam* are ethnic entrepreneurs. It is in their financial interest to further traditional values and perpetuate and defend ethnicity. Assimilation into the indigenous culture would not assist their own business enterprises. Ironically, this sub-section of the Muslim community often involves those individuals in the most contact with the majority society.[76] There have been instances where the *imam* has been dismissed by the mosque committee because of his religious views. Where this has taken place, the *imam* has usually been preaching a revivalist form of religion which places its emphasis on the universals of Islam and attacks cultural accretion as a corruption of the faith.

So far, there are no real indications that Muslims in Britain are following that path towards complete assimilation that has already been trodden by the majority of Britain's Catholics and to a lesser extent the Jews. Many young Muslims claim that assimilation is not a genuine choice in that the indigenous white culture would always discriminate against them on the grounds of colour. Integration is criticised by many in the receiving culture. Remaining separate is seen as a critique of the British 'way of life', and very often it is. Migrants in general are often attacked for not assimilating. Some young Muslims see three choices being presented to them by the receiving culture (i) Develop individuality and avoid group identity. This would leave them even more isolated than they are now. (ii) Take on the cultural norms of the indigenous culture. (iii) Be more subservient and obedient - a form of internal colonialism.[77] Equally, for reasons already discussed, they are ill at ease with the ethnic isolationism of their parents and grandparents. Embracing Islam as a religious experience rather than a cultural heritage is providing increasing numbers of young Muslims with an alternative to pressure to assimilate into British culture on the one hand, and on the other to respond to parental persuasion to conform to various strands of imported ethnic culture. Thus it can be seen that the situation is not a straight choice between assimilation and integration. The indigenous culture will have to come to terms with two major groups demanding the right to integrate: one on ethnic/racial grounds; the other on purely religious grounds. This can create considerable confusion. Both will call on Islam to support their case, and it will not always be easy for the receiving culture to distinguish between the two. It is likely that the latter group will become increasingly larger and more vocal.

Sufism v. Reform Islam

The religious and ethnic situation is further complicated by the history of Islam in the subcontinent. Sufism has always been a major influence in that part of the world, and Sufi *pirs* were a major factor in the propagation of Islam amongst the Hindu population. Many were converted under the inspiration of these charismatic figures.[78] Their attitude to *tawhid* was often far more flexible than the orthodox; they focussed on inner union with the immanent rather than on the uniqueness of the transcendent Allah.[79] Hindus would have been far more sympathetic to this outlook. The Sufis in turn were often not so strict on the externals of Islam and consequently there developed a highly syncretistic version of the religion, especially in rural areas. This version of Islam has been under constant attack from reformers who have criticised the Hindu influences in its style of worship. The reformers have focussed their attention on the universals of the faith as based on the Qur'an and the *Hadith*.[80]

The arrival of subcontinent Muslims in Britain has transplanted into this country all the divisions and controversies which have historically split the community in India and Pakistan. The major Sufi orders, *Naqshbandiya*, *Qadriya* and *Chistiya*, are all influential at a local level in Britain. The *pirs* have always been the bearers of regional culture and language. They have taught in the vernacular, and carried the message of Islam deep into the hearts and minds of rural people who are often illiterate. This custom-laden version of Islam emphasises popular devotion, the intercession of saints, *barakha*, shrines, tombs of holy men, peculiar powers and miracles, singing and dancing and, above all, the importance of the *pir/murid* relationship. Asian food, candles, incense, rosewater offerings, holy water and amulets are all used in religious worship. These may be used to cure the sick, to secure the birth of a male child, or even to protect the worshipper from magical forces such as evil *jinn*.

Obviously this form of Islam, unique as it is to the villages of the subcontinent, evokes very powerfully for many migrants the feeling of never-forgotten places of origin. It is debatable whether this strand of the faith can survive beyond the generation of migrants that was actually born in the subcontinent. Its powerful link with the villages of the migrants' past will have no association for British-born Muslims, and they may well ally themselves with the reformist critique of the Sufi tradition. Their need to distance themselves from their parents' Asian origin and to assert their British identity will leave them disenchanted with this folk form of Islam.

Status within migrant community v. Class position in British society

Any analysis of class in the Muslim community must take place on two levels. There is the social structure operating within the Muslim community itself which may be influenced by the stratification of society in the country of origin; and there is also the class position of the Muslim migrants within the receiving society. Pnina Werbner suggests that migrant men are likely to have dual status.[81]

In the wider society they are likely to be perceived as working-class or even as an underclass. The economic position of the Muslims in Britain has changed very little in the last thirty years; the majority are still concentrated in the semi-skilled and unskilled sectors of industry. They suffer disproportionately from unemployment due to their concentration in manufacturing industries[82] and the continuation of racist attitudes in job allocations. They are likely to be in low-paid, menial work that is unattractive to the indigenous population. In 1984 Muhammad Anwar and Roger Garaudy argued that the typical Muslim worker was likely to be young and male. They found that the overwhelming majority were employees in relatively few industries notably textiles and engineering. Large numbers were often found making up the workforce of a particular factory or mill. They calculated that 11% of the Muslim community were of professional class.[83]

The most noticeable change is in the growing number of self-employed Muslims. This may reflect a shift away from focussing on the country of origin and an acknowledgement that the future is in Britain. Money that was once sent home to relatives in the subcontinent may have been used to establish small businesses. Essentially these enterprises were set up to serve the requirements of the growing communities. This was facilitated by the way in which various migrant groups gathered together in relatively small areas of particular towns and cities. These entrepreneurs concentrated on providing goods and services that reinforced the ethnic identity of their customers. This has resulted in a further closing of ranks amongst the migrant populations. As the Muslim community becomes more autonomous, Muslim men and women can define their status within their own group thus the class position thrust upon them by the host community becomes largely irrelevant in terms of self-esteem. Amongst fellow-Muslims class status can be derived from several sources. Community leaders are given considerable prestige based on their education, their economic status, the length of time their family has been in Britain (original settlers are well respected as community elders), the status of their family in the country of origin, Islamic scholarship, and membership of voluntary organisations such as welfare organisations and mosque committees. The membership of the latter is likely to be dominated by those with high status in the community. Pnina Werbner confirmed that most Pakistani cultural, religious or political associations are run by educated members of the community; intellectuals of middle-class background.[84]

Pnina Werbner goes on to suggest that the mosque has become 'the highest locus of communal involvement'.[85] It is not only the centre of religious worship and learning but also the source of very high status within the community. The committee which runs each mosque in Britain is usually controlled by businessmen and the professional middle-class. Very often these are also early settlers in the area. Pnina Werbner argues that the mosque is 'the ideological, regional, denominational, economic and social "core" or centre of the community.[86]

This control of the mosque will have important consequences for the development of Islam in Britain. The firm grip of the older-generation early migrants is often resented by the generation born in Britain, the latter feel that the issues which are important to the old-timers are not relevant to them. Previously, it was explained that it is often in the interest of local Muslim entrepreneurs to maintain ethnic identity and that this has sometimes resulted in conflict with the *imam*. This conflict, however, can also happen in reverse. Sometimes the *imam* will be entrenched in a more tradition-based form of Islam that is influenced by Sufi beliefs and village practices. This may not please all the members of the mosque committee. It has been noted by Pnina Werbner that ritual and religiosity become vehicles for the display of social differences within the ethnic group, even as they continue to uphold the distinctiveness of the group as a whole.[87] This link between religion and class goes back to economic and social changes in the country of origin.

Village society is characterised by rigid adherence to traditional norms and values. Social control is maintained by everyday life in a close-knit community. Illiterate villagers are largely dependent upon the ceremonial aspects of religions and daily rites for their apprehension of Islam. Landless labourers in Pakistan are increasingly migrating to the cities. Werner Schiffauer argues that a quantum change occurs in the religion of migrants moving from the countryside to the city. In his study of Turkish peasants in their home villages in Anatolia and Germany, he notes what he calls 'Islamicisation of the Self' amongst urban immigrants and migrants to Europe. Schiffauer notes that religious thought in the villages takes 'the form of collective self-certainty', in which the legal norms, the do's and do not's of Islam are central.[88] He argues that 'in sacred times the village turns into a religious community', but that in the city one leaves the society and enters a religious community. This often becomes 'a counterweight to secular society, as well as a place of retreat, a haven where, in contrast to the outside society, one is treated with respect and esteem'.[89]

The move of the family from the village to the city may well result in better education for the children and more lucrative employment for the parents. For the first time the family will have access to the Qur'an and *Hadith* for themselves, and urban *imams* are likely to be better educated in the principles of Islam. Village practices and traditions may well be denigrated by 'sophisticated' urban dwellers. In Pakistan, the move to the city may well lead the migrant to identify with the values of *ashraf* culture to improve status. This includes a knowledge of classical Islam and a critique of village practices. All of these factors link the change in class status involved in the move from village to city to a change in religious identity. Revivalist and 'fundamentalist' groups flourish in the cities of the subcontinent. Badr Dahya estimates that 95% of Pakistani migrants to Britain were of rural origin.[90] Virtually all that move to Britain live in urban areas. The impact of this change will be considerably more than the move to a city in Pakistan. The bulk of the migrants were small landholders in their place of origin, people who considered themselves a class above landless labourers. In migrating to Britain they have not hesitated to take on work as labourers in mills, factories and foundries. Despite this apparent loss of status and their low position vis-a-vis the receiving culture, it can be argued that all migrants improve their class position by the actual process of migration to cities. This, in turn, has a radical effect on the kind of Islam they practise, as religion can be used to improve standing in the Muslim community. Thus Muslim migrant communities are likely to be in considerable flux in regard to their religious position. These changes will be uneven in different parts of the community, and thus generate considerable tension and inter-communal rivalry.

Regional Languages v. English

Language is able to express beliefs which are widespread in particular social groups. It is also the main means of transmitting culture from one generation to another. Particular usage of language can reinforce the values and goals of a particular section of society, as opposed to the values of the mainstream culture. In India during the nineteenth century, Urdu became the preeminent symbol of Muslim identity. Islamic revival was fuelled by the publications of the reform *ulema* in Urdu, and the translations of scripture from Arabic and Persian.

Breton has observed that the range and variety of ethnic institutions constitute an 'index of institutional completeness' in the migrant community.[91]Language must be included in this category of 'completeness'. The Muslims in Britain speak a variety of tongues, both national and regional. These local dialects will help to maintain the values and norms of the place of origin. They will also, however, restrict any attempt to create a unified *ummah* in Britain by circumscribing the community at the level of place of origin. This process is reinforced at the mosque where preaching is usually done in the local dialect of the congregation.

This influence of the vernacular language is counteracted by some Arabic phrases and by the increasing use of English. Certain expressions in Arabic that are derived from the Qur'an are used all over the Muslim world. They are well-known to all Muslims. Phrases like *'Allahu Akbar'*, *'Inshallah'* and *'Bismillah'* become symbols of the universal *ummah*. Their usage by all Muslims reminds them that they are united in the membership of their common faith. Thus these phrases in Arabic help to counteract the divisive tendency of ethnic languages.

The transmission of vernacular languages to a generation born and educated in Britain is problematic. The latter are much more likely to be fluent in English, and quite often this English is the working-class dialect of the region where they have grown up. This familiarity with a particular English idiom will also make up for an ease with local indigenous cultures in Britain such as their parents will never achieve as long as their main communication is in a language from the subcontinent. The older generation's control of the mosques has established a link between religion and the vernacular language from the place of ethnic origin. Many children are still taught Urdu, Bengali and Punjabi in the relevant mosque schools by the *imam*. British-born Muslims are, however, fluent in English. Unlike the first generation of migrants, English is their mother tongue. There are growing indications that these British-born Muslims will insist on English becoming the language in which Islamic beliefs and practices are taught and communicated.[92] A unified community in Britain can only be seen as a possibility when Arabic (the lingua franca of the *ummah*) and English become the sole linguistic modes of inter-generational transmission of Islam.

Majority v. Minority (Racism)

The Muslim psyche does not find it easy to come to terms with being a minority in a non-Muslim society. The *Shari'ah* makes no provision for Muslims living as a minority except to suggest that they should migrate to the nearest Muslim state. Although there is advice concerning obedience to legitimate rulers even if the latter do not practice Islam, Muslims are inherently uncomfortable as a religious minority under a non-Muslim government. The idea of 'manifest success'[93] has programmed Muslims (with the exception of the Shi'a minority) for victory. The initial rapid success of Islam led to the development of a theology of power which sits uneasily in the minds and hearts of Muslims experiencing powerlessness.

The South Asian Muslim community, however, was nurtured in the antagonistic environment of the subcontinent. Always a minority, it has had to face major challenges from Hinduism, Sikhism, Christianity and British colonialism. The loss of power to the British led to an increase in the feeling of insecurity; there was a constant threat that Muslims would lose their Islamic identity. The community developed a sense of distinctiveness based on an embattled or siege mentality. It thrives on conflict and persecution.

Despite the recent experience of Pakistan, this minority in the subcontinent has become a minority in Britain. Inevitably, these people brought with them to Britain the strategies which they had developed in the subcontinent in order to cope with their position there as an historical minority. The experience of Britain was, however, bound to increase the feeling of uncertainty. Familiar points of reference, cultural certainties, and South Asian moral codes were no longer there. The need to hold on to a consistent idea of selfhood became imperative. The ethnic institutions in the area of settlement serve as an anchorage for the migrant community; they were also used as a means of making explicit to outsiders the Muslims' refusal to adopt local norms or to surrender their religious and cultural identity.

One aspect of British identity has always been based on skin colour. The arrival of large numbers of non-white immigrants has created racial tension, and British culture is now believed by many to be under threat. Politicians and journalists have begun to speak of 'the British way of life' which must be preserved. There is a constant affirmation of a British identity which is felt to be threatened by the immigrants' culture. Although assimilation is presented as the ideal, many in truth know that it is not likely.

Muslims are beginning to function as a focal point in this racial conflict in Britain and Western Europe. Right-wing political activity is overtly directed at the presence of Islam in Europe. In France this campaign is based on an attack on what is termed the 'Islamicisation of the nation'. There have been demands to make the right to French nationality dependent on blood. In Germany racial attacks are on the increase since unification, and the Muslim migrants have been the major target.[94] The polemic of racism describes Muslims as dangerous, as a dark, sinister force in our midst. They are seen as barbarians, scroungers, a challenge to the indigenous culture, and a possible shelter for terrorists. During the Gulf War Muslims in Britain were sometimes regarded with suspicion as a fifth column. During the war, Charles Moore wrote in *The Spectator* that a large family of Muslims were living next door. Their prayers heard through the wall alarmed him. He did not feel that dark-skinned alien, non-Christian people should be allowed to settle here.[95]

Throughout the European Union, immigration laws are becoming tougher. This idea of a

'Fortress Europe' is formed at least in part as a response to the perceived threat from Islam. Paul Gordon suggests that Islam is becoming Europe's Other.[96] Edward Said in his illuminating book *Orientalism*[97] argues that European identity is always seen as superior to other cultures. The Orient is perceived as opposed to both Christianity and rational thought. The West is seen as rational and culturally superior, the Orient as undeveloped, irrational and culturally inferior, as something to be feared and to be controlled by pacification. Paul Gordon argues that immigration laws have to be understood in the context of Orientalism. Firstly, he explains that immigration policies are not based on rational criteria. There is a perceived need to control people who are regarded as undesirable. The criteria for 'undesirable' is non-European. Secondly, he makes the point that immigration discourse is not about those coming in but about those already here. An example of this is that in 1988 new Immigration laws were passed in Britain forbidding entry of more than one wife per man. Only an average of twenty cases per year were in this category, yet the passing of this law signalled to the white population that alien Islamic familial practices would not be permitted in Britain. Thus immigration controls are justified on cultural grounds.[98] It is significant that more immigration controls in Western Europe are using Muslims as an example.

For years Muslims have told themselves that Islam and the West are two mutually exclusive hostile systems. This is reinforced by conspiracy theories based on the 'West' being hell-bent on destroying Islam. These fears are simply confirmed by the rising polemic of racism in Britain and Western Europe that is being directed towards Muslim migrant minorities. Islam is perceived to be under attack, and consequently the Muslim religion becomes the most powerful banner under which the minorities can be united. This has given added urgency to the need to identify those universals of faith with which all Muslims can agree. The West can therefore be seen as having undoubtedly contributed to Islamic revival.

Dar al-Islam v. Dar al-Harb

Traditionally the awareness of an overriding Muslim *ummah* has been reinforced by the idea of *Dar al-Islam* and *Dar al-Harb*. The former constituted all the geographical territory that was ruled by Muslim rulers and under the jurisdiction of Islamic law. The latter was the world outside Islamic control, territory which could be conquered and converted. The idea of *Dar al-Harb* as the world of unbelievers has been reinforced by the concept of *jahiliyya*. Originally Muhammad had used this term to describe the condition of pre-Islamic Mecca; it denoted a Godless society ruled over by the pursuit of individual wealth and pleasure. The concept of *Jahiliyya* is a powerful precedent for viewing or identifying secularised British culture. Muslim revivalists use the term in much the same way, and with the same connotations, as Rastafarians draw on the concept of 'Babylon'.

Muslim minorities have to be careful about declaring as *Dar al-Harb* those non-Muslims nations that they have migrated to voluntarily for their own economic betterment. This is particularly poignant for British-born Muslims whose national loyalty is to their place of birth. There is no doubt that many of the relatives in the subcontinent and some of the migrants themselves considered that life in Britain was full of risk to moral health; it was seen as exerting a potentially corrupting influence on the newcomers. Britain is thus considered to be a land where people are too lax in their moral standards. This is particularly the case with sexual standards. The indigenous population, especially the women, are perceived as promiscuous.

The first-generation migrants used the concept of *jahiliyya* defensively; it was used to justify a 'ghetto' mentality. Once wives and children began to arrive, the newly-formed communities consolidated around a flurry of ethnic activity in well-defined areas of Britain's manufacturing and industrial centres. When the ethnic group begins to feel, as did the Muslims in Britain, that their way of life is threatened by acculturation, it can react with a conscious organised effort to preserve its religion and culture. Ralph Linton describes this organised reaction as 'a perpetuative-rational nativistic movement'.[99] He argues that to make such a movement successful, the group needs to use a number of 'boundary maintaining mechanisms'. These mechanisms can be both psychological and physical. An example of the latter is the organisation of both formal and informal provisions for welfare within the community. Those who needed assistance could go to fellow-migrants or members of a welfare association rather than to outsiders. Barth has argued that ethnic groups can only survive by maintaining distinctive cultural traits. He suggests that where people of diverse cultural backgrounds interact, it would be expected that these differences would break down. He concludes that the persistence of ethnic groups indicates that 'there is a structuring of interaction which allows for the persistence of cultural differences'.[100] The idea that Britain was *jahiliyya* operated as a powerful religious deterrent against assimilation. These boundary-maintaining mechanisms that were pursued by Muslim organisations and leadership in Britain were operated at the local level. They reinforced and created rivalry between religious and ethnic factions. They therefore also worked against the development of a national organisation and a shared Islamic identity.

Many young Muslims involved in establishing their Islamic identity use the concept of *jahiliyya* in a quite different way. Their Islam is militant and unapologetic. The portrayal of Western society as meaningless and aimless, as plagued by delinquency, crime, psychiatric disorder, immorality and the collapse of the family, can be used to establish Islam as an alternative lifestyle in Europe. They are given a sense of purpose by the feeling of being involved in an ideological movement which confronts the secular capitalism of the West. The strong moral precepts of the Qur'an, the emphasis on family values and collective responsibility in Islam, can be viewed as the cure for the ills of corrupt Western cultures. For many Muslims born in Britain the whole issue of *jahiliyya* cannot be ignored. The perceived atheistic and corrupt culture of Britain is not to be hidden from. It gives a raison d'être. A tremendous sense of individual and group identity can be found by stimulating the first Muslims who rallied round the Prophet and destroyed the *jahiliyya* that was Mecca, turning it into the first city of Islam. This '*Jihad*' must begin by liberating their fellow Muslims who have either fallen prey to its corrupting influences, or ignorantly allowed themselves to pollute Islam with the cultural accretions of South Asia.

Ethnicity v. Islam

This dichotomy is in some ways at the heart of everything that has been looked at so far. It is a central issue not only for Muslims in Britain seeking to establish self-identity in a new land, but also in that it links what is developing here to the struggle taking place in Islamic communities throughout the world. Historically, Islamic revival has always involved a search for the fundamentals of the faith - a purification based on rooting out cultural additions to the teachings of Qur'an and *Sunna*. Usually this search for a 'pure' Islam sets up as an ideal the Muslim community in Medina at the time of the Prophet and continuing during the reign of the four rightly guided Caliphs.

It can be argued that the British Muslim population has so far undergone two major religious revivals. The first was not unique to Islam; it was part of a process apparently common to all the migrant communities. Roger and Catherine Ballard isolated four chronological stages of development in the South Asian settlements in Britain.[101] The third stage involved a general consolidation of ethnic settlements following the large-scale entry of wives and children throughout the 1960's and 1970's. The reuniting of families was accompanied by a strong ethnic awareness, and the organisation of religious practices on a communal basis. Festivals, holidays and life-cycle rituals began to be celebrated here in Britain. These were all inextricably bound up with the religions of the various communities. Maintaining religious and ethnic customs provided status to the migrants amongst their peers. Gradually communities were formed, based on shared memories, values and goals that were all located in the area of origin. In the case of Muslims, Islam has always been the main basis of group cohesiveness. At this point the major symbols of Muslim communities began to appear in Britain.

Verity Saifullah Khan has argued that ethnicity is not a manifestation of the traditional but is something quite new. She suggests that it is a reaction to an unacceptable external definition, a perceived restriction of choice.

> The new minority demands resources inaccessible to, and distinct from the majority. Traditional mechanisms and resources are adapted to reorganise disrupted relationships and institutions within the minority - traditional symbols, ideologies, forms of behaviour, became strategies for articulating a distinctive self, a distinctive grouping.[102]

If this is true, then the phenomena associated with the Ballards' third stage of development should be seen not as a religious revival amongst the migrants, but rather as the use of religious symbols and institutions to ensure that the cultural traditions of the old country are transmitted to children. Thus, the separate identity of the communities concerned is maintained.

The Muslim communities in Britain are still very localised. They are formed along local as well as national lines. They are often structured around a handful of families who have all migrated from the same small group of neighbouring villages. This is particularly true of the Pakistani migrants. Akram in a study of Muslims in Huddersfield found that the majority of families were from villages in the Lyallpur district of Pakistan.[103] The majority of original Pakistani settlers relate to their village kin, home area and culture of origin. Although labelled Pakistanis by the indigenous population, in their own day-to-day activities they are neither reminded or involved with a wider notion of the Pakistani population. It is kinfolk, the village and the *biradari* network which command their attention. The notable exceptions to this were the perceived attack on Islam made in Salman Rushdie's novel *The Satanic Verses*, and any international conflicts involving Pakistan or to a lesser degree other Muslim nations.

The above characteristics of the Muslim population in Britain have resulted in the proliferation of a diverse range of ethnic concerns. These have kept the communities relatively closed since the migrants do not have to go outside their boundaries to satisfy everyday needs.

There are, however forces which counteract this tendency. The diverse nature of the Muslim population has resulted in their encountering other modes of Islamic cultural expression which have equally strong claims to validity as their own. This creates questions concerning the 'true' form of Islam. The majority of Muslims believe in the fundamental tenet of the faith that Allah is sovereign. This sovereignty does not reside in a human being or a territory. In Islam, religion is held to be the essence of culture. There is a widespread belief in a universal Muslim culture and lifestyle; the very search for an Islamic lifestyle in Britain brings this into focus. Many Muslims are seeking to define their faith in terms of the universals of the religion. This links up with the concept of the world-wide *ummah*, and also with the international phenomenon of revivalism. This has led to British-born and educated Muslim children questioning their parents' values. Muhammad Mushaq Ibn Ally argues that Muslims' perceptions of self-understanding must take into account that they consider themselves to be members of a universal community taking its membership from several diverse national, racial and linguistic groups.[104] Muslims from India, Pakistan and Bangladesh cannot help but be aware of tensions between this joint membership of the *ummah* which is the ideal in Islam, and the actuality of different ethnic groups. Stephen Barton discovered in his research undertaken in Bradford that when Muslims face tension and conflict, they take shelter in the communities in which they were born and raised.[105] To be a Muslim in Britain is to be a Bengali, or a Punjabi, a Sylheti, or a Mirpuri. He states: 'Bengalis in Bradford seek the company not of fellow Muslims, members of the world-wide *ummah* but of other Bengalis'.[106]

Contacts with developments in the heartlands of Islam however, are inevitable. Pakistanis have brought with them a history of conflict between tribal and regional divisions. The attempt to forge a nation state in Pakistan has revolved around this question. Islam was the single element which provided a basis for the foundation of Pakistan in 1947. The attempts to establish and preserve Pakistani identity have centred upon Islam. The Constitution of Pakistan begins with the declaration that:

> Sovereignty over the entire Universe belongs to God Almighty alone and the authority which He has delegated to the State of Pakistan through its people, for being exercised within the limits prescribed by Him, is a sacred trust.[107]

Clause 3 states that the Constitution must be based on:

> the right of Muslims to order their lives, in the individual and collective spheres, in accord with the teachings and requirements of Islam, as set out in the Holy Qur'an and the *Sunna*.[108]

This has resulted in considerable and still unresolved controversy in Pakistan. Several powerful religious groups are struggling for the establishment of an Islamic state based on *Shari'ah* law. This debate has taken on a new significance in Britain amongst Muslims who are seeking an Islamic identity over and above ethnic differences. It is significant that the same religious/political groups have been imported to Britain, and are competing for the loyalties of the Muslim population here.

Dr. Zaki Badawi has said:

Our adjustment is inevitable. The first sacrifice we shall make is the individual cultures within the faith. Nigerians, Egyptians, Pakistanis all carrying bits of their culture around their necks like a dead weight, slowing down progress. That will be shed, allowing a return to the basics of our religion.[109]

This is not as straightforward as Dr. Zaki Badawi claims it to be. He himself is a qualified member of the *ulema* who was trained in Al-Azhar, Egypt. His definition of the fundamentals will be debated strongly by various other factions in Britain.

Individual v. Community

Much has already been said about the pressures to conform to the norms and values of the group as experienced by Muslims in Britain. As already ascertained, these pressures can arise simultaneously from the local ethnic group and from the sanctified beliefs and practices of the world-wide Islamic *ummah*. The relationship between these two is complex, and the latter can often be used to reinforce the former or even vice versa. Conformity to group values is also reinforced within the family group. At this level the concept of *izzat* functions as a powerful agent to maintain conformity. The various obligatory aspects of Islamic worship (*salat, Ramadan, Hajj*) also function to maintain a very strong awareness of communal religious identity as opposed to a more individual relationship with the Divine.

In an early study Eric Butterworth has questioned the degree to which Muslims are a community. He argues that even though the lives of many are circumscribed within relatively narrow group tenets, this certainly does not apply to all of them. He emphasises that there are definite differences between the generation that arrived here as adults and those born and being brought up here.[110] Young Muslims will find themselves coming into daily contact with the core values of secular Britain through their education.

A change in the family structure has resulted from the geographical fragmentation of the extended family and the relatively young composition of the Muslim migrant population. Badr Dahya has observed that the village kin groups as a residential unit have gradually begun to transform into nuclear households.[111] Large numbers of Muslims in Britain are adopting the nuclear family as their own choice of ideal lifestyle. Although many still adhere to the system of arranged marriages, both Muslim boys and girls are demanding the right to refuse their parents' choice. Many would ideally marry a partner born in Britain rather than someone brought over from the country of origin. These changes in family structure will eventually lead to a lessening of those controls and strictures which are maintained through the extended family network. This process will be reinforced by the move away from the inner city migrant zones to the suburbs, a move which the Ballards identified as the fourth stage of migrant development.[112]

Muslims brought up in Britain are likely to find themselves being brought into contact with a culture which sanctifies the rights of the individual. At a Day Seminar on Islam in Britain at the Department of Peace Studies, Bradford University[113] the conclusion was that there were problems arising out of the conflict between maintenance of community values and identity and acceptance within the wider society. This has manifested in some Muslim girls running away from home, and a high incidence of attempted suicide amongst young people. The Salman Rushdie controversy highlighted the conflict between these opposing ideologies. Muslims as a community felt that they had been insulted by *The Satanic Verses* and its apparent attack on Islam. No less fervent was the reaction from various Western writers and creative artists. The latter attacked the Muslim critics by vigorously defending the rights of the individual to free expression. Very often the ideology being expressed by these Western critics of Islamic values was that contained in the term 'modernism'. This is defined as the search for

> individual autonomy driven by a set of socially encoded values emphasising change over continuity, quantity over quality, efficient production, power and profit over sympathy for traditional values.[114]

This lessening of the strength of traditional community structures does not necessarily mean an embracing of the values of the receiving society. The development towards increasing individualism may well lead to a change in the understanding of Islam. Muhammad Anwar sums up this process from his own experience of studying the Qur'an for himself:

> Contrary to what I may have expected, I find it very logical and very, very beautiful. That came as a surprise because of the Islam I had learnt from my father. He relied merely on habit. What I could work out for myself was much more exciting'.[115]

Tradition v. Modernity

Bruce Lawrence defines 'modernity' as:

> the emergence of a new index of human life shaped, above all by increasing bureaucratisation and rationalisation as well as technical capacities and global exchange unthinkable in the pre-modern era.[116]

Modernity is accompanied by the ideology of modernism which the Oxford English Dictionary defines as: 'modern view(s) or method(s), especially a tendency in matters of religious belief to subordinate tradition to harmony with modern thought'.[117] Ahmed states that 'the drive towards industrialisation and reliance upon the physical created an ideology which emphasised materialism as a way of life'.[118] It is often assumed that as modernisation sweeps across the world, traditional religion would lose its grip on culture. Ahmed is concerned with the question of how a religion like Islam which is based upon a revealed code of behaviour, and which zealously guards the uncorrupted and final revelation in the Qur'an can come to terms with an ethos which 'puts aside the past and exults in diversity'.[119]

This clash of values is further reinforced by the fact that Western imperialism is associated with the ideology of modernism. In the early twentieth century many Muslim leaders attempted to come to terms with the success of European colonialism by adopting a modernist stance. Most Muslim nations attained their independence led by movements whose leaders had embraced secularism, democracy, socialism, and a desire to model the newly-formed nations on a European model. They wished to transform their societies by introducing western education, technology, and legal codes.[120] This was resisted by religious leaders who asserted the values of traditional Islam over the influence of the west.

Ahmed discusses the relationship between postmodernism and Islam. Although he acknowledges that postmodernism incorporates a loss of faith in the ideological certainties of modernism, it retains the scepticism of traditional orthodoxy.[121] It is doubtful whether many devout Muslims would be able to make the distinction between modernism and postmodernism. The Islamic reform organisations like the *Deobandis* founded in the subcontinent in the nineteenth and early twentieth century are still engaged in a critique of modernism. Akhtar maintains that the orthodox will never be able to come to terms with 'the impulse to uncertainty so characteristic of modern pluralistic culture'.[122] Their response is often chauvinism and a retreat into isolation.[123]

Ahmed argues that the fundamentalist movements characteristic of the second half of the twentieth century are a response to the world of doubt which is a characteristic of postmodernism.[124] Sahgal and Yuval-Davis agree that the rise of fundamentalist movements is connected to the crisis of modernity. They argue that disillusionment with both capitalism and socialism has resulted in a feeling of despair which has resulted in some turning to religion as a source of solace.[125] They acknowledge that fundamentalist ideology has made a concerted attack on the ideology of secularism.[126] Many contemporary social scientists who maintain that western society has become secularised argue that any hold that religion might continue to have over individuals would be transformed into forms of privatised belief where religious belief became only a matter of individual consciousness rather than remaining a collective force with potential for social change. According to this argument, the contact of traditional South Asian Muslim culture with secularised Britain should result in the process of Islam becoming more a matter of individual private consciousness. The comment of Muhammad Anwar at the end of the last section may be interpreted in this light. In fact, it may be an example of a very different reaction to contact with western culture. As modernity becomes a global phenomenon, its ideology of modernism is meeting stubborn resistance from religion in the form of fundamentalism.

Fundamentalism v. Secularisation

Karel Dobbelaere has summed up the secularisation thesis as:

> The higher the degree of functional differentiation the more advanced secularism will be, and the less impact religious organisations will be able to exert on the culture. Functional differentiation produces social sub-systems in polity, economy, education, family etc. They are increasingly autonomous and specialised. Religion is reduced to a sub-system of society rather than an overarching system of values and beliefs. Secular values replace religious ones.[127]

This viewpoint assumes that at some point in the past religion and the world were once one, but that now religion and modernity are in basic contradiction. The secularisation theorists tend to be opposed to religious ideology, but fail to realise that secularism is in itself ideological. The concept is value-laden rather than value-free. The ideas of the secularisation theorists generally reveal the view that the so-called 'factual knowledge' of modern societies will obliterate the religious superstitions of traditional cultures.[128]

It cannot be denied that totally secular economic, scientific, governmental and educational institutions have developed in the West. These are often linked by sociologists to the transition of social life from *Gemeinschaft* to *Gesellschaft*. Secularisation is perceived as *Gesellschaft* rationality dissolving the customs and sentiments of religion. Hadden and Shupe contend that secularisation is a part of a 'globalisation' process in which there is increasing homogeneity with respect to modes of production, institutions and structures and patterns of social relationships.[129] This has come about from the increasing economic interdependency between nations and the success of technology. Alex Inkeles argues that this means that as 'human life experience becomes more alike; attitudes, values, and basic disposition will also become alike'.[130] He goes on to suggest that 'distinctive cultural traditions' and 'historically determined institutional arrangements' deriving from the precontemporary era will operate as the main brakes on this process.[131] If this is true, then the culture of the Muslim migrants in Britain is considerably at risk. If their original culture is being undermined by the spread of Western values, then they have put their heads into the lion's mouth by immigrating to the very Western European nations from which the global culture originated.

Hadden and Shupe also pose the possibility that fundamentalism is a global phenomenon in response to secularisation. They note the world-wide appearance of religious/political movements which base their claim to legitimacy on the fundamentals of a religious tradition. They all seek to direct social changes by claims based on scriptural authority.[132] Bruce Lawrence points out that fundamentalism is a modern phenomenon.[133] Although fundamentalists try to reclaim what is authentic in their pasts as there must be a clear discernible continuity between them and the faith tradition their movements claim to restore, they also accept implicitly that the modern movement is the credible guardian of the past, but in order to combat secularisation they are prepared to use modern technology to the full. Lawrence suggests that they are 'moderns but not modernists'.[134] They reject modernism as an ideological framework, asserting instead a religious authority expressed through the collective demand that specific credal or ethical imperatives derived from scriptures be publicly recognised and legally enforced. They reject the modernist apostasy that change is absolute and in some way always beneficial.

Muslim fundamentalists have attacked the values of Western Europe and the USA. They condemn Western culture as morally decadent and argue that colonialism has not ended. They link themselves to ideologies that attack third world exploitation by the West, and contend that even after independence Western ideology still rules the Islamic world under a so-called Muslim mask. Islamic fundamentalism must be seen as a protest movement promulgating an ideology which evokes a response from those groups which are the most acutely aware of the tensions presented by the contemporary world. Many Muslim fundamentalist groups are comprised of young people who have had some contact with Western values through education. They are educated enough to understand the possibilities denied to them by the inequalities of the world system. Trained and educated, often in science and technology, law and accountancy, they still face unemployment or underemployment on low wages.

It is not surprising that many young Muslims in Britain are attracted to the fundamentalist message as a solution to the problems that they face. The Muslim fundamentalist groups are addressing many of the dilemmas discussed above. Although British, many Muslims still feel exploited by Western colonialism. They also face unequal opportunities even though promised success if they achieve the academic goals of education. Many of them feel let down by both the culture of their birth and the culture of their parents. The latter they perceive as riddled by traditional attitudes and beliefs that have no bearing on their own situation. Fundamentalism attracts them because it is quintessentially modern; that is to say, it constitutes a response to events and conditions in the present. The problem of Muslim minorities in Britain encapsulates many of the problems facing the majority communities in the heartlands of Islam. It is not surprising that they seek similar solutions. In Britain, the values of modernity call for increasing assimilation into the cultural mainstream of the society into which the migrants have settled. At the same time, opportunities to do this on an equal footing are denied. On the other hand, the emergence of migrant communities which preserve group solidarity by defining identity ethnically cannot offer very much to young Muslims who firmly know themselves to be British. Fundamentalism, in its affirmation of religious authority as absolute and holistic, offers a solution to this dilemma. Although the establishment of an Islamic state is clearly an unrealistic goal in a British inner city where Muslims are a small minority, it should be apparent why it still remains the ideal for some. Religion is not just an individual commitment entailing personal piety nor a group loyalty which requires the formal ecclesiastical membership implicit in the arguments of secularisation theorists. The phenomenon of fundamentalism indicates that religion can be the corporate public action of religiously motivated individuals to change the social system on behalf of what they perceive to be their deepest spiritual loyalties. Thus for many Muslims in Britain and elsewhere, the concept of the *ummah* becomes of central importance in their religious ideology. In Britain, it links many British-born Muslims to an identity which transcends both their allegiance to nationality and the culture of their parents. The concept of the *ummah* can also be used as a challenge to that overriding secular view of the world they find in the indigenous culture which is so often unaccepting of their presence.

Conclusion

This chapter has looked in some depth at the dilemmas facing the Muslim population in Britain. Before a clear direction for a uniquely British Muslim community can be ascertained, it will be necessary to resolve the dichotomies which have been the subject of examination. The form that the community takes will be forged out of the process of resolving these difficult problems.

Islam is, in one form or another, the heritage of all Muslims who have come to live in Britain. Initially the society they joined was virtually devoid of all symbols of Islam. Many of these symbols have now appeared in Britain. Muslims can observe the familiar outlines of mosques complete with dome and minarets on the skylines of British industrial cities. Islam is here to stay. Along with the symbols have come the controversies. The Islamic world is involved in the process of rediscovering what it means to be Muslim; this too is the focus for British Muslims. They must be prepared to be rooted in Britain. This will make it imperative to evolve and generate a new pattern of life which is in harmony with the values and norms of Islam but which, in the context of life chances, is based firmly here in Britain. Many have already discovered that minorities need distinctive or alternative systems of resources to give them a greater degree of resistance. They are finding this is their common Islamic identity.

This will involve a continuous process of bargaining and negotiating between (a) the British social, economic and cultural environment, (b) the ideals and expectations of various components of countries of origin, and (c) the ideational forces of orthodox Islam in its several forms.[135] There is clearly no one group or grouping which on its own has the strength to impress itself on the majority of the Muslim population. All the main theological/political organisations will need to be examined in the context of the issues raised in this chapter. *Jamaat-i Islami, Deobandis, Tabligh-i Jamaat* and *Barelwis* will each have an influence on the shape of the community in Britain. They all have a definite ideological programme and a specific Islamic world outlook. Each one challenges the dominant secular ideology in Britain, albeit to differing degrees. They oppose the corruption and decadence of a materialist society which they perceive to have lost its moral values. It is important to establish whether their ideological programmes clearly perceive the need to find a place for Islam in Britain in the context of Britain as a non-Muslim society in which the historical controversies and solution of the subcontinent simply cannot work.

For this reason, as Islam becomes a rallying flag around which the various Muslim ethnic and national groups in Britain can rally, it is important to be aware of the religious background inherited from the subcontinent. It is especially noticeable that out of the main groups currently at work in Britain (*Deobandis, Barelwis, Ahl-i Hadith, Tabligh-i Jamaat, Jamaat-i Islami*), only the last two were formed in the twentieth century. The nineteenth century groups were all part of the phenomenon of Islamic reform in India, even the *Barelwis*, who need to be seen as an organised reaction to the reformers.[136] The twentieth century *Tabligh-i Jamaat* is a continuation of the reform trend, and even the fundamentalist *Jamaat-i Islami* incorporates many features of the earlier reform movement.[137] Therefore it is necessary to examine the origins of these movements within the wider context of the unique development of Islam in the subcontinent in order to discover the reasons why various strands of Muslim belief that arose there should be so important to Muslim migrants in Britain. The organisations which represent these strands will continue to have considerable impact on the direction that the Muslim community takes in the future.

Endnotes

[1] To name but a few: Jeffery, Patricia, 1972, 'Pakistani Families in Bristol', *New Community*, 1:5; College de France, 1983, 'Muslim Immigration and Settlement in Britain, colloquium on *Islam in Europe Today*, October, Association Pour L'Avancement Des Sciences Islamiques, Paris; Nielsen, Jorgen, 1984, 'Muslim Immigration and Settlement in Britain', *Muslims in Europe*, No.21, Centre for the Study of Islam and Christian/Muslim Relations, Selly Oak, Birmingham Joly, Daniele, 1986, 'Making a Place for Islam in British Society: Muslims in Birmingham', *Centre for Research in International Migration and Ethnic Relations.*

[2] Rex, John, 1990, 'Muslims in a Multi-Cultural Society', paper presented to Anglo-French workshop on Islam in France and England, 24th February, University of Warwick, p.5.

[3] The following figures, derived from the 1981 Census on the basis of place of birth of the head of household, demonstrate the rapid growth of the Muslim population from Pakistan and Bangladesh. This figure is distorted by including those born in Britain.
1951 5,000
1961 24,900
1971 170,00
1981 360,00
(Nielsen, op.cit).

[4] The 1991 Census was the first to include a question on ethnic origin, however, it did not ask for any information on religious affiliation. To estimate the total Muslim population in Britain it is necessary to combine information derived from the ethnic question with the country of birth information for people who originate in Muslim nations. This will not include Muslims born in non-Muslim nations like India or the number of converts amongst the Afro-Caribbean and indigenous white population. The estimate of the total Muslim population is as follows:

Country/Region of Origin	Population (in thousands)
Pakistani/Bangladeshi/Indian	770
Other Asians	80
'Other other'	29
Turkish Cypriot	45
Other Muslim countries	367
African Muslims (New Commonwealth)	115
Total	1,406

Information taken from Anwar, Muhammad, 1993, 'Muslims in Britain: 1991 Census and Other Statistical Sources', *CSIC Papers*, No.9, September, Centre for the Study of Islam and Christian/Muslim Relations, Selly Oak, Birmingham, p.7.

5 The 1981 census has percentages for this proportion of the population as follows:

1951 —
1961 1.2%
1971 23.5%
1981 37.5%

(College de France, op.cit., p3).

The 1991 Census figures reveal that 60% of Pakistanis and Bangladeshis are under 25 as compared with only 32% whites.

Age Breakdown of Pakistanis and Bangladeshis, 1991 (%)

Age.						
	0-4	5-15	16-24	25-44	45-64	65+
Pakistani	13.13	29.52	17.47	25.79	12.35	1.73
Bangladeshis	15.06	32.17	17.60	20.46	13.51	1.20

(Anwar, op.cit., p.14).

6 Smith's 1974 survey showed that the regional breakdown of subcontinent Muslims was as follows:

Pakistan	Punjab	37%
	Kashmir	37%
	Karachi	6%
	N.W.Frontier	4%
	Other	7%
East Pakistan (now Bangladesh)		9%
India	Punjab	49%
	Gujarat	16%
	Other	35%

(College de France, op.cit., p.4).

7 Ethnicity is something to do with group distinctiveness based on cultural characteristics (Rex, John, 1986, *Race and Ethnicity*, Open University Press, Milton Keynes, p.22). Knott has stated that 'ethnicity is a certain form or condition of identity, that is experienced by migrants or settlers with a continuing awareness of difference' (Knott, Kim, 1992, 'The Role of Religious Studies in Understanding the Ethnic Experience', *Community Religions Project Research Paper*, University of Leeds, p.15). Rex points out that recent writing on ethnicity utilises a 'situational' view rather than a 'primordial' view (Rex, op.cit., p.26). The primordial view perceives ethnic characteristics such as religion, language, particular social customs as givens containing an 'overpowering coerciveness in and of themselves' (Geertz, Clifford, 1963, *Old Societies and New States - the Quest for Modernity in Asia and Africa*, Free Press, Glencoe, p.109). Barth lists the following charac-

teristics of ethnic groups utilised by anthropologists:

'1. they are biologically self-perpetuating;

2. they share fundamental cultural values, realised in overt unity in cultural forms;

3. they make up a field of communication and interaction;

4. they have a membership which identifies itself, and is identified by others, as constituting a category distinguishable from other categories of the same order.'

(Barth, Fredrik, 1970, *Ethnic Groups and Boundaries*, George Allen & Unwin, London, pp.10-11).

Barth argues that the critical feature of ethnic groups is item 4 as it allows for self-ascription and ascription by others (p.13). This situational view sees ethnicity as a resource which the agent can utilise or which can remain dormant. Alternatively, it can be ascribed by more dominant groups to deny rights (Rex, op.cit., 1986, pp. 27-28). Verity Saifullah Khan is aware of this element of choice when she defines ethnicity as 'something to do with people of one culture realising its distinctiveness and utilising its distinctive resources in interactions with outsiders' (Khan, Verity, Saifullah, 1976, 'Pakistanis in Britain:Perceptions of a Population', *New Community*, 5:3, p.223).

[8] This stage of community development was classified as the third phase by Catherine and Roger Ballard. It is signified by the mass entry of wives and children, and 'a general consolidation of the ethnic settlement' (Ballard, Roger, and Ballard, Catherine, 1977, 'The Sikhs: The Development of South Asian Settlements in Britain', *Between Two Cultures*, ed.Watson, James, Basil Blackwell, Oxford, p.22).

[9] Nielsen, Jorgen, 1992, *Muslims in Western Europe*, Islamic Surveys, Edinburgh University Press, Edinburgh, p.44.

[10] Barton, Stephen, 1986, *The Bengali Muslims of Bradford*, Community Religions Project, Monograph Series, University of Leeds, p.179.

[11] Barth has argued that it is the ethnic boundary that defines the group (Barth, op.cit., p.15). Wallman states that it is the 'identity element in ethnic processes which moves the boundaries' (Wallman, Sandra, 1986, 'Ethnicity and the Boundary Process in Context', *Theories of Race and Ethnic Relations*, eds. Rex, John and Mason, David, Cambridge University Press, Cambridge, p.230). She argues that 'differences between groups of people turn into ethnic boundaries only when heated into significance by the identity investment of either side' (ibid).

[12] Knott has stated that 'the predominant view in Britain and the U.S.A, is that religion is the passive instrument of ethnic identity' (Knott, op.cit., p.12). Typical of this viewpoint is Francis' statement that 'it is the ethnic group which sanctions a particular church affiliation, and which supports a religious congregation and its institutions as an effective means for its own maintenance and the preservation of its cultural traditions' (Francis, E.K., 1976, *Interethnic Relations*,

Elsevier, New York, p.157). This viewpoint is helpful to analyse the religious symbols and organisations developed by the first-generation migrants but the relationship between ethnicity is complex. Anwar sees both ethnicity and religion as variables of identity, independent but inter-related (Anwar, Muhammad, 1980, 'Religious Identity in Plural Societies: The Case of Britain', the *Journal of the Institute of Muslim Minority Affairs*, 2:2/3:1, pp.110-121). There are certainly occasions when religion plays a central role in ethnic group identity (Knott, op.cit., p12).

[13] Examples of this include certain gender attitudes belonging to the subcontinent; the insistence upon defining South Asian Muslim dress as Islamic; certain marital customs; and a complex network of customs and behaviour belonging to the religious practices of the village which can be loosely defined as folk-Sufism. Mol has argued that religion is used in this way as the sacraliser of identity, ethnic or otherwise (Mol, Hans, 1977, *Identity and the Sacred*, Free Press, New York).

[14] This is an example of where ethnicity influences the religiosity of groups (Knott, op.cit., p.5). Many young Muslims are joining revivalist groups associated with the Islamic Movement like *Jamaat-i Islami* which criticise the influence of ethnicity on Islam as cultural accretion and *bida*. They are organising themselves around religion rather than ethnic affiliation with a direct critique of ethnic customs.

[15] Clarke, Peter, 1985, 'Islam in Britain', *Religion Today*, 2:3.

[16] Ally, Mushaq Muhammad Ibn, 1989, 'Stranger Exiled From Home', *The Salman Rushdie Controversy in Interreligious Perspective*, Ed. Cohn-Sherbok, Dan, Symposium Series, Vol.27, The Edwin Mullen Press, Lampeter, pp.140-141.

[17] Rex, op.cit., 1990, p.5.

[18] Schiffauer, Werner, 1988, 'Migration and Religiousness', *The New Islamic Presence in Western Europe*, Ed. Gerholm, Tomas and Lithman,Yngve Georg, Mansell Publishing, London, pp.146-158.

[19] Khan,Verity Saifullah, 1979, 'Mirpuris in Bradford', *Minority Families in Britain: Support and Stress*, ed. Khan, Verity Saifullah, London, p.37.

[20] Dahya, Badr, 1972-3, 'Pakistanis in England', *New Community*, 2:1, p.30.

[21] Longley, Clifford, 1987, 'At the Crossroads of Belief', The Times, August 17th.

[22] Shaw, Alison, 1988, *A Pakistani Community in Oxford*, Blackwell, Oxford, p.22.

[23] Werbner, Pnina 1987, 'The Fiction of Unity in Ethnic Politics: Aspects of Representation and the State among British Pakistanis', *Black and Ethnic Leadership in Britain: The Cultural Dimensions of Political Action*, eds. Werbner, Pnina & Anwar, Muhammad, Routledge,

London, p.131.

[24] Nielsen, op.cit, 1992, pp. 44-45.

[25] ibid., p.47.

[26] Badawi, Zaki, 1986, 'Religions in Britain: Islam in Britain', *World Religions in Education: Shap Mailing 1986*, Shap Working Party/CRE, London, p.14.

[27] Alavi, Hamza, 1985, 'Pakistan and Islam: Ethnicity and Ideology', unpublished paper to *the Middle East Discussion Group*, November, Oxford, p.17.

[28] The most prominent of these are the nineteenth century *Deobandis* who developed as a movement out of the establishment of the *Deoband dar al-Ulum*. The most important twentieth century movements are the *Jamaat-i Islami* and the *Tabligh-i Jamaat*.

[29] Anwar, Muhammad, 1980-81, 'Religious Identity in Plural Societies: The case of Britain', *Institute of Muslim Minority Affairs*, 2:2/3:1, p.110.

[30] The notable exception here is the Barelwis who cannot really be defined as revivalists or reform. They actually came into being as a conscious reaction against the Reform movement of 19th century India. Ahmad Riza Khan of Bareilly formed a theological movement which defended the folk/Sufi syncretistic practices and beliefs widespread among subcontinent Muslim villagers.

[31] The *Barelwis* have accused *Deobandis* of being *Wahhabis*, whom they believe to be a sect. Some *Barelwis* go as far as to accuse them of being outside the pale of Islam. The *Deobandis*, on the other hand, condemn the *Barelwis* as guilty of *shirk*, and many of their practices as *bida*. The *ulema* of both factions have issued *fatwas* which denounce the other group as non-Muslim. The rivalry has manifested in Britain in the form of conflicts over the control of mosques.

[32] Azam, Sher, quoted in Ruthven, Malise, 1990, *A Satanic Affair - Salman Rushdie and the Rage of Islam*, Chatto and Hindus, London, p.82

[33] Badawi, Zaki, quoted in James, Brian, 1987, 'Which path leads to Paradise', *The Times*, August 16th.

[34] Anwar, op.cit., 1980-81, p.112.

[35] Anwar, Muhammad, 1982, *Young Muslims in a Multi-Cultural Society - Their Educational Needs and Policy Implications: The British Case*, The Islamic Foundation, Leicester, p.4.

[36] Nizami, Farhan, quoted in James, op.cit, *The Times*.

[37] Quoted from Whyte, Alison, 1989, 'Flying in the Face of Tradition', *The Guardian*, 25th

July.

[38] College de France, op.cit., p.7.

[39] ibid.

[40] Sharif,R., 1985, 'Interviews With Young Muslim Women of Pakistani Origin', *Muslims in Europe*, No.27, Centre of the Study of Islam and Christian/Muslim Relations, Selly Oak, Birmingham, p.11.

[41] ibid., p.3; Mirza, Kauser, 1989, 'The Silent Cry: Second Generation Bradford Muslim Women Speak', *Muslims In Europe*,No.43, Centre for the Study of Islam and Muslim/Christian Relations, Selly Oak, Birmingham, p.6.

[42] Rashid, S., 1981, 'The Socialisation and Education of Pakistani Teenage Girls in London', M. Phil Thesis, School of Oriental and African Studies, London, p.97.

[43] Knott, Kim & Khokher, Sajda, 1993, 'Religious and Ethnic Identity Among Young Muslim Women in Bradford', *New Community*, 19(4), July, p.596.

[44] Mirza, op.cit., p.7.

[45] ibid.

[46] ibid.

[47] Shaw, op.cit., pp.165-166.

[48] Knott & Khokher, op.cit., p.595.

[49] Examples of this are South Asian *purdah* and prescribed dress codes; certain kinds of arranged marriages which are kept within the kin network, especially those where the consent of the daughters is not respected. In the subcontinent the right of widows to remarry is still an issue.

[50] Knott & Khokher, op.cit., p.596.

[51] ibid.

[52] Quoted from Bunting, Madeleine, 1990, 'A Meeting of Two Worlds', *The Guardian*, 13th June.

[53] Knott & Khokher, op.cit., p.596.

[54] Yaseen, Moeen, 1992, of the Islamia Schools Trust, 'Islam and the Educational Systems of Europe', Paper presented at the Conference on *Islam in a Changing Europe*, 9-11th September, Bradford University.

[55] Afshar, Haleh, 1992, Paper presented to the Conference on Islam in a Changing Europe, Sept 9-11th, Bradford University.

[56] Taylor, Monica & Hegarty, Séamus,1987, *The Best of Both Worlds*, Nfer Nelson, Newcastle-Upon-Tyne; Bhachu, Parminder, 1985, *Twice Migrants*, Tavistock Publications, London, p.171.

[57] Mirza, op.cit., p.10.

[58] ibid., p.11.

[59] Barton, op.cit., p.161.

[60] Link International, November 1987, 'Muslim Institutions for Muslims in Britain'.

[61] Sharif, op.cit., p.3.

[62] Mirza, op.cit., p.15.

[63] Sharif, op.cit., p.5.

[64] ibid., p.4.

[65] Mirza, op.cit., p.16.

[66] Sharif, op.cit., p.4.

[67] ibid.

[68] ibid.,p.23.

[69] Mirza, op.cit., p.16.

[70] Ali, Yasmin, 1992, 'Muslim Women and the Politics of Ethnicity and Culture in Northern England', *Refusing Holy Orders: Women and Fundamentalism*, eds. Sahgal, Gita, & Yuval-Davis, Nira, Virago, London, p.130.

[71] Husband, Charles & Ahmad, Waqar, 'Social Welfare', *Islam in a Changing Europe*, 9-11th September 1992).

[72] Unemployment rates as % of the relevant population:

Whites	7%
Indians	13%
Afro/Caribbean	15%
Pakistan/Bangladesh	21%

(ibid).

[73] Taylor, Monica, Ethics, Ethnicity & Education

[74] Anwar, op.cit., 1980-81, p.110.

[75] Khan, op.cit., 1976, p.222.

[76] Werbner, Pnina, 1981, 'Manchester Pakistanis: Lifestyles, Ritual and the Making of Social Distinctions', *New Community*, 9:2.

[77] Hussein, Ali, 1992, 'Culture, Faith and Political Ideology: Islam in a Changing Context', *Conference on Islam in A changing Europe*, 9-11 September, Bradford University.

[78] Mujeeb, M., 1966, *The Indian Muslims*, George Allen & Unwin, London; Titus, Murray, Y., 1979, *Indian Islam - A Religious History of Islam in India*, Munshiram Manoharlal, New Delhi, both confirm the impact of the Sufis on conversion to Islam in India.

[79] Forbes, A.D.W., ND, 'Two Concepts of Monism: The *Wahdat Al-Wujud* of Ibn Al-Arabi and *Wahdat Al-Shuhud* of Shaikh Ahmad Sirhindi', Submitted for M.A., University of Leeds, Leeds.

[80] Metcalf, Barbara Daly, 1982, *Islamic Revival in British India: Deoband 1860-1900*, Princeton University Press, New Jersey.

[81] Werbner, Pnina, 1987(a), 'Taking and Giving: Working Women and Female Bonds in a Pakistani Immigrant Neighbourhood', Manchester University, p.5.

[82] The 1982 Government Trend Survey states that Ethnic minority groups between the ages of 16-19 were suffering 50% unemployment compared to 25% whites in the same age group.

[83] Anwar, Muhammad & Garaudy, Roger, 1984, 'Social and Cultural Perspectives on Muslims in Western Europe', *Muslims in Europe*, No.24, Centre for the Study of Islam and Christian/Muslim Relations, Selly Oak, Birmingham, p.7.

[84] Werbner, op.cit., 1987(a), p.9.

[85] ibid.p.11.

[86] ibid.

[87] Werbner, op.cit, 1981, p.223.

[88] Schiffauer, op.cit., p.149.

[89] ibid., p.150.

[90] Shaw, op.cit., p.17.

[91] Breton,R., 1964, 'Institutional Completeness of Ethnic Communities and the Personal Relations of Immigrants', *American Journal of Sociology* 70.2, 193-205.

[92] *The Young Muslims UK* are an example of an organisation which insists on English as the medium for propagating Islam. The ISB (*The Islamic Society of Britain*) has been established to function as an umbrella organisation for all Islamic youth movements which use English as their first language.

[93] The success at the Battle of Badr (623AD) had a deep significance for Muhammad and the first Muslims. For the first time Muslims were in a position of strength, not weakness. This success was interpreted as a vindication of their faith in God, a divine intervention on their behalf. The victory was regarded as proof that God was on their side. Success and victory were to be seen from then on as proof of Islam's message.

[94] Gordon, Paul, 1992, 'Islam as Europe's Other: Restrictive Immigration Policy as a Response to the Muslim Presence', Conference on *Islam in a Changing Europe*, September 9-11th, Bradford University.

[95] Moore, Charles, 19th October 1991, 'Time for a more liberal and "racist" immigration policy', *The Spectator*, p.7.

[96] Gordon, op.cit.

[97] Said, Edward, 1985, *Orientalism*, Penguin, Middlesex.

[98] Gordon, op.cit.

[99] Linton, Ralph, 1943, 'Nativistic Movements', *American Anthropologist 45*, pp.230-240.

[100] Barth, op.cit., pp.15-16.

[101] Ballard, Roger & Catherine, op.cit., 1977, pp. 21-22.

[102] Khan, op.cit., 1976, p.223.

[103] Akram, M., 1974-75, 'Pakistani Migrants in Britain: A Note', *New Community*, 4:1, p.117.

[104] Ally, op.cit., pp.137-138.

[105] Barton, op.cit., p.34.

[106] ibid., p.34.

[107] Newman, K.J., 1956, *Essays on the Constitution of Pakistan*, Pakistan Co-operative Book Society, Dacca, p.3.

[108] ibid.

[109] James, op.cit.

[110] Butterworth, Eric, 1967, 'A Muslim Community In Britain', Church Information Office, p.11.

[111] Dahya, Badr, 1974, 'The Nature of Pakistani Ethnicity in Industrial Cities in Britain', *Urban Ethnicity*, ed.Abner Cohen, ASA Monographics, p.87.

[112] Ballard, C & R., op.cit., p.22.

[113] *Islam In Britain*, 20th June 1992, Day Seminar, Department of Peace Studies, Bradford University.

[114] Lawrence, Bruce B., 1990, *The Defenders of God: The Fundamentalist Revolt Against the Modern Age*, I.B. Tauris, London, p.27.

[115] Quoted from Ruthwen, op.cit., p.137.

[116] Lawrence, op.cit., p.27.

[117] Ahmed, Akbar, 1992, *Postmodernism and Islam*, Routledge, London, p.6.

[118] ibid.,p.7.

[119] ibid., p.5.

[120] ibid., p.31.

[121] ibid.,p.10.

[122] Akhtar, Shabbir, 1990, *A Faith For All Seasons: Islam and Western Modernity*, Bellew, London, p.22.

[123] Ahmed, op.cit., p.45.

[124] ibid., p.13.

[125] Sahgal & Yuval-Davis, 1992, 'Introduction: Fundamentalism, Multiculturalism and Women in Britain, Refusing Holy Orders, Virago, London, p.5.

[126] ibid.,p.7.

[127] Hadden, Jeffery K. & Shupe, Anson, 1989, *Secularisation and Fundamentalism Reconsidered- Religion and the Political Order Vol III*, New Era Books, New York, p.xvii quot-

ing from Karel Dobbelaere, *The Secularisation of Society ? Some Methodological Suggestions.*

[128] Wilson, Brian, 1966, *Religion in a Secular Society*, Pelican, London, pp.10-13.

[129] Robertson, Roland, 1989, 'A New Perspective on Religion and Secularisation in the Global Context', *Secularisation and Fundamentalism Reconsidered*, New Era Books, New York, p.69.

[130] Inkeles, Alex, 1981, 'Convergence and Divergence in Industrial Societies', *Directions of Change*, ed. Attir, Mustafa O. et al, Boulder, Colorado, Westview Press, p.3-38.

[131] ibid.

[132] Hadden & Shupe, 1989, 'Is There Such A Thing as Global Fundamentalism?', *Secularisation and Fundamentalism Reconsidered*, New Era Books, New York, p.109.

[133] Lawrence, op.cit., p.1.

[134] ibid. p.17.

[135] Joly, Daniele & Nielsen, Jorgen, 1985, 'Muslims in Britain: An Annotated Bibliography 1960-1984', unpublished, p.3.

[136] This viewpoint is affirmed by Metcalfe, Barbara Daly, 1982, *Islamic Revival in British India: Deoband 1860-1900*, Princeton University Press, New Jersey.

In a paper entitled 'South Asian Sunni Reform Movements in the West: The Lang Scots Mile from Delhi to Dundee', presented to the Conference on New Islamic and Related Movements in the West, 11th December 1993, The Centre for New Religious Movements, King's College, London, p.13, Andrews, Ahmed asserts that 'the Barelwis represent a movement of resistance to reformism, and became centred around the personality of the scholar, Ahmad Riza Khan (1856-1921)'.

[137] Geaves, Ronald, 1989, 'Maulana Mawdudi: A Pure Islam or Cultural Inheritence', submitted for partial fulfilment of M.A., University of Leeds.

5 Barelwis in the subcontinent

Introduction

In Chapter III there is a section on Gellner's analysis of the division between rural and urban forms of Islam. Gellner points out that in rural areas, the kind of Islam practised is likely to rely on a multiplicity of ritual and mystical practices, devotion to charismatic personalities, and finally, a tendency towards this-world and other-world hierarchies. The subcontinent is particularly rich in this version of Islam and it manifests in countless varieties from region to region, village to village. The predominance of this strand of Islam in the subcontinent arises from two causes: the powerful influence of Sufism in the area and syncretic developments arising·out of the meeting of Islam with Hinduism. It would have been also reinforced by the work of Maulana Ahmad Riza Khan (1856-1921) to defend the beliefs and traditions of this strand of Islam against the vehement attacks of the reform groups. Raza Khan's activities established a common identity known as *Barelwi* to this wide-ranging diversity of belief and practice. Since the majority of the first-generation Muslim migrants arrived from rural areas of the subcontinent, it is inevitable that they would have brought with them religious beliefs and practices steeped in local customs legitimised by precedent.

Obviously the impact of practices derived from Hinduism would be less apparent in the Muslim nations of Pakistan and Bangladesh but in both these countries the tradition of Sufism has been, and still is, very powerful. Historically, many Sufis had been far more tolerant of Hinduism than the *ulema*, and some of them had not been very strict concerning the externals of Islam. This had assisted the development of syncretistic varieties of Islam and a trained eye familiar with both religions may still observe the Hindu origin of various practices even in Pakistan and Bangladesh.

Sufis and Shrines

Although the invasion of parts of India by Muslim forces would have resulted in forced conversion, the majority of Indians converted to Islam through contact with wandering *faqirs* and Sufis.[1] These charismatic figures would have easily gained the respect and veneration of Hindu villagers familiar with wandering *yogis* and *sadhus*. It is arguable that they did not always differentiate between them. This is still the case today in Indian villages where there are many examples of *sadhus* and *faqirs* being welcomed by both Muslims and Hindus alike. Village shrines of holy men are attended by adherents of both faiths regardless of the original faith of the tomb's occupier. Indian temples and sacred places were taken over by Muslims and continued to be visited by the local unconverted population.[2] If the place had become a centre of teaching by a

Sufi some of the Hindu population would have been converted, possibly feeling more at ease with Sufism's spiritual interpretation of Islamic precepts. Others would have incorporated the Islamic cult based around the Sufi into their own system of beliefs by identifying the Muslim saint with Hindu mystics or even with one of the Hindu deities.[3]

One of the central tenets of Hinduism is reverence for the spiritual guide or *guru*. Disciples have gathered in large numbers around some of the more charismatic of these figures, and after their death many cults have developed. The holy man is a venerated figure, often being perceived as a link to the divine or as even participating in divinity himself. At the same time, traditional Sufi doctrine insisted upon the need for a spiritual guide and encouraged reverence and devotion towards him. It is not surprising that the Sufi *shaikhs* or *pirs* collected disciples from both communities. The Hindu reverence for holy men did not end with their deaths; it was believed that their link with divinity ensured that their power survived the demise of the body. Shrine centres focussed the attention of devotees who hoped that the saint could intercede with or propitiate the divinity on their behalf. The institution of shrines was already prevalent amongst Hindus before the arrival of Islam, and played an important part in local religious tradition.[4] Pilgrimage to these shrine centres was regarded as a sacred act.

Sufism, too, has stressed the master/disciple relationship. A *pir* is expected to undertake responsibility for his *murids'* spiritual development. A formal oath of allegiance or *bai'at* is made by the *murid* to the *pir*. Once taken the *murid* is taken into the spiritual protection of the *pir* and his old sins are forgiven.[5] The *pir/murid* relationship is prevalent in the Muslim villages of the subcontinent. Usually children will follow the *pir* of their parents. The Urdu adjective '*be-pir*' (without *pir*) which means pitiless, vicious or cruel, indicates the importance of the *pir* in traditional Muslim society.[6]

A Sufi was expected to have *karamat*, supernatural power which enabled him to perform miracles. This power, it was believed, was not lost at death, but was retained and later attributed to his tomb in the *dargah* or *khanqah*.[7] Relics, such as the personal belongings of the saint are maintained in the *khanqah* and believed by the pilgrims to be endowed with *baraka*, the power to bless.[8] The saints were also attributed with the power to intercede and answer prayers on behalf of *murids* or visitors to the tomb. The deaths of Muslim holy men thus created a new network of local shrines, and sometimes in the case of prominent Sufis, national centres of pilgrimage.[9] Imtiaz Ahmad argues that these shrines created local cults which 'involved what may be called the localisation of Muslim spiritual geography to correspond broadly with the confines of their region with some extension to the great all-India shrines'.[10]

Many Sufis wandered as itinerant holy men but as the great Sufi orders developed, the advantages of remaining in one place and working with a particular community became apparent. The *khanqah* or *dargah* was established, as a teaching institution usually by those Sufis who belonged to one of the orders, this ensured that the orders would survive the lives of founders and individual inmates.[11] After the saint's death it was essential for his successors (*pirzade*) to legitimise their claimed closeness as soon as possible. This was usually done by stressing bloodties to the saint himself or to his immediate successor (*khalifa*) if he had nominated one.[12] The main duties of the successors was to cherish the memory of the dead saint, to observe the proper rites at the tomb and to guide the pilgrims and visitors to the tomb so that they may receive the blessings of the dead saint via the mediation of his successors. The sanctity of the *khanqah* increased with proximity to the tomb. Generally women are not allowed into the tomb itself but perform prayers, light incense and make offerings outside the walls of the inner sanctum. Very often the shrine consisted of several tombs containing the bodies of the saint's wives and children.[13] Sometimes these become special places of worship for women denied entry to the tomb of the saint.[14] In general, however, women form an important constituent of the shrine cults. Although mosque attendance for women is generally disapproved of in the subcontinent, shrine attendance is not. Many *pirs* accept women as *murids* and some shrines are specifically to women saints.[15]

Depending on the fame of the *pir*, the number of visitors to the shrine can range from a handful to hundred each day. This number increases dramatically during *urs*, the annual celebration of the deathday of the saint, when thousands can gather at the fair which is held at that time. The annual *urs* functions as a social event for the surrounding population who are entertained by music, games, and food. Pilgrims can attend the shrine to receive the saint's blessing and intercession on all manners of ills. The sick can pray for a cure and couples who are childless may bring a red thread which is tied to the wall of the tomb. Those in debt seek the blessings of the *pir*. The poor, the destitute and those who find the social well-being of their families threatened may stay in the *khanqah* for a short period. Some *khanqahs* maintain public kitchens which distribute free food to the poor and to travellers. This is known as the *langar*.[16] The *langar* is also an essential feature of the *urs* celebrations. Depending upon the Sufi order to which the saint belonged, many of the *khanqahs* provide *qawwali* singing; this usually occurs on a Thursday night. The musicians sing of the life and death of the *pir* together with popular songs of the Sufi tradition. There is also worship and prayers in the attached mosque, and generally *dhikr* would be held here: ordinarily once a week, but also on special occasions like *urs* and *Milad Nabi*. Most visitors donate to the *khanqah*, often on the tomb of the saint. This money is collected by the *mujawars* or *pirzade*, the descendants of the shrine and to assist the local poor.

In the saint's lifetime people would have come for blessings and for the cure of ailments. This was done by the issuing of *ta'widhs*, amulets each containing a verse of the Qur'an written on a small piece of paper. At the larger *khanqahs* the *mujawars* continue this function at the shrine by mediating the power of the *pir*. On arriving at the shrine the visitor is met by the *mujawars* who offer their services. They guide the visitors to the tomb, assist their offerings and prayers and issue blessings on written *ta'widhs*.

Despite the processes of urbanisation and the sharp attacks of the critical reform movements, folk-sufism based around the shrine cults and the figure of the *pir* remains popular throughout the subcontinent. It is difficult to envisage its decline in the region. In Pakistan and Bangladesh some *pirs* have considerable political influence, and since the work of Ahmad Raza Khan established the *Barelwi* tradition, this popular strand of Islam has been represented by powerful bodies of *ulema*.

Local customs

Besides the Sufi tradition which has developed into folk-religion based around the *pirs* and their tombs there is also widespread practice of customs and rituals which some Muslims, particularly those from the reform organisations, would argue were unIslamic and a product of incomplete or faulty conversion. These customs usually predominate in rural areas and concern religious activities involved with rites of passage. In contrast to the reform argument, however, many Muslims claim that it is completely acceptable within Islam to follow both local custom and the universally prescribed laws of the *Shari'ah* as long as there is no compromise with the central tenets of Islam. This debate over the legitimacy of local custom is central to the antagonism between the *Barelwis* and the reform movements. The reform movements criticise many local customs as *bida*, innovation deriving from contact with Hinduism. This syncretic influence is likely to be stronger in India and Bangladesh than in Pakistan. The following examples demonstrate the kind of customs shared by both Muslims and Hindus in the villages of the subcontinent.

Several studies have examined this aspect of Muslim culture in the subcontinent.[17] Fruzzetti explores birth rituals in Bengal and finds striking similarities between those observed by both Hindu and Muslim women.[18]She notes that in the fifth month of pregnancy a black thread containing a *ta'widh* is tied around the mother's neck and a red thread is tied around her waist. The purpose of the treads is to protect the mother and the child against *bhutas* (spirits) which can take life. Both Hindu and Muslim women bury the placenta as it is regarded as vulnerable to attack by the *bhutas*, who it is believed can harm the child.[19] Various rituals of protection for the newborn child are identical for both Muslims and Hindus, and both groups believe that the child must be protected by these for the first twenty-one days after birth. After twenty-one days it is believed the child is partially protected by *Sasthi*, Hindu deity of children. Amongst the spirits which can harm a child the most feared is the Hindu godling *Chutti*.[20] Amongst Hindus and Muslims alike the mother and child must be kept in seclusion as both are believed capable of polluting people who come in contact with them. Fruzzetti concludes that a dual system of thought operates among these rural Bengali Muslims: they clearly state that they belong to the universal Islamic *ummah*, but the rites and practices which bind them to this *ummah* are by no means their only concern. In everyday life they share in a 'Bengali culture' which is common to both them and Hindus.[21] In an earlier piece of research Fruzzetti concludes that these customs and practices which belong to Bengali culture combined with the universal prescriptions and practices of Islam to form a 'folk religion of Islam unique to Bengal'.[22]

Saiyid has examined the phenomenon of celebrating *Moharram* amongst some *Sunni* communities in India.[23] He discovered that in several cases the festival involved the entire community regardless of religious affiliation. He noted that this was not the case with the universal Islamic festivals of *Eid* and *Ramadan*, which were only observed by Muslims.[24] At some *Moharram* festivals he observed that on the final day the custom of *possi* was maintained. In the morning groups of Muslims banging drums collected donations from all the houses in the village, both Muslim and Hindu. The collection was later spent on alcohol which was drunk that night while dancing. The drinks were served to the dancing men by the village womenfolk. It was discovered that this custom was also followed at the Hindu festivals of *Dussehra* and *Diwali* when the roles were reversed. The Hindus collected the donations and the Muslims contributed and joined in the celebrations.[25] It is possible that these *Sunni* communities regarded the *Moharram* festivities as part of local culture as it is traditionally a *Shi'a* festival. This allowed them to participate in the festival with the Hindu neighbours. By contrast *Eid* and *Ramadan* are considered to be part of their belonging to the universal *ummah*, and therefore purely Muslim occasions.

The above examples are only a few selected at random from detailed research carried out in the subcontinent. Undoubtedly in every region in India where Muslims live similar examples can be found. When combined with the tradition arising out if Sufism they form a varied, regional folk-Islam that is vigorously practised throughout the subcontinent. Even the Muslim nations, Pakistan and Bangladesh, have not lost these traditional folk customs amongst rural Muslims, though in this case the *Sufi* variety is stronger than syncretic influences arising out of contact with Hinduism. As mentioned previously, one of the main devisions between the *Deobandis* and the *Barelwis* concerns the permissibility in Islam of these local customs arising as they do either out of contact with Hinduism or from a bedrock of popular Sufism.

The Barelwis

The Barelwis are the only major nineteenth century Islamic movement in the subcontinent whose teachings were not derived from the ideas of Shah Wali-allah. Rather than emerging out of a desire to change standards of religious practice, they adhered to the custom-laden style of *Sufism* and closely allied themselves to the teachings of the mediaeval *pirs*. They gave less importance to individual responsibility, and believed in the intercession of the *pirs* and their *ulema*. Their leader Maulana Ahmad Riza Khan Barelwi defended vigorously any custom that elevated the stature of the prophet and the saints. He emphasised the pre-eminence of Muhammad and often spoke of the *Sufi* doctrine of *Noor-i Muhammad*. This doctrine regarded the Prophet as an emanation of God's light, and saw the Prophet as pre-existing the beginning of creation. The world was seen as having been created specifically to demonstrate the Prophet's glory, and his true form was believed to be self-existent light. He was human, but his humanity was different from other men. He possessed a unique knowledge of the unknown, and complete awareness of all spiritual matters. Consequently, he could be called upon to intercede with God on behalf of the believer. The saints were at once part of and aware of the light of Muhammad, and after death they were believed to be able to intercede with God on behalf of ordinary believers just as the Prophet himself could. Ahmad Riza Khan elaborated on Ibn Arabi's belief that there was a secret hierarchy of saints whose presence in every age sustained the universe itself.

The *Barelwis* can be seen as a conscious reaction to the *Deobandi* reformers. Obviously every Muslim from the subcontinent who does not follow the strictures of the revivalist message can be described as *Barelwi*, but Ahmad Riza Khan and the *Barelwi ulema* used their status and legal scholarship consciously to justify a mediatory, custom-laden Islam that was closely linked to the intercession of shrine-based *pirs*. Unlike the *Deobandis*, there was no attempt to blame the colonial rulers for the threat they made to Muslim culture, but the *Barelwis* under the leadership of Ahmad Riza Khan worked hard to inspire Muslims to devote themselves to Islam. The aim was to revive and maintain the Islamic status quo as it existed currently. Its present state was seen as an organic and hence valid development from the past. The reformers of Deoband were accused of practising an idealised Islam that was based on texts and historical past and was not properly aligned to the present. More significantly, they were accused of lack of respect for Allah's prophets. It is not surprising that the *Barelwi* message appealed to the rural population and the uneducated. It supported and justified the faith that they were already practising. Especially significant is the fact that it made far less demand for individual responsibility in its followers than did the reform movements.

Ahmad Riza Khan did agree with the reformers in one respect: he sought to make religion play an intensely vital part in daily life. Unlike the reformers, he and his movement initially placed little value on the establishment of schools and institutions. The success of Deoband, however, caused the *Barelwis* to found a number of schools of its own in order to train its *ulema*. The most famous of these is Ahmad Riza Khan's *dar al-Ulum* in Bareilly. Like Deoband the college has attracted students from abroad, but these have been generally the sons of prominent *Barelwis* who have migrated from the subcontinent. One distinctive difference between the two colleges is their respective treatment of the graves of their founders. The original *Deobandi ulema* are buried in the college graveyard. These graves are marked by simple headstones. Sometimes students will enter the graveyard and stand quietly with closed eyes by the grave of a famous *ulema*. In Bareilly, Ahmad Riza Khan is buried in a splendid tomb in the mosque hung with fabric and surrounded by carpets. His immediate family have tombs around him and are venerated equally. Any day a number of people may be seen at the shrine as at any of the other famous shrines of saints and *Sufis* in the subcontinent. Ahmad Raza Khan's *Urs* is celebrated at the college which functions as a shrine as well as a *dar al-Ulum*.

It is difficult to assess the degree to which the beliefs of Ahmad Raza Khan were followed by the nineteenth century Indian *ulema*. Many of the *ulema* were untouched by the reformist position, and already practised the type of religion advocated by the *Barelwis*. Today there are many *ulema* and *pirs* that would describe themselves as *Barelwis* merely because they practise a certain type of Islam. This certainly indicates the success of Ahmad Raza Khan in establishing a unified identity for a strand of Islam which is by nature disparate and lacking central organisation. On the other hand, many adherents more closely identify themselves with their individual *pir* or *tariqa* than a wider *Barelwi* consciousness. Organisation still takes place around the former although there are groups of *ulema* trained in *Barelwi dar al-ulums* who consciously represent the latter. There is no doubt that Ahmad Raza Khan enabled Muslims who practised the type of Islam condemned by the reform groups to feel a common identity and to fight back against the success of the criticism made against them. It is not the actual type of religion practised by the *Barelwis* that made them an independent sect, but rather the conscious use of it as an oppositional stance to the reformers.

Conclusion

Fruzzetti's conclusion that Muslims in Bengal feel that they belong both to the universal Muslim *ummah* and to a Bengali culture which is common to them and Hindus is important. It demonstrates that Muslims who follow this tradition will have no opposition between ethnicity and Islam. The *Barelwi* tradition is strongly represented in Britain and is often used to reinforce identification and loyalty to ethnic origins. As mentioned in Chapter IV, the folk-Sufi strand of Islam, which is followed throughout the Muslim villages of the subcontinent, powerfully evokes memories and feelings of never-forgotten places of origin for the first-generation migrants. Although the influence of Hinduism is nowhere near so apparent as in the villages of India and Bengal, many Muslims associate the lifestyle and beliefs of those who practise this kind of Sufi-inspired Islam with Hindu influence. While researching in Leeds, a prominent local businessman and chairman of a *Barelwi* mosque committee, was described to me as 'a devout Muslim who lived a Hindu lifestyle'. In reality, it is a strand of Islam which is inextricably interwoven with the customs pertaining to ethnic origin. Consequently, it is difficult to foresee the form that this tradition will take in Britain as British-born Muslims may have little sympathy with this highly idiosyncratic form of Islam unique to the subcontinent. The following chapter hopes to throw some light on the development of the *Barelwi* tradition in Britain.

Endnotes

[1] Mujeeb, M., 1966, *The Indian Muslims*, George Allen & Unwin, London; Titus, Murray, Y., 1979, *Indian Islam - A Religious History of Islam in India*, Munshiram Manoharlal, New Delhi; Von Schwerin, Graeffin, 1985, 'Saint Worship in Indian Islam', *Ritual and Religion Amongst Muslims in the Subcontinent*, Ahmad, Imtiaz, Vanguard Books, Lahore all support this view.

[2] Von Schwerin, Graeffin, 1985, 'Saint Worship in Indian Islam', *Ritual and Religion Amongst Muslims of the Subcontinent*, Ahmad, Imtiaz, Vanguard Books, Lahore, p.145

[3] ibid.

[4] Bhardwaj, S.M., 1973, *Hindu Places of Pilgrimage in India*, University of California Press, Berkeley.

[5] Lewis, P., 1985, *Pirs, Shrines and Pakistani Islam*, Christian Study Centre, Rawalpindi, p.11.

[6] Ibid., p.12.

[7] Pfleiderer, Beatrix, 1985, 'Mira Datar Dargah: The Psychiatry of a Muslim Shrine', *Ritual and Religion Amongst Muslims in the Subcontinent*, Ahmad, Imtiaz, Vanguard Books, Lahore, p.196

[8] Lewis, op.cit., p.8.

[9] The tomb of Mu'in ud-Din Chishti, the founder of the *Chishti* Sufi order, at Ajmer is prominent among these. It is attended by Hindus as well as Muslims. This is true of several of his descendants including the well-known Shaikh Farid whose poetry is included in the Sikh scripture, the *Guru Granth Sahib*.

[10] Ahmad, Imtiaz, 1985, 'Introduction', *Ritual and Religion among Muslims of the Subcontinent*, Vanguard Books, Lahore, p.17-18

[11] Mujeeb, M., 1967, *The Indian Muslims*, George Allen and Unwin, London, p.147.

[12] Jeffery, Patricia, 1985, 'Creating a Scene: The Disruption of Ceremonial in a Sufi Shrine', *Ritual and Religion Among Muslims in the Subcontinent*, Ahmad, Imtiaz, Vanguard Books, Lahore, p.179

[13] Pfleiderer, Beatrix, op.cit., p.198.

[14] Lewis, op.cit., p.7.

[15] Ibid., pp.70-71.

[16] ibid., p.199.

[17] Fruzzetti, Lina M., 1985, 'Muslim Rituals; Household Rites vs. the Public Festivals in Rural India'; Mines, Mattison, 1985, 'Islamicisation and Muslim Ethnicity in South India', Saiyid, A.R., 'Ideal and Reality in the Observance of Moharram; A Behavioural Interpretation', 1985, can be found in Ahmad, Imtiaz, 1985, *Ritual and Religion among Muslims of the Subcontinent*, Vanguard Books Lahore.

[18] Fruzzetti, Lina, M., op.cit., p. 95.

[19] ibid., p.97.

[20] ibid. p.90.

[21] ibid., p.92-93.

[22] Fruzzetti, Lina, M., 1970, 'The Idea of Community Amongst West Bengal Muslims', ed. Bertocci, P., *Prelude to Crisis: Bengal and Bengal Studies in 1970*, South Asia Series Occasional Paper, No.18, Duke University.

[23] Saiyid, A.R., op.cit.

[24] ibid., p.114.

[25] ibid., pp.124-125.

6 Barelwis in Britain

Introduction

Most of the original migrants from the subcontinent came from a few very defined areas of the region. Large numbers of Pakistanis came from the poorer rural communities of Mirpur district in southern Kashmir and the Campbellpuri districts of north-eastern Punjab. Many of the Bangladeshis originated from Sylhet district. These are all places where Sufism has been traditionally very strong. Although the evidence suggests that religion was not a major factor to the first-generation migrants when they first arrived, it was soon to become so once wives and children began to settle.

This apparent religious revival very strongly featured the reinforcement of ethnic identity and awareness. In order to achieve this, the focus of religious activity and customs centred upon the way of life that was followed in the villages of origin. When mosques were established in Britain's industrial cities, the *imams* were often employed from the area of origin. The *imams* themselves very rarely challenged the kind of Islam practised, being indeed selected to reinforce it. Problems did emerge, however, when the wishes of the often better educated mosque committee diverged from the wishes of the congregation. This could result in the appointment of an *imam* who preached the teachings of the reformers when by contrast the congregation hankered for the folk-Sufism and more syncretistic oral traditions of the faith associated with their home villages. The problem was compounded by the fact that the reform groups such as the *Deobandis, Ahl-Hadith*, and *Tabligh-i Jamaat* were quicker to organise themselves in the context of Britain (see Chapter IX). They were aided by the fact that they were already tight-knit organisations created for the express purpose of reforming Islam in the subcontinent. They were all committed to *dawah* activity amongst Muslims. Definite dilemmas were created when many Muslims from rural backgrounds arrived in the economically and socially advanced industrial cities of Britain; the reformers were quick to use these dilemmas to their own advantage. Despite the activity of the reformers, however, the majority of first-generation subcontinent Muslims in Britain who continued to practise their faith retained their loyalty to the traditions they had received back in their villages.

It is this geographical and social background of the migrants that gives credence to the suggestion made by Maulana Shahid Raza Khan, *imam* at the Leicester Islamic Centre and Executive Secretary of the *Shari'ah Council of Britain*, that most of the Muslims in Britain are *Barelwi*.[1] Shahid Raza Khan's statement is accurate to the degree that the majority of practising Muslims who migrated from the subcontinent are happy with the traditional version of Islam that they brought with them from their places of origin. This, however, does not mean that they consciously identify themselves with being *Barelwi*. Even in mosques that I visited which were associated with the teachings of a particular *pir*, many of the congregation said that they prayed there because it was the nearest mosque to their home. Only in cases where a Muslim was consciously active in a reform movement, or was, equally, the *murid* of a *pir* did I find that they went to a mosque that was further away than the local one. It is this majority of first-generation Muslims and their offspring, people who do not consciously identify themselves as *Barelwi* yet practise the kind of Islam that the *Barelwis* assertively defend, that has become the target of *dawah* activities from the activists amongst both the reform groups and *Barelwi* organisations.

The fact that this kind of Islam is practised by rural people throughout the subcontinent, involving as it does a wide range of local customs established by oral tradition or kept to a particular locale through being focussed around a Sufi shrine, makes it difficult for its adherents to organise themselves on a national basis in Britain. Barton in his study of Bradford states that at the shrines in Sylhet,

> the Muslim is not only made aware of the centuries of tradition that link him to his ancestors, but is able to engage in a form of devotion that is significantly different from the performance of the formal prayer-rite.[2]

He argues that it is unlikely that the shrines can be replicated in Bradford, and indeed that it is not necessary so long as the migrants focus their attention on Sylhet through remittances and journeys home.[3] The very nature of this kind of Islam has meant that its adherents have not usually engaged themselves in a debate concerning unification through using the universal symbols of Islam. There is instead an awareness of belonging to the wider Muslim *ummah*, but in everyday life we find rites and rituals legitimised by custom functioning to strengthen kinship ties and localised identity within the country of origin. Maulana Shahid Raza Khan indicates that this a problem confronted by *Barelwis* trying to organise themselves in Britain:

> That is why sometimes for an outsider, or for a person who is just having a quick view of the community he or she (can) think that they are not a major group; they may be a minor group (based) here or there. The *Barelwis* in this country are (also) divided into several groups. You will find mosques of *Barelwi* Muslims who have come from Bangladesh who are working among their own people. They have no strong links with Muslims from other countries. (But) I think that the Pakistani *Barelwis* have got the dominant hand here in this country in the Muslim community but they are divided on the basis of their regional background. Again they have their own Sufi orders. There are *Qadiris*, *Chishtis*, (and) *Naqshbandis*.[4]

Within the major Sufi *tariqas* the prime loyalty is not to the *tariqa* itself but to the individual *pir*. Although those amongst the *Barelwis* who follow a *pir* acknowledge his *tariqa*, they do not organise themselves around their identity as *Naqshbandis*, *Chishtis*, or *Qadiris*. Each group of *murids* following a particular *pir* creates its own organisation in which membership is restricted to the *murids* and the *pir*. This fragmentation of the community is maintained in many of the *Barelwi* mosques which are not affiliated with a Sufi *tariqa*. The mosque will often serve a community which lives in the streets surrounding it. Through the process of chain migration, very often this community will consist of Muslims who have all come from the same small area of the subcontinent and the *imam* will have been recruited from the district of origin. In this way the mosque provides a sense of security in an alien world by continuing the familiar customs of the original migrants' place of birth. The *imam* may well not speak English but his presence becomes a focal point for legitimising and reinforcing those customs from a particular rural locale in the subcontinent that have been transported to a few terraced streets in a British industrial city. Here the mosque functions more strongly as a means of reinforcing kinship and ethnic ties than as a means of intensifying the sense of belonging to the wider *ummah* whether in Britain or the Islamic world. This kind of mosque will demonstrate the symbols of being *Barelwi* without necessarily identifying with any larger attempt to establish a *Barelwi* consciousness throughout the country.

Maulana Shahid Raza Khan suggests that there are further reasons for the *Barelwis* not being unified. He argues that there are divisions between some of the *Barelwi ulema* and some of the *pirs*. These divisions are based on a number of factors. He suggests that though the *ulema* believe in the *tariqas*, all is not well within those institutions:

> There are so many wrong things that have cut into these institutions, and the existing *pirs* who come here frequently from Pakistan or other parts, certainly their ancestors they (were) real Sufis and *pirs*, but they themselves do not hold those moral and spiritual values up to their standard.[5]

He goes on to suggest that in many cases the *pirs* who visit from the subcontinent have suspect motives. He claims that:

> most of them come here for their material objectives; they come here to raise funds to build a school, or a spiritual centre, and because the people are simple, most of them have come from villages, they have no education, or they are not well-educated, so they respond very warmly.[6]

Furthermore, he says, the *pirs* coming from the subcontinent to Britain have brought with them long-standing differences between themselves. These imported historical differences have yet further fragmented the community to which the pirs come.[7] He also criticises some of the *pirs* for their lack of knowledge of Islam. He states that:

> a number of *pirs* and Sufis who are coming to this country from the subcontinent (they) are not qualified *ulema*. They have no degrees from a *dar al ulum* or a *madrasa* at all. They are just here on the basis of their family heritage, family name. 'Look I am the grandson of that big *pir*.' 'I am the great-grandson of that great, great Sufi.' So they have got that sort of link in their mind and they think that is the greatest qualification that they are holding.[8]

It is difficult to substantiate these criticisms of the motives of visiting *pirs* by prominent members of the *Barelwi ulema*, but two important points emerge that will have repercussions for the development of the community here in Britain. Firstly, there are obviously divisions amongst the leaders of the Barelwi *communities* which will further set back any attempts towards creating a unified *Barelwi* front in Britain. Secondly, whatever the motives may be of some visiting *pirs*, as long as they direct the focus of the community towards projects in the subcontinent, they will undermine the development of a Muslim community centred upon Britain.

The *Barelwi ulema* in Britain are also divided along political lines. These lines reflect historical disputes over authority which originate in Pakistan and India. The founding of the *Jami'at al-Ulema-i Hind* and its equivalent organisation, the *Jami'at al-Ulema-i Islam*, in

Pakistan brought the *Deobandi ulema* into the field of politics. The *Barelwi ulema* were quick to realise that there would be a significant loss of status and power if they did not similarly organise themselves. Subsequently these bodies which represent the *ulema* were established in Britain. The first *Barelwi* organisation established here was the *World Islamic Mission*, which runs several mosques. The *World Islamic Mission* has branches in a number of Western European countries, in the Middle East and in Africa. Although its headquarters is in Britain, the prominent figure is the Chairman, Maulana Murani, who is an important politician in Pakistan. The *World Islamic Mission* is active in publishing books and magazines. A second *Barelwi* organisation, the *Jamaat-i al Sunnat* was created here in Britain echoing divisions between the *ulema* in Pakistan. This organisation is not involved in publishing but it is active in organising annual conferences. These conferences bring together *ulema* and scholars from the subcontinent to discuss various theological and political issues with the *Barelwi ulema* here. Recently there has been a breakaway from the *World Islamic Mission* which has resulted in the founding of a third *Barelwi* organisation, the *International Muslim Organisation*; this was founded by Pir Abdul Wahhab Siddiqi from Coventry who died in 1994. Despite a strong local following in Coventry, Pir Abdul Wahhab Siddiqi did not appear to have much support throughout the country. He was, however, very active in Holland, Canada, the U.S.A., and parts of Central America. The most important development in the context of Britain is that Pir Abdul Wahhab Siddiqi had allied himself with the newly established *Muslim Parliament*.

Despite these various factors which create tensions and further fragmentation amongst the *Barelwis* here in Britain, there are other forces which have pulled them towards a common consciousness and a degree of unity. The *Barelwi ulema's* reassertion of the more popular expressions of the Sufi traditions has resulted in strong criticism from the reform groups, particularly the *Deobandis* and the *Ahl-i Hadith*. As a result of this, a common *Barelwi* identity has developed as a defence mechanism against the attacks of the better organised, often tightly-knit, reform groups. Ahmad Riza Khan (1856-1921) has been the focus for this organisation of *Barelwi* practices and beliefs into a recognisable and coherent group in the subcontinent. His followers have presented themselves as *Ahl-i-Sunnat wa-jamaat* rather than as *Barelwis*. This has allowed them to identify themselves as the true *Sunni* Muslims who follow practices legitimised throughout the Islamic world by popular usage. In this way they can transcend being labelled a regional sect within Islam. Maulana Shahid Raza Khan says on this subject that:

> there is a group of *Barelwi ulema* and *imams* who say 'look there is a great danger that the real name, "the *Sunni*", the word "*Sunni*" will be highjacked by others, and then we will be introduced all over the world as "*Barelwi*", and the word "*Barelwi*" is not known all over the Middle-East at all'. (Because) "*Barelwi*" is not a legal or recognised term in Islamic history. There is a danger they (will) think we are only in Pakistan, India and Bangladesh, (but) what we do is done by Muslims all over the world. So they (the *ulema*) say, the *Barelwis* of the subcontinent (that we) are a part of that Muslim community who are all over the world.[9]

Identifying themselves as the true *Sunni* community has allowed the *Barelwis* to counter the reform groups' central criticism that their Islam is impure and full of innovations and cultural accretions. In response, they reply that the Islam they practise is legitimised by being followed by the wider *Sunni* community throughout the world. They accuse the reform groups of being *Wahhabis*. The *ulema* of the Bareilly *dar al-Ulum* founded by Ahmad Riza Khan have issued *fatwas* which declare that *Wahhabism* is outside the fold of Islam. This counterattack by the *Barelwis* against the reform movements has resulted in several struggles for control of mosques in British cities. Usually these incidents have been between *Barelwis* and *Deobandis*, the traditional antagonists with a history of conflict going back to their roots in the subcontinent. Maulana Shahid Raza Khan, although a prominent *Barelwi alim*, has been active in trying to resolve these conflicts in his role as the Executive Secretary of the *Shari'ah Council*. He suggests that, although these conflicts between the *Barelwis* and the *Deobandis* still happen, they are on the decrease. He is confident that dialogue and negotiations will begin between these traditional enemies in Britain. They will be brought together by crises in the community that demand a unified Muslim response.

> I am sure that the first positive thing to begin in this country among various sects of the Muslim community will be dialogue among these groups. We are experiencing it now and then on common issues. (Like) during the Rushdie affair it happened for a short while. And again at the moment regarding the Babri Mosque issue. I can see that *Ahl-i Hadith* and *Barelwis* and *Deobandis* are attending meetings with each other. Having dialogue and talking to each other sincerely.[10]

He is more concerned that many of the conflicts that he is now called upon to conciliate are between various *Barelwi* groups fighting amongst themselves for control.

> It has happened in so many places. This type of thing has happened in the past in High Wycombe, in some of the mosques in Birmingham, in Bradford, in Manchester. So there is internal rivalry going on between *ulema* or *imams* and *pirs*. Though both are *Barelwis*, both have got (the) same *apida* but it has become a matter of their authority in this country and that is why such things are happening in this country at the moment.[11]

Ahmad Riza Khan definitely established the *Barelwis* as a self-aware tradition within sub-continent Islam. Nielsen suggests that there are three elements which identify this tradition. First is the centrality of the Prophet.[12] This is so strong that the Reform groups have accused the *Barelwis* of *shirk*. Maulana Shahid Raza Khan says that the *Barelwis* have distinctive beliefs concerning the Prophet.

> They believe that the Prophet Muhammad, peace be upon him, has been given by God the knowledge of the Unseen. Similarly the *Barelwis* believe that Prophet Muhammad, peace be upon him, is going to intercede on the Day of Judgement for the *ummah*, for the believers. They also believe that he has been given by God such a power (in) which he can hear whatever we say in our address to him. They believe that he is alive as he was alive in this world and whatever we are saying for him here, he is listening.[13]

According to Nielsen, the second distinctive feature is that religious authority is mediated through the descendants of the Prophet and the descendants of the saints and *pirs*. Finally, this piety towards the Prophet and the saints has resulted in a succession of celebratory popular holidays. The most important of which is the birthday of the Prophet himself but also includes celebrations known as urs, on the deathdays of the saints, which commemorate their reunion with Allah.[14] The holidays celebrating the Sufis and saints are usually held locally at the respective shrine. Maulana Shahid Raza Khan adds to the above several unique customs which also distinguish and unite all the *Barelwi* factions. *Barelwi* mosques are usually decorated with fairy lights and coloured tinsel; above the *minbar* '*Ya Allah*' is written on the right-hand side and '*Ya Rasul Allah*' is written on the left-hand side. When the *Barelwis* gather for congregational prayers they include a number of additional practices such as *Du'a* (prayers of petition and intercession usually addressed to the Prophet); *dhikr* (formula for the constant remembrance of God usually consisting of repetition of Allah's ninety-nine names or the first part of the *kalima* '*la ilaha illa Allah*'); and a *na't* (song) sung in Urdu by the congregation gathered around the *imam*, in which the Prophet is praised and his blessings called for (see Appendix C). At the end of the prayers the congregation will often form a line to greet and kiss the hand of the *imam* or any descendants of *pirs* that may be present.[15] These features have given the *Barelwis* a distinct identity and have helped them towards forming a cohesive group.

In Britain three other factors have worked together to overcome the usually disparate nature of the *Barelwi* tradition. The *Barelwis'* veneration for the Prophet meant that they reacted much more strongly to the publishing of Salman Rushdie's book, *The Satanic Verses*. Nielsen reports that their communities were 'collectively more prepared to register the insult contained in the book'.[16] Maulana Shahid Raza Khan supports this view:

> In the campaign against Rushdie the support of the masses was on the basis of *Barelwi* support. *Barelwis* were the major group who were attending rallies, demonstrations and giving the campaign a boost everywhere. They were in the forefront but unfortunately as the majority of the *imams* amongst the *Barelwis* cannot speak English; they are not organised; (and) they do not know how to approach the press, so the leaders on the forefront were other people, but the real support to this campaign was given by the *Barelwis* in this country.[17]

This experience not only helped to unite the *Barelwi* factions but also provided openings for their leaders to work with the leaders of other *non-Barelwi* groups on issues which affected the Muslim community in Britain as a whole. Undoubtedly the various Muslim factions were impressed by the value of unity on this occasion, but it is still unclear just how this realisation will manifest in the future.

Another factor which is bringing the *Barelwis* together is their shared fears for the future of the younger generation. This fear exists not only in the context of children growing up in a non-Muslim environment, but in the anxiety that these children will be attracted towards the message of the better organised and more vocal reform organisations. When I asked Maulana Shahid Raza whether it was not more important that the younger Muslims in the community became strong in their faith than that they belong to particular factions, he personally agreed but stressed that,

> they (the Muslims) wish to identify themselves in terms of their own group title. They think for their children that it is essential to be a *Barelwi* or a *Deobandi* or a *Tablighi* or something like that. These differences are very, very deep and serious, and those devoted *Barelwis* or *Deobandis* or *Tablighis* (they) think that if my child goes into another group he almost loses his faith. He is not a Muslim.[18]

He insists that the *Barelwis* are particularly afraid because the reform groups, especially *Jamaat-i Islami* and *Tabligh-i Jamaat*, are exceedingly well-organised. He states that,

> These are well-organised organisations having good leadership, and working in a dynamic way in

this country, (and) they might affect their future, and many of our children might fall in the trap of these groups. That is the general feeling of the *Barelwis* at the moment. And they are very keen on doing something in order to neutralise the effect of other well-organised and well-financed groups. A lot of meetings are going on.[19]

A third element has amplified the above factors in terms of pointing the *Barelwis* towards greater cohesion: the arrival in Britain of resident charismatic *pirs* who are forming powerful groups of *Barelwis* amongst Britain's Muslims.

In order to highlight the various changes which are taking place within the *Barelwi* community it has been essential to acknowledge the disparate nature of the *Barelwi* tradition. To render analysis possible three case studies have been chosen to represent the *Barelwi* scene in Britain. All are in the Sparkbrook area of Birmingham. The first is a *Barelwi* mosque with no association with a *pir* or Sufi *tariqa*. The mosque functions as the focus for a Mirpuri community living in the streets which surround it. The other two examples examined are connected with Sufi *tariqas*. One is grouped around the example and charisma of a living *pir* based in Britain; the other is a traditional Sufi structure centred around the descendants of a thirteenth century Sufi whose shrine is in Pakistan.

1. The Barelwi Imam
Noor ul Uloom Mosque, 51 Somerville Road, Birmingham

The mosque is situated on the other side of the Moseley Road from Sparkbrook, at the edge of the Mirpuri-dominated Alum Rock area. It is in a new building on the site of a former house mosque in a quiet street made up of Victorian terraces and larger detached houses of the same period. Inside, the only indications that you are in a *Barelwi* mosque are the many multi-coloured strands of tinsel that crisscross the ceiling, the fairy lights that decorate the relatively simple *minbar*, and 'Ya Allah' and 'Ya Rasul Allah' in Arabic on either side of the *minbar*.

My visits were made during the last ten days of *Ramadan*, and the mosque was always packed for prayers. This was probably considerably more than the usual attendance, but the Friday *juma namaz* was obviously always packed as there had been a history of complaints from the non-Muslim residents of the area concerning lack of parking facilities. The congregation is essentially Mirpuris living in the streets which surround the mosque. There is, however, a small minority which consists of Muslims originating from around Peshawar, Lahore and Bengal. As usual in a *Barelwi* mosque, the customary *na't* in praise of the Prophet is sung by the congregation at the end of the prayers but a considerable proportion of the congregation leave before this event. This and the composition of the mosque congregation suggests that the mosque is filled with Muslims who attend because they live locally rather than for ideological reasons. For those Muslims in the area that are either *Deobandi* or *Jamaat-i Islami* there are mosques nearby that belong specifically to those groups.

Despite the fact that the dominant group is made up of Mirpuris, the *imam* is not from that region and neither does he preach the weekly Friday sermon and the Sunday Qur'an interpretation in their dialect. He speaks to them in a very fine educated Urdu. The *imam* reflects the fact that the mosque committee is composed of some very prominent local businessmen whose allegiance to the *Barelwi* tradition is more consciously ideological than merely a matter of imported customs from a cluster of villages of origin. This is particularly demonstrated in the way that the *imam* was chosen. He comes from Bihar state in India, and was educated first in a *madrasa* in Faisalabad and then, finally, in Bareilly *dar ul Ulum* itself. After completing his education he was invited to teach children in Bareilly, and he remained in this post for two-and-a-half years. At this point an invitation arrived from the mosque in Birmingham. The *imam* explains:

> So I taught there for two-and-a-half years, and then someone wrote a letter from here to Bareilly asking that we need a preacher. And then the manager of the school chose four names and sent their speeches here with a cassette.[20]

After being chosen the *imam* arrived from India. Initially he intended to stay for only three months, but the congregation of the mosque was reluctant to let him leave.

> I gave admission to the manager of the mosque and to the *madrasa* in Bareilly that I wanted leave for three months to preach. A call to preaching. And they were agreed. But here people stopped me (from returning). We couldn't move back there.[21]

The training which the *imam* has received in the centre of *Barelwi* theological thought means that he is very consciously *Barelwi*, but in a way that is markedly different from the type of *imam* who is chosen because he lives in the region from which the mosque congregation originates. Imam Razwi, in common with many in the congregation, arrived in Britain unable to speak any English, but he was also unable to communicate in their dominant language. He has, however, managed to learn a considerable amount of both English and Punjabi since his arrival. He is very conscious that the language used in the mosque should incorporate more English, especially if the younger generation are to be kept interested.

> The younger generation of Muslims understand English well. So the *ulema* must also learn English. This is the necessity of this country. So we try, in some schools, and some mosques, to appoint a teacher or *imam* who will learn English, like in the big mosques, the central mosque. It is very necessary.[22]

His attempts to achieve this, however, have been limited in scope and marked with little success. As in other mosques, the *imam* runs traditional classes for the children every evening from 5pm to 7pm. Between eight to ten assistants help him in this teaching. Each teacher has a class of about twenty children. Although there are a large number of children attending these classes, the lessons are only in memorising the Qur'an and learning Urdu. The *imam* is proud that the lessons have succeeded in creating ten *hafiz*, but his attempts to incorporate English into the syllabus so far have been limited only to facilitating the students' ability to learn Urdu.

> When I teach Urdu, I explain the difficult, the new words in English. Yes. And then they write the word easily. And if I explain the new word in Urdu they feel many difficulties. The children feel more difficulties. If I say it in English they understand quickly. And sometimes I say some sentences in English, and they become active and they have more interest.[23]

Attempts by the Mosque committee to find someone who could teach the children Arabic, Urdu, and English through the medium of English have failed. Although there has been little actual success in this direction, it is notable that the *imam* and the committee are both aware of the need to correct this situation.

The *imam* is also keen that the *Barelwi* tradition should not be linked to specific practices or beliefs which pertain only to the subcontinent. He suggests that the word '*Barelwi*' was invented by the *Deobandis* in order to create the perception that the *Barelwis* were a sect in Islam. The *imam*, however, believes that the *Barelwi* tradition follows the beliefs of the majority of *Sunni* Muslims since the time of the Prophet.[24] As a consequence of this belief, he attempts to legitimise the *Barelwi* tradition by removing it away from the locale of the subcontinent out to the wider Islamic world. In common with many other active *Barelwis* interviewed he recounts the same hagiographical event from the life of Ahmad Riza Khan in order to achieve this.

> Some *Deobandi ulema* wrote in their books wrong things. And then one person called Maulana Ahmad Riza Khan took action against them and wrote a book which said that this was a lie, is wrong against Islam, and he wrote like a judge. He went direct to the Arabs on the occasion of the Pilgrimage. And he showed the thing (his book) to the Arab *ulema*, and the Arab *ulema* agreed with him, and said 'indeed these things are wrong'. And they wrote and supported him. They supported Maulana Raza Khan and said that the persons who had written these things were wrong according to the Qur'anic verses and Islamic traditions.[25]

In order that the *Barelwis* in Britain should not be considered a sect of subcontinent Islam, the *imam* believes that not only should the *ulema* be trained in this country but that they should also be sent outside to the Muslim world to complete their training. He is very pleased that a *Barelwi* mosque in Milton Keynes is sending children to complete their education in al-Azhar, Cairo.

Although it is difficult to ascertain all the beliefs held by the Mosque congregation, it is clear that the *imam* and the mosque committee are holding to a theologically conservative version of the *Barelwi* tradition as followed by the qualified *ulema* from Bareilly and associated *dar al Ulums*. There is no *dhikr* in the mosque, and the only *urs* celebrated are the birthday of the Prophet and the night of *Miraj*. There have been attempts to introduce *Naqshbandi dhikr* into the mosque by one of the congregation who is a son of a *pir* in Pakistan, but the *imam* has refused permission. He has, however, allowed him and his sympathisers to eat and to read from the Qur'an in the mosque on certain festive occasions. The *imam* does not believe that real *pirs* inherit their position, but rather that they earn the title through their spiritual practice. He asserts that the great Sufis of the past combined spiritual experience with study of the Qur'an and the *Hadith*.

> Pir is not an inheritance. It depends on knowledge and especially knowledge of God. If there is a good or a real *pir* I will respect him because in Islam there were a lot of *pirs* who were educated and were good leaders but nowadays, I think, as I know here, a lot of *pirs* are uneducated. They cannot explain to people the Qur'an and *Hadith*, and if any person asks them to please explain anything, they will say, 'go to a *maulvi* to understand. I am a *pir*'. In the past history of Islam all *pirs*, *faqirs* and Sufis were well-educated. These *pirs* are only (*pirs*) in appearance.[26]

There are no social welfare activities taking place from the mosque, but the *imam* feels that it is a good thing when a mosque is able to organise this kind of activity. He blames the lack of these activities on the size of the mosque and its lack of facilities. He praises Sufi Abdullah for organising social welfare activities at his centre in Birmingham and has attended meetings there. These are meetings to which all the *ulema* and prominent Muslims in Birmingham are invited regardless of sectarian affiliation. Imam Razwi admits, however, that generally only the *Barelwi ulema* attend. The *imam* expressed sentiments of unity to me, an expression of his feelings that the divisions between Muslims of the subcontinent should not be continued here in Britain. He attempted to confirm this belief in unity by citing the mosque's membership of the *Sunni Configuration of Mosques Midlands*. This is an umbrella organisation founded in 1984 to which fifty-two mosques belong. All of the mosques, however, are *Barelwi*, and so far their activities have been limited to such activities as fixing the timetables of prayers and establishing the beginning and end of *Ramadan*. Birmingham council has now made the *Eid* at the end of *Ramadan* an official public holiday for Muslim employees. Through the efforts of the *Sunni Configuration of Mosques*, the majority of Muslims celebrated *Eid* on the same day in Birmingham in 1993. This was the first time such a majority agreement had been reached. The *imam* felt that this was a great step forward in achieving a common identity for the Muslim community in Britain. He emphasised, however, that each mosque still maintained its independence.

It is apparent that this mosque is not the typical small house mosque serving a group of Muslims united by their place of origin in the subcontinent which employs an *imam* from the same area, even though it does provide facilities for a predominantly Mirpuri population living nearby. The Mosque committee and its choice of *imam* has ensured that the traditions of the mosque belong to the more self-conscious *Barelwi* school as linked with Ahmad Raza Khan and the Bareilly *dar al Ulum* rather than with the religion of local customs or folk-Sufism as originating in specific areas of the subcontinent.

2. The Living Pir
Dar ul Uloom Islamia, Golden Hillock Road, Birmingham

The *Dar ul Uloom Islamia* buildings occupy two blocks on either side of a stretch of the Golden Hillock Road between two roundabouts. On one side of the road a very large mosque is under construction; it will dominate the area's skyline. The mosque will offer facilities for several thousand Muslims to congregate and pray, and there is also a large car park and buildings which will be used as a supplementary *maktab* for the children.

On the other side of the road, various buildings are contained within a courtyard which is entered through arched gates constructed in traditional Islamic style. The buildings which front the street are all obviously a part of the complex as their windows are designed to match the arch of the entrance. Fairy lights cover the arches. Inside the complex there is a mosque decorated with gold tinsel. The *minbar* is particularly ornate; it is a painted wooden structure which is itself a small mosque complete with two minarets. This model of a mosque is illuminated with coloured fairy lights. There is also a large meeting hall which is used as a *langar* and a place of prayer for women; a small *dar al Ulum* in which a few older male students come from other parts of Britain to study; an Islamic bookshop and printing press; and two Asian job clubs, one for males and the other for females. Once the buildings are completed in the new mosque complex, there are plans to extend the school facilities so that they become a large *dar al Ulum* and hostel. The overall intention is to create an Islamic village or, to be more specific, a model Sufi community in the centre of Birmingham; this is envisaged as taking place over the next five to ten years. The energy and the vision manifesting in this once run-down part of inner city Birmingham is the product of the inspiration of one man, Sufi Abdullah Khan.

Like the *imam* of the *Noor ul Uloom* mosque many of Sufi Abdullah's *murids* argued that the term '*Barelwi*', although acknowledged, created a false picture of their lineage. They did not wish to be confined to a sectarian conflict that was limited to the subcontinent, but wanted rather to be identified with a much larger tradition as found throughout the Islamic world.[27] Ahmed Riza Khan's work is acknowledged and highly respected for challenging the claimed false ideas of *Deoband*, *Ahl-i Hadith*, and the *Shi'as*. He is perceived as a *mujaddid*, a purifier of Islam, and a Sufi saint of the *Qadiriyya* order. Here at the *Dar ul Uloom Islamia* too, they told in great detail and with many embellishments the story of Ahmed Riza Khan's defence of his beliefs in Mecca before the Arabian *ulema*. The *Deobandis* were accused of creating a major schism in Sufism by adopting and spreading the ideas of Muhammad Ibn 'Abd Wahhab.

At this centre, however, as opposed to the *Noor ul Uloom* mosque, the stress is on Sufism and the role of the great Sufi teachers in Islam.

> The great Sufi *shaikhs* have done great work in accordance with the way of the Prophet to put people on to the right knowledge, the right guidance, and they propagated Islam from that point, and they fought against whatever was not Islamic. And a Sufi's rank can go as far as where prophethood begins, but it does not supersede or become the rank of a prophet.[28]

The major focus of respect is the person of Sufi Abdullah himself and his *pir*, Hazrat Shah, who is usually referred to as Zindapir; Zindapir means 'the living *pir*'. The followers of these exemplary or charismatic living Sufis are to some degree critical of the *sajjada nashin*, those descendants of famous Sufis who usually function today as guardians of the shrines based around their illustrious ancestor's tomb. The followers of the charismatic living Sufis described above still acknowledge and respect the *sajjada nashin*, but see the latter's charisma as merely derivatory. They are not regarded as 'real' saints as the original Sufi was, or, indeed, as Zindapir and Sufi Abdullah are today. As the Chairman of *Dar ul Uloom Islamia* explained:

> Our religion is not coming from inheritance. A *pir* is a *pir*, we respect them because their fathers did a good thing, but in the meantime he or she has to earn that thing. Sufi Abdullah is not the son of a *pir*; he is not the relative of *Pir Sahib* but at the moment we are witness that he is near to *Pir Sahib*. He has got a very, very, very big place in front of our Zindapir. He has earned this seat.[29]

The history of the *Tariqa*

The *Naqshbandi silsilah* of the followers of Zindapir and Sufi Abdullah begins with Abu Bakr. Several famous subcontinent Sufis are contained within this spiritual genealogy, amongst them Bayazid and Naqshband (see Appendix D). The teacher of Zindapir was Muhammad Qasim Mori, a Kashmiri; his shrine named Mohara Sharif is in the Muree hills, to the north of Islamabad. He had established his *khanqah* there in the late 19th century. Muhammad Qasim died in 1947. Zindapir, a *sayyid*, although from a family of *Qadiriyya* Sufis himself, had travelled from his home in Kohat on the North-West Frontier in search of a teacher. The story of this meeting, told in the words of Abid Hussein, demonstrates the hagiographical accounts of Sufis' lives that are constantly being recounted by their followers.

> When he went there at that time Baba Ji (Muhammad Qasim) had finished with the world, he had gone into total devotion and seclusion. He had passed permission to his son to see to the murids, the people, the *khalifas*. And he went into seclusion to see no-one, to initiate no-one, to meet no-one. When a Sufi master reaches a certain rank, and that rank is very high, when that stage takes place then he begins to lose his shadow. When you develop the great *Noor*, the great light of Allah, and you are totally merged into the Prophet, into Allah, and then your physical form is there but it doesn't have a shadow. It has developed as pure light. So that was the position with Baba Ji. When Zindapir arrived his intention was to meet Baba Ji but everyone was going towards his son, Shaikh Nazir Ahmed. Whoever wanted initiation to join the *tariqa*, they were asked to go to Nazir Ahmed. But Zindapir heard a voice. I heard this direct from Zindapir. He said that he heard a voice in his ear which said 'your initiation is with Baba Ji'. Three times the voice said the same thing to him. So he requested one of the grandsons of Baba Ji, who was the doorman, who took food in, washed Baba Ji's hair, did everything, looked after him, and that grandson's son is here with us. So Zindapir spoke to him, and all he did was to go into Baba Ji and stand before him. He didn't say a word. And Baba Ji said, 'Go and call him in'. Baba Ji was expecting him. So when Zindapir went in they spent a long time together. What they exchanged together, what took place, only those two people know, only Allah knows. So he was given initiation and he was given the *juba* from Baba Ji and then Baba Ji walked out with him and told all the people 'this is my khalifa'.[30]

It is of interest to note here that the congregation of the *Harounia* Mosque in Alum Rock, Birmingham are followers of the *pir*, Haroun Rashid, the son of Nazir Ahmed; Haroun Rashid visits this country periodically from Pakistan. This group considers itself to be in a direct line of descent from Muhammad Qasim. Although the group respects the efforts of Sufi Abdullah in Birmingham, it only acknowledges Zindapir as one of the *khalifas* of Muhammad Qasim.

After initiation, Zindapir joined the army, married and had four children. In the army he worked as a tailor, but also he began to teach, to organise *dhikrs* and to initiate followers. It was here in 1948 that he was met by Sufi Abdullah, an instructor in the Signals section. In 1951, Zindapir left for the mountains around Kohat and went into retreat within a cave. He claims that this was under the direction of the Prophet who appeared to him in a vision. He has remained there ever since. Abid Hussein describes this with great piety and respect:

> He is just called Zindapir which is a title but his own name he has forgotten because he has totally annihilated himself, finished himself and this is the spiritual name which means the living *pir*. The place where he lives is called Gamkol Sharif in Kohat. It is about six kilometres from Kohat City in the mountains. I have only been there once. It is situated in such a place that before the *shaikh* sat there in 1951 there was no life there. Huge mountains. All around mountains. And caves there. And in 1951 he sat there in a cave in that mountain. There wasn't any vegetation, or any green, or any tree, or any water, or any animal.[31]

From 1951 to 1971 he did not leave the area at all, but since 1971 he has made the *Hajj* annually in the company of many of his followers from all over the world. Since 1951 the efforts of Zindapir's followers have transformed Ghamkol Sharif. Pnina Werbner visited the centre in 1989 and describes the *khanqah*:

> It is a lovely, prosperous, tranquil scene. The orchards bear apples, oranges, lemons. Tomatoes, cucumbers, cabbages, and chillies grow in well tended vegetable beds. A fifty strong cattle and buffalo herd grazes in the valley. Chicken and geese honk in the coop. A herd of goats bleat in the hills. Wild honey bees have made a hive in one of the trees of the orchard groves. The courtyards of the houses and hospices are surrounded by green lawns and bordered with flower beds and shady trees. The beautiful mosque, elaborately decorated in white, green and dark red, its three domes and delicate minarets set against the blue sky and the hills beyond, is a scene of perfection... All is quiet apart from the sound of *dhikr* echoing in the mountains and the splashing of water fountains. Ghamkol Sharif is, perhaps, as close to paradise as a Muslim can get on this earth.[32]

Sufi Abdullah had accompanied Zindapir to Ghamkol Sharif and remained there with him until 1962. In that year his *shaikh* made him a *khalifa* and sent him to Britain. Pnina Werbner records that Zindapir told her that he had sent Sufi Abdullah to Britain because the Pakistani migrants had forgotten Islam. They no longer prayed, celebrated *Eid*, maintained *Ramadan*, or performed *dhikr*. He felt that they needed a guide to direct them back to the path of Allah.[33] Sufi Abdullah's followers in Birmingham compare his journey to the West with Zindapir's retreat to Kohat. Both have raised the flag of Islam in a desolate, God-deserted wilderness. This is the mark of the true Sufi. Pnina Werbner states that it is the hardship of the saint's journey, whether to the land of infidels or to the wilderness, which constitutes the ordeal that makes him who he is.[34] The Sufi saint literally sanctifies the godless ground where he takes up residence. In Sufi Abdullah's case, the ordeal was to include twenty-four years of manual work in the iron foundries of the Midlands. At the same time, he was beginning his spiritual work. Initially, he taught Qur'an classes to a handful of children and only two people joined him for *dhikr*. Slowly his work progressed and then gathered pace. He purchased a house in Warwick Road and converted it into a mosque. Originally he knocked out the downstairs walls but as more and more people joined him in prayer and *dhikr* he enclosed the complete back garden to form an extension. In 1983 Sufi Abdullah expanded his work by instructing his followers to purchase the present site in Golden Hillock Road. He continues to live with his family in the Warwick Road Mosque, however.

Personal Impressions of Sufi Abdullah

Sufi Abdullah spends most of his time living in extreme simplicity in a small room downstairs. I was told that often he spends many days there fasting and in retreat. This room has become the equivalent of Zindapir's cave. The *shaikh* keeps to the rules of fasting, required of all Muslims during *Ramadan*, all the year round. The same room is also used to meet people. A *darban* (doorkeeper) controls the visitors and ensures that Sufi Abdullah is not disturbed unnecessarily. Women visitors are taken upstairs to the family quarters, and from time to time he goes up to see them. During the time that I spent sitting with Sufi Abdullah he dealt with many problems; these ranged from advice on illnesses and family matters to simply giving his blessing.

He had just returned from keeping *itikaf* in the Prophet's mosque in Medina and hundreds of followers wished to see him and to receive the enhanced blessings that such an action could provide. Sufi Abdullah had brought water from the spring in Medina, and this was given to all the visitors to drink along with raisins and nuts from the same area.

There is no doubt about Sufi Abdullah's charisma. My first meeting with him was at Heathrow Airport on his return from Medina. I travelled with a coachload of *murids* from Birmingham who were going to meet him there and bring him back to the city. The excitement was immense. Many of them told me of the blessings I would receive in seeing the *shaikh* when he was himself in such a state of holiness. On the journey the followers continuously performed *dhikr*, chanting '*la illa'llah illallahu*' melodiously. Many of them told me stories of miraculous events either in their own lives or in the lives of Sufi Abdullah and Zindapir. These events usually involved some kind of synchronisity. At Heathrow many other followers from different parts of Britain had gathered to meet Sufi Abdullah. Altogether there were about four hundred people, many of them carrying welcoming garlands. Just prior to the *shaikh's* arrival everyone formed a double line and began to perform *dhikr*. I was not prepared for Sufi Abdullah's physical appearance. He is a giant of a man, probably close to seven feet tall in his turban. He was dressed that day in white robes with the *juba* given to him by Zindapir thrown over the top. His grey beard is long and full, and his eyes are still, fixed and penetrating. Sufi Abdullah passed down the double line of joyful followers, and they all garlanded him. At the end of the line the *murids* encircled him, continuously performing *dhikr*, while he removed the garlands and placed them over their heads. After this, before beginning our journey back to Birmingham, Sufi Abdullah led the evening prayers in Terminal 4 of Heathrow Airport. Carpets were produced from the bags of various followers and the Airport became a *masjid* for a short while. The prayers also marked the end of the *Ramadan* fast for the day, so on the coach back everybody celebrated with a meal eaten with their *shaikh*. Before arriving in Birmingham, the coach stopped in the carpark of a motorway service station to allow everyone to perform the final prayer of the day. Observing the followers of Sufi Abdullah with their *shaikh* demonstrated that they are clearly inspired by the example of his piety and devotion. Muhammad Saleem Akhtar expresses this exemplary role of Sufi Abdullah and his shaikh Zindapir in the following words:

> Our shaikh is doing it. And those followers who have seen it, can see in him the shape of the Prophet. They can see in him the teachings of the Prophet. They can see in him the deeds and the character of the Prophet. And they love it.[35]

Although I was to meet Sufi Abdullah several times, he usually directed me to one of his followers to answer my questions. He was concerned only with my spiritual state, not my academic research and constantly reminded me to prepare myself for the Day of Judgement.

The Special Features of Worship (*Adab*) in the *Dar ul Uloom Islamia*

The *Naqshbandi* order of Sufis can be found throughout most of the Muslim world, but it is not a unitary organisation. There will be variations unique to each individual group within the order, all of which are recognised as a means towards final unification with the Prophet and God. Very often these variations will be based upon the lifestyle, dress, habits and spiritual practices of the *shaikh* that founded the group. His followers will base their own spiritual disciplines on attempting to emulate him. This is known as *adab*. The followers of Zindapir form a distinct regional cult within the *Naqshbandi* order as centred upon the *Pir* and Ghamkol Sharif. Sufi Abdullah has extended the borders into Britain. All Sufis taught that the heart can be purified through *dhikr* but the form of the *dhikr* will change from group to group. The followers of Zindapir practice both the silent *dhikr* of the *Naqshbandis* and the spoken *dhikr* of the *Qadiriyya* Sufis. This is because Muhammad Qasim's father was a *shaikh* of the *Qadiriyya* but he received *bai'at* from the *Naqshbandi*, shaikh Nisamuddin. In the silent *dhikr* the practitioner internally remembers the sound 'Allah' as he inhales, and the sound 'hu' as he exhales. The loud or spoken *dhikr* consists of a series of short phrases from the Qur'an constantly chanted over and over. These phrases are usually connected with the ninety-nine names of God. Amongst these are the phrases *'Allahu 's samad'*; *'la ilaha illa 'llah'*; *'la ilaha 'llahu ill 'llah'*; and *'Allah hu'*. The male followers of Sufi Abdullah, including some young boys, gather in the mosque late each Saturday night to perform communal *dhikr* around their *shaikh*. The *dhikr* goes on for about two hours. Each one of the above chants is repeated; they begin slowly and pick up speed until the sounds seem to run into each other. The *dhikr* always finishes on the silent repetition of Allah's name in the breath. This is an intense, powerful religious experience.

Although gathered around the *shaikh* in a circle, the practitioners cannot see each other. The mosque is kept in darkness so that whatever experiences of ecstasy they may have, no-one else can see what must be kept private between the worshipper and Allah. In the dark I could only perceive silhouettes rocking back and forth rhythmically to the ever-increasing speed of the beat of the *dhikr*. After completion of the *dhikr* Sufi Abdullah asks the young men and children to recite passages from the Qur'an. During this recital bottles of water were brought in to be blessed by the sanctity of the *dhikr*. First Sufi Abdullah blew into the top of the bottle, and then it was passed around for each participant to do likewise. I was told that this water was distributed to the sick in the community. After this, the participants eat and drink tea together. The *dhikr* ends with the followers of Sufi Abdullah lining up to embrace the *shaikh* and then to kiss his hand. Individual disciples practice *dhikr* in their own time whenever they can. The aim is that the name of Allah should be remembered constantly and automatically in all their activities.

Sufi Abdullah and his followers celebrate two major occasions in addition to the universal festivals of Islam. The first is the *Milad e Nabi*, or the celebration of the Prophet's birthday in August. This is celebrated, of course, in common with all the *Barelwis*. The other, an *urs*, held since 1962 with the permission of Zindapir, is the *urs* of Baba Muhammad Qasim. This is held after the *Hajj* in July. Sufi Abdullah has made both these celebrations unique events in Birmingham by having a procession, or *julus*, pass through the city from Small Heath Park opposite the *Dar ul Uloom Islamia* to the Central Mosque. The followers of Sufi Abdullah come from centres in Manchester, Derby, Slough, Burton, Watford, High Wycombe, and Maidenhead to join with thousands of *Barelwis* in Birmingham who either watch or join the procession. Sufi Abdullah leads the procession himself, followed by a group of seven or eight *khalifas*. Each *khalifa* wears a black *juba* over new white cotton robes. Behind come the followers wearing white *shalwar kamis* and green caps; they carry banners inscribed with the *kalima*. A group of highly decorated cars leads the way, one of these is fitted with a loudspeaker to lead the procession in *dhikr*. The celebration ends late at night in the mosque when Sufi Abdullah recites the final *du'a*. It is believed that at this last *du'a* all the living souls of past Sufis attend along with the congregation.

Sufi Abdullah visits Mecca and Medina twice a year. Since 1971 he has attended the *Hajj* with Zindapir. In 1980 he obtained permission to do *'Umra*, the lesser pilgrimage which may be performed at any time of the year, during the last ten days of *Ramadan*. He keeps *itikaf* in the Prophet's mosque in Medina. The *Hajj* provides an opportunity for any of Zindapir's followers to spend time with him. Both men are accompanied by as many of their followers as can attend; between one hundred and four hundred *murids* usually attend the *Hajj* with their *pir*.

The *langar* is an important institution to Zindapir, and he insists that everyone who comes to visit him in Ghamkol Sharif is fed before their audience with him. In Mecca, Zindapir provides free food to all needy pilgrims. It is the duty of Sufi Abdullah to organise the *langar* on the *Hajj*. There is a *langar* in the centre in Birmingham too, and Sufi Abdullah follows in his *shaikh's* footsteps by organising a *langar* during the two *urs*. The food is distributed freely at the end of the procession. The food is *tobarrak*, blessed, and the cooks perform *dhikr* as they prepare it.

The spiritual world of the followers of Sufi Abdullah in Britain is a contained universe of specific communities linked together in veneration of one man and his religious life. The centre of this universe is the space sacralised by Zindapir's presence in Ghamkol Sharif. Sufi Abdullah's piety and commitment to the work of his *shaikh* has made the *Dar ul Uloom Islamia* an important centre in its own right. By following Sufi Abdullah, the *murids* are linked to Zindapir in Ghamkol Sharif.

> It is true that the *pir* is in Pakistan but his representative is with us here. So that fills the gap. When people wish to see the *pir* there is *Hajj*, and also in Pakistan they visit him. They get the full flower of the knowledge from Sufi Abdullah.[36]

It should be noted that the *murids* in Britain are comprised of those who received *bai'at* from Zindapir in Pakistan, and the majority who have received it from Sufi Abdullah in Birmingham. The relationship of these two groups of *murids* towards Sufi Abdullah is different. Both groups respect him and follow his leadership but those who received *bai'at* from Zindapir regard Sufi Abdullah as a fellow disciple or *pirbhai*, albeit a very respected one as he is a *khalifa* with the right to appoint *khalifas* of his own. The majority regard Sufi Abdullah as their *pir* but retain immense respect for Zindapir as the *pir* of Sufi Abdullah.

Other Features of the *Dar ul Uloom Islamia*

Obviously this is a community of Muslims which focuses its attention upon the charismatic figure of Sufi Abdullah. The *shaikh* leads the *dhikr*, and at the *juma namaz* on Friday he says the *du'a* supplicatory prayers on behalf of the congregation and the wider Muslim community. A living saint is a *wali*, a friend of God and his ability to intercede on behalf of the worshipper is firmly believed in. This central role of the *shaikh* is indicated by the number of supplicants who come to him with various problems and ailments. The *shaikh's* role is not theological or scholarly. Questions concerning *tafsir*, *fiqh*, or the *Shari'ah* are resolved by the *imam*; the latter appointed by the *shaikh* from amongst the *ulema* who follow Zindapir.

The mosque congregation does not consist solely of Sufi Abdullah's followers. This mosque is not situated in the Alum Rock Mirpuri community. Around Small Heath there are Punjabi communities and Campbellpuris from the North-West Frontier, and Sufi Abdullah is himself a Pathan. Several of Sufi Abdullah's followers are from these communities, and the mosque provides a place of worship where the other members of these ethnic communities can gather together. Although not members of the *tariqa*, they are, nonetheless, pleased at the external signs of success in this centre as it enhances the status of their community, and of Islam in Birmingham. As in the other *Barelwi* mosques which I visited, a large percentage of the congregation left the Friday prayers before the final *du'as* and *naths*. Some young Muslims I met, members of various reform groups, told me that they once prayed in the *Dar ul Uloom Islamia* but that they now refused to go there. They were scathing of the *Barelwi*/Sufi practices and compared them to witchcraft.

The charisma of Sufi Abdullah and the piety of his followers has attracted converts to Islam; there are several young white and West Indian males who attend the mosque. Their knowledge of Islam is very basic, and in my discussions with them, I found that many did not seem to be aware that they were involved with a Sufi group. They did not realise the distinctiveness of the various different elements within Islam, and in the case of the white converts, they did not seem to realise that the Islam they had adopted had many practices which belonged to the subcontinent. Most of them were dressed in *shalwar kamis* and had adopted beard styles that were copied from the *tariqa's* elders. When I challenged them on the question of why they had taken on a style of appearance which belonged to a subcontinent ethnic minority rather than to Islam, they were surprised. In the main they had never thought about such issues. The converts, on the whole, were far less analytical of this kind of issue than were the young British Asians of such reform groups as *Young Muslims UK*; to these Muslims such questions are crucial.

The people I interviewed were aware that it was important to ensure that the practice of Islam remained strong in the younger, British-born generation. They did not, however, critically analyse what was required to achieve this beyond ensuring the continued practice of those time-honoured customs which for generations had been used in the education of subcontinental Muslims. Muhammad Saleem Akhtar believed that the problem of the young could be resolved by training new members of the *ulema* who were well-educated and skilled in the medium of English. He accepted that the original migrants were generally uneducated and made no attempt to integrate themselves into the receiving culture.

> As a result the first generation managed, it was needed, to bring with them a piece of their original country. They came with the culture of their town. They were not equipped with English. With the passage of time we have realised that this is a gap that we have to fill up.[37]

The solution, however, has been to send ten boys to a *dar al Ulum* in Lahore where the Islamic education is completed through the medium of English. Muhammad Saleem Akhtar also acknowledges that the general feeling in the institution has been to emphasise reading the Qur'an in Arabic because that bestows more blessings on the reader. He agrees that it does not answer the requirements of the present generation of young Muslims.

> Today's need is not that. Today's need is to understand it. And to understand it the teachers must speak your language. If I speak in my own language I cannot make any communication. That is missing. We are not getting the results as we ought to be having.[38]

I saw very little attempt to use the medium of English in the mosque or the supplementary school at Warwick Road. The latter was very traditional in its methods of education. The children sat on the floor in lines and were taught by rote to recite the Qur'an; when they failed the teacher verbally bullied them and sometimes beat them.

A much more progressive attempt to work with young people is the provision of space on the premises for an Asian Job Club. Abid Hussein suggests that this was the brainchild of Sufi Abdullah:

> He says that Islam and Sufism, and being a good Muslim is your personal thing, but you have other needs, recreational and social, and educational needs which Islam emphasises. Encourages. So he is very much in favour of that.[39]

There are two Job Clubs, one for women and the other for men. They are staffed both by followers of Sufi Abdullah and by professional career advisors. They not only help to find jobs but also provide training and educational programmes for young Asians in the city, regardless of their faith.

The followers of Sufi Abdullah do express the need for greater unity amongst the Muslims in Britain. In order to further this unity of the *ummah* they have been instrumental in forming the *Configuration of Sunni Mosques Midlands*. This organisation was created to link together all the *Barelwi* mosques and institutions. Muhammad Saleem Akhtar, a *murid* of Zindapir and the Chairman of *Dar ul Uloom Islamia*, is a founder member of the Configuration. He is the chairman of the Configuration's executive committee, which consists of each individual mosque's chairman and secretary. Obviously this organisation provides a strong show of unity when dealing with local officials. Muhammad Saleem Akhtar admits that it was not easy to get all the mosques to work with each other:

> When people got together and they came to know the written constitution and that they were not going to lose their own religious identity then I think it became popular because our intention was for there to be a unity among the Muslims.[40]

So far the Configuration has been successful in achieving agreement on the times of prayers and the dates of the beginning and ending of *Ramadan*, but it has not attempted to resolve the ideological and religious differences that divide the community. The members of the Configuration are very proud that these times and dates are now agreed upon by most mosques in the Midlands, and feel that unifying these externals of the faith is the way forward to unify the community. This search for unity extends outside the *Barelwi* groups but only in very limited forms. The *Dar ul Uloom Islamia* holds meetings which are attended by many prominent members from all the Muslim denominations. These meetings can be on specific topics, for example a lecture on Malcolm X held while I was there, or on the occasion of a Muslim holiday celebrated by all the community. There is a deliberate policy at these meetings not to discuss issues which divide the members of the various groups that attend. At one such meeting that I attended during *Ramadan*, the guest speaker was Dr. Surti of the Muslim-Christian Relations Institute at Selly Oak. The theme of the lecture was *Ramadan in the Qur'an*. The unusual feature was that the lecturer admitted that he was a member of *Ahl-i Hadith*, and identified himself with the *Salafis*, an extreme reform group from Saudi Arabia. These special occasions hosted by the *Dar ul Uloom Islamia* should not be regarded as being necessarily an indication of closer links or co-operation between traditional rivals. In Birmingham, the leaders of the Muslim community have always demonstrated considerable unity on key issues concerning all Muslims without giving up internecine conflicts.[41] As a consequence of working together on such issues as education, the Rushdie affair, and the provision of *halal* food, the Muslim community leaders know each other well. It is a sign of the prestige of Sufi Abdullah that his institution can organise and host these social events.

3. Sajjada Nashin
Sultan Bahu Trust, 17 Ombersley Road, Birmingham

The *Sultan Bahu Trust* mosque is to be found in a maze of Victorian terraced streets in what was once obviously an industrial area full of factories. Just before the railway bridge over Ombersley Road there are two large double gates that lead into a cobbled courtyard. On the left-hand side there is an old Victorian factory about four to five stories high. On the right-hand side there are buildings which were once the offices of the factory management. There is nothing about these buildings which would suggest to a casual passer-by that here is one of the biggest *Barelwi* centres in Birmingham. A more observant person might notice the sign on the gates in Urdu and English; this indicates that what we have here is not an old Victorian industrial site but a centre of Islamic worship.

Directly in front of the viewer, at the end of the courtyard, stands the recently constructed building which is the new mosque. Until recently the factory had been used for prayers, and one of the floors is still maintained for that purpose. Thousands could gather here in these huge Victorian galleries. At the present time this area is used by the women for Friday prayers and for the supplementary classes for boys and girls. The offices opposite contain the rooms used by the mosque administration; these are also used as a hostel for the *dar al Ulum* which the *Sultan Bahu Trust* is trying to establish. In August 1994 there were thirty-five students.

The mosque is a large hall which could accommodate several hundred Muslims at prayer. I first visited it during the last ten days of *Ramadan*, and observed an area of the mosque had been closed off with white sheets to form a separate compound. This area was being used by several old men who were maintaining *itikaf*. The mosque is relatively simple by *Barelwi* standards; it is not decorated with tinsel, and the *minbar* is a very basic structure. There is, however, the usual 'Ya Allah' and 'Ya Rasul Allah' on the wall on either side of the *minbar*. The same *na't* is sung at the end of *namaz* as is sung by *Barelwis* everywhere in Britain and the subcontinent. As in the other mosques that I visited, a large proportion of the congregation left the mosque immediately after completing their prayers and before the *na't* began. This mosque, like the others

I studied, is used by the community which lives around it regardless of whether they are followers of Sultan Bahu or even consciously *Barelwi*. The mosque serves both the local community as a place of prayer and the committed followers of Sultan Bahu's *tariqa* as their centre of activity in Birmingham.

Despite the relative lack of decoration, this is not only a *Barelwi* mosque but also a centre of *Naqshbandi* Sufism committed to the teachings of Hazrat Sultan ul Ahrafeen Sultan Bahu. The latter was an seventeenth century mystic, and his shrine, Durbar Sultan Bahu, is in Jhung near Multan in Pakistan. The *tariqa* and the shrine of Sultan Bahu have been maintained by his descendants to this day.

Biography of Sultan Bahu

Although well-known in Pakistan, there is a Sultan Bahu Chair in the Punjab University,[42] very little material is available on the saint's life and teachings in English at the present time. Hazrat Sultan Bahu's family were wealthy landowners of the Awan clan who ruled in the South Punjab. It is said that originally the Awan clan migrated to Pakistan from Medina.[43] His father, Sultan Muhammad Bazid was one of the leaders of the Awan and his mother, Rasti was also known as a Sufi. According to the hagiography of Sultan Bahu, it was his mother who was responsible for the saint moving to Shorkot in the Jhung District where he settled and established his *khanqah*.

Although Hazrat Sultan Bahu travelled extensively in search of a *pir*, he claims that his attempts to find one who could satisfy him were unsuccessful. In his most famous book, *Risala Rouhi*, he writes that he received *bai'at* directly from the hands of the Prophet. He claims that he received no formal education and that he was directly educated by the Prophet himself. These accounts of Hazrat Sultan Bahu's spiritual experiences also state that Abdul Qadir Gilani was present in the gathering of saints around the Prophet. As a result of this the original *tariqa* of Sultan Bahu is known as *Qadiri/Sarwariyah*. Succeeding *pirs* took *bai'at* at the hands of *Naqshbandi* *shaikhs*.[44] thus linking themselves to the *Naqshbandi tariqa*. Although Hazrat Sultan Bahu acknowledges only the Prophet as his *pir*, there is no doubt of his own conviction to teach through the path of direct personal experience. In *Risala Rouhi* he writes that if you are in search of Allah, then come to me, I will make the connection in one moment.[45] Despite his denial of any formal education Hazrat Sultan Bahu was, however, a prolific author, writing over one hundred works on the Qur'an, *Hadith*, and *fiqh* in either Arabic, Punjabi or Persian.[46]

The Sultan Bahu Trust in Birmingham

There are several descendants (*sajjada nashin*) of the saint who lay claim to the title of *pir* as based on direct family lineage traced back to him. In Pakistan these men manage the shrine at Jhung, preach, and maintain the centres of the Sultan Bahu Trust around the country. In 1980 one of them, Sultan Fiaz ul Hasan Bahu, visited Britain and set up the *Sultan Bahu Trust* in Birmingham. He stayed here and was joined by his two brothers, Niaz and Riaz. The efforts of the three brothers have resulted in the establishment of mosques dedicated to Sultan Bahu in Bradford, Leicester and London. There are also groups of followers in Leeds, Newcastle and Glasgow. Fiaz ul Hasan Bahu is regarded as the present *pir* of the *Sultan Bahu Trust*, and his brother Sultan Riaz ul Hasan Bahu is the chairman of the centre in Birmingham. The President of the *Sultan Bahu Trust* in Birmingham is Yousef Kamaur, a very prominent community leader and the Director of the *Asian Advisory Centre* in the city. Yousef Kamaur is also a member of the *Muslim Liaison Committee*, an umbrella organisation which attempts to represent all Muslims in Britain. Yousef Kamaur informed me that the *Sultan Bahu Trust* had recently spent £350,000 on developing the centre at Ombersley Road. This money was used on the new mosque and the *dar al Ulum*.[47]

The *imam* of the Sultan Bahu mosque discussed with me the Trust's intentions concerning the *dar al Ulum*. Imam Pirzade is aware that it is necessary to provide a thorough Islamic education for young Muslims born in Britain. He feels that *imams* brought to Britain from the subcontinent should be trained in modern teaching methods by attending courses here, and that English should become as soon as possible the medium for the transmission of Islam to the British-born generation.

> In the mosque there should be two languages: Arabic and English. Of course the language of Islam should be Arabic. You should know Arabic and English because it is the language of this country. Punjabi and Urdu are the other languages (spoken); they should be personal not the language of the mosque. The *imams* which are coming from Pakistan are mostly educated in Urdu medium or Punjabi medium so they do not know English. I have often said that some of our Muslim scholars have very orthodox thinking. If you want to make your ideas progressive then you must learn English.[48]

In order to provide for the needs of young *Barelwi* Muslims from around Britain, the Sultan Bahu trustees want to provide hostel accommodation and educational facilities. There will be two courses: one for children starting at the age of eleven and lasting for three years; and the other will be a six year course for boys aged sixteen or above. The courses will begin by providing a basic introduction to Islam; English, Arabic and Urdu will also be taught. The students will go on to study the Qur'an, *Hadith*, *fiqh* and *tafsir*. While the children are still at school or college they will stay at the hostel and study their Islamic curriculum every evening. The intention is to provide qualified teachers who can assist the children in the subjects they are learning at school. As a result it is hoped that the students will become knowledgeable in both the culture they live in and the religion they belong to.

The appointment of Imam Pirzade at the *Sultan Bahu Trust* reflects the ambitions and the religious orientation of this institution. The *imam* himself is from a long line of *Naqshbandi* Sufis. His grandfather was a *pir* and a graduate of Bareilly *dar al Ulum*, and Imam Pirzada had studied Islam with him. He told me how his father had taught him the use of specific *ta'widhs* to achieve various ends. He knew different *ta'widhs* to make people fall in love with each other, to prevent toothache, to cure the bite of a mad dog, and to protect people from the evil eye. These amulets contain verses from the Qur'an written in Arabic, Urdu, Persian, or even in local dialects and they are worn on the hand, the throat, or the shoulders. For example, Imam Pirzade explains how the *ta'widhs* can be used to cure rabies:

If a mad dog bites someone, then write this *ta'widh*, and say to the person that he must bring some clay, and mix the *ta'widh* in the clay, and then rinse it on his body. The hair of the dog who has bitten the person, this hair will come out through the skin, and the effect of the madness will disappear.[49]

The *imam* told me that the *pirs*, or anyone to whom they have given permission, can give *ta'widhs* to people. He himself distributes them, and he informed me that the practice is widespread amongst *Barelwi* Muslims in Birmingham. On the other hand, Imam Pirzade is very educated compared to many *imams* in this country. He completed his M.A. in English in Pakistan and taught as a lecturer there. His ambition was to open his own school. In order to achieve this he came to Britain to study the education system here. He has now enrolled for a part-time M.Phil. at the *Institute for the Study of Islam and Christian/Muslim Relations* in Selly Oak. He chose to study in Britain because he knew people here who were his *pirbhai*. He was persuaded by them to remain here as the *imam* of the mosque on the grounds that he was educated, knew the English language, and could establish the school for Islamic studies. He admits that his background is Sufi but that his education has been secular.[50]

The Religious Practices (*adab*) Unique to Sultan Bahu

The religious practices in the *Sultan Bahu Trust* mosque are an example of the wide range of minor variations that can exist within the *Barelwi* tradition whilst remaining recognisably *Barelwi*. As mentioned before, the customary *nath* is sung after prayers. Here, however, the *nath* is preceded by a poem written by the original Sultan Bahu, and followed by the *silsilah* of Sultan Bahu chanted in Urdu. As in the other mosques that I visited, the *tariqa* is *Naqshbandi*, and the *dhikr* is a variation of the essential *Naqshbandi dhikr*. There are no *qawwalis* sung in the mosque, although they are not disapproved of if listened to or participated in by any Muslims elsewhere. The *dhikr* is held every alternate Friday and Sunday evening. It begins with the chant '*La ilaha illallah*', then the '*la ilaha*' is dropped and only '*illallah*' is repeated; then only '*Allah*' is chanted repeatedly; finally '*Allah hu*' is repeated with the breath. It is claimed that this variation of the *Naqshbandi dhikr* can be traced back to Abdul Qadir Gilani of Baghdad who is held in very high regard by all the *Barelwis*. I found a qualitative difference between the *dhikr* as practised by the Sultan Bahu followers on the one hand and that of Sufi Abdullah on the other. The Sultan Bahu *dhikr* is much shorter in duration and less intense. It is a part of a formal religious ritual in which are included other set prayers and the repetition of the *silsilah*. The *dhikr* with Sufi Abdullah, however, is an intense shared emotional experience in the company of the *shaikh*, whose purpose is to induce ecstasy. Often the *sajjada nashin* of Sultan Bahu are present in the mosque during *juma namaz*. At the completion of the prayers the remaining congregation will line up to greet them and the Sultan Bahu elders. I felt that I was witnessing a time-honoured *Barelwi* tradition but it lacked the electricity which was always present when Sufi Abdullah was with his followers.

The *dhikr* is also chanted at the *urs*. There are two *urs* celebrated at the *Sultan Bahu Trust*. There is the annual *Milad Nabi* and the *urs* of Sultan Bahu but the followers also celebrate the birthday of the Prophet every Monday night after *isha* prayers. This occasion consists of recitation from the Qur'an, a sermon in which stories from the Prophet's life are told, several *nat's*, the *dhikr*, the *silsilah*, and prayers of intercession on behalf of the sick and needy. Finally, there is *Giarvin Sharif*, a monthly celebration of the teachings of the Sufis. The *Giarvin Sharif* is also held quarterly and annually in a more elaborate form. The women also observe these celebrations, gather for *juma namaz*, and study Islam. The *Sultan Bahu Trust* has a formally organised women's section which uses the prayer hall in the former factory. The young girls are taught by a qualified primary school teacher. Sometimes the *imam* teaches the women and the girls if there is something that cannot be explained by the usual teachers.

The *Sultan Bahu Trust* has both informal and formal relations with the *Dar ul Uloom Islamia*, with Harounia Mosque in Alum Rock, and with several other *Barelwi* centres in Birmingham. At the *Eid* prayers on the completion of *Ramadan* I noticed the presence of several prominent members of other mosque organisations in the Sultan Bahu mosque. This interchange was made possible by having four sessions of *Eid* prayers between 8am and 10.30am. Imam Pirzade confirmed that, although the *Barelwi* mosques were independent, there was interchange between them, and that members of the different groups do visit each other on special occasions. He attributed much of this to the work of Sufi Abdullah and the *Configuration of Sunni Mosques Midlands* to which the *Sultan Bahu Trust* belongs, as do most *Barelwi* mosques in Birmingham.

Conclusion

The claim that the *Barelwis* form around 90% of the subcontinent Muslims in Britain has to be viewed critically. It is true that the great majority of Muslims do not belong to the various reform movements. Most of the first-generation migrants were uneducated villagers, and the religion in which they practice and believe has been passed on to them from generation to generation. There has been little reason to analyse or challenge that which they have received. They have attempted to reproduce their faith in Britain, but not without criticism from their children. Both the *Barelwi ulema* and the Sufis who are beginning to step up their missionary activities amongst the Muslims in Britain claim that this majority are their supporters. In fact, this population of Muslims is the target of both the activists of the reform groups and the consciously aware *Barelwis* led by the inspiration of Sufi *pirs*. The *Barelwi* leaders acknowledge that the *Deobandis* began to organise themselves in Britain far earlier than they did:

> In 1973 there were only two *pirs* resident in this country. Pir Marouf of Bradford and Sufi Abdul-lah Khan in Birmingham. These were the only two personalities in the whole of the country who were actually resident. Other used to come in those days, make a visit and go back. They still come. Obviously the *Deobandis* had been here a long time before. And they settled. They had their mosques.[51]

The conflicts that took place over the control of mosques throughout the 1970s and '80s point to an attempt by the *Barelwi* leaders to organise their followers into a self-conscious *Barelwi* movement in Britain which would offset the start which the *Deobandis* and the other reform groups had over them. Despite the work of Ahmed Riza Khan, the *Barelwis* were, however, still not a unified religious movement. There was remarkable disparity and diversity amongst them based on place of origin, language, degree of organisation, religious practice, education, and involvement or non-involvement in varous Sufi *tariqas*. Pir Noor ul-Aqtab Siddiqi states that the *Barelwi* mosques are 'connected with people, personalities' rather than organisations.[52] This has worked against any attempt to create unity of purpose amongst the *Barelwis*. The recent change in pattern of mosque conflict from *Barelwi* versus *Deobandi* to *Barelwi* versus *Barelwi* indicates that important changes could be taking place amongst themselves. The conflict with the *Deobandis* and other reform groups helped to define a common *Barelwi* identity. The in-fighting amongst *Barelwi* groups suggests a leadership struggle as various factions attempt to make themselves more influential. I would suggest that this is an aspect of the changes that are taking place amongst the *Barelwis*. I would argue that the conflict is an indication of a shift towards greater *Barelwi* awareness of common identity and a need to organise themselves around this identity despite the prevalence of disparity. The conflicts are a power struggle amongst *Barelwi* personalities out of which the most dominant could emerge victorious as leaders of the community. This search for unity and common identity is further demonstrated by organisations like the *Configuration of Sunni Mosques Midlands* which respects the autonomy of each individual mosque but promotes the awareness of the benefits of working together.

None of the mosques that I visited conformed to the traditional scenario of a *Barelwi* mosque that is comprised of a congregation which originates from a small group of villages somewhere in the subcontinent and an *imam* imported from the same region. This picture seems to be rapidly changing. There are obviously still mosques of this type to be found throughout Britain, but the demands of the younger generation that was born and educated here are making themselves felt. The mosque committees are often led by men like Yousef Kaumar who runs the *Asian Advisory Centre* in Birmingham, and Muhammad Saleem Akhtar, who is a successful accountant. These men are in touch with wider British society and the problems of young British Muslims. Although staunch *Barelwis* and Sufis, they are aware of the need for a wider unity which must include all Muslims in Britain if Islam is to prosper here. These successful and educated community leaders are appointing *imams* whose viewpoint is wider than the rural *imam* imported from the subcontinent. It is essential that their viewpoint includes the younger generation of both sexes. Certainly, one spur of this new emphasis on young people is the success of some of the reform groups in this area. Noor ul-Aqtab Siddiqi confirms this:

> Slowly there is a movement growing up that we have to do something about our younger generation. The reason why at this particular moment in time even the *Barelwis* have to accept that they (the reform groups) are working harder is because of the fact that they have more resources.[53]

As a result of this concern for the younger generation, the more organised *Barelwi* groups have begun to establish *dar al-Ulums*. In 1982 Pir Abdul Wahhab Siddiqi set up the *Islamic Study Centre* in Coventry to help create a British *Barelwi ulema*. At the moment the college has facilities for fifty pupils, but the *International Muslim Organisation* founded by the *pir* is buying a school from Coventry City Council which can take three hundred students. The *pir's* long-term ambition was that the school will grow to become Britain's first Islamic university. Noor ul-Aqtab Siddiqi claims that his father' school was the first *Barelwi dar al-Ulum* in Britain.[54] and that it was inspired by his father's ideas concerning the future of Islam in this country.

> He said that we need those *ulema* who are going to be successful in Western society. Those *ulema*

who are familiar with Western ideas, Western concepts, and have gone through the Western system of education, and also they have that ability, they have the knowledge of the *din*, the knowledge of Islam.[55]

Pir Abdul Wahhab Siddiqi also believed that the next generation of *imams* has to be chosen from amongst the educated in the community. He believed they should also be 'doctors, lawyers, and engineers'. He felt that the most important aspect of the *imam's* work is preaching rather than leading the prayers.[56] There are now two *dar al-Ulums* in Bradford belonging, respectively, to Pir Marouf and Habib Rahman Shah. In Birmingham, there are the *dar al-Ulums* of Sufi Abdullah and the *Sultan Bahu Trust*. So far, all these establishments are very new. Despite the awareness of the needs of young people and of women that is developing amongst the foremost *Barelwi* leaders, I saw little happening in practice. The *dar al-Ulums* may now be established in Britain but so far they have offered little beyond the traditional Islamic education as prevalent in the subcontinent.

One problem is that the teachers know only the system of education which they themselves were taught when they were students in Pakistan, Bangladesh and India. The other problem is the innate conservatism of most of the first-generation migrants. They are suspicious of any kind of innovation in terms of religion which they inherited from their ancestors. In my visits to *Barelwi* mosques I did not find one that was using English either in the mosque or in the mosque schools. The prevalent feeling amongst the members of the mosque congregation was that these changes would take place organically as the older generation died. The mosques which are organised around the Sufi *tariqas* in Birmingham were at least providing separate prayer facilities for women but this was not happening in other *Barelwi* mosques.

There is no doubt that the arrival of resident Sufi *pirs* is inspiring the *Barelwis* in Britain. The teachings of the Sufis pervade *Barelwi* thought and practice. The lives of the saints are a focus for the piety and devotion of the majority of ordinary subcontinent Muslims. The arrival of living charismatic *pirs* based on British soil does much to redirect the focus of *Barelwis* away from their place of origin in the subcontinent to the community here. The respect which the *Barelwis* have given to the Sufis has focussed the attention of *Barelwi* worship upon the shrines that have grown up around the tombs of the saints. These shrines cannot be imported to Britain, but living Sufis can. Sufi Abdullah, for example, through his activities and obvious piety, has done much to extend the focus of his followers in Britain from Ghamkol Sharif in Pakistan to an inner city block in Birmingham. Pnina Werbner asserts that the 'spirituality of a Sufi *pir* is embodied in the space that he has sacralised. His divine blessing purifies his spatial dominion and endows it with sanctity'.[57] The presence of living *pirs* resident in Britain is sacralising buildings, parks, city blocks, and procession routes. Parts of inner city Britain are becoming as sacred as shrines in the subcontinent. It is tempting to speculate that the death of *pirs* that have lived their lives in Britain, as in the case of Pir Abdul Wahhab Siddiqi who has been buried in Coventry, could produce future shrine locations here in this country.

Pnina Werbner also points out that there is a constant historical process of 'waxing' and 'waning' amongst the local cults within the broad encompassing *tariqa*. She suggests that new cults appear, 'energised through the emergence of a charismatic saint', which revitalises the *tariqa*.[58] She argues that the shrines of departed saints cannot function in this way.

Although shrines of illustrious saints, once established, remain points of personal pilgrimage and seasonal ritual celebrations, such shrines no longer extend as organisations far beyond a relatively localised area, and cannot continue to control, as the cult founder did, a series of sub-centres, and sub-sub-centres over a vast region.[59]

The situation in Birmingham indicates the complexity of the full picture of the relationship between charismatic living *pirs* on the one hand, and on the other, descendents of past Sufi saints, the *sajjada nashin*, who usually maintain and lead the activities of a cult based upon a shrine. The *sajjada nashin* have been visiting Britain for some time; ever since, in fact, they became aware that followers of their localised cults had migrated here. They have created centres in Britain that are based on the original cult but the needs of the community, however, are different here than in the country of origin. In the subcontinent the *sajjada nashin* find themselves acting principally as custodians of the shrine but here they are involved in the propagation of Islam. Due to the need to ensure the survival of Islam on foreign territory, these Sufi cults have spread to form sub-branches in other British cities. The *Sultan Bahu Trust* is an example of this kind of organisation. What is most interesting, however, is the relationship between the Sufi groups organised around the efforts of the *sajjada nashin* and the groups growing up under the leadership of living charismatic *pirs*.

If Pnina Werbner is correct, the former should be declining or static whilst the latter flourish. I do not disagree with Pnina Werbner that this is the usual cyclical pattern of development amongst Sufis cults in the subcontinent or elsewhere in the Muslim world. What appears to be happening in Birmingham, however, is that the presence of charismatic *pirs* like Sufi Abdullah, together with the activity which their presence inspires, is reawakening the old cults led by the *sajjada nashin*. This is given impulse by the need of Muslims to protect their religion in an alien environment. Groups like the *Sultan Bahu Trust* are old in the subcontinent but new in Britain. It is difficult for them to lie dormant when half-a-mile down the road so much inspired activity is taking place. This is especially so when it is the followers of Sufi Abdullah who are taking the lead in promoting *Barelwi* unity and who have persuaded them to join the *Configuration of Sunni Mosques Midlands*. The timing of the increase in the activities of the Sufi groups would suggest that they have been accelerated by the publishing of *The Satanic Verses* by Salman Rushdie. As previously noted the *Barelwis* were particularly upset by the novel because of their great veneration for the Prophet. They were foremost in public expressions of anger but lacked the leadership to organise. This role of organising the Muslims' reaction fell to the better educated and structured reform groups. The *Barelwi* masses, however, experienced for the first time the results of organised protest and the power of unity. It is not surprising then that the growth of the groups led by the *pirs* has occurred since the late-1980s even though the *pirs* themselves have been here longer. The diverse nature of the tradition is still the dominant feature amongst *Barelwis* in Britain as it is in the subcontinent. There are indications, however, that a stronger sense of unity and identity is growing amongst them as they tackle the problem of being part of a Muslim minority in Britain. The roles of Sufism and, above all, of charismatic *pirs* will be crucial in this process.

Endnotes

[1] Interview with Maulana Shahid Raza Khan, 13th December 1992, Leicester Islamic Centre, Leicester. Shahid Raza Khan claims that 90% of Muslims in Britain can be defined as *Barelwi*. This figure is problematic. He is using the term *Barelwi* to describe any Muslim who is not consciously a member of a reform group such as the *Deobandis*, *Ahl-i Hadith*, *Tabligh-i Jamaat* or *Jamaat-i Islami* to name the most prominent. It must also be taken into account that Maulana Shahid Raza Khan is a prominent *Barelwi alim*. This figure is more likely to describe the proportion amongst the first genereration Muslim migrants.

[2] Barton, Stephen, 1986, *The Bengali Muslims of Bradford, A Study of their Observance of Islam with Special Reference to the Function of the Mosque and the work of the Imam*, Monograph Series, Community Religions Project, University of Leeds, p.102.

[3] ibid.

[4] Maulana Shahid Raza Khan, 13th December 1992, Leicester.

[5] ibid.

[6] ibid.

[7] ibid.

[8] ibid.

[9] ibid.

[10] ibid.

[11] ibid.

[12] Nielsen, Jorgen, 1992, *Muslims in Western Europe*, Islamic Surveys, Edinburgh University Press, Edinburgh, p.133.

[13] Shahid Raza Khan, 13th December 1992, Leicester.

[14] Nielsen, op.cit., p.133.

[15] Shahid Raza Khan, 13th December 1992, Leicester.

[16] Nielsen, op.cit., p.159.

[17] Shahid Raza Khan, 13th December, 1992, Leicester.

[18] ibid.

[19] ibid.

[20] Interview with Imam S.M. Razvi, 27th March 1993, Noor Ul Uloom Mosque, Somerville Road, Birmingham.

[21] ibid.

[22] ibid.

[23] ibid.

[24] ibid.

[25] ibid.

[26] ibid.

[27] Several of Sufi Abdullah's *murids* were keen to demonstrate that the *Waqf Ikhlas Publications* published by the Sufi group, *Hakikat Kitabevi*, in Istanbul were also arguing that the true *Sunnis* were those which acknowledged Sufi doctrine and practice. Some of the publications produced by this group also denounce the reform movement as *Wahhabi*. Muhammad ibn 'Abd al-Wahhab (1699-1791) is denounced as a spy of the British whose mission was to subvert Islam (*The Sunni Path*, 1993, Waqf Ikhlas Publications, Istanbul ,p.61). These publications were used to prove that the *Barelwi* tradition was part of the true *Sunni* tradition practised by millions of Muslims throughout the Islamic world.

[28] Interview with Abid Hussein, a murid of Sufi Abdullah, 20th March 1993, Golden Hillock Road, Birmingham.

[29] Interview with Muhammad Saleem Akhtar, Chairman of the *Dar ul Uloom Islamia*, and the *Configuration of Sunni Mosques*, 29th March 1993, Golden Hillock Road, Birmingham.

[30] Abid Hussein, 20th March 1993, Birmingham.

[31] ibid.

[32] Werbner, Pnina, 1990, 'Stamping the Earth with the Name of Allah: Zikr and the Sacralising of Space Among British Muslims', unpublished paper, University of Manchester, pp.9-10.

[33] ibid., p.21.

[34] ibid., p.22.

[35] Muhammad Saleem Akhtar, 29th March 1993, Birmingham.

[36] Abid Hussein, 20th March, 1993, Birmingham.

[37] Muhammad Salem Akthar, 29th March 1993, Birmingham.

[38] ibid.

[39] Abid Hussein, 20th March 1993, Birmingham.

[40] Muhammad Saleem Akhtar, 29th March, 1993, Birmingham.

[41] Interview with Dr. Jorgen Nielsen, 23rd March 1993, Institute for the Study of Islam and Christian/Muslim Relations, Selly Oak, Birmingham.

[42] Interview with Pir Sultan Fiaz ul Hasan Bahu, 13th August, 1994, Abu Hariara Mosque, Hardy Street, Leeds.

[43] Ibid.

[44] Ibid.

[45] Ibid.

[46] Ibid.

[47] Interview with Yousef Kaumar, 31st March, 1993, Ombersley Road, Birmingham.

[48] Interview with Imam Pirzade, 19th March 1993, Sultan Bahu Mosque, Birmingham.

[49] ibid.

[50] ibid.

[51] Interview with Maulana Noor ul-Aqtab Siddiqi, son of Pir Abdul Wahhab Siddiqi, 30th March 1993, Coventry. Since my interview Pir Abdul Wahhab Siddiqi has died. His son, Noor, is now the pir.

[52] ibid.

[53] ibid.

[54] ibid.

[55] ibid.

[56] ibid.

[57] Werbner, op.cit., p.28.

[58] ibid.

[59] ibid.

7 The rise of Islamic reform movements in India and their role for Muslims in Britain

Introduction

The conditions which paved the way for the essential message of the reformers can be traced right back to the introduction of Islam into India. Chapter V has established that right from the beginning there were various compromises with Hinduism particularly amongst the Sufis. This example of tolerance towards the Hindus became the normal policy of the state although the more orthodox *ulema* were often opposed to this.[1] This pragmatic approach made it easier for a minority to rule, but it also facilitated the gradual encroachment of Hindu ideas and customs. Several of India's Muslim rulers and courtiers, together with many noblemen, married Hindus. Titus suggests that the influence of these wives would sometimes affect their husbands' views towards Hindus and their religion, to say nothing of the influence of the mothers on children.[2]

Besides the influence of their high-caste Hindu wives on the Muslim ruling class, there was also the fact that the greater part of the Muslim population was converted en masse from Hindu low castes and outcast groups. Regardless of whether the conversion had come about as a product of conquest or to improve status by joining the faith of the new rulers, or, even by religious persuasion, complete Islamicisation of the converts had not been accomplished thoroughly. Often, hastily converted people were left behind by the conquering forces, and for many of these there would have been little follow-up when it took place. Very often the original conversion would have been at the hands of itinerant Sufis following in the footsteps of the military forces. Besides the formative influence of the Sufis and the impact of Hindu ideas and customs, there were also powerful *Shi'a* elements which led to the creation of many diverse religious movements which were eclectic and syncretistic in their message.[3]

The Origins of the Reform Movement: Akbar and Sirhindi

The syncretistic tendency was to reach its zenith during the reign of the Mughal emperor Akbar (1556-1605).[4] Akbar's abandonment of *Shar'iah* law and the establishment of his new religion which placed him above the law was anathema in Islam, and appalled the orthodox.[5] Akbar came to be viewed as an apostate by the orthodox *ulema*, as a symbol of the corruption and decline of Islam and the pollution created through its contact with Hinduism. This situation brought to a head the idea that Islam was in danger of being engulfed in an all-embracing sea of Hinduism. Shaikh Ahmad Sirhindi (d.1625) of the *Naqshbandi* Sufi order[6] was to lead the reaction against Akbar and the cultural impurities that he perceived to be entering Islam. Sirhindi's ideas of reform became the basis of the later reform movements, which really began with Shah

Wali-allah and his descendants (see Appendix E). Sirhindi was determined to unite the *ummah* under the rule of the *Shari'ah*,[7] to destroy the innovations (*bida*) which he saw creeping into Islamic belief and practice, and to persuade Muslims to shun religious contact with the Hindu population.[8] This attempt by orthodox Islam to reassert itself became the seed of that Muslim separatism which continued to develop, culminating in the establishment of the separate Muslim state of Pakistan in 1947.

Despite his own Sufi affiliation, Sirhindi asserted the prominence of the *Shari'ah* over the *Tariqa*, insisting that Sufis themselves should be exemplary in their obedience to the law.[9] Simple conformity to the *Shari'ah* would base the Muslims' faith firmly on revelation rather than on the mystic's intuitional awareness of unity. The heart of Sirhindi's attack on the heterodox forms of Sufism was its openness to pantheistic and monistic ideas, which in turn led to alliances with Hinduism. He considered that education in theology and law should take precedence over Sufi teaching, and that the Prophet and his companions were superior to all the saints of Sufism. A core idea in Sirhindi's plan for revival, central to all the later reform movements, was the return of Muslims to perceived standards of the Islam of the Prophet and the *Rashidun* (the first four rightly guided caliphs). Sirhindi's voice of protest against syncretistic movements and liberal trends was an attempt to protect both Sufism and the Muslim masses from the ideas and morals of Hinduism's pantheistic views. Essentially, Sirhindi saw Hindus as infidels not entitled to their *dhimmi* status; the revival of Islam thus meant the reimposition of *Shari'ah* and the removal of cultural accretions and innovations arising out of Sufism, *Shi'a* and, in particular, Hinduism.[10] True Islam must rest on the Qur'an and the *Sunna* of the Prophet. The correct *Sunna* was established in approved *Hadith*. Sirhindi's deep awareness of the need for reform, combined with his intense suspicion of innovation and his distrust of any contact with the non-Muslim world, made him the pioneer of Muslim isolationism. Consequently, his restoration of orthodoxy led inevitably to a widening gulf between the Hindu and Muslim communities.

Shah Wali-allah (1702-1763)

Shah Wali-allah, often described as the greatest Islamic scholar India ever produced,[11] picked up the major strands of Sirhindi's ideas and developed them into a coherent ideology that was to form the basis of Islamic revival in the subcontinent right through to the present day. Very few Muslim thinkers from the region have not been influenced by him. Appendix C indicates graphically the extent of his influence on modern Islamic history in the Indo-Pakistan subcontinent. He himself lived in an age that saw the rapid decline of Mughal power, but the Battle of Plassey, which placed the East India Company in effective control of Bengal, occurred four years after his death. It was left to his sons and successors to develop his ideas into a coherent movement dealing with the transfer of power of Islamic rule to the British. The decay, however, had begun to set in long before the East India Company established its dominion over Bengal; it had begun with the death of Aurangzeb in 1707. Since his demise there had been a decline which led to the disintegration of Muslim political power and culture.[12] Feudal lords were no longer prepared to act as vassals, and now established their own kingdoms.[13] There were rebellions by Marathas, Sikhs and Rajputs, and, in 1739, Nadir Shah of Persia sacked Delhi.[14] There was no longer any strong central government or leadership.

India had never been a theocracy, but matters of religion had always been seen as a function of the Muslim state. The need to maintain Muslim rule in India was very rarely disassociated from the necessity to establish the religion of Islam. During the era of Muslim domination the unity of the faithful was expected to be maintained by the ruler, who was seen as the defender of the faith and the custodian of the law.[15] A truly Islamic temporal order was that in which the *Shari'ah* as understood by the consensus of scholars was enforced by a righteous Muslim ruler. The anarchy and degeneration of the eighteenth century, and the loss of Mughal territory to the Hindu Marathas and the Sikhs, helped to create a desire for the renewal or purification of Islam. The Qur'an states that God has confided the world to His righteous servants;[16] for many Muslim thinkers, the decline in temporal power was an indication that they were no longer to be counted amongst the righteous.

As so often in Islam's history, the pattern of decline in temporal power was accompanied by a religious revival. Ikram states, 'that the political disintegration of the eighteenth century in the subcontinent was not partnered by religious collapse is largely due to the work and inspiration of Shah Wali-allah'.[17] Through his inspiration, the religious leadership came to believe that political leaders could no longer hold onto the empire without the motivating force of religion. In fact, Shah Wali-allah throughout his life never ceased from turning to various Muslim potentates in an attempt to restore the glory of the Muslim way of life. None of these rulers, however, responded to his call. It was difficult for him to conceive of any solution other than the discovery of an enlightened ruler who was strong enough to re-establish the rule of the *Shari'ah*.[18] This failure, however, did not stop him from communicating his message of renewal.

Like Sirhindi before him, Shah Wali-allah reiterated that the lack of moral standards which led to the decline of Muslim fortunes was due to contact with Hindus and badly converted Muslims.[19] He accused the Muslims of India of becoming Indians rather than identifying with the larger worldwide *ummah*.[20] He was especially afraid that Islam, the only religion that had not been corrupted by innovation, was itself in danger of losing its pristine and final revelation.[21] This he felt to be coming about as a result of Hindu contacts that encouraged the admittance into Islam of non-Islamic practices. He insisted that Indian Muslims should see themselves as an integral part of the larger Muslim world.[22] He saw the intolerable political situation as proof that Indian Muslims had failed to fulfil the requirements of the *Shari'ah*. It was incomprehensible to him that Islam itself could be at fault. Recommitment was required, and no true Muslim should accept the contemporary decline. He was convinced that a regenerated Islam could again be strong enough to counteract the effects of internal decay and external domination.

Although Shah Wali-allah's call for revival had a strong Sufi influence,[23] he attacked many Sufi practices of his time as corrupt and as aberrations of true Islam. He rejected the local popular style of Islam in favour of scripturalist emphasis on the original practice of the faith. He criticised both the attribution of divine powers to saints and the habit of worship at their tombs. It is, however, possible to find various aspects of Sufism, for example, the *pir/murid* relationship, *dhikr*, and silent meditation being practised in the nineteenth century reform groups like Deoband. Essential Islam was contained in the revelation to the Prophet, and the exemplary inspiration was the life of Muhammad himself. Shah Wali-allah's belief in revelation made it impossible for him to question the *Shari'ah*.[24] This final perfection of the *Shari'ah*, which he was to champion with great energy, enabled him and succeeding generations to rally around the banner of a system that could not be improved upon and therefore should not be changed. The renewal of the reformers was a return to what they considered to be the pure Islam of the founder. Shah Wali-allah's emphasis on the exemplary role of the Prophet led him to stress the importance of a renewed study of *Hadith*.[25] He urged Muslim scholars to study the Qur'an and the *Hadith* directly, rather than studying the interpretations made by the four schools of law.

If the Muslims could not be united by being citizens in *Dar al-Islam*, Shah Wali-allah believed that there must be an integrated Muslim brotherhood which could reach out to bring everyone into a united religious social grouping: a kind of *ummah* within the *ummah*. In his attempt to create unity out of discord, Shah Wali-allah presented a comprehensive statement of Islamic belief and practice in which all *Sunni* scholars could find guidance and inspiration. Ikram suggests that Shah Wali-allah's translation of the Qur'an into Persian connected him with a broad-based movement to carry the knowledge of the Qur'an to 'the average literate Indian Muslim'.[26] Although he was to have little effect in his own lifetime, his habit of training students in the different branches of Islamic knowledge and entrusting them with the teachings of others, thus allowing him to be free to write, was to achieve great success as the model for the reform movement developed by his successors. Ikram argues that 'by working out a system of thought upon which most extremes of view could agree, he helped to supply a religious base for later national cohesion'.[27] He was not, however, able to reconcile the basic divisions in Indian Islam, despite the fact that all the various movements that emerged, including the *Barelwis*, acknowledged him as a scholar, reformer and mystic.

The Issuing of *Fatwas*

In 1803 Lord Lane occupied Delhi.[28] Around the same period Ranjit Singh was consolidating Sikh power in the Punjab, and Western India was experiencing an upsurge of Hindu revivalism inspired by the success of the Marathas. By the opening of the nineteenth century, real power over the heartlands of the old Mughal empire had passed into non-Muslim hands. Although a Mughal remained as titular king in Delhi until after the uprising in 1857, from now on the Muslims would have to come to terms not only with being a minority in Hindu India but also with being relatively powerless under British rule. The first decades of British rule were to worry pious Muslims. No longer able to control a whole range of issues relating to the organisation of the law, there was a proliferation of the direct issuing of *fatwas* from the *ulema* to believers.[29] Common penal laws and separate judicial courts meant that they were mainly concerned with the small detailed concerns of everyday life, and although they had no coercive power, they were essential to Muslims searching for a way to preserve a true expression of their faith under foreign domination.[30] The issuing of *fatwas* indicated a move towards creating self-contained communities in matters of religion and everyday behaviour.[31] The thousands of *fatwas* issued by various *ulema* were to help maintain the boundaries of the various movements that appeared throughout the nineteenth century. *Fatwas* were issued to condemn the beliefs and practices of other groups and to give authority to one's own. The *fatwas* functioned to form group identity and they also allowed for some control over keeping Muslim life within the bounds of the *Shari'ah* when there was no Muslim state to enforce the law. The detailed restrictions on daily activity also functioned as a boundary which isolated those Muslims who observed these practices from both Hindu and British India. Furthermore the issuing of *fatwas* confirmed that India was no longer *dar al-Islam*; it was now *dar al-Harb*. The *fatwas* functioned as a recognition that organisation of the state was no longer in Muslim hands.

Many of the *fatwas* were issued by the descendants of Shah Wali-allah. The nineteenth century saw his ideas organised into energetic socio-political religious movements. Mujeeb states that Shah Wali-allah's sons, Shah Abdul Aziz (1746-1824), Shah Rafi'uddin (1748-1817) and Shah Abdul Qadir (1753-1827), 'turned to the study of the Qur'an, the popularisation of religious knowledge, and the creation of a new aspiration to study, to understand and live by the *Shari'ah*'.[32] As part of their aim of popularising the correct interpretation and practice of Islam, two of the brothers made translations of the Qur'an into Urdu,[33] which was rapidly taking over from Persian as the language of educated Indian Muslims.[34] The reformers were to encourage the use of Urdu as the basis of communication amongst the religious elite. In time Urdu was to become one of the most important symbols of Muslim identity in India. Shah Abdul Aziz took over from his father as spiritual leader in Delhi, and became the central figure in an important circle of reformist teaching.[35] He was a prolific issuer of *fatwas* in an attempt to ensure thereby that instruction in a *Shari'ah* should spread beyond his circle of followers and students.[36] In continuation of his father's message, many of his *fatwas* were explicit commands to follow the *Sunna* of the Prophet by continuous reference to *Hadith*.[37] When the British entered Delhi, Shah Abdul Aziz issued his famous *fatwa* which declared India to be outside *Dar-al Islam* and inside the world of *Dar al-Harb*.[38] The declaration that India was *Dar al-Harb* opened up the possibility of *jihad* as an activist alternative to the more scholarly issuing of *fatwas*.[39]

Sayyid Ahmad of Rae Bareilly

The charismatic Sayyid Ahmad of Rae Bareilly (1782-1831) established a small kingdom in the North-West Frontier from which he waged *jihad* against the Sikhs of the Punjab.[40] He defeated the Sikhs at Akora Khattak in November 1826, and began to establish the rule of *Shari'ah* in the area he had carved out for himself and his followers. Despite the opposition of local tribes to his reforms, he had established himself in Peshawar by 1830. In 1831 he was trapped at Balakot by the Sikhs, and he and six hundred of his *mujahiddin* were killed.[41]

Sayyid Ahmad was closely connected to the family of Shah Wali-allah. As a young man (1806-1811) he had studied with Abdul Qadir in Delhi. Abdul Aziz's son-in-law Abdul Hayy (d.1828) and Shah Wali-allah's grandson Muhammad Ishmail (1781-1831) were both to become followers of Sayyid Ahmad after he returned to Delhi in 1818. Both took an oath of allegiance to him as their Shaikh.[42] They assisted him in writing his two influential works, the *Siratu'l - Mustaqim* (The Straight Path) and the *Taqwiyattu'l - Imam* (The Strengthening of the Faith), in which he stressed the centrality of *tawhid* and condemned all practices and beliefs that in any way compromised the essential teachings of Islam.[43] Metcalf suggests that his commitment to the reform of custom and practice was even stronger than that of his teachers from the family of Shah Wali-allah. They had interpreted the renewal and purification of Islam in a more intellectual form.[44] Despite Shah Wali-allah's insistence that his successors forsake cultural accretions, some refused to abandon the practices involved. Even Shah Abdul Aziz distributed food after reading the *fatihah* at his father's grave. The younger members of the family quietly left when such practices were carried out.[45] Sayyid Ahmad's more radical reformist approach was consequently more attractive to the younger generation of reformers.

In the years prior to his *jihad*, Sayyid Ahmad established the method of spreading the reform message that was to last throughout the nineteenth century, long after his military operations had failed. Particularly in the period after returning from his *Hajj*, he began to orchestrate his followers into the type of organisation that was to become the model for the future *jamaats* (a well-knit group of workers, preachers and reformers). He established a network of centres through word-of-mouth preaching in villages and the distribution of tracts. Leaders of prayer were appointed to mosques to teach the basic beliefs of reform Islam, subscriptions were collected, and Islamic courts were set up to administer the *Shari'ah* amongst Muslims. The followers of Sayyid Ahmad, like those of the later nineteenth century reform movements, felt themselves to be a part of a special community with access to the true teachings of the faith. They had a sense of being unique, of exclusiveness. Metcalf suggests that this gave meaning to people whose lives appeared to be beyond their own control.[46] Sayyid Ahmad used the Delhi nucleus of reformers centred on the descendants of Shah Wali-allah to give him contacts with a network of *ulema* and students from the most important religious families of the Doab.[47] Also, inspired by the methods of the Christian missionaries, the reformers made considerable use of the printing press, publishing both tracts and books in Urdu. Many of the reformers undertook extensive preaching tours, and Sayyid Ahmad's tours were especially renowned.[48]

Sayyid Ahmad's death finished the possibility of re-establishing Islam through the means of *jihad*, although some of his followers regrouped in Sittana where they kept alive the idea of *jihad* until the 1860's, when the British backlash to the 1857 uprising finally destroyed their hopes.[49] Sayyid Ahmad, however, left behind him two important ideals: the possibility of an Islamic society made actual, and a means of revitalising Islam through reform-movement *jamaats*. After his death the reformers focussed their attention on the latter.

Strategies towards the British

In 1824, Shah Abdul Aziz died and was succeeded by his grandsons Muhammad Ishaq (1778-1846) and Yaqub. Although Abdul Aziz and the Bengali reformer Shari'atullah (1781-1840) established the trend of the reform movement to co-operate with the British, maintaining the ideal of renewal rather than *jihad*, the *ulema* hated not only the British but everything to do with British culture - the British way of life, British dress and British-style education. In all these areas, the reformers encouraged Muslims to assert their own unique identity. Shah Abdul Aziz insisted that it was improper for Muslims to learn English in order to secure jobs in the administration or to promote better relations with the British.[50] Mujeeb states that several sensational murders were committed by Muslim servants who became aware that is was sinful to serve British masters.[51] Before 1857 Indian Muslims were far more concerned with purifying their own religion than imitating a culture which in their eyes was barely worth the name. After 1857, that culture would have to be taken seriously, not for its own worth but in view of its material success. In their efforts to keep Muslim society distinct from the British invaders and the taint of Christianity, the reformers began to construct a wall of isolation that was cemented together by religion.

Although both Abdul Aziz's grandsons emigrated to Mecca in 1841, they had continued the work of spreading Shah Wali-allah's vision of reform. They left behind them a committed nucleus of students[52] who in turn were dramatically to influence the direction of Islam in the subcontinent (see Appendix E). Their call to reform, rejecting mediaeval Indian Islam in favour of classical Islam, attempted to demonstrate that such a message had the possibility of uniting Indian Muslims who were otherwise divided by class, education, language and regional culture.

As the nineteenth century progressed, the British consolidated their power in India. The Muslims were far from being in one mind in regard to British rule. The activist option of *jihad* was to decline in importance as the hold of the British tightened. After 1857, very few Muslims believed that the British could be removed by force. The ideal of a separate Muslim state governed by *Shari'ah* and led by a righteous Muslim leader, however, lived on. Some came to accept that as the British did not interfere with the practice of Islam, it followed that India was still *Dar al-Islam*. The British government was an established, legitimate regime, and therefore it would be breaking the law to rebel or create disaffection against it.[53] Increasingly, the reformers understood the necessity of using their zeal and enthusiasm to establish their vision of an Islam that could be capable of existing in the absence of an Islamic state. There is no doubt that they succeeded in this, but the price paid was an isolationism which they justified by perceiving the culture of the British as *jahiliyya*, to be avoided. The other problem was that the *jamaats* that had been formed by various reformers suffered from the members' sense of exclusiveness. Islam was rescued in a time of extreme crisis and then renewed, but the reformers did not succeed in uniting Indian Muslims, as can be seen by the fact that the various movements began to develop sectarian tendencies. This was especially pronounced in the conflict between *Deobandis* and *Barelwis*, but even the reform movement itself experienced problems between the various *jamaats*; a good example of this is the conflict between *Deoband* and the *Ahl-i Hadith*.

It is debatable whether the Indian Muslims could ever have been defined as a separate nation, even before losing power to the British. There was no common race, little common history, and a proliferation of conflicting interests. Some Indian Muslims were descended from converts, others from Arabs, Turks, Persians, Afghans and Central Asians. Some spoke Urdu while others communicated in a wide variety of dialects. Some had been in India for as long as a thousand years, others had been converted for no more than a hundred. Many of these people had more in common with the local Hindu population than with their fellow-Muslims. Being Muslim did not make them a nation, but being Muslim under British rule did provide them with a common experience upon which to draw. They all had to deal with the problems created by the increasingly secular culture of the imperial power, which was itself undergoing a huge transformation through the processes of modernisation and industrialisation. The reformers' main strategy was to devote their energies to the Muslim community, preaching a renewal of Islam which they felt could resolve the historical diversity of Indian Muslims and bring about a unified *ummah*.

Mediaeval Islam had not thought of itself as a nation. It was at best held together by a few common rituals and by the aspirations of its scholars. The nineteenth century reformers helped to create a unique national identity for Indian Muslims based on faith.[54] They came to hold a special position that was defined by monotheism, a unique revelation, and a remembrance of the days when they had reigned supreme in India. By the time of Partition in 1947, a very large number of Muslims in British India felt themselves to be part of a special community. All the reform movements that were formed in the previous hundred years contributed to the substantial religious self-consciousness of the period, demonstrating and encouraging as they did the growing awareness that the Muslims of British India were all linked together by the practice of their faith. Despite the internecine squabbles that resulted from the conflicts between the various reform movements, the very existence of these different movements led to substantial Muslim homogeneity. It was crucial for Muslims to define themselves as just Muslims; those united in conflict shared a powerful sense of belonging. The overall result was a proliferation of mosques in cities and villages alike; new schools everywhere; literacy and elementary religious knowledge for girls; printing and publishing houses for religious books and tracts; and ever-increasing numbers of pilgrims doing the *Hajj*. Religion became a badge of pride, and the reformers who were committed to the ideal of return to classical Islam believed themselves to be in the exalted company of the great Muslims of the past. The reformers felt great strength in the fact that they were engaged in a renewal of the Prophet's teachings. There was a sense of continuity with the past together with a sense of community in the present, plus an enhanced awareness of meaning and direction in the life of the individual.

The Relevance of the Reformers in Britain

It is not really surprising to find that the same organisations are preaching the same message in British cities in the second half of the twentieth century. This is because the Muslim presence in Britain continues the colonial relationship between the two cultures. The British Muslims still find themselves a relatively powerless minority in the midst of a non-Muslim majority. In their homeland, the indigenous British occupy twin roles: they are both the rulers and the majority faith. Muslims living in Britain experience themselves as a community under threat, socially underprivileged and isolated from their home culture. Once again it is appropriate for them to rally around Shah Wali-allah's old familiar cry of 'Islam in danger!',[55] and just as it once attempted to unite all the disparate Muslim strands in India, so now the reform message can hope to bring together the many ethnic divisions amongst the Muslims in Britain. The reform message can serve to unite a Muslim minority community from the subcontinent to a wider world-wide movement of Islamic revival.

The reform movements offer guidance in changed circumstances. Although they have not yet taken to issuing *fatwas* on the scale of their Indian forbears, they are excellent vehicles for the dissemination of detailed information on religious matters, especially those applying to everyday life. In the absence of an Islamic state, it is once more essential that a Muslim minority seeks methods to preserve an authentic religious expression and to maintain its identity. The nineteenth century movements have stockpiled two hundred years of experience in performance of this task.

Mattison Mines notes that the reformist tradition provides a common cultural identity amongst Muslims. In particular, Muslims uprooted from their local societies have been influenced by reform beliefs and values. In his study[56] he observes the behaviour of a group of Muslims who travel to the city to find employment. He demonstrates the importance to them of identification with the 'high tradition' of Islam for securing a place in their new community. In the city they explicitly identified themselves as Muslims in dress, religious activity and patterns of association, something which they had not done in their villages. Adherence to the 'classical tradition' of Islam can also be a mark of being '*Ashraf*', well-born Muslims claiming Arab or foreign ancestry.[57] Those who wish to improve their status but are unable to change their economic position can acquire signs of *Ashraf* behaviour such as refined language or a degree of religious learning. In some way, the knowledge gleaned from reform Islam can still bestow a sense of cultural worth. This process of social mobility provides a means of obtaining status and respect within the migrant community that is independent of the receiving community's attitude, which may be hostile or disinterested.

The Indian reformers of the nineteenth century had already established the psychological ploy of improving their self-esteem by defining their morality and beliefs favourably against those of outsiders. They had given this ploy the sanctity of legitimacy. British culture in India had already been labelled as sinful, corrupt, materialistic and godless. The followers of the reform movements operating in Britain can draw upon this already developed theme, and label the receiving culture as *jahiliyya*. In this way, they can feel themselves linked with the difficulties experienced by the Prophet himself in Mecca. Muhammad was the first to use the term '*jahiliyya*'; he used it to describe the condition of the materialistic Meccan merchants. The migration to Britain can be seen in terms of '*Hijrah*', a journey which furthers the cause of Islam as did the original flight of the Prophet from Mecca to Medina. This provides a religious sanction to the situation of being an embattled minority. By living an exemplary Islamic life it may be possible to return a godless society to the true path. It also justifies the community in turning inwards upon itself, even though the receiving community would allow it little opportunity to do otherwise should it wish to do so.

The rivalry for power and leadership amongst the various reform factions provides an opportunity for the ambitious in the community to consolidate their position and gain prestige as defenders of the faith. Sandra Freitag suggests that this type of conflict is actually positive in that it satisfies the needs of those involved. It endows them with a sense of uniqueness, of being misunderstood, of being wronged by society, but it also allows them to relish the fact that they are morally superior.[58] Where self-esteem is shaken by change in general, and by the racism inherent in both direct and economic colonialism in particular, sectarian membership and its rivalries can provide a sense of value.

Economically, the reform movements have already learned the lesson of being self-supporting. Experienced in being without the support of a state apparatus, they succeeded in raising all the significant symbols of Islam during alien rule. In Britain, custom-built mosques and Muslim schools become equally important symbols of Islamic presence. The various communities can feel a great sense of achievement and pride if they utilise the experience of the reform groups in the subcontinent and manage to fund their enterprises without endowments or assistance from outside. In Britain, however, many of the reform groups have been accused by their critics of receiving large endowments from oil-rich Muslim states.

Conclusion

Life in a modern Britain can provide several parallels with the experience of the nineteenth century Indian Muslims. There are economic factors at work just as there were then.[59] The reform message can be used to support and unite an underprivileged class, and the added legitimacy of the heritage of Shah Wali-allah can be as powerful an agent of identity for the Muslims in Britain now as it was for their ancestors in British India. The 'internal conversion' to the scripturalist tradition, as found for example in *Tabligh-i Jamaat*, is, in Weberian terms, part of the process towards rationalising religion. It leads to a religion which is more self-conscious, systematic, and based upon abstract principles. Consequently it is a faith that travels well, since it has the potential to escape the confines of ceremonies and rituals that bind the believer to a particular site, such as the tombs of saints or festivals that need to be at a definite location. Shah Wali-allah's warning that the endangered Muslim minority in India must identify themselves with the world-wide *ummah* through determining and then practising the universals of Islam is also valid for the Muslims in Britain.

Endnotes

[1] Titus, Murray T., 1979, *Indian Islam - A Religious History of Islam in India*, Munshiram Manoharlal, New Delhi, pp.18-19.

[2] ibid., pp. 153-154.

[3] An example of the efforts made to adapt the esoteric teachings of *Shi'a* to Hindu beliefs is found amongst the *Khojahs*. Sadr-ud Din (15th C.) wrote the *Das Avatar* (the Ten Incarnations) for the use of his converts in Sind. He endeavoured to demonstrate that Ali was in fact the long-expected tenth incarnation of *Vishnu* (ibid., p.102).

[4] There is considerable controversy over the degree of Akbar's apostasy. Titus notes that the emperor established Thursday evening discussion groups in the audience hall at Fatehpur Sikri to listen to the views of theologians of various religions, including Hindu *pandits*, Parsees and Roman Catholic priests from Goa, as well as learned *maulvis* and Sufis. During these discussions, the very principles of Islam were debated (ibid., p.158). He argues that Akbar had come to the point of stating, 'there is no god but God, and Akbar is God's apostle' but was too fearful to do so (ibid., p.160). Mujeeb is more circumspect. He argues that Akbar had lost confidence in the *ulema*, and wished merely to form a body of men who shared his outlook and were willing to attach themselves to him (Mujeeb, M., 1967, *The Indian Muslims*, George Allen & Unwin, London, pp.260-261).

[5] Akbar made the *ulema* sign a decree of infallibility which in effect placed the decisions of the monarch over and above the *Shar'iah*. 'If there be variance of opinion among the *mujaddids* upon a question of religion, and His Majesty, in his penetrating understanding and unerring judgement should incline to one option......and give his decree for the benefit of mankind, and for the due regulation of the world, we do hereby agree that such a decree is binding on us, and on the whole nation' (Budayuni, *Muntakhab-ut-Tawarikh*, p.70 quoted in Titus, op.cit., p.160).

[6] ibid., p.124.

[7] Mujeeb, op.cit., p.244.

[8] Ikram, 1964, *Muslim Civilisation in India*, Columbia University Press, New York, p.172.

[9] Mujeeb, op.cit., p.246.

[10] Haq, M. Anwural, 1972, *The Faith Movement of Maulana Muhammad Ilyas*, G. Allen & Unwin, London, p.130.

[11] Iqbal described Shah Wali-allah as 'the first great theologian of Islam' (Metcalf, Barbara Daly, 1982, *Islamic Revival in British India: Deoband 1860-1900*, Princeton University Press, New Jersey, p.36).

[12] ibid., p.8.

[13] Ikram, op.cit., p.261.

[14] ibid., p.258.

[15] Ala'ud -din Khalji (1290-1320) declared that polity and government are one thing, and the rules and decrees of Islamic law another. This becomes the pattern for Muslim rule in India. The early *ulema*, realising the complexity of the Indian situation accepted this. They did not interfere in the affairs of state (Mujeeb, op.cit., pp.73-74). Aurangzeb did introduce reforms intended to make the empire a genuine Islamic state. He opposed all taxes not authorised by Islamic law and appointed censors of public morals to ensure that the *Shari'ah* was implemented (Ikram, op.cit., pp.198-199)

[16] Ali Yousef (trs), 1992, *The Holy Qur'an, Sura An-Nur* 24:55, Mushaf Al-Madinah An-Nabawiyah, Saudi Arabia.

[17] Ikram, op.cit., p.263.

[18] He invited the Nizam of Hyderabad (1724-1748) to come and save the empire. The Nizam was disinterested, so Shah Wali-allah turned to Najib-ud-Daula (d.1790) of Rohilkhand, and even Shah Abdali of Afghanistan. All without success. Abdali did respond, and assisted by Najib-ud-Daula, defeated the Marathas at the Panipat in 1761 but like Nadir Shah he looted and left (Karandikar, M.A., 1968, *Islam in India's Transition to Modernity*, Orient Longmans, Bombay).

[19] ibid., p.127.

[20] ibid.

[21] ibid.

[22] ibid., p.128.

[23] Shah Wali-allah was a *Naqshbandi*. The *Naqshbandi* order was introduced into India relatively late by Muhammad Baqi Bi'llah (1563-1603), during the reign of Akbar. They were more legalistic than other Sufi orders in their approach to the *Shari'ah* and many of them opposed local customs such as ecstatic dancing at the tombs of saints. It was the increasing influence of the *Naqshbandiyya* in the eighteenth century which shaped the views of many of the *ulema* towards a rigorous emphasis on the *Shari'ah* and moderation in spiritual experience (Metcalf, op.cit., p.28).

[24] Despite his conviction that the *Shari'ah* should be implicitly followed, Shah Wali-allah took up the middle ground between those who argued external obedience to the law and those who insisted upon individual spiritual experience. He wrote, 'We must understand that the proper balance which is inherent in man as man, cannot be fully attained without (1) certain kinds of knowledge, which only those endowed with the keenest insight can acquire, and whose guidance

others follow; (2) a *Shari'ah* which encompasses religious knowledge, the science of beneficial living as well as those rules in which voluntary acts are discussed and their detailed division into meritorious, the permitted, the undesirable, and the forbidden is laid down, and these theses in which the degrees of virtue are explained. Therefore it is considered necessary by God in His wisdom and mercy to provide sustenance for intellectual power in the Holy Unseen, and to select and to set apart the person with the highest intelligence to obtain every kind of knowledge from the world of holiness' (Shah Wali-allah, *Al Hujah Allah al Balighah*, Himayat-i Islami Press, Lahore, p.26 quoted in Mujeeb, op.cit., p.280).

[25] Metcalf, op.cit, p.37.

[26] Ikram, op.cit., p.264.

[27] ibid.

[28] Metcalf, op.cit., p.48.

[29] ibid., p.49.

[30] ibid., p.50.

[31] ibid., p.52.

[32] Mujeeb, op.cit., p.390.

[33] ibid.

[34] Metcalf, op.cit., p.49.

[35] Ikram, op.cit., p.281.

[36] Metcalf, op.cit., p.47.

[37] ibid.

[38] Mujeeb, op.cit., p.390.

[39] ibid., p.391.

[40] *Jihad* had to be fought in accordance with the *Sunna*. It was not simply rebellion. In order to do this, Sayyid Ahmad had to carry out his campaigns from a Muslim area. He chose the Sikhs of the Punjab as his opponents, blaming them for interfering in Muslim religious life. In 1826 he had set out on a journey of 3,000 miles through Rajasthan, Sind, Baluchistan and Afghanistan to the tribal territory he had determined to fight from (Metcalf, op.cit., p.52).

[41] ibid.,pp.52-54.

[42] Sayyid Ahmad never denounced Sufism. He rejected the idea of intermediaries between the believer and God, circumambulation, sacrificing animals, burning lights, sanctifying water, the consecration of ritual dishes, and any form of worship at the tombs of saints. He gave, however, initiation into all the traditional Sufi orders but also into the *tariqat - i Muhammadiyya* (the way of the Prophet), which he characterised by external obedience to the *Shari'ah* rather than personal devotion (ibid., p.57).

[43] ibid., p.56.

[44] ibid., p.55.

[45] ibid.

[46] ibid., p.61.

[47] ibid., p.63.

[48] Karandikar states that during Sayyid Ahmad's journey from Delhi to Calcutta, he preached to thousands of Muslims at Allahabad, Mirzapur, Benares, Gazipur, Patna and Calcutta. He cites a famous story from Abul Hasan Ali Nadwi who wrote 'When it became impossible for the *Bai'at* to be administered to everyone individually, it was arranged for aspirants to collect in a large house where Sayyid Sahib went and initiated them into his fold. Seven or eight turbans were un-rolled on the ground when he went there and the aspirants were told to hold them at different places, while one end of them was held by Sayyid Sahib himself. He then taught them the funda-mental principles of Islam and read out the vow in a loud voice like the *azan* which they repeated and thus the ritual was completed. This was done seventeen or eighteen times a day' (Karandikar, op.cit. p.138).

[49] ibid., p.134.

[50] Mujeeb, op.cit., p. 398.

[51] ibid.

[52] Abdul Ghani Naqshbandi (1819-1878), who succeeded Muhammad Ishaq; Fazlur Rahman Ganjmuradabadi (1793-1895), a famous *pir* of post-1857; Sayyid Nazir Husain Muhaddis Dihlawi (d.1902), the founder of *Ahl-i Hadith*; Imadadullah (1817-1899) who was *shaikh* to many of nineteenth century reform *ulema*; Ahmad Ali Saharanpur; and Sayyid Ahmad Khan (1817-1898), political and educational leader of the post-1857 modernists (Metcalf, op.cit., p.72).

[53] Muhammad Ishmail declared that Muslims under British rule were not being persecuted, and were also subjects of the British government. 'They were bound by their religion not to join a *jihad* against it' (Agwani, M.S., 1986, *Islamic Fundamentalism in India*, Twenty-First Century India Society, New Dehli, p.17).

[54] November 1988, The Viceroy of India, Lord Dufferin (1826-1902) described the Muslims of India as a nation of 50 million, with their monotheism, their iconoclastic fanaticism, their social equality, and their remembrance of the days when, enthroned in Delhi, they reigned supreme from the Himalayas to Cape Cormorin (Dufferin's 'Minute of November 1988 in Provincial Councils', enclosed with a letter dated 11th November 1988 to Viscount Cross, Secretary of State for India, *Letters from Dufferin to Cross, Vol V.*, India Office Library).

[55] Karandikar, op.cit., p.127.

[56] Mines, Mattison, 1973, *Towards a new Perspective on Muslim Identity and Integration in Contrasting Social Settings*, Typescript, University of California.

[57] ibid.

[58] Freitag, Sandra, 1980, *Religious, Rites, and Riots: From Community Identity to Communalism in North India 1870-1940*, PhD, Berkeley University.

[59] Bengal in particular had suffered from the import of cheap manufactured goods from Britain. Consequently, the revivalist movement was directed against the new landed classes, and adapted to fit the needs of peasants suffering from the effects of loss of both land and employment (Metcalf, op.cit., p.69).

8 Nineteenth century reform movements: Deoband and Tabligh-i Jamaat

Introduction

The previous chapter has explored the history of Islam in the Subcontinent in order to demonstrate the conditions which paved the way for the message of the reformers in the nineteenth century. It is clear that the various necessary compromises with Hinduism, the incomplete Islamicisation of converts, and the prominence of Sufis in the propagation of the faith resulted in powerful syncretistic developments within Islam in India. The tradition of reform grew from various attempts to purify Islam from these accretions and to establish what was perceived to be, in the ideals of the reformers, a pristine faith identical to that practised by the Prophet and his companions. These two strands of the faith have divided the religious tradition of the Muslims in India into two distinct elements: one proximate and local, validated by custom; the other ultimate and formal, derived from Islamic texts.

Islam in India had never been able to function as an organic unity. It had been unable to develop the kind of organisation required in order that all the diverse strands of the community could act as one in religious matters. In order to achieve this aim, effective control would have to have been maintained by acknowledged representatives and a formal hierarchy. However, this did not exist. It had been a powerful but unrealised dream since the very beginning of Islam, this vision of an integrated Muslim brotherhood which would include all the faithful in one united social grouping. This dream of an united *ummah* has always existed in the religious consciousness of Muslims. Its power has been unaffected by the fact that the unity of Islam was shattered within a few years of the Prophet's death, when Muslims were already fighting fellow-Muslims. This fact of disunity, however, strengthened the ideal of unity rather than weakening it. Again and again, reformers of the faith were to preach that unity and success would be restored to the *ummah* by returning to the basics of the faith as based upon the message in the Qur'an and reinforced by the *Sunna* of the Prophet.

Developments in the Subcontinent Reform Movement Prior to the Establishment of Deoband

Confronted with British rule, Muslim loss of power and the threat of Hindu majority, undergoing its own revival, the nineteenth century Muslim reformers looked aghast at the fragmented condition of Islam in India. They, like their predecessors, were to draw heavily on the ideal of a brotherhood united together by a pristine Islam. They confronted the fact of Islam's reduced condition with a firm belief that the way to salvation and renewal was through strict adherence to the *Shari'ah* in its purest form. They were convinced that it was only by a renewal of their faith and by living an exemplary pious life that Muslims could regain their former glory. After 1857, the reform movements retreated from political activism to religious quietism. Sayyid Ahmad's militant methods were dropped, but not forgotten. His more peaceful methods of dissemination were retained and developed. The result was a forceful and active propagation of scripturalist legal norms in all aspects of social and religious life. Although preaching and distribution of religious tracts became a dominant method of spreading the reform message, a new and very important thrust of dissemination was to develop. To counteract the establishment of schools in India by Christian missionaries and the British government, the reform *ulema* turned their energies towards education. Suspicious of British education, either because of its secular or its Christian element, the reformers decided to establish institutions that would educate young Muslims in the classical traditions of their faith. The graduates of these colleges would spread the message of reform throughout the subcontinent.

Delhi College

During the first half of the nineteenth century the most important Muslim educational institution was Delhi College, founded in 1825 and closed down after the 1857 uprising. The college had been established by the government to educate middle-class Indian youths to occupy positions in the administration. Taking over the buildings of the *Madrasa-e Ghazi al-Din*, the college had a British principal and was expanded by endowments from the Nawab of Oudh in 1828.[1] The curriculum combined Western and Oriental subjects including English language and literature, sciences, Arabic, Persian, Sanskrit, Geography, History and Mathematics.

Barbara Metcalf argues that the success of the school was due to the use of Urdu as the primary means of instruction.[2] The school certainly encouraged the use of Urdu, and its Muslim intake comprised between one-third and one-half of its pupils. Many of these Muslim pupils were attracted by the presence of Mamluk Ali, the school's head of Arabic. Mamluk Ali had close connections with the family of Shah Wali-allah (see Appendix E). He had come to Delhi in 1842 with the express purpose of studying under the descendants of Wali-allah. The first head of Arabic at Delhi College had been Maulana Rashiduddin Khan.[3] Mamluk Ali studied under him and later succeeded him. Rashiduddin Khan had been the disciple of Shah Rafiuddin, the youngest son of Shah Wali-allah. He had also studied under Shah Wali-allah's other two sons, Shah Abd al-Aziz and Abdul al-Qadir.[4] Mamluk Ali's involvement with the Delhi reformers is further demonstrated by the fact that he went on the *Hajj* with Muhammad Ishaq and Yaqub (see Appendix E) in 1842.

There were mixed feelings concerning their contact with the government amongst these members of the reform movement associated with Delhi College. Barbara Metcalf suggests that the students of Muhammad Ishaq and Yaqub shared a common experience created by their commitment to reform and their exposure to Western institutions. The latter influence was created by the missionary societies and the educational institutions of the British.[5] She argues that it was the varying balance between their two formative influences that determined the different directions in which their followers were to develop their ideology throughout the remainder of the nineteenth century and into the twentieth.[6] Some, despite their fears of contact with the missionaries and the government, went on to prestigious positions either in government schools or in the administration. Through Mamluk Ali they achieved not only a firm commitment to Islam but also access to government service so it is not surprising that among Mamluk Ali's pupils were the founders of the *Aligarh* movement (see Appendix E). Others were to go in a different direction. Heirs to the early nineteenth century programme of reform, they turned their attention to the establishment of educational institutions which could train men to give guidance in their faith to Muslims of all backgrounds. They were suspicious of Western education, and were only interested in reviving religious education along the lines of the traditional Arabic *madrasas*. They were primarily concerned with the Islamic quality of individual lives and they were sceptical of the *ulema* who served the British. Amongst this group can be found the originators and first teachers of Deoband, Muhammad Qasim Nanautawi, Maulana Rashid Ahmed Gangohi, Maulana Zulfiqar Ali, and Maulana Fazl al-Rahman Usmani who studied with Mamluk Ali. Of the six founders of the *Dar al-Ulum*, four had studied with Mamluk Ali at Delhi College.[7]

Deoband

The founders of Deoband were also connected with the descendants of Shah Wali-allah through their association with Shah Muhammad Ishaq, the leader of the Delhi reformers and the grandson of Shah Wali-allah (see Appendix E). Maulana Muhammad Qasim Nanautawi, Maulana Rashid Gangohi, Maulana Muhammad Muzhar Nanautawi, and Maulana Muhammad Munir Nanautawi had all fought against the British in 1857.[8] This fact links the founders of Deoband back to the militant *Jihad* movement of Sayyid Ahmad of Rae Bareilly. After the defeat of 1857, however, this group of *ulema* eliminated any further thought of political activity from their programme. They did not want any more direct confrontation with the British so they chose to protect Islam from both the British conquerors and the Hindu majority by eliminating all apparent cultural accretions from the faith.[9] In order to achieve this they focussed their attention on the Muslim community. They left Delhi and established themselves in Deoband, Saharanpur, Khowlah, Gangoha and Bareilly, all in the North-East corner of Uttar Pradesh. These were places with large established Muslim communities. There had been Muslims in Deoband since the thirteenth century.[10] The British presence was less noticeable than in Delhi and the cities of North India, and it was here that they made their centres for preserving classical Muslim culture and religious life along the lines taught by Shah Wali-allah. They made the *madrasa* the institutional centre of their activity. It was felt that the establishment of a religious academic institution was necessary in order to keep the Muslim religious consciousness awake and to organise on a national scale.[11]

Deoband *dar al-Ulum* was founded in 1867 on a site ninety miles north-east of Delhi, and the school was to become the pattern for all the other *madrasas* which were established throughout the subcontinent by so many of the Deoband graduates. The school was conceived in discussions which took place in the old Chhatta Mosque in Deoband between Maulana Muhammad Qasim Nanautawi, Maulana Zulfiqar Ali, Maulana Fazl al-Rahman and Hajji Muhammad Abid.[12] The first classes took place in the same mosque, and apparently began with only one student and one teacher.[13] The rapid expansion of the classes resulted in the school moving, first from the

Chhatta Mosque to the Qazi *Masjid* and then to the Deoband *Jama Masjid* where cells and courtyards were constructed in the style of the old *madrasas*. By 1869, when this too proved inadequate, land was purchased near the Chhatta mosque on which the original school was built. This is still the site for the college, although several buildings have been added to the original as growth continues.[14]

It is possible that the founders, influenced by their time in Delhi, had been impressed by the British bureaucratic style of educational institution as opposed to the old informal teaching style of the *madrasas*. Although the growth of the academy was organic, it would appear that the founders always thought that it would be more than a class held in the corner of a mosque or at the home of a Muslim teacher. Within the first year of its existence it had acquired a library and classrooms; professional teachers were appointed; the students were admitted for a fixed course of study and required to take annual examinations, and a *majlis-e shura* (council) was appointed for administrative purposes and to function as a board of governors.[15]

The curriculum developed as the college expanded and it took some time to evolve to the state it is in today (see Appendix F). In 1956 an official publication issued by the government of India stated that the college taught *Tafsir, Hadith,* Islamic law, philosophy of law, principles, astronomy, *Unani* medicine, and mathematics, but with the greatest emphasis being on *Tafsir* and *Hadith*.[16] The original curriculum was basically that devised by Farangi Mahal in Lucknow in the eighteenth century. This curriculum was known as the *Dars-i Nizami*. It was divided into two parts: the *Manqulat*, which consisted of study of the Qur'an and *Hadith*, and the *Ma'qulat*, which was the study of law, logic and philosophy[17]. The *Deobandi ulema* were opposed to the emphasis on *Ma'qulat* which existed at Farangi Mahal and had become the norm in most of the old-style Arabic *madrasas* before the arrival of the British; they accordingly reversed this trend. More emphasis was given by them to the traditional sciences of *Tafsir, Fiqh* and *Hadith* as opposed to the rational sciences. In particular the six authorised collections of *Hadith* were studied as they were regarded by them as the basis of correct belief and practice. The curriculum was certainly not innovative, but the focus on *Hadith* gave the graduates knowledgeable access to popular material for teaching the Muslim masses.

The aim of the school was to train well-educated *ulema* who would be committed to the cause of reform Islam as taught by Shah Wali-allah and his successors. The *Dar al-Ulum* at Deoband has never considered itself to be only an educational institution. The staff and students have always regarded themselves as an independent school of thought, and as an effective and active movement within Islam.[18] The main aim of this movement is to protect and revive Islam by continuing Shah Wali-allah's efforts to purify the faith. Rizvi in *The History of the Dar al-Ulum Deoband* quotes from Shah Wali-allah's work, *Rasala al-Jaz al-Latif*:

> I have been gifted with the expertise whereby I can distinguish between what is the original teachings of religion brought by the Holy Prophet and what are those things that are accretions or later additions as the result of interpolation of certain schismatic sects.[19]

Rizvi himself writes:

> This movement cleansing the Muslims' beliefs and actions of all the rubbish and trashery, acquainted them with pure and unalloyed Islam, liberated them from polytheism and superstitions,

and, removing fear and awe from their hearts, capacitated them politically to raise the prestige of the Muslims as a community.[20]

The *ulema* were seen to have a central role in this rejuvenation of Muslim society. The school set out to provide the structure for a religious leadership of India's Muslims without the support of the state. In order to achieve this, Maulana Muhammad Qasim Nanautawi insisted that the school and the students' education should be financed by donations from well-wishers. By means of private donations he hoped that it would remain independent of the government and feudal landlords.[21] In the early years people donated books, food for the students and furniture for the premises as well as cash. The network of donors both provided financial support and helped to disseminate the reform message.[22] It also engendered the development amongst Muslims who were not students or staff of a genuine consciousness of being part of a movement. This special bond was reinforced amongst the staff and the *ulema* as many of them belonged to reform Sufi orders; in particular, many were *murids* of Imadadullah (see Appendix E) who was known as the *shaikh* of the *ulema*.[23] As many as five hundred *alim* of North India were reputed to have taken *Bai'at* from him.[24] Barbara Metcalf suggests that marriage was also used to strengthen links between the reformers of Deoband.[25] The combination of these factors reinforced the unity already existing through commitment to reform and together they defined a separate sense of community within the wider *ummah*. Increasingly Deoband came to represent a distinct style, a *maslak*, of Islam in India.

Within six months of the founding of the Deoband school, another *madrasa* run on the same lines was opened in Saharanpur. This college, named *Madrasa Mazahir-i Ulum*, is regarded as being second only to Deoband. By 1880 there were over a dozen schools identified as Deoband and this number had tripled by the end of the century with schools existing as far away as Madras, Peshawar and Chittagong. By the time of Deoband's centenary celebration in 1967 they claimed that there were 8,934 *Deobandi* schools in the subcontinent.[26] Many of the graduates from the *dar al-Ulums* went on to establish schools themselves, and so the system became self-perpetuating. In 1971 a census in Pakistan of 915 *madrasas* found that 458 were *Deobandi*. The remainder belonged to *Shi'as, Ahl-i Hadith* and *Barelwi* groups.[27] As well as opening new *madrasas*, many of the existing ones affiliated themselves with Deoband and were provided with the same structure in regard to syllabus and examinations. All the schools exchanged staff and the personnel were linked by family, common experience and cooperation. The combination of this network of schools and the dominance of *Deobandi* graduates in the *Jami'at-i Ulema-i Hind*, the most influential organisation of the *ulema* in India and its equivalent organisation in Pakistan, the *Jami'at-i Ulema-i Islam*, has resulted in Deoband having a status in the subcontinent that goes far beyond the numerical strength of the reformers.

The success of Deoband was partly achieved by the synthesis of the two main streams of Islamic tradition: intellectual learning and spiritual experience. The *Deobandi ulema* actualised Shah Wali-allah's theorising on the unity of the *Shari'at* and *tariqat*; both were placed firmly within the fold of Islamic orthodoxy. The *Deobandi ulema* were not totally opposed to Sufism. Many of them received *Bai'at* from *Naqshbandi Sufis* such as Imadadullah, and the *pir/murid* relationship cemented the teacher/student relationship in the colleges. The *ulema* were often themselves *shaikhs* and this combined the two disciplines. The *Deobandis* were totally opposed to the kind of Sufism that arose around the tombs and shrines, condemning the celebrations of *urs* and most of the practices associated with 'popular' or 'folk Sufism' and refusing to believe in the intercessionary role of the *shaikh*. In contrast to the *pirs* of the shrines, the *Deobandis* emphasised that the most important activity of the disciple was obedience to the *Shari'ah*. In common with most Sufis, however, the *Deobandi* Sufis did practice *dhikr* and *tasawuf* but obedience to the *Shari'ah* was nonetheless always central.[28]

Soon it was not only Indian Muslims who began to be attracted by this successful mixture of *Shari'at* and *tariqat*. The combination of this and the *Deobandi's* emphasis on conduct was successfully promoted by high profile visits of the *ulema* to other Muslim nations. Thus its success in propagating the message of reform was furthered by the college's ability to attract students from outside the subcontinent. Even in the first few years of its existence the Deoband *dar al-Ulum* received students from Afghanistan and from South India. From its founding in 1867 to its centenary in 1967 the college had produced graduates form Afghanistan, Burma, China, Malaysia, Iraq, Iran, South Africa, Thailand, Russia, Indonesia, Kuwait, Ceylon, Saudi Arabia and the Yemen, although obviously the vast majority were from India and Pakistan.[29] Foreign students still come to Deoband, but I was told, not in the same numbers as before. The students themselves claimed that this was both because of the difficulties of obtaining visas from the Indian government and because many students from the Islamic world now find it easier to go to Pakistan. Most of the foreign students presently at Deoband are the children of either Indian and Pakistani migrants to other parts of the world or of Malaysians. Some of the teachers complained that the foreign students were corrupted by Western values and were not as compliant to discipline as were the Indian students. Some of the Malaysian students complained that they were pressured to attend the *dar al-Ulum* because their parents were afraid that they would become tainted by contact with Western culture in Malaysia. This was compensated for, however, by some foreign students' ideological commitment to reforming Islam in their home nations, this being particularly the case with those students from Britain, Trinidad and South Africa. The present *Shaikh al-Hadith*, Niyamatullah, commented that it had become a custom amongst some Indian Muslims to send the least bright of their children to receive the very economical *dar al-Ulum* education whilst sending the brighter children to state universities. He was concerned that this would effect the quality of the future *ulema*[30]. Despite these problems, however, the foreign students have helped to spread the *Deobandi* message of reform outside the subcontinent and have helped to link it to the wider world of Islam.

Deoband used several methods of spreading the reform message. For this purpose they made great use of *fatwas*. Within ten years of the college's foundation, *istafta* (legal queries) began to arrive in increasing numbers.[31] Muhammad Qasim Nanautawi had taught that false custom led to *shirk*, certainty was required to avoid this danger, particularly in periods of *fitnah* (disorder). To ensure that this certainty was provided Deoband produced *fatwas* in great numbers. From 1911 a register was kept of *fatwas*. In the first century of the college's existence 269,215 *fatwas* were issued, most of which focused on belief and ritual.[32] The *ulema* closely examined customs and beliefs associated with Sufism to see if they contained *bida* or innovation. They attacked anything which sought to elevate the status of the saints. In addition to *fatwas* the *Deobandis* took part in preaching and religious debates. This activity was often directed against Christianity and militant Hindu organisations like the *Arya Samaj*, but much of the debating was between groups within Islam on points of custom and law. These debates helped to establish the boundaries between different Muslim points of view, and assisted the growth of diverse reform movements such as *Ahl-i Hadith* and *Ahl-i Qur'an*.

The *Deobandi* emphasis on custom and *Shari'ah* means that they are deeply conservative; the proliferation of *fatwas* reinforced this conservatism. They had decided that the *dar al-Ulums* would teach only a traditional religious curriculum and would not incorporate any of the syllabus of Western education. Muhammad Qasim Nanautawi had stated that this was so because the tremendous increase of government schools throughout the nineteenth century made it a futile exercise to attempt these Western-style subjects, and it was much more important to concentrate on the religious sciences.[33] He suggested that Deoband graduates could continue in secular education after leaving the college. In practice, however, this is difficult, because the full term of study at the *dar al-Ulum* takes eight years. The question of the curriculum has been a source of considerable debate and criticism within the subcontinent to the present day. It is argued that this puts the *Deobandi* graduates and *ulema* completely out of touch with the modern world and the problems faced by ordinary Muslims living in it. Some of the contemporary students at the college explained that they felt that they only qualified to become members of the *ulema* or teachers in religious institutions, that they felt inadequate to deal with the problems of the modern world. *The Hindustan Times* has criticised the institution of Deoband for being socially and academically backward, and has stated that it needed to 'moderate its methods of work in accordance with present circumstances'.[34]

I attended *Hadith* classes with Shaikh Niyamatullah. The only concessions to the modern world were electric lighting and the *Shaikh's* microphone. The students were seated on the floor before the *Shaikh* who himself sat on a raised wooden platform. He would command a student to read from the relevant *Hadith*. When the *Shaikh* wished the student to stop reciting, he raised his arm. The *Shaikh* then commented in *Urdu* on the passage. When he had ceased his commentary, he again raised his arm and the student continued. Both the *Shaikh* and his students were proud of the fact that this traditional style of teaching *Hadith* was still maintained.

This conservatism further manifests in the *Deobandi* attitude towards *ijtihad*. Cantwell Smith states that 'the door of *ijtihad* is closed tight'.[35] This accusation is also critically made by the members of *Jamaat-i Islami* against the *ulema* of Deoband; the *Deobandis* defend themselves against the accusation by arguing that the door of *ijtihad* remains open but that great caution has to be exercised. Shaikh Niyamatullah argued that:

> if you give permission to do *ijtihad* to every person then there will be a lot of opinions and differences which will cause chaos in the community. You will find a *mujaddid* in every corner. And who is going to follow who. So now we have *ijtihad* for those things which are not being presented in the old books, which have not been dealt with. When we have a new problem to solve, it can be done in a group -*ijma* - the system of *ijma* can be done here, and if all the *ulema* get together and want to do *ijtihad* then it is proper.[36]

It is new problems arising out of the modern world that seem to worry the *Deobandi ulema*. The Vice-Chancellor of Deoband told a meeting of the *ulema* at Cairo in 1963 that *ijtihad* must not be used to establish new views in support of something arising out of present-day Western civilisation that had impressed Muslims. He said, 'we must not be anxious to bring them within the limits of legitimacy (*jawaz*) by searching (for) supporting evidence in the Qur'an and the *Hadith*'.[37] The *Deobandi* conservatism is further reinforced by their emphasis on correct religious practice. This has been reinforced by a lessening of the Sufi influence with its focus on inner experience throughout the twentieth century. When I asked Shaikh Niyamatullah who has been a student and a teacher in Deoband since 1945 what changes he had seen in that time, he replied that:

> before they not only studied, they also meditated, what we call *tasawuf*. They were master in both........so what I am trying to say is that we also have to have master-teachers not just ordinary teachers who just come to learn for the sake of learning, or just to teach for the sake of teaching, or just to learn for the sake of knowledge; there must also be some meditation and inner experience.[38]

This conservatism is joined to the *Deobandis*' belief that they have a special understanding of the reality of God. This belief gives than a feeling of specialness, a sense of being unique. All the reform movements created a sense of conviction amongst their followers that they alone conformed to the *Sunna*. This conviction is central to *Deobandi* belief and self-perception. Their self-definition is that they are the true *Sunni* Muslims, whereas others are deluded or confused by following cultural additions which jeopardise their Islam. Although there is empathy with other reform groups similar to themselves, the *Deobandis* have difficulties with most of the new 'Islamic Movement' organisations such as *Jamaat-i Islami* as they are often critical towards the *ulema* or even actively opposed to them.

Throughout the nineteenth and the first half of the twentieth centuries the *Deobandis*, though increasingly conscious of their differences from other communities, defined themselves in opposition to the ruling non-Muslims. In the face of British power, scientific knowledge and material mastery, the *Deobandis* asserted moral superiority. They urged their followers not to wear British dress or to buy British goods. Many of the *fatwas* encouraged this attitude of moral and spiritual self-confidence. The emphasis on correct religious practice provided a means for people to express their own value in a situation where they were powerless in other areas. There was satisfaction to be gleaned from identifying themselves as morally correct, and in separating themselves from others whom they judged to be wrong.

A sense of pride and self-esteem also resulted from the rejection of local Sufi-based practices in favour of the emulation of regulations demonstrated to be from an authentic text or identification with an idealised historical period in Islam's past. The *pir*-based style of religion of the Sufis made the follower dependent on others for spiritual development. The *pir* mediated between his followers and God, and his position often rested on descent rather than accomplishment. The *Deobandis* taught that the believers were responsible for their own practice. This shift in emphasis put much more weight on individual initiative. Furthermore, the adherence to the high tradition of Islam provided the means for identification with Muslims throughout the world rather than merely with the followers of a local Indian variety of the faith.

Tabligh-i Jamaat

Tabligh-i Jamaat was founded in the late 1920s by Muhammad Ilyas.[39] Ilyas had studied *Hadith* in Deoband in 1908, and continued as an instructor at *Mazahir-i Ulum* in Saharanpur until 1910.[40] After the death of his brother in 1916 he returned from *Hajj* to teach in his father's *madrasa* in Nizzamuddin, South Delhi.[41] The mosque and *madrasa* in Nizzamuddin is now the headquarters of *Tabligh-i Jamaat* activity in India and worldwide. In 1926 Ilyas again visited

Mecca, and returned with the burning conviction that he should take on the task of teaching Islam to the Muslim masses. To achieve this he went on extensive preaching tours.[42] He began his work in Mewat, a district south of Delhi among the Mewatis. The population was only nominally Muslim, and Hindu customs and traditions were prevalent amongst them. *Holi* and *Diwali* were celebrated along with *Moharrum* and *Eid*.[43]

Unlike the members of Deoband, Ilyas did not feel that it was necessary to be a member of the professional *ulema* in order to reform Islam. He believed that every Muslim had a responsibility to generate an awareness of Islam to others. He was not interested in reaching out to non-Muslims, but wanted to create a grassroots movement amongst Muslims to inspire religious renewal. The organisation created to achieve this had no central administrative structure, but Ilyas felt that there was a need for a central leader to co-ordinate the voluntary activities of a network of preaching teams.

The organisation of these preaching teams remains basically unchanged to the present day. They consist of an *Amir* or leader, a *Mutakallim* or speaker, and a *Rahbar* or guide. The size of the team can range from a minimum of three people to a maximum of ten. The *Amir* co-ordinates, selects the speakers and checks the content of the preaching. The *Mutakallim's* task is to inspire the audience into faith and right conduct. The main emphasis is on performance of prayers and instruction in the Qur'an. The *Rahbar* takes care of practical arrangements such as travel, food, laundry and accommodation. Meetings are held with both prominent Muslims in the neighbourhood and with the common people, both singly and in groups. Large gatherings are then organised in halls and mosques. Each member of the preaching team has to pay for his travel and board, and private hospitality is avoided. The teams sleep in the *madrasa* or mosques. There is a strong emphasis on humility and piety, and the overall aim is the self-reform of the members of the teams themselves; others are to be encouraged by example. As the teams progress, those that have been inspired by them are formed in turn into new preaching teams and sent out. In this way the circle of preachers is constantly extended.

Ilyas taught that Muslims should make religious effort a part of their daily lives. When he was teaching in Mewat he insisted that volunteers should preach weekly on basic religious principles in their own locality, and form a group that would tour the neighbourhood. For three days out of every month they should go to nearby villages to hold meetings and to persuade other people to undertake similar tours. In addition to this, they should spend at least four months out of every year away from their homes, visiting centres of religious learning and studying there. Ilyas maintained that the natural way to learn Islam was to follow the Prophet's method of creating a group which, through travel and personal effort, would effectively transmit the religious call to all sections of the community.[44] So as to meet these demands, he felt that Muslims needed to spend time away from their home and vocation in order to concentrate on their faith.

If the preaching team was operating in an urban environment, the group members would preach in a city mosque. After sunset prayers they should go from door-to-door inviting people to come to the mosque where, after prayers, they could listen to the message. If the preaching was taking place in a rural area, however, schools for the poor were to be established at the roadside. The shade of a tree was sought, a sackcloth spread, and water and a *hookah* provided for the sake of hospitality.[45]

Like the *Deobandis*, Ilyas was tolerant of Sufism so long as it was concerned to maintain the *Shari'ah*. Like Deoband and *Ahl-i Hadith*, he considered himself to be true successor of Shah

Wali-allah. In common with Shah Wali-allah, Ilyas believed that the Muslims of his time were ignorant of their faith.[46] He regarded true Muslims to be those who led a life of true faith, observing the Law as revealed by God to His Messenger. He based the aims of the *Tabligh-i Jamaat* on two verses from the *Qur'an*:

> You are the best community sent forth to mankind, you command that which is reputable, and you prevent that which is disreputable and you believe in Allah.

> And let there be of you a community calling others to do good, commanding that which is reputable and prohibiting that which is disreputable.[47]

Ilyas believed that the British were the main opponents of Islam in India at the time, but he never allowed himself to be drawn into political activity. He was unique in his belief that religion and politics should be kept strictly separate. Haq states that Ilyas believed the religious quest to be the sole reason for the emergence of the Muslim *ummah*.[48] In this respect *Tablighi-i Jamaat* differ radically from the views of Maulana Mawdudi and *Jamaat-i Islami* (see Chapter X). Ilyas stated that 'never can a government or any kind of political authority be the objective of Muslims'.[49] Purely as individuals, volunteers were free to hold any individual political view they wished, and there was no objection to their participating in political activities so long as they did not bring their politics into religious affairs. Political discussion was forbidden in the preaching groups. Haq suggests that Ilyas was attempting to adapt the teachings of Islam to the policies of a secular state.[50]

Ilyas's work was primarily directed towards people who were totally ignorant of the basic principles of Islam; he aimed to acquaint them with at least the minimum correct religious observances. He emphasised the fundamentals of the *Shari'ah* and acknowledged the influence on him of Shah Wali-allah, Ahmad Sirhind and the reform *Naqshbandiyya* Sufis.[51] Nielsen describes *Tabligh-i Jamaat* as 'the active pietism of the *Deobandi* movement'.[52]

During Ilyas's lifetime the *Tabligh-i Jamaat* spread out from Mewat to U.P. and the Punjab. After Partition it was carried to Bombay, Gujarat, Maharashtra, Hyderabad and Madras. In 1950 the *Tabligh-i Jamaat* began in Pakistan. Ilyas was succeeded in 1944 by his son Muhammad Yusef who expanded the work phenomenally, both in the subcontinent and abroad. Preaching began in Saudi Arabia, Iraq, Syria, Turkey, Britain, Holland. France, Malaysia, Indonesia, Algeria, Japan and the U.S.A. Of all the subcontinent reform groups, the *Tabligh-i Jamaat* has been the most successful at transforming itself into a worldwide organisation transcending local ethnic and geographical divisions.

Conclusion

Through its network of *dar al-Ulums*, Deoband was able to formalise the ideas and activities of the reformers into a coherent body of knowledge and practice that could be transferred from generation to generation through education. Wherever they were in the world, the *Deobandi*-trained *ulema* would preach the same basic message to Muslims. Education enabled the reform tradition to be passed on in places where Muslims no longer held political power. The emphasis was on strict obedience of the *Shari'ah* and study of the Qur'an and *Hadith*. The reform message of an unsullied Islam required the *Deobandis* to avoid the influence of *Shi'a*, Hinduism, and the British.[53] The resulting isolation combined with the organising of reform doctrine into an institutionalised education system caused the *Deobandis* to develop into a distinct group within subcontinent Islam. This led to fervent discussion between the reformers over aspects of belief and practice, resulting in various other reform groups appearing each with a distinct group identity. The debates and arguments over right practice which went on between the groups helped to reinforce the boundaries between them, and membership thus became an important factor in defining self-identity. Although a Muslim's faith and knowledge of Islam was enhanced by membership and a sense of identity was provided by being a committed member of the *ummah*, on the other hand, sometimes violent antagonism could be felt towards Muslims belonging to other groups.

Francis Robinson surmises that if the '*Deobandis* in Britain are true to their original purposes, they will form a bastion of conservative *Sunni* orthodoxy in the *Hanafi* mould' which will be concerned to continue proselytising through education a 'particular religious personality'.[54] Robinson also indicates that *Tabligh-i Jamaat* is probably the most successful reform movement in the Muslim world.[55] He argues that the missionary activity of *Tablighi Jamaat* carries the energy and orientation of the nineteenth century reformers and Deoband into the twentieth century, and enables the message to reach the Muslim masses.[56] The next chapter will explore the two movements and the relationship between them in the context of Britain.

Endnotes

[1] Rizvi, Sayyid Mahboob, 1980, *History of the Dar al-Ulum Deoband Volume I*, Maulana Abdul Haqq, *Dar al-Ulum*, Deoband, p.76. The two volume official history of the *dar al-Ulum* which was compiled by Rizvi, is more in the nature of primary source material as it contains letters, timetables, curriculums, lists of staff members, numbers of students and their place of origin, and much more data of this kind.

[2] Metcalf, Barbara Daly, 1982, *Islamic Revival in British India: Deoband 1860-1900*, Princeton University Press, New Jersey, p.72.

[3] Rizvi, op.cit, Vol I, p.76.

[4] ibid., p.75.

[5] Metcalf, op.cit, p.72.

[6] ibid.

[7] Rizvi, op.cit., Vol I, p.93.

[8] ibid., p.71.

[9] ibid., p.107.

[10] ibid., p.99.

[11] ibid., p.113.

[12] ibid.

[13] ibid., p.118.

[14] On my visit in 1991 a very large mosque was being constructed within the college grounds as the old one could no longer accommodate the number of students for prayer.

[15] ibid., pp.122-123.

[16] ibid., p.298.

[17] Robinson, Francis, 1984, 'The *Ulema* of Farangi Mahall and their *Adab*', *Moral Conduct and Authority: The Place of Adab in South Asian Islam*, University of California, Berkeley, pp.154-155.

[18] Rizvi, op.cit., Vol I, p.336.

19 ibid., p.67.

20 ibid., p.107.

21 ibid., pp.116-117.

22 Metcalf, op.cit., p.97.

23 ibid., p.80.

24 ibid.

25 ibid., p.156.

26 ibid., p.136.

27 Rizvi, op.cit., Vol.I p.364.

28 Metcalf, op.cit., pp.180-183.

29 Rizvi, op.cit., Vol I, p. 340 cites the college record of graduates. 11,714 from the sub-continent; 1,672 from abroad.

30 Interview with Shaikh Niyamatullah, *Shaikh al-Hadith*, 30th October, 1991, Deoband *dar al-Ulum*, Deoband, India.

31 Rizvi, op.cit., p.143.

32 Metcalf, op.cit., p.146.

33 Rizvi, op.cit., Vol I, p.132.

34 ibid., p.265, cites *The Hindustan Times*, July 16th 1957.

35 Smith, Cantwell, W., 1946, *Modern Islam in India*, Minerva, Lahore, pp.320-321.

36 Interview with Shaikh Niyamatullah, 30th October, 1991.

37 Rizvi, op.cit., Vol.I, p.292.

38 Interview with Shaikh Niyamatullah, 30th october, 1991.

39 Robinson, Francis, 1988, 'Varieties of South Asian Islam', *Research Papers in Ethnic Relations*, no.8, Centre for Research in Ethnic Relations, University of Warwick, p.15.

40 Haq, M. Anwarul, 1972, *The Faith Movement of Mawlana Muhammad Ilyas*, George Allen

& Unwin, London, pp.86-87.

[41] ibid.

[42] ibid., p.91.

[43] ibid., p.100.

[44] ibid., p.145.

[45] ibid., p.151.

[46] ibid.,p.72.

[47] ibid., p.73.

[48] ibid.,p.74.

[49] ibid., p.137.

[50] ibid., p.171.

[51] ibid.,p.179.

[52] Nielson, Jorgen, 1992, *Muslims in Western Europe*, Islamic Surveys, Edinburgh University Press, p.133.

[53] Robinson, 1988, op.cit., pp.4-5.

[54] ibid.,p.6.

[55] ibid.,p.15.

[56] ibid.

9 The reform movement in Britain: Deoband and Tabligh-i Jamaat

Deobandis in Britain

In 1971 the Vice-Chancellor of Deoband *dar al-Ulum* visited Britain. He stayed for a few months and spoke in most of cities in which South Asian Muslims have settled. After leaving Britain, he visited France and Germany. After returning to India he expressed his opinion that:

> Such preachers and *ulema* are urgently required there who, having full command over the English language, may explain the basic principles of Islamic sciences with insight and discrimination to the people of those places and may also live for some time amongst them with financial independence.[1]

The *Deobandis*, however, were established in Britain well before 1971. An examination of the major South Asian Muslim communities in Britain shows that the first mosque to be established often became a *Deobandi* one. Research in Birmingham, Leeds and Bradford reveals a similar pattern of development in each.[2] There the first mosques were established in the late 1950s-early 1960s, and according to the people interviewed had no obvious affiliation to any particular school of thought within Islam. Sher Azam describes the early days in Bradford:

> What happened is that when we came to Britain, the people who were praying in the mosque, I remember, we were praying together. There were no *Deobandis*, no *Barelwis*, no *Ahl-i Hadith*, nobody. We were glad to have a mosque and to be able to pray. Whoever established it usually was going to do it his own way, in his own tradition, but we were glad to see him whether *Deobandi* or *Barelwi*. We didn't mind what it was as long as Islam was practised. I remember that Pir Marouf Husain Shah who was a *Barelwi* used to pray at Howard Street.[3]

A similar pattern occurs in the Jinnah mosque, the first to be established in Leeds.[4] The Howard Street mosque, the Jinnah Mosque and the Walford Road mosque in Birmingham are all now firmly within the *Deobandi* tradition. The key to what happened lies in Sher Azam's statement that 'whoever established it usually was going to do it his own way, in his own tradition'. The founders of the earliest mosques were usually the better-educated migrants who had come from the cities of the subcontinent. They were more confident to organise in a strange environment and were the natural leaders of the community. Initially they founded mosques in various cities wherein all members of the small but growing communities could pray. There are, however, two reasons why the founders of the first mosques would have been sympathetic to the reform tradition of Islam. Firstly, it is generally true to say that the *Deobandi/Barelwi* division is along an urban/rural divide. Sher Azam acknowledges this:

I think it is fair to say that a large number of people who have the *Barelwi* tradition happen to be from the rural areas, while the situation from the *Deobandi* tradition is almost the reverse, they are from the cities and towns. Educated urban migrants were therefore statistically more likely to be sympathetic to the Islam of the reform tradition. Secondly, if a mosque was to be founded in which all the community could pray, it would be necessary to include only the very basics of Islam within the style of worship and the mosque architecture. This was a stripped-down, supposedly culturally-unadulterated, basic style of Islam that was practised to find the common denominator amongst mosque attenders, so that there would be no disagreements within the congregation. Significantly, this also coincided with the basic ethos of the *Deobandis*. The *Barelwis* and other groups were happy to go along with this until the community grew big enough to sustain another mosque. When this happened, the prominent leaders of the other communities founded their own places of worship. This left the original mosque free to declare openly its *Deobandi* sympathies.[5]

The establishment of *Deobandi* mosques did not happen without controversy. Tariq Modood notes that South Asian Muslim migrants in Britain are 'only one generation from rural peasantry'.[6] Many of them originated from Azad Kashmir, one of the poorest and most back-ward areas in Pakistan. The majority of Britain's original Muslim migrants were from rural areas of the subcontinent that were more familiar with the traditional folk-Sufism of the *Barelwis* than with the more orthodox message of the nineteenth century reformers. Many of the Bengali population came from Sylhet, an area famous for its Sufi traditions.[7]

Initially, when all the community attended one mosque, there were almost no members of the *ulema* in the community. The congregation often prayed behind an *imam* who was chosen from amongst their number on the basis of age, education and background. Very often the *imam* would have been selected from the members of the mosque committee, the small group of educated urban, middle-class Muslims who had founded the mosque. With the arrival of families from the subcontinent and the subsequent growth of the community, these mosque committees organised for qualified *ulema* to be sent from the subcontinent as *imams* for the mosques. These *imams* reflected the beliefs of the mosque committee and were often graduates of *Deobandi dar al-Ulums* throughout the subcontinent. This created tensions between the *imam* and the mosque committee on the one hand, and the predominantly *Barelwi*-orientated congregation on the other. Even the more moderate mosque committees, more aware of the very different circumstances in Britain, were not always happy with the fervour of some of the *Deobandi ulema*. Sher Azam graphically describes this situation:

> I think that conflict is...what happens is we have sometimes teachers, *alims*, who are very orthodox, rigid believers in one tradition. They come to speak and they naturally speak in favour of one and they combat the other. And the people who are from other traditions don't like this or have problems... And because of this the Council of Mosques and other institutions have discouraged it in the last few years. And they have also asked the Pakistan government to help us in that, so that they do not send us the identified troublemakers.[8]

This kind of pragmatic realism was arrived at only after several years of painful experience. Often the *imam* would preach against the time-honoured customs still believed in by the congregation, and conflict would break out. Once the *Barelwis* managed to organise themselves behind their own leaders, several very bitter conflicts broke out for control of mosques.[9]

In the late 1960s and throughout the 1970s, the Muslims set about recreating in Britain as many of the institutions of Islam as they could. Religious life was used to reinforce an intense awareness of ethnicity. Amongst the South Asian Muslims this process is reflected in the increase in the number of mosques in Britain. At the end of the 1960s there were only nine, but by 1974 there were 81 registered mosques. Between 1975 and 1980 twenty mosques were registered each year. By 1983 it was estimated that there were 450 mosques in Britain.[10] This number is thought to have increased to around 900 in 1993.

This rapid expansion in the number of mosques resulted in a dramatic increase in the number of *imams* employed from the subcontinent. The *imams* of the first mosques were chosen from the community to lead the prayers (*imam ratib*). Some basic instruction was also given to children. Daniele Joly in her research in Birmingham noted a disapproval in the better organised mosques towards those mosques that only had an *imam ratib*. She suggests that the 'revitalisation of Islam' required an *imam khatib* who was able to preach and instruct the congregation in Islam.[11] She noted that the *imam khatib* was usually a qualified *alim* trained in Islamic theology.[12]

Many of these members of the professional *ulema* as employed from the subcontinent were trained in *Deobandi dar al Ulums*. Deoband education provided its graduates with a thorough training and a unified, consistent curriculum. It also had the reputation in the subcontinent of being the most famous Islamic university after Al Azhar in Egypt. To the middle-class Muslims dominating the mosque committees in Britain, Deoband's reputation for scholarship and religious orthodoxy appeared to provide the essential qualities necessary for strengthening Islamic values amongst the migrants. The *Deobandi* style of Islam had two main aims: to purify the faith from superstitions and folk-belief and to rediscover the pristine faith of the Prophet and his companions through direct study of the Qur'an and the *Hadith*. This suited the new status of the Muslim migrants.

I agree with Werner Schiffauer that the migration of workers has to be seen as a process of urbanisation.[13] Changes in religious consciousness arising from the migration from rural areas to the cities of the subcontinent will inevitably be accentuated by migration to the inner cities of Britain. Schiffauer claims that 'the development of specifically urban (and modern) structures of consciousness can be more clearly observed than in the native country'.[14] Philip Lewis points out that those involved in the transmission of Islam are faced with the dilemma of a culture that is in the process of transformation from orality to literacy.[15] Lewis shows that three traditional features of the transmission of Islamic knowledge are being challenged. He identifies these as 'the essential orality of the Qur'an, a highly personalised transfer of knowledge through accredited teachers and the popularity of *sama*', a state of ecstasy achieved through music and dance.[16] He argues that the introduction of printing to nineteenth century India, so successfully utilised by the *Deobandis*, not only assisted the process of the shift from oral to written culture but also made possible a diminution in dependence on rote learning. Increasing literacy brought a new emphasis on understanding.[17] Schiffauer explains that, in the village, little emphasis was placed on inner conviction. He demonstrates that when Muslims migrate to the city, religious practices are no longer an obligation but become part of a process of 'Islamicisation of the self'[18]. He suggests that in the new environment the individual no longer belongs automatically to a given community but can choose a religious group and a leader on the basis of how convincingly Islam is represented.[19]

In this context, the *Deobandis* were initially in a better position to supply the religious demands of the migrants in the context of their radically altered situation in Britain. Although the migrants were economically and socially at the bottom of the overall British class structure, within their own framework they had risen a class. They had moved from a rural location to an urban one. They were better off financially than they had been in the subcontinent, and they could demonstrate this new-found wealth by sending money and gifts back to relatives in the place of origin. Many were able to build new homes in the villages they had come from and to improve the economies of those areas. In Chapter IV I have argued that identification with the classical tradition of Islam demonstrates improved social status. The *Deobandi* tradition provided the migrants with a means of showing both their new status within their own culture as well as a more rational approach to religion as founded on self-knowledge through a study of the Qur'an and *Hadith*.

Despite the *Deobandis'* claim that the Islam to which they are committed is freed from the accretions of South Asian culture, that it is a universal Islam which unites the *ummah* in the central tenets of orthodoxy, they are in fact linked to various class and ethnic groups of the subcontinent. The South Asian background to this has been discussed in detail in the previous Chapter. This is manifested in Britain by the predominance of Muslims committed to Deoband and originating from India, either via East Africa or as *muhajirs*, Indian Muslims who migrated to Pakistan in 1947.[20] John King and Philip Lewis point out that the Gujarati community plays a significant role in *Deobandi* leadership, a role that is disproportionate to its numerical strength in Britain.[21] The Gujarati migrants are traditionally self-employed merchants who have spread throughout the world. They are familiar with the processes of migration, and compared with other ethnic groups they are highly urbanised. The Urdu-speaking *muhajirs* came from the heartlands of the old Mughal empire where Sufism had never been as prominent as orthodoxy. As they are not native Pakistanis, they have raised the slogan of Islam to fight for their position in Pakistani society. This position is increasingly involved in a power struggle between ethnic and regional groups.[22] For other Muslims in Britain, status may be enhanced by being connected to these two better-educated or materially successful groups through religious affiliation.

The *Deobandi* ethos also coincided with the consolidation of the community around religious/ethnic identity in the third stage of migrant development. The emphasis of the *Deobandi ulema* had always been on the minutiae of correct religious custom and behaviour derived from the *Hadith* rather than on the legalistic interpretation of *fiqh*. This was so in spite of their allegiance to the *Hanafi* school of jurisprudence. As a consequence of this the *Deobandis* stressed correct dress, length and style of beards and correct Islamic manners, all these dictates being derived from the *Sunna* of the Prophet. Essentially, this attitude arose out of the colonial situation in nineteenth century India, in which the Muslims were a powerless minority. In order to protect the community, they set out to construct a fence of correct ritual and practice which defined the parameters of Muslim life. Maulana Muhammad Raza explained that when *Deobandi* students first went to study at Al Azhar, they were surprised to find that Egyptian Muslim scholars were not at all concerned with such issues as the length of beard permissible in Islam.[23] This obsession to copy the details of the Prophet's lifestyle and appearance was not paramount in a Muslim majority state. Such an obsession was a defence mechanism against inundation by the ways of a stronger, more powerful non-Muslim ruling group. Metcalf points out that threaded through all these issues was the essential underlying concept of community. The *Deobandis* needed to define the limits for a group of Muslims where unity was obtained by this kind of shared correct perspective on all issues.[24]

The Muslim migrants in Britain underwent the same process after the arrival of wives and children from the subcontinent. They felt the need to protect themselves as a viable separate religious and cultural community. They were also concerned to protect their womenfolk from the perceived immorality which they saw as innate in the Western liberal ethos of freedom, and to pass on their culture and faith to the younger generation. The *Deobandis* already had a respected tradition of strategies by which to define and protect the community from outsiders. It is not surprising, then, that they were initially successful amongst Muslims in the new environment. The statistics support this. Maulana Muhammad Raza suggests that 90% of Muslims who came to Britain were from a rural background, and that although they were not self-consciously *Barelwi*, in general they believed in the kind of traditional rural Islam as defended by the *Barelwi ulema* and *pirs*. He admits, however, that although there are no official figures of the ratio of *Barelwi/Deobandi* control of mosques nationwide, it is something like 60:40.[25] This ratio is surprising considering the rural backgrounds of the majority of first-generation Muslim migrants and indicates both the *Deobandis'* organisational abilities and the success of the reform message in the new environment of urban Britain.

By 1967 the *Deobandi ulema* had founded the *Majlis Ulema UK*, an organisation designed to coordinate their activities in Britain. The *ulema* needed to come together to organise conferences, to plan tours of visiting preachers, to print calendars and posters, to establish the correct times for prayers and the beginning and end of *Ramadan*, to coordinate their activities against *Qadianis* and *Ahmadiyyas* in Britain[26], to discuss what was *bida* in the British context, and to issue *fatwas* to ensure correct practice by Muslims in Britain, and to operate politically in the campaign for separate Muslim schools for girls, the provision of *Halal* food, and the acceptance of Muslim family law by Parliament.[27]

In spite of the *Deobandi* emphasis on a uniquely religious community as one bound together by observing the essentials of Islam stripped of South Asian cultural accretions, members were not able to override the considerable strength of original national and ethnic identity. In 1974, the *Majlis Ulema UK* divided into the *Jami'at Ulema Britannia* and the *Markazi Jami'at Ulema Britannia*. In 1980, the *Jami'at Ulema Britannia* divided again, and the *Hizbul'ulema* was established for predominantly Gujarati *ulema* who have always been influential amongst the *Deobandis*.[28] The *Jami'at Ulema Britannia* has recently divided again, both organisations keeping the same name. Besides these organisations, there are smaller national groupings of *ulema* that are organised from London, Nottingham and Manchester.[29] There is also the *International Mosque and Muslims Defence Council*, which focuses on welfare activities. It is extremely difficult for an outsider to obtain the precise information on why there are so many splinter groups among the *Deobandi ulema*. Certainly ethnic origin will have an important role to play, since all the organisations involve themselves in the politics of the various subcontinent nations. Nonetheless division has also arisen over arguments on sighting the new moon in order to establish the beginning of *Ramadan* and the dating of *Eid*. Various new organisations have arisen or split off from existing ones when the management have divided amongst themselves. I was not able to establish the details of these internal politics amongst the *Deobandi ulema*, but Sher Azam admits that ethnic background is significant.

> What seems to be happening is that there are people who have come from different areas, and (that) although they have the same tradition, they have come from different countries or different areas; and therefore sometimes it is a language problem, or cultural problems.[30]

The *Deobandi* tradition of issuing *fatwas* has continued in Britain but on nowhere near the scale reached by the *Dar al-Ulum* in India. The *Jami'at Ulema Britannia* has established a sub-committee to function as a *Shari'at Council*.[31] The members of this committee answer the questions of individual Muslims who approach them on matters of the law. Most of the questions are on matters of births, marriages, deaths, wills and mortgages. The collection of *Deobandi fatwas* issued in Pakistan and India is referred to but new *fatwas* are being issued here in Britain. New situations are creating questions unique to the community's presence in Britain. Typical of these concerns are questions about artificial insemination or the method of slaughtering animals. The Council meets every month and liaises with solicitors and barristers who advise them on British law.

Deobandi *dar al-Ulums* in Britain

Although the *Deobandis* have successfully created a network of mosques in Britain and established various organisations of their *ulema*, the most important development is the foundation of *dar al-Ulums* in this country. Deoband came into being originally as a college which was a separate institution from the mosque. The *Deobandi* influence on the community came through their graduates becoming *imams* in the mosques and establishing further colleges. Up to the present time, *Deobandi ulema* have been invited from the subcontinent to become *imams* of the mosques. There has been no central organisation to coordinate this, and each mosque committee has made its own arrangements in the subcontinent. As a result, the *imams* reflect the regional background of the congregation. During my travels around the various communities I found very few *Deobandi imams* who were able to converse in English. This fact has been noted by a number of prominent *Deobandis*, both lay and *ulema*, who are increasingly concerned for the future of the younger generation. Although they voice their concern in regard for the continuation of Islam, like all the groups studied they believe that theirs is the genuine expression of the faith. In practice, therefore, the well-being of Islam really means the perpetuation of their own tradition.

In order to solve this problem, the *Deobandis* have opened several *dar al-Ulums* designed to train qualified *ulema* who are familiar with the problems of life in Britain. These *ulema* also have to be conversant with English, and able to carry the tradition forward to the next generation. I have been able to identify *Deobandi dar al-Ulums* in Bury, Dewsbury[32], Birmingham, Bolton, and the girl's college in Bradford, but Sher Azam states that there are seven in the country.[33] Of these, the most influential are in Bury (founded in 1975) and Dewsbury (founded in 1982). The *dar al-Ulums* provide the means to liberate the *Deobandi* mosques from their dependence upon the subcontinent. They also function to forge links between the mosques, as so many of the latter have sent students to the *dar al-Ulums*.[34] This is especially true of Bury and Dewsbury, which cater for about six hundred students between them.[35] Over the last few years, the leaders of the community have agreed to modify the original *Dars i Nizami* curriculum of Deoband so that it may be more suited to Muslim requirements in Britain.[36] The main addition is a secular timetable in the afternoon that is taught in English. This section of the curriculum is known as *Duniawi*. This addition of a secular curriculum is something which Deoband in India fiercely refuses to do[37]. At Bury and Dewsbury these subjects are chosen from amongst Science, Computer Studies, Mathematics, English Language, Geography, Social Studies, History, Urdu and

Arabic and taught up to GCSE level. It is unlikely that the students will study all of these. Some Bury students informed me that it depended upon the availability of staff and the demands of the timetable.

In the afternoons the sole priority is *Hifz*, the traditional method of learning to recite the Qur'an in Arabic without understanding the meaning.[38] At the age of sixteen the students can enter the full seven year course to study to become *ulema*. It is not until the third year of this course that they can begin to study the Qur'an in order to understand its meaning.[39] In this second period the students will study not only the Qur'an but also the *Hadith*, Arabic, Urdu, Persian and *Hanafi fiqh*. The main text for this is the twelfth century Central Asian work the *Hidayah*, written by Burhanu'd-Din Abu'l-Hasan 'Ali Marghinani. This text consists of fifty-seven volumes covering such topics as basic religious duties, purification and cleanliness, apostasy, criminal offences, peace and war, the status of non-Muslims, commercial transactions, and the administration of government. Each chapter contains the opinions of several jurists and scholars.[40] Persian and Urdu have to be learnt because most of the books which are studied are in those languages. The *Deobandis* were influential in making Urdu the language of Islam in the subcontinent. The language is immensely important to them and has become sacralised second only to Arabic. For three years the students have to learn *tajwid*, the proper pronunciation of Urdu. The language is still the medium of instruction both in the morning classes of the younger boys and in the senior college. When the Qur'an is studied to ascertain its meaning, it is the Urdu translation which is used, not English.[41]

The students still learn in the traditional method of the *dar al-Ulums* in the subcontinent. They sit on the floor and wear traditional South Asian Muslim dress. Television, radio and videos are forbidden.[42] Philip Lewis notes that the method of learning is to master a series of set texts from the *Hadith*. These are read aloud in Arabic and translated into Urdu by the student. The teacher then provides a commentary on the text in which he offers various interpretations of the meaning as offered by different scholars. There is no speculation or individual interpretation of the text by the students. The successful student is able to memorise the text and reproduce the official interpretations.[43] This is exactly the same process that I observed when I sat in on *Hadith* classes in Deoband itself. After completing their studies, the brighter students go on to further studies in Al Azhar or Medina University. Sher Azam told me that the first batch of Bury graduates completing their studies at those universities are due back in Britain next year. He feels that this will correct the situation whereby the present *ulema* have an inadequate command of the English language.

> The main problem is that we have a shortage of teachers, a shortage of *alims* who are as you have quite rightly said that they do not have enough command of English as well as the religion. So we need to fill that gap.[44]

He admits that there is a reluctance on the part of the mosque committees and other *Deobandi* institutions to switch from Urdu to English in the mosque and at meetings.[45]

Sher Azam estimates that there are about 1500 students in the *dar al-Ulums*, including the girls' college in Bradford. He suggests that the present number of colleges does not accommodate the demand from Muslim parents for their children to attend. He states that this demand is growing, and that more *dar al-Ulums* will need to be opened. He admits that this is one reason for the secular curriculum.

> If we just prepare them for *imams* then there are not enough mosques in Britain. It is a lifetime work and unless the person dies there is a tradition that he carries on[46].

He believes that the *dar al-Ulums* have to equip the students to live in Britain, carrying out other professions.[47] He is also concerned that the *ulema* should not become a priesthood.

> It is one of the religions that does not confine you to a life which says that you must not do any other worldly thing. Therefore we have to demonstrate that Islam, being a Muslim, or being an *alim*, or *imam*, you are not forbidden to be taking part in anything else. You can be an *imam* and you can be a barrister, you can be shopkeeper.[48]

There are two problems with this approach. The course already takes seven years, which means that the students graduate at the age of twenty-three if they complete the full course. If the *dar al-Ulum* teaches an 'A' level curriculum it will add another two years. If the students then goes on to a Western university they will be close to thirty before completing their education. Sher Azam admits that very few students would be sufficiently committed for such a long duration of study.[49] He concedes that the emphasis on correct Urdu is very demanding for young British Muslims who are more fluent in English. The demands of learning Urdu prevent the *dar al-Ulums* running 'A' level courses along with the Islamic curriculum.[50] The problem here is that the texts are written in Urdu, and the *Deobandi ulema* are reluctant to abandon a teaching medium with which they are so emotively involved. Sher Azam acknowledges that the problem has been identified, and says that discussions have taken place as to how Urdu may be phased out.[51]

The Problem of Deobandi Isolationism

Previous chapters have explored the history of the development of Deoband in the context of the British conquest of India and the decline of Muslim power. The *Deobandis* responded to the social and political changes brought about by colonialism by creating a self-conscious ideology and constructing a fence around themselves in which the primary focus was group loyalty. This loyalty was expressed as loyalty to the pristine faith of Islam. Barbara Metcalf states that the 'colonial appropriation of public and civic institutions encouraged a kind of retreat to domestic and religious space as sites where cultural values could be reworked and renewed'.[52] In order to ensure that the correct cultural values were maintained within the walls of the threatened community, the *Deobandi ulema* issued *fatwas* on the minutiae of everyday life.

The *Deobandi ulema* kept their distance from the British, suspecting their motives, condemning their lifestyles, and ignoring their secular educational reforms. The *ulema* and their supporters despite their isolation, were vigorously anti-colonial.[53] Their campaign to purify Islam was dynamic and, notwithstanding their traditional orthodoxy, revolutionary and modern in four major areas. Firstly, they defined the world of religion as a private domain that was separate from the public arena of politics and government. This is explicit in Maulana Hasan Ahmad Madani's statement that:

(1) faith was universal and could not be contained within national boundaries, but

(2) nationality was a matter of geography and Muslims were bound to the nation of their birth by obligations of loyalty along with their non-Muslim fellow-citizens.[54].

This allowed the *Deobandis* to liberate themselves from the politics of confrontation as implicit in the dichotomy of *dar al Islam* and *dar al Harb*. It became politically acceptable to live as a minority in a non-Muslim environment if that nation could be defined as *dar al Amn*, a place of tolerance where Muslims could be guaranteed the freedom to practise their faith.[55] Secondly, the *Deobandi ulema* were engaged in an attempt to rationalise the faith. There was the beginning of a move away from rote learning towards a new emphasis on understanding.[56] Thirdly, the *Deobandis* continued the work of the earlier reformers in making classical Islam more accessible to the people by preaching, printing and teaching in the vernacular Urdu. They were able to reach both secular educated elites and educated women, and to move outwards to the populace as a whole. Fourthly, the *Deobandis* were concerned to include women in their vision of Islam.

These four areas of change should enable the *Deobandis* to establish themselves in Britain as a group capable of leading the community forward, but as Daniele Joly notes, the *Deobandis* appear to be 'the least open to British society'.[57] It has to be remembered that the *Deobandis* are a nineteenth century movement of reform. The strategies developed for the reformation and protection of Islam are now routinised and institutionalised into *Deobandi* practice and ideology. Despite the claims of Muslim leaders in Britain that Islam is flexible and able to accommodate modern technological society, the *Deobandis* are still utilising the strategy of withdrawal that they used so successfully in British India in order to protect Islam from the threat of secularisation in modern Britain. The *ulema* are not sufficiently educated to take the move towards the self-understanding of Islam a step further. They hold to the idea that the door of *ijtihad* is closed, which means that all the knowledge required to implement Islam is contained within the interpretations of the classical jurists. All new rulings must not contradict these original pronouncements. The work of the *ulema* is to interpret modern problems in the light of these ancient legal ordinances. They have little knowledge of the criteria of the British educational system and, unless the *dar al-Ulums* can radically transform their approach from the traditional religious education of the subcontinent, it would appear that their graduates are going to be at a disadvantage in relation to Muslim youth who attend state schools and universities. Even the newly-trained British *ulema* may find it difficult to reach those of their own generation who have been educated in Western institutions. Most of the texts which they have studied reflect the problems of pre-industrial rural India. Even though the majority of the pupils will not become members of the *ulema*, the demand for places in the *Deobandi dar al-Ulums* reflects the traditional *Deobandi* fear of contamination by British society.

The *Deobandis* were able to bring their version of Islam to the people of the subcontinent through their use of the vernacular. They established Urdu as the foremost language of South Asian Islam. In Britain, they now cling to the language as an expression of religious elitism. Their children are more fluent in English, and care must be taken to ensure that Urdu does not become a religious language that is used exclusively in worship and the study of revered sacred texts. In Britain the majority of the *Deobandi ulema* fail to see that the original spirit of Deoband was to communicate in the language of the people which is rapidly becoming English.

The *Deobandis* have provided religious education for girls by opening a boarding school in 1987 in Kidderminster, the *Madina ul Uloom Al Islamiyya*, which moved to Bradford in 1992. The school is under the supervision of Bury *dar al-Ulum* and provides the same curriculum. The girls are educated to the level of *alima* and thus become qualified to teach Islam to other women and girls.[58] The *Bihishti Zewar* is still the most influential text for women, in spite of the fact that it is more concerned with eliminating customs and superstitions commonplace in rural India considered to be un-Islamic. Examples of these practices are: trying to cure illnesses by feeding meat to kites or purchasing an animal and setting it free, and placing food at crossroads to appease ghosts.[59] Very few *Deobandi* mosques in Britain have any facilities for women, and they are discouraged from praying there. The *Deobandis* traditionally believe that women should pray at home and not join the congregational prayers at the mosque. It is unlikely that this approach will satisfy future generations of British Muslim women.

The reforms begun by the *Deobandis* have now been continued and surpassed by the radical programmes of the twentieth century lay Islamic movements with their political agenda to revolutionise Islam (see Chapters X & XI). The generally insular and conservative *Deobandis* are still trying to preserve the way of life they established in the subcontinent. This approach ensures that they continue to expend more energy fighting battles imported from the subcontinent concerning the true practice of the faith than in meeting the demands of Islam in Britain. This can be seen both in their vehement criticism of *Shi'as* and *Ahmadiyyas*, and in the contents of the Friday sermons where their *imams* still focus on eliminating those customs of subcontinent Muslims which are considered *bida*.

Deoband and Tabligh-i Jamaat

The *Tablighi* missionary groups first visited Britain in 1956, and continued to come on a regular basis throughout the 1960s.[60] The leaders of the world-wide *Tablighi* organisation in Nizamuddin, Delhi, were intensely aware of the situation of Muslims in Britain and sent the groups to stay and preach in sympathetic mosques.[61] They were concerned that as the prosperity of the Muslim migrants increased in the materialist environment of the West, their worldly ambitions would lead them away from Islam.[62] As the Muslim presence in Britain increased, permission was sought from India to establish a purpose-built centre which could function as the headquarters of *Tabligh-i* activity in Britain and Europe.[63] John King states that they were told to find a place where there was already an established Muslim population which would be familiar with the work of *Tabligh-i Jamaat*.[64] Dewsbury was chosen. Land was purchased in 1972. Construction of the *Markazi Mosque* began in 1977 and was completed in 1980. In 1982 the *dar al-Ulum* was opened.[65]

The mosque and *dar al-Ulum* are situated in South Street in the district of Saville Town, whose population is almost exclusively Muslim. The mosque is very large and impressive, and its green dome and tall minaret dominate the skyline at the end of South Street. Inside, in addition to the two spacious prayer halls there are numerous offices and meeting rooms. These are used by the *imam*, by visitors, and by *Tabligh-i* members in transit. As in Nizamuddin, the mosque functions as the centre of *Tabligh-i* missionary activity. The *qush* (missionary tours) begin and end at Dewsbury. This coming and going is constant. There are missions to be organised throughout Britain, and visitors arrive from India, Pakistan and other centres in Europe and Africa where *Tabligh-i* is active. The centre is used for work, rest and retreat.[66] The *dar al-Ulum* reflects the international structure of *Tabligh-i Jamaat* and has students from Canada, Norway, Denmark, Belgium and France. They all study the *Deobandi* curriculum in Urdu. The presence of the *Tabligh-i* students is noticeable in Dewsbury. They traditionally dress in a white cap, a long *kurta* well below the knees, and pyjamas shortened to above the ankles. They are bearded and often wear sneakers.

The spokesman for the *Tabligh-i Jamaat* in Dewsbury is Muhammad Ishaq Patel, who has been active in Britain since 1956. Ishaq Patel, a Gujarati, denies the title of leader on the grounds that the *Tablighis* are run by a *shura* which meets every Thursday night to discuss strategy. Thursday night is also an open night for Muslims where they can listen to guest *Tabligh-i* preachers. The missionary groups are also briefed and de-briefed.[67]

The *Tabligh-i Jamaat* operates entirely within the Muslim community and is relatively invisible to outsiders. The *Tabligh-i* activists are concerned only with *dawah* amongst Muslims. There is no qualification to join but neither is there any doubt concerning the piety and enthusiasm of *Tabligh-i* volunteers. Their experience of Islam is through internal conversion and conviction since they were all brought back to their faith by the preaching and exemplary lives of the *Tabligh-i* members with whom they came into contact. Their success internationally indicates that they are flexible, and that they adapt well to the diversity of Muslim cultures around the world. They would appear to be capable of transcending both cultural and linguistic differences and the internal divisions amongst the various traditions of Islam as practised by Muslims. *Tabligh-i Jamaat* manages to succeed in this by focussing its efforts strictly upon the essentials of Islam. Kandhalvi states that the *Tablighis* spread the message of reform through a missionary spirit which encourages people to acquire a knowledge of Islam and to work together in brotherly love.[68] It is through the missionary tours that they communicate this message of a return to the true elements of the faith. Volunteers under the leadership of experienced *Tabligh-i* preachers go from house to house, inviting Muslims to attend the mosque and to learn how to pray. They avoid religious controversy and political issues, and focus only on personal religious observation.

The aim of *Tabligh-i Jamaat* is very simple. It urges the members of the Muslim community to remember their faith and return to it. Sher Azam describes them as, 'an Islamic movement that do not want to have anything to do with any sect, politics, or political view... they want to work for self-purification.[69] The *Tabligh-i Jamaat* may indeed welcome Muslims from any background, but their ideological orientation is definitely towards the simple and puritanical ideas of Deoband. Muhammad Ilyas, the founder of *Tabligh-i Jamaat* had been a student of Rashid Ahmad Gangohi (see Appendix E), the founder of Deoband, and was a qualified *Deobandi alim*. The key difference between Muhammad Ilyas and the *Deobandi ulema* was Ilyas's strong missionary impulse.

Sher Azam admits that 'they say that they are not connected with any tradition, but it is fair to say that in Britain most of the work which they do is mainly in *Deobandi* mosques'.[70] The relationship between *Tabligh-i Jamaat* and Deoband has been described in various ways.[71] Muhammad Raza claims that 'all *Tablighis* are *Deobandis* but not all *Deobandis* are *Tablighis*'.[72] This is certainly true only in terms of the inter-relationship in Britain. In other parts of the world where *Tabligh-i* are active, Deoband has no relevance to local Muslims. In the subcontinent, despite the historical and ideological links, *Tabligh-i* preachers are not dependent on the *Deobandi* mosque network as they are in Britain. In this country their preachers are reliant on the mosques both for accommodation and meeting places and in order to know the whereabouts of local Muslims. They have been banned from *Barelwi* mosques, so the old affiliation with Deoband takes on a new and crucial significance.

Felice Dassetto argues that *Tabligh-i Jamaat* has four major ways of disseminating its message: pilgrimage to Mecca; the network of Gujarati merchants in Asia, Africa and Britain; the immigration of workers to European and North American countries; and the Deoband connection.[73] The last three all relate to the Deoband connection. Philip Lewis, Ahmad Andrews and John King all find evidence of *Deobandi* mosques being used by *Tabligh-i Jamaat* when on tour.[74] Andrews does a network analysis of *Deobandi* mosques in Scotland using a computer programme which conclusively demonstrates the role of both the *Deobandi dar al-Ulums* at Bury and Dewsbury, and the activities of *Tabligh-i Jamaat* in maintaining links between the *Deobandi* mosques in Scotland.[75] Once the lines of communication caused by contacts with the *dar al-Ulums* and *Tabligh-i Jamaat* are removed there is little communication at all. This reinforces Nielsen's suggestion that *Tabligh-i Jamaat* and the *dar al-Ulums* are forging and maintaining the *Deobandi* network in Britain.[76]

Philip Lewis notes the relationship between *Tabligh-i Jamaat* and the two *Deobandi dar al-Ulums* in Dewsbury and Bury.[77] The Bury *dar al-Ulum* lacks the very close relationship with *Tabligh-i Jamaat* that exists in Dewsbury but it was established by Yusef Motala, a graduate of Deoband's second most important *dar al Ulum* in India, the *Mazahir-i Ulum* in Saharanpur. The Saharanpur school has maintained a special link with *Tabligh-i Jamaat* as Muhammad Ilyas was a teacher there.[78] Yusef Mutala was directed by his teacher Maulana Zakariya (d.1982) to establish a *dar al-Ulum* in Britain. Maulana Zakariya was an important figure in *Tabligh-i Jamaat* and the writer of their standard text, *Tabligh-i Nisab* (the Preaching course). In Dewsbury, the first aim of the *dar al-Ulum* is to train *Tabligh-i Jamaat* preachers. The students in Dewsbury are expected to spend a weekend every month, some of their holidays, and then a whole year at the end of their studies in missionary activity.[79] Lewis claims that the main method of recruitment for both colleges is the international informal *Tabligh-i* networks.[80]

Lewis's most important discovery concerning the closeness of the relationship between *Deobandi* mosques and *Tabligh-i Jamaat* in Britain is the way in which the *Tabligh-i Nisab* is used by *Deobandi* congregations in Bradford. This book, a compilation of Qur'anic and *Hadith* verses, contains stories of the Prophet's companions. Lewis notes that 'it is a merit/blessing literature rather than application or interpretation of the law to society'.[81] Lewis's research in Bradford demonstrated that sections of the *Tabligh-i Nisab* are daily recited in *Deobandi* mosques for around fifteen minutes after *asr* prayers.[82] Maulana Tassawar ul Haq in Birmingham confirmed that this was *Deobandi* practice throughout the country.[83] These particular passages from the book have become a part of institutionalised *Deobandi* practice that is as unique to their mosques as is the *na't* sung after communal prayers in *Barelwi* mosques.

This connection between British *Deobandis* and *Tablighi Jamaat* is significant for both groups. *Tabligh-i Jamaat's* appeal outside Britain lies in its universal message, but in this country it is limited largely to the *Deobandi* section of the community because of the way in which it spreads and operates. The effect of the *Tabligh-i Jamaat* on the already introverted *Deobandis* is to isolate them even further from the receiving community as *Tabligh-i Jamaat's* activities are contained exclusively within the Muslim community. Dassetto states that 'the relationship with the outside is entrusted in a relatively exclusive way to particular persons'.[84] *Tabligh-i Jamaat* discourages interfaith contacts, and ecumenical approaches by Christian religious leaders have been rebuffed.[85] Members believe that the truth of Islam excludes any kind of attempt to find common ground with other religions. They condemn reading newspapers, watching television, and listening to the radio, fearing the contaminating contact that such practices would bring with the secular culture of Britain. They also condemn videos, music and dance. Lewis argues that the *Deobandi* tradition, heavily influenced by the ethos of *Tabligh-i Jamaat*, is consequently not sympathetic to youth work unless that youth work is a part of revivalist activity.[86]

This stance of isolation from the wider British society was confirmed by my own attempts to gain entry to Dewsbury and Bury. After several telephone calls to Bury I gave up any attempt to visit. On my first few calls I was told that it was not possible to visit or to interview because the principal, Mufti Shabbir, was away. Finally I was told that there was no possibility of visiting the *dar al-Ulum* as no contact was wanted with the non-Muslim world, and that they were not interested in the type of Islamic study pursued by Western academics. I also felt that there was an atmosphere of perhaps justifiable paranoia concerning British media enquiry. This attitude was confirmed by my attempts to visit Dewsbury. An initial telephone inquiry asking for Muhammad Ishaq Patel was met by an invitation to the 'open' Thursday night meeting. On arrival at the mosque I was greeted by a cordon of students surrounding the building and young *Tabligh-i* activists who were acting as security. This was surprising as I had never before been stopped from entering a mosque in this way. On mentioning my appointment, I was escorted to an office where the *shura* was meeting. Muhammad Ishaq Patel apologetically informed me that a mistake had been made; I should never have been invited to the mosque at all. The 'open' night was for Muslims only. Since an error had been made he allowed me to attend the meeting in the mosque, but informed me that I was not allowed to return. When I mentioned that I was personally interested in Islam, he told me to visit my local mosque. He furthermore informed me that the *Tabligh-i Jamaat* were not interested in non-Muslims that were attracted to Islam, only after conversion could they attend *Tabligh-i* meetings.

Inside the mosque I joined several hundred mainly younger Muslims who were having the preaching translated to them in English by a *Tabligh-i* member. The preaching was of an anecdotal style consisting of stories about the Prophet and his companions. Generally these stories emphasised the faith and conviction that existed amongst the first Muslims. The overwhelming message was one of faith. Muhammad Ilyas preferred to call *Tabligh-i Jamaat* 'the faith movement' or *Tahrik-i Iman*.[87] There were a few English converts to Islam in the congregation, but they were all dressed as Pakistanis in *shalwar kamis*. Even their beards were cut to the style of subcontinent Muslims. All the South Asian Muslims were dressed in the same style. Only a few Africans wore their own style of clothes. At the end of the preaching, a *Tabligh-i* member began to call on the congregation to come forward to the front to offer themselves for preaching tours. He stressed that they could volunteer as much time as they had available. I was told that the family system in the West was not strong enough to allow breadwinners to leave on a full preaching tour. Other students, however, were dismissive of this, claiming that faith in Allah should be the Muslim's first priority. Everything else would be taken care of. The invitation to missionary work was made in a fervent manner.

When Muhammad Ishaq Patel noticed that I was still in the mosque and seeing the call to missionary activity and speaking to members of the congregation, he came and took me outside. The atmosphere was one of intense secrecy and a defensive fear of attracting attention from the wider British society. The connection between Deoband and *Tabligh-i Jamaat* was played down. Muhammad Ishaq Patel admitted that there was sympathy for the Deoband school of thought but insisted that the *Tabligh-i Jamaat* were a simple movement existing only in order to strengthen faith and to bring Muslims back to prayer as the basis of their religion. His last words to me told me politely but firmly never to return.

The *Tabligh-i* priority is with *dawah*. The *Deobandi* mosques form a relatively static network, fixed in a geographical location. The mosques serve as a focal point for Muslim communities sympathetic to *Deobandi* traditions. *Tabligh-i Jamaat*, however, is dynamic and mobile, with its teams of preachers moving from mosque to mosque. The itinerant missionaries serve to reinforce the values of introversion already prevalent amongst the *Deobandis*.

Conclusion

In spite of the fact that individual *Deobandi* mosque congregations are often found to be more ethnically diverse in Britain,[88] the *Deobandis* in this country are not free from that tendency of South Asian Muslims to bring the rallying cry of Islam to the defence of particular class structures or ethnic groupings, as in the case of the *muhajirs* in Pakistan. The symbols of doctrine have been called up to defend ethnic, class and/or kinship networks within the South Asian Muslim community. They have also been used by the *Deobandis*, as they were in nineteenth century India, against the external forces of British culture. The policy of the *Deobandis* is still one of isolation and retreat from the old colonial enemy, even though they themselves are now British citizens. They are the products of colonial experience, affected by the social and political changes engendered by that experience. Their relationship with modern Britain is still determined by the strategies that they developed in order to deal with the British presence in India, and the resultant loss of Muslim power. Their attitude to the receiving culture of Britain is consequently fearful and defensive. The first generation of migrants is more likely to respond to the orthodox conservatism of the tradition because, while its members seek a new alternative from the apparently outmoded folk-religion of rural Islam, they do not want to compromise their identity as a people firmly rooted in South Asia. The *Deobandi* tradition is familiar and authoritative.

John King's informants in Birmingham told him that the younger members of the community are statistically under-represented in mosque attendance.[89] One of the problems is that the *Deobandis* are reluctant to enter into social activities outside the sphere of worship. The influence of *Tabligh-i Jamaat* has reinforced this tendency considerably. Members' refusal to participate in Western entertainment and media will alienate many younger British-born and British-educated Muslims. My overall impression confirms that of John King's: the network of mosques representing Deoband and *Tabligh-i Jamaat* has its emphasis firmly placed upon an introspective concern with a particular stance towards the practice of Islam amongst Muslims[90]. Most of the activity with which *Tabligh-i Jamaat* is involved in Britain is designed to reinforce the internal cohesion of a particular ideological section within the British Muslim community. Since this group is still not free from the historical confines of either South Asian politics or South Asian ethnic divisions, the ethos of *Tabligh-i Jamaat* that it is universal is severely compromised by its connection with *Deobandis* in Britain. The *Deobandi* association with *Tabligh-i Jamaat* will further reinforce their insularity. On the other hand, the Deobandis will benefit from the *Tabligh-i Jamaat's* use of their mosque network for their missionary activities as those attracted to the message will continue to frequent the mosques. The close contact will also connect the insular Deobandis to the activities of Tabligh-i Jamaat worldwide and thus help to provide a wider frame of reference than the subcontinent.

Endnotes

[1] Rizvi, S.M., 1980, *The History of the Dar al-Ulum*, Deoband, Vol.I, Maulana Abdul Haq, Deoband, India, p.307-308.

[2] Lewis, Philip, 1993, *Bradford's Muslim Communities and the Reproduction and Representation of Islam*, PhD, University of Leeds, p.75); Geaves, 1989, *Muslims in Leeds*, paper presented for M.A., University of Leeds.

[3] Interview with Sher Azam, ex-President of the Council of Mosques, Bradford, President of Howard Street Mosque, 1st December, 1993.

[4] Geaves, op.cit., p.14-15.

[5] Interview with Sher Azam.

[6] Modood, Tariq, 1990, 'British Asian Muslims and the Rushdie Affair', *Political Quarterly*, 61:2, p.145.

[7] Adams, Caroline, 1987, *Across Seven Seas and Thirteen Rivers*, London.

[8] Interview with Sher Azam.

[9] This happened in several British cities for example Manchester, Birmingham, Oxford, Coventry, Luton amongst others. Alison Shaw explores a typical conflict for control over a mosque between *Deobandis* and *Barelwis* in Oxford (Shaw, Alison, 1988, *A Pakistani Community in Britain*, Blackwell, Oxford).

[10] These figures are taken from 'Muslim Immigration and Settlement in Britain', 1983, *Colloquium on Islam in Europe Today*, College de France, Paris. The 1993 estimate was provided by Maulana Muhammad S. Raza, Muslim College, Ealing.

[11] Joly, Daniele, 1988, 'Making a Place for Islam in British Society: Muslims in Birmingham', *The New Islamic Presence in Western Europe*, ed. Gerholm,Tomas & Lithman, Yngve, George, Mansell, London, p.42.

[12] ibid.

[13] Schiffauer, Walter, 1988, 'Migration and Religiousness', *The New Islamic Presence in Western Europe*, ed. Gerholm, Tomas & Lithman, Yngve, George, Mansell, London, p.156.

[14] ibid.

[15] Lewis, Philip. op.cit., p. 60.

16 ibid., p.63.

17 ibid., p.64.

18 Schiffauer, op.cit., p. 155.

19 ibid., p.154.

20 King, John, 1993, 'Tablighi Jamaat and the Deobandi Mosques in Britain', Paper presented to the Conference on *New Islamic and Related Movements in the West*, 11th December, 1993, The Centre for New Religious Movements, Kings College, London, p.7.

21 ibid. Philip Lewis notes that both Bury and Dewsbury *dar al-Ulums* are managed and run by Gujaratis (op.cit., p.77). All the staff of the girls college in Bradford are also Gujaratis (ibid., p.87).

22 Alavi, Hamza, 1988, 'Pakistan and Islam: Ethnicity and Ideology', *State and Ideology in the Middle-East and Pakistan*, ed. Halliday, Frank and Alavi, Hamza, Macmillan Education, London, pp.71-73.

23 Interview with Maulana Muhammad Shahid Raza Khan, Leicester Islamic Centre, 13th December, 1992.

24 Metcalf, Barbara, Daly, 1992, 'Imagining Community: Polemical Debates in Colonial India', *Religious Controversies in British India - Dialogues in South Asian Languages*, ed. Jones, Kenneth. W., State University of New York Press, New York, p.230.

25 Interview with with Maulana Muhammad Shahid Raza Khan, 10th January 1994.

26 The *Ahmadiyya* are not accepted as Muslims by many Islamic organisations and some Muslim nations, including Pakistan. The orthodox *ulema* of the reform groups are particularly antagonistic towards them. In Britain, the *Ahmadiyya* are well-organised and therefore attract the attention of the *Deobandi ulema*. They produce *anti-Ahmadiyya* literature and warn their communities against them in their sermons.

27 Interview with Maulana Abdul Rashid Rabbani, *Imam* of the Madni Mosque, Dewsbury, 15th January 1994.

28 ibid.

29 Interview with Maulana Tassawar ul Haq, *Imam* of the Tayyabah Mosque, Washwood Heath Road, Birmingham, 3rd January 1994. The *Imam* identified the following as organisations of *Deobandi ulema*: Ahl i Jami'at al Sunnat whose headquarters is in Nottingham; *Jami'at Ahl i Sunnat Wa' Jamaat* in Manchester; *International Majlis Ta'afuz at Nubwat* and the *World Islamic Forum* both in London.

[30] Interview with Sher Azam.

[31] Interview with Maulana Abdul Rashid Rabbani.

[32] The Dewsbury *dar al-Ulum* is part of the European headquarters of *Tabligh-i Jamaat* and is closely linked with their activities. It uses the *Deobandi* curriculum and is staffed by *Deobandi*-trained *ulema*. This arrangement expresses the close relationship between *Deobandis* and *Tabligh-i Jamaat* in Britain.

[33] Interview with Sher Azam.

[34] Lewis, Philip, op.cit., p.76.

[35] Interview with Sher Azam.

[36] ibid.

[37] Interview with Shaikh Niyamatullah, Deoband *dar al-Ulum*, Deoband, U.P, India, 30th October 1991.

[38] Lewis, Philip, op.cit., p.78.

[39] ibid.

[40] Metcalf, Barbara, Daly, 1982, *Islamic Revival in British India: Deoband, 1860-1900*, Princeton University Press, Princeton, pp.20-21.

[41] Lewis, Philip, op.cit., p.79.

[42] ibid., p.80.

[43] ibid.

[44] Interview with Sher Azam.

[45] ibid.

[46] ibid.

[47] ibid.

[48] ibid.

[49] ibid.

[50] ibid.

[51] ibid.

[52] Metcalf, 1992, p.230.

[53] Alavi, op.cit., p.81.

[54] ibid., p.83.

[55] ibid.

[56] Metcalf, 1990, *Perfecting Women: Maulana Ashraf 'Ali Thanawi's Bihishti Zewar*, partial translation and commentary, University of California Press, Berkeley, p.20, notes that Thanawi recommends that teachers using the book must ensure that: 'the girls should always repeat the lesson in their own words.....and if there are two or three of them they should ask each other questions.' Written in 1906, the book is one of the most influential *Deobandi* texts, specifically aimed at Muslim women. The book includes discussions on religious law, household management, Islamic medicine, correct practice of life-cycle rituals, and biographies of righteous women (Metcalf, ND, 'Islam and Custom in Nineteenth Century India', *Contributions to Asian Studies*, Vol.XVII, p.65-6.

[57] Joly, op.cit., p.38.

[58] Interview with Sher Azam.

[59] Metcalf, op.cit., p.74.

[60] Interview with Muhammad Ishaq Patel, Markazi Mosque, *Tabligh-i Jamaat*, Dewsbury, 9th December 1993.

[61] ibid.

[62] King, op.cit., p.10.

[63] Interview with Muhammad Ishaq Patel.

[64] King, op.cit, p.10.

[65] Interview with Muhammad Ishaq Patel.

[66] ibid.

[67] ibid.

[68] Kandhalvi, M., 1931, *Tabligh-i Nisab*, Vol I, Book 5, Anjuman - e Islahul Muslimeen, Dewsbury, p.8-47.

[69] Interview with Sher Azam.

[70] ibid.

[71] Nielsen describes *Tabligh-i Jamaat* as 'the active pietism of the *Deobandi* movement' (Nielsen, Jorgen, 1992, *Muslims in Western Europe*, Islamic Surveys, Edinburgh, p.13).

[72] Interview with Muhammad Raza

[73] Dassetto, Felice, 1988, 'The Tabligh Organisation in Belgium', *The New Islamic Presence in Europe*, ed. Gerholm, Tomas & Lithman, Georg Yngve, Mansell, London, p. 171 Note 4.

[74] King, op.cit, found that *Deobandi* mosques in Birmingham were used by *Tabligh-i Jamaat*; Andrews found the same phenomenon in Scotland (Andrews A., 1993, 'South Asian Sunni Reform Movements in the West: The Lang Scots Mile from Delhi to Dundee, paper presented to the Conference on New Islamic and Related Movements in the West, The Centre for New Religious Movements, 11th December 1993, Kings College, London). Lewis notes that the Howard Street Mosque in Bradford received *Tabligh-i* preachers. Other *Deobandi* mosques in Bradford sent people to the *Tabligh-i* 'open night' in Dewsbury (Lewis, op.cit., p.76).

[75] Andrews, op.cit.,pp.20-22.

[76] Nielsen, op.cit., p.45.

[77] Lewis, op.cit., pp.77-78.

[78] Robinson, Francis, 1988, *Varieties of South Asian Islam*, Research Papers in Ethnic relations, No.8, Centre for Research in Ethnic Relations, University of Warwick, p.15.

[79] Lewis, op.cit., p.78.

[80] ibid., p.77.

[81] ibid., p.82.

[82] ibid., p.80.

[83] Interview with Imam Tassawar al Huq.

[84] Dassetto, op.cit., 1988, p.163.

[85] King, op.cit., 1993, p.13.

[86] Lewis, op.cit., 1993, p.88.

[87] Robinson, op.cit., p.15.

[88] Lewis, op.cit. p.75.

[89] King, op.cit., p.27.

[90] ibid., p.29.

10 Jamaat-i Islami in India and Pakistan

Introduction

Chapter VII and VIII demonstrate the responses of the subcontinent reform movements in the eighteenth and nineteenth centuries to the loss of Muslim power. Their policy of isolating themselves and focusing on reform amongst Muslims was initially successful in safeguarding the community from the impact of invading non-Muslim culture and ideas. In the twentieth century, however, many Muslims felt that the *ulema* had become hidebound, conservative, and totally out of touch with the problems of the modern world. The new political situation demanded confrontation with the Western colonial powers. As the Muslim nations struggled for independence, the question arose of how the newly-emerging nation states should be governed. The *ulema's* conservative attitudes to the modern world placed them in a weak position to influence this debate. In particular, their attitude to *ijtihad* made it particularly difficult for them to adapt to the rapid changes brought about by science and technology.

In the twentieth century, throughout the Muslim world, groups arose that challenged the secular and nationalist ideas of the ruling classes on the grounds that they were tainted by Western imperialism and were not Islamic. They also criticised the *ulema*. The twentieth century revivalists were not prepared to be apologists for Islam; they condemned the West and its values and asserted the self-sufficiency and superiority of Islam. They attacked both the ethos of personal piety and the rise of ethnic or national consciousness.[1] Islam, they urged, had to be a comprehensive ideology for personal and public life. It had to be the only foundation upon which Muslim society and state could be built. They combined their religious ideas with social and political activism; true believers were distinguished from their fellow Muslims and were to be totally committed to the struggle to transform society along Islamic lines. These groups mobilised opposition against what they saw as corrupt Westernised elites. This situation was exacerbated by the contradiction between the poverty of the masses and the affluence of the privileged classes.

Pakistan

The creation of the independent state of Pakistan was inspired by the Muslim League's claim that the Muslims of India formed a separate nation. This communal definition of nationhood was reinforced by arguments emphasising a distinct Islamic way of life. This campaign for the creation of an independent Muslim state was reinforced by the idea at the heart of Islam of an independent political community as the best arena for religious activity. It has been demonstrated in Chapter VI that in the subcontinent this impulse for Muslim separatism had stemmed from the 19th century revivalists inspired by Shah Wali-allah.

The important point here is that to the Muslims of the subcontinent, the attainment of a state of their own was a religious as well as a political event. One of the new state's main aims was to enable Muslims once more to be able to implement their faith in the political realm. This aspiration is explicit in both the 1949 *Objective Resolution* presented to Parliament by the Prime Minister, Liaqat Ali Khan, and the 1956 *Constitution of Pakistan*. The *Objective Resolution* categorically states that Islam is the raison d'être for the creation of the nation in that it should serve as the main source of inspiration for 'the principles of democracy, freedom, equality, tolerance, and social justice as enunciated by Islam', and that these ideals should be fully observed in Pakistan.[2] The *Constitution* itself begins with the declaration that

> Sovereignty over the entire universe belongs to God Almighty alone and the authority which He has delegated to the State of Pakistan through its people, after being exercised within the limits prescribed by Him, is a sacred trust.[3]

Ironically one of the new state's first problems arose out of this Islamic ethos that was inbuilt into the logic of Muslim nationalism. There were those who took the ideal of an Islamic state far more literally and much more seriously. There were those who believed that the new nation had been created for the sole purpose of showing the world a model Islamic state that was based on the sovereignty of Allah rather than on the secular idea of the sovereignty of the people. These groups emphatically declared that Islam was a better alternative to both capitalism and communism. They argued that in Islam there is no distinction between the spiritual and the temporal realm: the matter of worldly life is not left to the discretion of human beings; there is a clearly defined path based on revelation; and God has commissioned the state to enforce these commands. The Medinan state under the Prophet and the first four Caliphs was used as the standard reference for this ideal.

The new state of Pakistan needed to establish an industrial base. This required the expansion and dissemination of modern skills through an education system that was secular and not dependent on received religious wisdom. This transformation of Pakistani society was a challenge to traditional views. The *ulema* had failed to come to terms with the modernisation process; increasingly the urban educated sectors of the population saw them as superstitious and clinging on to outmoded traditional ideas which were irrelevant in the modern technological world. The secularisation of culture, however, which accompanied the processes of urbanisation and the development of modern science and technology, was seen by many as the heritage of the West and as a legacy of the colonial period. Independence had not freed the Muslim nations from the colonial influence of the Western powers; it had merely changed the form of the oppression. The modernist trend in Islam was suspected of compromising with the exploiters. The old reform message that Islam needed to be cleansed of any kind of cultural influence, whether it originated in the West or in the historical heritage of Hindu India appeared in a new form. The message of the new revivalists was that a purified Islam practised within the context of an Islamic state would provide the proper ideological framework for the nation to address itself to modernisation. This new Islamic Movement was to appear in the Arab world in groups like *Ikhwan*. In the subcontinent it was spearheaded by *Jamaat-i Islami*, led by its founder Maulana Mawdudi (1903-1979).

Maulana Mawdudi - a brief biography

Maulana Mawdudi was born in Aurangabad, Hyderabad, India to a family with a long tradition of spiritual leadership within the *Chishti* Sufi order.[4] His father (Ahmad Hasan), a lawyer and a highly religious man, an early companion of Sir Sayyid Ahmad Khan,[5] sent his son to be educated at *Madrasa Fawqaniyah*, which combined modern Western and traditional Islamic education.[6] Mawdudi went on to be an undergraduate at the *dar al-Ulum* in Hyderabad, but had to abandon his studies when his father fell ill and died.[7] From this point onwards, he was essentially self-educated. During the 1920's he learnt Arabic, Persian and English.

During this period his interest in politics began and he turned to journalism in order to make a living. He moved to Delhi to become the editor of *Muslim* (1921-1923) and, later, *Al-Jam'iyat* (1925-1928). Both of these newspapers were organs of the orthodox *Deobandi Jam'iat i Ulema i Hind*.[8] His principle interests during this period were journalistic and academic. In 1928 he resigned from *Al-Jam'iyat* and returned to Hyderabad, where he concentrated on research and writing. In 1930 he published his first major book, *Al Jihad Fi al Islam*, a scholarly treatise on the Islamic laws of war and peace.[9]

In 1932 Mawdudi started his own journal, *Tarjuman al Qur'an*. This he used as the main means of propagating his ideas on Islamic revival, a movement which he described as 'Islamic renaissance'. In *Tarjuman al Qur'an* he focussed upon issues arising out of the conflict between the Islamic and the Western world view. His methodology was to study everything concerning both, passing judgement according to their conformity with the teachings of the Qur'an and *Sunna*[10]. On Islamic grounds he condemned the ideologies of democracy, nationalism, and secularism which were growing apace amongst Indians of all religious affiliations in the Independence Movement.[11] Mawdudi was particularly hostile to nationalism, which he saw as totally incompatible with Islam and the concept of *ummah*.

Between 1937 and 1947 he opposed the Indian nationalist position of Madani and the Deoband *ulema* because of their alliance with the Congress Party. In 1939, however, Mawdudi began to attack ,Jinnah and the Muslim League, denouncing its secular leadership and arguing that the League was only a Westernised elite that desired Muslim nationalism, declaring that it wanted this solely to further its own interests. Mawdudi declared himself to be interested not in self-determination or the political freedom of the Indian Muslims, but in the rule of Islam; he sought to establish a purely Islamic theocracy. He argued that Jinnah's concept of Pakistan would lead to the formation of a pagan state and he criticised the League's leadership as follows:

> Not a single leader of the Muslim League from Jinnah himself to the rank and file has an Islamic mentality or Islamic habits of thought, or looks at political and social problems from the Islamic viewpoint...their ignoble role is to safeguard merely the material interests of Indian Muslims by every possible political manoeuvre or trickery.[12]

He moved to Pathankot, in the eastern part of the Punjab, where in collaboration with Iqbal, he established an academic research centre called *Dar al Islam*. Their vision was to train scholars who would produce works of outstanding quality on Islam and carry out the reconstruction of Islamic Law in the post-colonial era.[13]

This move began to give actuality to Mawdudi's belief that the capabilities of the best minds at a given moment in history should be mobilised into a *Jihad* movement to bring about Islamic revolution. In 1941 he was to make a much more ambitious and comprehensive step in this direction. He established *Jamaat-i Islami*, appointing himself *amir*, a position which he held until his retirement on the grounds of ill-health in 1972.[14] In 1947, despite his opposition to the formation of Pakistan, he migrated to the newly-formed nation. In 1948 he modified his attitude to the existence of the state of Pakistan. He decided to support Pakistan under the principle of 'gradualism'. The resources of *Jamaat-i Islami* were utilised in the political arena to work towards the Islamicisation of the law and constitution of the state. Throughout the 1950s until his death, Mawdudi and the *Jamaat* were particularly active in any issue which related to the Islamic identity of Pakistan.

The ideas of Maulana Mawdudi

Ishtiaq Ahmed states that 'Mawdudi is considered one of the ablest theoreticians of the Islamic state in the Muslim world'[15]. Mawdudi consistantly argued that the first step in bringing about a genuine Islamic renaissance was to convert the state to Islam. The *Shari'ah* had to be fully restored, and all laws from other sources repealed. Secular-minded officials had to be replaced, and all the media of education and mass communication had to be utilised towards the creation of an Islamic consciousness in the populaces.[16] This is because Islam is more than just a personal faith; it is a complete way of life (*Din*). He stressed that the *Shari'ah* does not recognise any division between religion and other aspects of life, especially between religion and the state. He saw the division between religion and state as a Western invention.

Mawdudi argued that the need for an Islamic state arose from the nature of universal order. God's law governs all creation, but man suffers from the delusion of independence. Nature is under the sway of Islam because it obeys God's natural law, but human beings have the capacity to choose to obey or disobey. In order that they may make the correct choice there is revelation. Human behaviour is governed, therefore, by revealed law just as the universe is ruled by natural law. The law which governs human behaviour is fully revealed in the Qur'an and *Sunna* of the Prophet.[17] The key to understanding Mawdudi's ideas on the necessity of the Islamic state is his interpretation of the *Kalima*. He saw the major problem of history not as mankind's denial of the existence of one God but as mankind's unwillingness or refusal to recognise the sovereignty of God.[18] Mawdudi interpreted the *Kalima* as a statement which not only proclaims the uniqueness of God as the Creator or sole object of worship, but also expresses the uniqueness of God as the Master, Sovereign, Lord and law-giver. God alone has the right to command.[19]

It is this revolutionary interpretation of the *Kalima* which provided Mawdudi with his main critique of the intrusion of Western ideas and philosophy into Muslim society. Secularism, nationalism and Western models for democracy are all based on the idea of the sovereignty of the people. Mawdudi argued that the acceptance of any other authority as sovereign is a form of *shirk*, and as such raises that authority to the status of being a partner with Allah.[20] The moral evil of the age, which all true Muslims should actively oppose, consists of accepting other sovereigns such as 'the will of the people' or the laws of worldly rulers and setting them over and above God. True Islamic faith must strive for the creation of an Islamic society as well as individual righteousness. Islam leads individuals to develop a community of faith which promotes social change by creating a society fully obedient to God's law. Mawdudi called this state 'the Caliphate based on the Prophetic pattern'.[21] It is a human caliphate under the sovereignty of God with no power to make new laws, but it will work within the limits prescribed by Allah by fully implementing the *Shari'ah*. Ideally, the state would be ruled by an *amir* in consultation with a council (*shura*). Mawdudi called this a 'theo-democracy' as it was based on the equality of all Muslims under the sovereignty of Allah. Again and again, Mawdudi returned to the period of the Prophet and the 'four rightly guided Caliphs' as his blueprint regarding everything he said about the Islamic state and its constitution.[22] Mawdudi, however, was not against the discoveries of science and technology, which he believed should be used to further the progress of the Islamic state. In order to achieve the goal of the Islamic state and the total change in consciousness that this would require, it is necessary that an organised movement should be launched that would culminate in in the establishment of a state committed to Islam. This organised movement would strive to achieve the revolutionary direction that Mawdudi's vision gives to Islam.

This movement is given organisational form in the *Jamaat-i Islami*. It would help to create a revolution to overthrow the new but sinful leaders of the Muslim world, and replace them with the faithful who would follow God as the legal sovereign.[23] A Muslim society that either creates its own constitution or borrows legal or constitutional elements from outside Islam breaks its covenant with God and therefore loses its right to be considered Islamic.[24] The *Shari'ah* alone is the codification of the contract laid down in the Qur'an.

Mawdudi, like Shah Wali-allah, emphasised the importance of the *Shari'ah* but also advocated tolerance and flexibility in interpretation.[25] He believed, like Shah Wali-allah, that the doors of *ijtihad* are never closed. In an Islamic state the Legislature can interpret laws but it cannot make them.[26] Mawdudi suggests that *Qiyas* (analogy) can be used. Legislators and scholars can also delve into the spirit of the *Shari'ah* and the intention of the Prophet in order to formulate specific rules accordingly.

He also attacked the conservative *ulema* for adding too many rules of their own invention to the fundamental commands of the Qur'an and *Sunna*. He criticised the *ulema* for being unable to distinguish between the complex structure of the mediaeval legal schools and the basics of Islam. He argued that a Muslim may use his or her own reasoning powers against the *ulema*, or even use personal *taffaqa* (legal deduction) to determine exactly what the Qur'anic commands mean to mankind. Mawdudi argued that most of the *ulema* deny the right of interpretation, because they consider it to have been completed by the great legalists of the past,[27] which meant that the gate of *ijtihad* was closed. Mawdudi's emphasis on the use of reason required a high level of understanding of their religion from individual Muslims. Certainly, he said, all should be able to read and understand the Qur'an for themselves; rote learning was not sufficient. Consequently, Mawdudi's *Jamaat-i Islami* placed great emphasis on education and training for laymen. Charles Adams suggests that Mawdudi's emphasis on reason links him to the modernists, influenced by Western ideas, who argue that Islam must be rational.[28] In fact, Mawdudi's ideas concerning the use of reason need not in fact be derived from Western sources, since they link him directly to the tradition of reformers following in the influential footsteps of Shah Wali-allah.

Maulana Mawdudi's direct legacy from Shah Wali-allah is also seen in his urgent plea for Muslims to return to the essence of an Islam firmly based on the Qur'an and *Sunna*. Although there can be no deviation from the fundamentals of Islam, Mawdudi did not enforce such outward forms as wearing special dress, certain kinds of appearance, extra prayers, or the adoption of an ascetic lifestyle. He is also tolerant on *fiqh*, recognising all the major legal schools of Islam. This is because Mawdudi believed that Muslims should go direct to the Qur'an and *Sunna*, and only then consult *fiqh*, if necessary. Despite this flexibility, however, Mawdudi was himself deeply conservative. His own *tafsir* of the Qur'an, *Tafhim al Qur'an*, is so literal that it barely leaves any scope for interpretation at all. In Gilani's observations of Maulana Mawdudi he notes that Mawdudi's beard was cut to 'one and half fist long' and that his hair was 'straight, combing backwards, sloping on to an evenly cut straight base at the back of the neck'.[29] Gilani comments that this is according to the Sunna. Despite Mawdudi teaching that there is no such thing as Islamic dress except insofar as people should be modest according to the Qur'an's command, Gilani states that 'In the matter of dress he (Mawdudi) is quite a nationalist. He accepts that certain dresses of other cultures are 'permissible' according to the *Shari'ah*, but he would not prefer those, lest it might express inferiority complex'.[30] This conservatism is demonstrated by Mawdudi's grave, which is simply an unmarked mound of earth on the lawn of his house in Lahore.

The most important example of Mawdudi's conservatism is his attitude towards Muslim women. Zakaria Bashier claims that although Mawdudi was not a traditionalist in many of his views, he certainly was on the question of women. He notes that Mawdudi analysed and defended the traditionalist position in regard to women in his book *al-Hijab*, in which he argued that covering the face is part of the Muslim woman's veil.[31] Mawdudi believed that Islam has different areas of activity for men and women and that women should remain in the confines of the home, while men devote themselves to activities in the socio-economic sphere. If women should have to go out of their homes for any reason, they should be fully veiled and covered.[32]

Above all, Mawdudi believed that the transformation of society required political power. To this end he deeply involved himself in the politics of Pakistan and India, although his stance is thoroughly religious in character. Mawdudi's political campaign is the inevitable conclusion of his belief in the sovereignty of God. He emphasised that he was not expounding a new interpretation of Islam or creating sectarian differences, but only attempting to return to the original faith stripped of cultural impurity. His deep involvement in the politics of Pakistan may have undermined this somewhat, but his stance based on a return to the principles of Qur'an and *Sunna* echoes the position of Islamic revivalists throughout the Muslim world.

Jamaat-i Islami - a vehicle for Mawdudi's ideas

Maulana Mawdudi created the organisation of *Jamaat-i Islam* in 1941 with the idea of training committed members who would work tirelessly towards the foundation of an Islamic state in the subcontinent. The organisation was a change from the earlier reform movements in that these had been primarily concerned with how to be Muslim under colonial rule. *Jamaat-i Islami* tackled the wider question of how to be Muslim when faced with the overall domination of Western civilisation. The solution was to create a state which would simultaneously embody the teachings of Islam and exemplify these to both the West and other Muslim nations. On Partition in 1947, Mawdudi divided the organisation into two separate and independent parts: one for India and the other for Pakistan. The organisation in Pakistan was given the task of implementing Maulana Mawdudi's four-point programme: the first aim was intellectual, in that there should be a campaign to educate Muslims in the teachings of Islam, purged of all foreign accretions and false ideas; the second aim was to carry the message of Islam to all people in Pakistan who were inclined to work for the establishment of righteousness in human society, and then to mould them into an efficient organisation; the third part of the programme was to persuade committed Muslims to dedicate themselves to bringing about a complete change in society based on the teachings of Islam; and finally, fourthly, they should work for a complete change of leadership, both intellectual and political. Thus the state could become truly Islamic once its affairs were directed by people of clear Islamic vision and commitment.[33]

To succeed in these goals, trained cells of Islamic activists were formed to work towards achieving social and political leadership. *Jamaat-i Islami* remained committed to the idea of the Islamic state in which there would be Islamic government, economic institutions, banking, and the implementation of the *Shari'ah* in both public and private life. The organisation functioned as an efficient opposition to the government, and played a major role in the overthrow of Bhutto in 1977. This resulted in some of their leaders becoming ministers under Zia al Haq, and in several of their policies being implemented. There were major reforms of the penal code, which reintroduced traditional Islamic punishments for certain offences. A *Shari'ah* judiciary was established, but it had to operate in tandem with qualified common law judges. There were also fiscal and economic reforms involving payment of *zakat* and experimental forms of free banking. Finally, the government introduced a national Islamic curriculum into schools; separate universities were opened for women; and Urdu replaced English as the language of higher education.

The major problem for the further progress of *Jamaat-i Islami* was its inability to capture the support of either the masses or the ruling classes. Its numbers have always remained relatively small. Even in 1974, during the regime of Zia, there were only 2,500 members, although there were several hundred thousand sympathisers who to varying degrees had participated in its training programmes.[34] The masses, although emotive in their loyalty to Islam, were uneducated. Their religion was not the ideological faith of *Jamaat-i Islami* member but the folk Islam of the village. Their loyalty was to the local *imam* or *pir*. Maulana Mawdudi's appeal was to the lower middle-classes, urban discontents, and idealistic youth. The members of *Jamaat-i Islami* tended to be drawn from the products of Western modernisation: engineers, teachers and lawyers. These were the new young rising middle-classes who were opposed to the ruling class with whom they competed for control. They were opposed to the *ulema* and *pirs* on the grounds that they found them ignorant and superstitious, and opposed to the West on the grounds of post-colonial exploitation. Mawdudi's rational but vehement attack on both Western ideology and the Islam of the clerics appealed to them. It gave them an ideology and an identity with which to fight for their place in their society.

The organisational structure of Jamaat-i Islami

Jamaat-i Islami is a lay organisation with a qualitative hierarchical pyramid structure. At the top of the pyramid is the *Amir*, who is elected by the members every five years. The Amir is assisted in running the organisation by a *Shura*, or consultative council. This council is comprised of one hundred and forty members, seventy of whom are directly elected by the wider membership and another seventy of whom are appointed. The *Shura* consists of scholars of Islam and 'persons of piety and activity'[35] who formulate its decisions on major issues and who also decide on the day-to-day policy decisions of the *Jamaat*. Sometimes the *Shura* nominates a committee of *ulema* to review certain issues relating to *fiqh*. Under this central *Shura* come the provincial organisations which are run by an elected General Secretary and committee. Again, this central organisation for each province in Pakistan supervises the activities of the branches in its area.[36] In October 1992 there were 75 district branches in Pakistan. Each branch elects its own organising committee. The branches are composed of members, associate members, workers, and sympathisers. This division is a qualitative one. The workers attend training programmes and become involved in *Jamaat-i Islami* activities. After this they progress according to their development in the training programmes, their involvement in the organisation, and the quality of the Islamic life they are seen to be leading. The training is rigorous, and the standard expected of members very high. In 1992 there were 7,000 full members. There are no figures for the other categories, but it is estimated that there are roughly a million active supporters of the *Jamaat* in Pakistan.[37] *Jamaat-i Islami* leadership is aware of its inability to attract a wide cross-section of the Pakistan population and has specialised sections which work with specific groups. In order to attract the rural population there is a separate organisation to improve the lives of peasant farmers. The objective of this group is to introduce the religious message whilst working with the people on a variety of agricultural and socio-environmental projects. The *Jamaat* has also organised its own trade unions for the workers in urban industries. Through these two operations the *Jamaat* hopes to increase its popularity amongst the common people.[38] This kind of activity has resulted in the establishment of a social work programme (*Paasban*). According to Maulana Shahid Raza this programme is criticised by many in the leadership of *Jamaat-i Islami* because they fear that an expansion of this kind of social activity will engulf the rigid selectiveness of the *Jamaat's* structure.[39] There are also separate professional organisations for teachers and doctors, and the very successful students' organisation.

The nerve centre of these well-organised and tightly disciplined groups is the national headquarters in Lahore. The Mansurah complex is situated in the suburbs of the city, and forms a self-contained township in its own right. Altogether about one hundred families are housed on the complex. About 25 people are employed full-time in running the central offices, while the remainder work outside the organisation in their chosen professions.

Many of the various buildings are concerned with education. The *Islamic Research Academy* engages fifteen scholars in translating books, editing papers, and producing some original works. There is also the *Centre for Islamic Education* situated in the large and recently constructed mosque complex. Some of the students live on campus and some live nearby. Besides teaching the Qur'an, *Hadith*, Arabic and Urdu, the school also has English Language, Economics and Political Science on the curriculum. The students are presented as private candidates to the examinations of the Punjab University or the Board of Secondary Education. The final level of achievement is accepted as an M.A. degree in Islamic Studies awarded by the Punjab University. There are also several other schools: a small primary school for girls and two high schools, one for boys and one for girls. These schools take in children from the surrounding area as well as the children of the families living in the complex. There is also a small school which specialises in memorising the complete Qur'an, and another Islamic college which takes in students from countries where Islam is weak and Muslims a minority. This college is primarily for students from China and the former Soviet Union. The predominance of schools and colleges in Mansurah indicates the importance which the *Jamaat* gives to education in its *dawah* activities.

Besides these institutions there is a small out-patient clinic for local people, and, very interestingly, an advanced surgical hospital set up for severely wounded Afghan *mujahiddin*. *Jamaat-i Islami* also had two hospitals nearer the Afghanistan border in Quetta and Peshawar. The hospitals and the college for educating Muslim minority students from Central Asia demonstrates that the activities of the Pakistan *Jamaat-i Islami* extend beyond the confines of the country, linking the organisation to the Islamic Movement worldwide.

Islami Jami'at-i Talaba

Islami Jami'at-i Talaba was founded on December 3rd 1947 to propagate the message to the campuses and schools of Pakistan. The *Talaba* is organised on the same hierarchical principle as *Jamaat-i Islami*, but the elections for office in the organisation are held annually. This is a practical arrangement since membership of the *Talaba* ends when the student completes full-time education.[40] There are six hundred full members, in addition to which the *Talaba* has widespread support in the campuses and schools of Pakistan. Membership of the *Talaba* does not constitute membership of *Jamaat-i Islami* in spite of the equally rigorous training programmes.[41] It says something for the quality of *Jamaat-i Islami* membership that the outgoing Secretary-General of the *Talaba*, who had also been President of the Students' Union at the Punjab University, was accepted only as an Associate Member of *Jamaat-i Islami*.[42] The *Talaba* operates independently of the *Jamaat*, and has its own headquarters in the city next door to the house where Maulana Mawdudi resided until his death in 1979. Every afternoon from their schools and colleges the students come to their *Talaba* headquarters. Here they engage in training programmes, run the various departments (Mass media, Publications, and Finance), and go out on various organised *dawah* activities. There is an atmosphere of intense activity.

The *Talaba* has a variety of programmes. There is literature aimed particularly at schoolchildren which includes stories from Islam's past. The *Talaba* organises picnics for schoolchildren in which Islam is taught through stories and games.[43] The main work, however, goes on in the universities. Typical of student organisations, the *Talaba* produces literature, holds debates, sells newspapers, and proselytises on campus, visits door-to-door in the student quarters, and holds large rallies and meetings.[44] The *Talaba* are also involved in student politics and social activities at a more general level. They have fought many campaigns to better the conditions of students and, on an individual level, they try to assist poor students with funds or even with clothes and food where necessary. To these activities they bring with them the level of organisation and discipline which is considered the normal standard in *Jamaat-i Islami*, but which is generally unusual in the subcontinent. As a result of this success the *Talaba* is popular amongst students, and its members are voted into student union positions right across the country.

The involvement of the *Talaba* in student union activities is particularly noticeable in the Punjab University, Lahore, which has been transformed by *Talaba* activity. For the last twenty years the *Talaba* have won every election on the university campus, despite attempts by other political groups to defeat them by forming alliances. A visit to the campus revealed the dominant influence the *Talaba* has over the students' activities and behaviour. Although the majority are not actually following *Talaba* principles, there is immense respect for those who do. Professor Zafarullah Sheikh, the Dean of the Faculty of Engineering and Technology, stressed the high moral standards of the *Talaba* youth, and observed that these days the campus is used for youth rallies which preach the standards and morality of Islam. He pointed out that the mosque, which had fallen into disuse, is now packed every Friday afternoon. After the prayers, the preaching is done by *Talaba* members. Dr. Sheikh claims that this transformation has come about because of the high standard of personal morality and behaviour amongst the *Talaba*, and their overwhelming success in holding all the higher offices in the Student Union for the last twenty years. Dr. Sheikh also commented that the students were now working harder and obtaining better degrees. He stated that this made the *Talaba* very popular amongst the staff of the University, regardless of their own religious or political affiliation.[45]

There is no doubt that the members emphasise academic performance as well as religious activity. The *Talaba* insists that its members get the best results possible in all their fields of endeavour. This echoes Mawdudi's belief that revolution had to begin at the top of society by replacing the traditional rulers with new leaders whose priority was Islam. The *Talaba* has established an organisation in conjunction with *Jamaat-i Islami* whose objective is to select the brightest students of the *Jamaat* as early as the intermediate high school level and bring them under special observation and training. The aim of this operation is to guide the careers of society's most gifted members into the armed forces, the bureaucracy, government, economy, technology and medicine.[46] In this way the *Jamaat* has long-term plans to bring about Mawdudi's hopes for a transformation of Pakistani society.

Jamaat-i Islami Hind

Jamaat-i Islami in India is a completely separate organisation with its own *Amir* and *Shura*. The organisational structure is the same as in Pakistan. The organisation is active in nearly all of India's states, but in keeping with the *Jamaat's* philosophy of a qualitative hierarchy, the membership is small. There are around 4,000 members, 15,000 associate members, 100,000 workers and a large number of sympathisers.[47] The organisation publishes magazines, newspapers, journals and books in almost all of India's major languages, and puts a lot of energy into translating into these languages many major Islamic works, including the Qur'an and *Hadith*. The organisation also has a students' wing called the *Students' Islamic Organisation* (SIO).[48] In the major states the *Jamaat* has organised women's branches of the students' wing and, like its Pakistan counterpart, provides equal training in Islam to both sexes. The GIO or *Girl's Islamic Organisation* is particularly strong in Kerala and Andhya Pradesh.[49]

There is an essential difference between the work of the *Jamaat* in Pakistan and the work of the *Jamaat* in India. Muslims in India comprise only 12% of the population, so consequently there is no overt ideology to make India an Islamic state. *Jamaat-i Islami Hind* is engaged in an active and well-organised programme of *dawah*. The thrust of this work is two-pronged. Firstly, there is an active outreach programme to non-Muslims.[50] There is a considerable literature devoted to explaining Islam to non-Muslims, and in Madras *Jamaat-i Islami* runs a successful campaign for converting *harijans* to Islam.[51] Whenever there is any natural disaster the *Jamaat* utilises its resources in humanitarian relief work. In the North the situation is complicated by the activities of the BJP (*Bharata Janata Party*) and the militant wing VHP (*Vishwa Hindu Parishad*). These extreme Hindu organisations have made it difficult openly to propagate Islam. *Jamaat-i Islami* members feel that Islam, Muslim culture, and the personal security of individual Muslims is threatened.[52] Thus it is engaged in protecting all of these from attack. The second major prong of the *Jamaat's* activities is directed at the Muslim community itself. It is acknowledged that India's Muslims are socially and economically backward. The *Jamaat's* main activity amongst the Muslim community is therefore in the field of education.[53] This, however, does not hinder their first priority: to teach a pure Islam which is in accord with the Qur'an and *Sunna*. Ejaz Ahmed Aslam sums up the work of the *Jamaat* in India as:

> Preservation of the Islamic identity, and provision of true Islamic norms in the society, and spreading the knowledge of Islam among the non-Muslims. These three are our basic works.[54]

Without the prime aim to achieve an Islamic state which involves the Pakistan and Bangladesh organisations so heavily in the political arena, *Jamaat-i Islami Hind* is committed to *dawah*. This commitment is the essential link between the independent *Jamaat-i Islami* organisations wherever they are established.

Jamaat-i Islami in Pakistan today

There is no doubt that the *Jamaat-i Islami's* central aim is still the same as that originally inspired by Maulana Mawdudi. The organisation is still committed to the ideal of an Islamic state in Pakistan, and its political work is always directed towards that aim. This central aim is formalised in the Constitution of both *Jamaat-i Islami* and *Jami'at-i Talaba*.[55]

According to Dr.Israr Ahmad, who formed a conservative breakaway organisation from *Jamaat-i Islami* called *Tanzim-e Islam*, Mawdudi retreated from his position of complete opposition to the secular state of Pakistan after his release from prison in 1956. Dr.Israr Ahmad contends that after this date Mawdudi sought alliances with other religious groups and even with avowedly secular political parties in order to further his aims. He argues that once Mawdudi began to work within the political system to achieve gradual reforms, he tacitly cooperated with the government which he had pledged to overthrow.[56] Today, *Jamaat-i Islami* has continued with this programme of gradual reform by working within the system. They are against violent revolution to achieve their aims[57] and they are currently a part of the *Islamic Democratic Alliance* (IJI), an Islamic Front which in 1991 had eight members in the National Assembly. Maulana Mawdudi's own shift in attitude towards the government of Pakistan and his flexibility on *fiqh*, dress and other non-essentials of Islam has provided *Jamaat-i Islami* with the opportunity to shift their position as Pakistan society undergoes various political and sociological changes. In general, these changes indicate a move towards a moderate stance on various issues. The influx of young, university educated, urban youth into their ranks has maintained the radical zeal but brought up fresh important issues. These include the role of women, style of dress, social and economic exploitation and Muslim sectarianism. The educated young of the new middle-class are the grassroots of *Jamaat-i Islami* support and activism. Muhammad Aslam Saleemi suggests that they give their support because Mawdudi was not apologetic in defending Islam against the values of European civilisation, and because his ideal of Islam was stripped of both Western and Indian adulterations.[58] Though his Islam did not compromise with the West, his tolerance on the above issues made his views seem more acceptable to Western-educated young people than those of the custom-bound *ulema*. Ishtiaq Gondal, however, stresses the ideological component of Mawdudi's message. He is concerned with social justice:

> The people of the middle classes they have minimum chances and they want to promote themselves. To get free from this miserable and unjust, you can say, polarised society. The programme with us provides them with such chances...Islam says there is always a share for poor people in the wealth of rich people.[59]

Universal education has created a new young middle-class in Pakistan but economic development has not kept pace with this development. The nation has not been able to create sufficient jobs for the many qualified accountants, lawyers, engineers, teachers, doctors and other such young professionals and graduates coming out of the colleges and universities. These people are naturally disillusioned, jealous of the power that is still retained in the hands of the dynastic families, and aware of exploitation from the West. They blame their own governments for selling out to Western capitalism, and turn increasingly to Islam for an ideology of revolution and social justice. The truth is probably a combination of the above factors. The interest shown in the *Jamaat* by this section of the community, however, has focussed attention on Mawdudi's tolerance rather than on his conservatism. His belief that the doors of *ijtihad* were always open and that Muslims should use their own powers of reasoning would naturally appeal to the educated young.

The *Jamaat* has shifted ground in regard to Mawdudi's conservatism on the subject of women. Universal education has resulted in more equal opportunities for women. In addition to the usual mixed education there are also universities which are only for women. *Jamaat-i Islami* has an active women's section, and the accountant for the national organisation is a woman who ran her own company before becoming a full-time member. There is a separate mosque for women in Mansurah and they are conspicuous by their presence on the complex involved in all kinds of activities. There are teachers and female doctors in the hospital. The women wear *hijab* but do not usually cover their faces; a headscarf is considered sufficient. Women are educated to the same standard of Islamic knowledge as the men, although this is controversial in Pakistan and India as theoretically it allows women to achieve the status of *mujaddid*. These changes indicate a shift from the 'traditional' position towards the 'moderate Trend'[60].

Mawdudi's tolerance towards the different schools of *fiqh* has allowed *Jamaat-i Islami* to adapt its position in regard to other Islamic groups. Many of the young people I interviewed in Pakistan were intolerant of their parent's sectarianism. They felt that Muslim groups should cooperate with each other. These feelings were echoed by the organisation's leadership. I was surprised to find that there were members of the *Jamaat* who had allegiances to other schools of Islamic thought. This was explained by the Secretary-General of the North-West Frontier Province:

> The basics of Islam if someone believes in those it is sufficient for us. In *Jamaat-i Islami* we require that person not to preach his specific sect in *Jamaat-i Islami*. To preach or make *dawah* of

those principles in which the whole Muslim nation believes. The universal principles. [61]

Ishtiaq Gondal also confirmed this trend:

> There are different schools of thought, *Barelwi*, *Deoband*, *Ahl-i Hadith* but we have collections of all their *fiqh*. We do not attract them on the basis of *Deoband*, *Barelwi*. We attract them on the basis of being Muslim. We insist (in order) to minimise these conflicts and these differences and become united.[62]

This attitude has allowed *Jamaat-i Islami* to work with other groups in Pakistan through political alliances and combined religious conferences. There is now closer association with the *Deobandi ulema* and *Tabligh-i Jamaat*. This has resulted in a more united Islamic front.

Mawdudi's death, and the system of voting in a new leader every five years, has taken the emphasis away from one charismatic leader. Although *Jamaat-i Islami* is still dominated by the ideas of Maulana Mawdudi, he is now more of an inspiration for them than a source of strict ideology. The organisation is prepared to question his ideas if necessary when responding to new political, social or economic developments. The criterion for change is whether such a change is permissible in Islam. Today it is the *Constitution* (see Appendix G) that controls the members of the *Jamaat*, rather than a charismatic leader. Ishtiaq Gondal expresses this succinctly:

> Our *Constitution* which is very comprehensive - we carry on our activities, our sessions, our programmes according to that *Constitution*. That is strictly implemented and violations against that *Constitution* are minimal, and whenever we find it we check it strictly'.[63]

Endnotes

[1] Mawdudi, Sayyid, 1986, *The Islamic Way of Life*, ed. Ahmed Khurshid, The Islamic Foundation, Leicester, pp.54-55; Donohue, John J. & Esposito, John L, (eds), 1982, *Islam in Transition*, Oxford University Press, Oxford, pp.94-97.

[2] The full text of this resolution can be found in Khan, M.A., 1982, *Pakistan's Long Autumn*, Iqdam Publications, Lahore, pp.232-234.

[3] Newman, K.J., 1956, *Essays on the Constitution of Pakistan*, Pakistan Co-operative Book Society Ltd, Dacca, p.3.

[4] Gilani provides a genealogy of Mawdudi's family which he claims is autobiographical. (Gilani, Syed Asad, 1984, *Mawdudi - Thought and Movement*, Islamic Publications, Lahore, pp.23-25).

[5] Mawdudi's father was one of the first students at Aligargh University. According to Mawdudi, Syeed Ahmad Khan collected the students from friends and relatives. Sir Syeed was related to Mawdudi's grandmother. Mawdudi claims that his father finished with the influence of the modernists, led by Sir Syeed Ahmad Khan, and eventually retired from practice in law, when he was instructed in Sufism by Maulvi Mohiyuddin. This took place when Mawdudi was one year old. (Gilani, op.cit, pp.26-27).

[6] Ahmad, Khurshid & Ansari, Zafar Ishaq, 1979, 'Mawlana Sayyid Abul A'la Mawdudi: An Introduction to His Vision of Islam and Islamic Revival', *Islamic Perspectives*, ed. Khurshid & Ansari, The Islamic Foundation, Leicester, p.360.

[7] ibid.

[8] ibid.,p.361.

[9] ibid.

[10] ibid., pp.361-362.

[11] ibid., p.362.

[12] Aziz, K.K., 1967, Islamic Modernism in India and Pakistan 1857-1964, Oxford University Press, London, p.214.

[13] Khurshid & Ansari, op.cit., p.362.

[14] ibid.

[15] Ahmed, Ishtiaq, 1987, The Concept of the Islamic State - An Analysis of the Ideological Controversy in Pakistan, Francis Pinter, London, p.33.

[16] 'A group of people or a society which consists of true Muslims can never break away from the Law of their Lord. Its political order, its social organisations, its culture, its economic policy, its legal system and its international strategy must all be in tune with the code of guidance revealed by Allah' (Mawdudi, Sayyid, 1986, *The Islamic Way of Life*, The Islamic Foundation, Leicester, p. 14).

'Finally, I should state one more important thing. This witness of ours would not be complete unless we establish a state based on the principles and teachings of Islam' (Mawdudi, Sayyid, 1986, *Witnesses Unto Mankind: The Purposes and Duty of the Muslim Ummah*, The Islamic Foundation, Leicester).

[17] Mawdudi, Sayyid, 1985, *Towards Understanding Islam*, The Islamic Foundation, Leicester, p.18.

[18] It does not consist in a mere profession of belief in Allah. It is an acknowledgement of the fact that Allah alone is our Lord, Sovereign and Ruler and that everything that man has, including his own life, belongs to Him and must be used in accordance with His directives. If a Muslim adopts a different course, he is insincere in his profession of faith' (Mawdudi, op.cit., p.15).

[19] 'We are slaves or servants of nobody save Him, nor is anyone also our Master or Sovereign. Our duty is to obey Him and abide by His laws and His alone. This is the covenant which you made with Allah as soon as you recite '*La ilaha illa'llah*', and while doing so you make the whole world your witness' (Mawdudi, 1985, *Let Us be Muslims*, The Islamic Foundation, Leicester, p.72).

[20] ibid., p.296 and Adams, Charles, 1966, "The Ideology of Maulana Mawdudi", South Asian Politics and Religion, ed. D.E.Smith, Princeton University, Princeton, p.382.

[21] *Khilafah 'ala Minhaj al-Nubuwah*' (Ahmad & Ansari, op.cit, p.20).

[22] Adams, op.cit.,p.127.

[23] 'The objective of the Islamic Movement, in this world, is revolution in leadership. A leadership that has rebelled against God and His guidance and is responsible for the suffering of mankind has to be replaced by leadership that is God-conscious, righteous and committed to following Divine Guidance' (Mawdudi, 1984, The Islamic Movement: Dynamics of Values, Power, and Change, The Islamic Foundation, Leicester, p.71).

[24] 'Islamic society that consciously resolves not to accept the *Shari'ah*, and decides to erect its own constitution and laws or borrows them from any other source in disregard of the *Shari'ah*, such a society breaks its contract with God and forfeits its right to be called Muslim' (Mawdudi, op.cit., *Islamic Way of Life*, p.17).

[25] Mi'raj, Muhammad, 1980, 'Shah Wali-Allah: Concept of the Shari'ah', *Islamic Perspectives*, ed. Ahmad & Ansari, Islamic Foundation, Leicester, p.345.

26 'The injunctions of God and His Prophet are to be accepted and obeyed and no legislative body can alter or modify them or make any new laws which are contrary to their spirit' (Mawdudi, op.cit., *The Islamic Way of Life*, p35).

27 Adams, op.cit., p.100.

28 ibid., p.395.

29 Gilani, op.cit., p.4.

30 ibid, p.5.

31 Bashier, Zakaria, 1985, *Muslim Women in the Midst of Change*, The Islamic Foundation, Leicester, p.17.

32 'Islam effects a functional distribution between the sexes and sets different spheres of activity for both of them. Women should in the main devote themselves to household duties in their homes and men should attend to their jobs in the socio-economic spheres. Outside the pale of the nearest relations between whom marriage is forbidden men and women have been asked not to mix freely with each other and if they do have to have contact with each other they should do so with *purdah*. When women have to go out of their homes, they should wear simple dress and be properly veiled. They should also cover their faces and hands as a normal course. Only in genuine necessity can they unveil, and they must re-cover as soon as possible' (Mawdudi, op.cit., *Towards Understanding Islam*, p.112).

33 Khurshid & Ansari, op.cit., pp.24-26.

34 Robinson, Francis, 1988, *Varieties of South Asian Islam*, Research Paper in Ethnic Relations No.8, September, Centre for Research in Ethnic Relations, p.19.

35 Interview with Muhammad Aslam Saleemi, Secretary-General of *Jamaat-i Islami*, Pakistan, 19th October, 1991, Mansurah, Lahore.

36 ibid.

37 ibid.

38 ibid.

39 The information on the *Paasban* programme was provided by Maulana Shahid Raza, Executive-Secretary of the *Shari'ah Council*, UK and *Imam* of the Leicester Islamic Centre, 6th December 1992, Leicester Islamic Centre. Maulana Shahid Raza stated that before the recent election for *Amir* he had 'read several articles against Kasim Husain Ahmed written by the leaders of the *Jamaat* that Kasim Husain Ahmad has become unpopular in the *Jamaat* hierarchy because he is giving open support to *Paasban*'. It should be noted, however, that the *Amir* was re-elected

in 1992 for a further five years.

[40] Interview with Ishtiaq Gondal, ex-Secretary-General of the *Jam'iat-i Talaba*, 21st October, 1991, Lahore.

[41] ibid.

[42] ibid.

[43] ibid.

[44] ibid.

[45] Interview with Professor Zafarullah Sheikh, President of the Pakistan Institute of Chemical Engineering, Dean of the Faculty of Engineering and Technology, 23rd October, 1991, Punjab University, Lahore.

[46] Interview with Ishtiaq Gondal.

[47] Interview with Ejaz Ahmed Aslam, Secretary-General of *Jamaat-i Islam Hind*, November 2nd 1991, Delhi, India.

[48] ibid.

[49] ibid.

[50] ibid.

[51] ibid.

[52] ibid.

[53] ibid.

[54] ibid.

[55] See Appendix G (*Constitution of Islami Jami'at-e Talaba*, Pakistan, Preamble p.8).

[56] Ahmad, Barakat, 1983, 'Mawdudian Concept of Islamic State', *Islam and the Modern Age*, No.14, November, p.10.

[57] 'We try to get things done in a proper manner, and we avoid violence' (Ishtiaq Gondal)

[58] 'You see regarding the values propounded by the European civilisations Mawdudi was not apologetic. He propounded the theories of Islam as they are. Without the adulterations of Indian civilisation and without the adulterations of Western civilisation.....Maulana Mawdudi had in

mind that he had to remove the non-Islamic manners and etiquettes and civilisation whether they be Indian or whether they be European.' (ibid)

[59] Ishtiaq Gondal.

[60] This is according to the categories in Bashier, op.cit., p.17-20.

[61] Interview with Professor Muhammad Ibrahim Khan, Secretary-General, Jamaat-i Islami, North-West Frontier Province, 19th October, 1991, Mansurah, Lahore, Pakistan.

[62] Ishtiaq Gondal

[63] Ibid.

11 Jamaat-i Islami in Britain

Introduction

Maulana Mawdudi saw the foundation of an Islamic state as essential in the achievement of a pure Islam which would encompass every area of life. This ideal was so dominant it would seem unlikely that any *Jamaat-i Islami* organisation could be successful where Muslims are in a minority. When *Jamaat-i Islami* activists find themselves in a situation where the chances of an Islamic state developing are slight, as in India, they change their approach. Instead they concentrate their efforts on *dawah*. Predominantly this consists of educating their fellow-Muslims to live an Islamic life individually which will encompass all their activities.

Like India, Britain is a nation with a Muslim minority and the same change of emphasis is evident here too. As with the other organisations and movements looked at in this thesis, *Jamaat-i Islami* entered Britain with the migrants from the subcontinent. Jorgen Nielsen identifies four separate organisations which he claims to have been developed by *Jamaat-i Islami* for specific purposes.[1] These organisations he identifies as *The UK Islamic Mission, Young Muslims UK, The Islamic Foundation,* and *The Muslim Educational Trust.* However, all four organisations claim to be fully independent of each other and from *Jamaat-i Islam* in the subcontinent, although all of them, with the exception of *The Islamic Foundation,* were once part of *The UK Islamic Mission.* This in itself does not necessarily disprove Nielsen's observation as *Jamaat-i Islami* tends to establish various specialised organisations which are officially independent, even in the subcontinent. There are, however, changes taking place in these organisations which suggest that the ideas of Maulana Mawdudi and the influence of *Jamaat-i Islami* in the subcontinent is becoming less central. This is particularly noticeable in the *Young Muslims UK* and *The Islamic Foundation.* These changes are caused by the unique situation in which Muslims find themselves in Britain, particularly the younger British-born generations, and by events in the wider Muslim world. In a later book Nielsen describes these organisations in Britain as '*Jamaat* related'.[2] This description tallies with my own findings. At a formal, official level *Jamaat-i Islami,* as established in Pakistan, India, and Bangladesh, does not exist in Britain. There are, however, organisations in Britain which are inspired by the teaching of Maulana Mawdudi and the work of *Jamaat-i Islami.* These organisations have close informal links with *Jamaat-i Islami* in the subcontinent but their allegiance is increasingly given to the Islamic Movement worldwide. *Jamaat-i Islami* is acknowledged as that part of the Movement working in the subcontinent, as *Ikhwan al-Muslimum* is acknowledged for its work in the Arab world. The organisation with the closest similarities to *Jamaat-i Islami* in the subcontinent is the *UK Islamic Mission.* Perhaps this is not surprising as it is the oldest *dawah* organisation in Britain and was established by first-generation migrants whose concerns were still located in their countries of origin.

The UK Islamic Mission

The *UK Islamic Mission* was founded in December 1962 by a small group of Muslim migrants who met at the East London Mosque to discuss the need for such an organisation in Britain.[3] Some of them had been already actively involved in establishing the *London Islamic Circle*, which started in the Saudi Arabian-influenced *Islamic Cultural Centre*.

The UK Islamic Mission's structure is definitely influenced by Maulana Mawdudi's idea that, in order to restore the *ummah* to its original purity of faith and political greatness, an organisation is required whose membership is selected on the basis of quality rather than quantity. As in *Jamaat-i Islami*, the membership is a small elite of well-trained and committed activists.[4] In 1992 they numbered 475, although the number of sympathisers was calculated as exceeding 50,000.[5] The *UK Islamic Mission* has modified the hierarchical structure from that prevalent in *Jamaat-i Islam*. There are only three categories of involvement: members, associate members, and sympathisers. These are distinguished by level of commitment to the organisation and by the quality of Islamic life lived. The level required for members and associate members is outlined in the *Constitution* (see Appendix H). An example of the kind of requirement expected of members is that they cannot be involved with *riba*. They cannot own a property that is mortgaged or have any kind of financial investment that earns interest, or insurance, unless it is illegal not to have it as in the case of car insurance. Great emphasis is placed on training programmes *(tarbiyah)* for members and associate members. As in the *Jamaat-i Islami*, this programme has been specifically designed by the organisation to train individuals mentally and spiritually to carry out the work of the movement. Every branch and circle holds weekly meetings which consist of studying the Qur'an, *Hadith*, and other Islamic literature sympathetic to the organisation's aims. They also discuss effective methods of communication. There are monthly sessions which cover specific ideological, spiritual and moral topics. It is interesting to note that the *Constitution Committee* is discussing the possibility of changing the three-tier model of involvement to a one-tier system.[6] If this is accepted by the majority of the membership, this will be another move away from the subcontinent *Jamaat-i Islami*-style structure.

The organisational structure of the *UK Islamic Mission* is also derived from the *Jamaat-i Islami* model. The organisation is run by a President in consultation with a *shura* made up of ten members. The President and the *shura* are elected by the membership every two years. Britain has been divided into three zones: North, South and Midlands. Each of these zones is run by a *Nazim* and an executive, who are also elected by the members and associate members of their respective zone. The zones consist of branches and circles.[7] There are thirty-nine branches and thirteen circles throughout Britain and the Mission has also established twenty-eight mosques throughout the country, usually in places where there are already branches. Once there is a mosque established the organisation has more influence over the local community, because Muslims tend to focus their activities around their local mosque.[8]

The Mission has recently begun to give attention to women. There is now a women's section which they hope will develop into an independent organisation. This effort is still relatively small. In 1992 there were only six members and thirty associate members, and assistance was required from the female members of the *Young Muslims UK*.[9] The training for women, as in *Jamaat-i Islami*, is identical to that of the men. The relative lack of progress with women is explained by the fact that when the Mission was formed, the subcontinent Muslim migrants were predominantly male. Once the families began to arrive the first generation wives remained generally in their homes raising their children. Many of them did not learn English or participate in the wider culture. This is not true of second and third generation Muslim women who may have the same educational opportunities as their brothers. Their first language is English and they are very often seeking employment in the wider society. The relatively young age of these women has meant that they are more likely to be involved with *Young Muslims UK*. The Mission is trying to redress this by working amongst the older generation women. Now that many of the mosques are larger than the earlier converted terraced houses there is space for facilities to be provided for women, and in the Mission mosques women are encouraged to attend.[10] For the last eight years the Mission has run a marriage bureau to assist Muslims to find suitable partners.[11] Tanzeem Wasti feels that this kind of involvement has encouraged women to participate as they are concerned with anything to do with the family, particularly the subject of marriage partners for their children. He believes that although the different ethnic communities are very strong, the younger generation will increasingly marry across ethnic lines simply seeking Muslim partners. Already they want to marry partners from Britain rather than the subcontinent, but he argues that the young activists in the organisation are more concerned with the quality of Islam in their prospective partners than in their ethnic origin.[12]

The Introduction to the UK Islamic Mission states that

> the task that we, Muslims in the West, face is not merely to safeguard our spiritual heritage and cultural identity and passively resist the onslaughts of foreign ideologies, but to participate fruit-fully and contribute positively to the moral and spiritual betterment of the society we happen to live in. This, however, presupposes a spiritually and culturally strong Muslim community established through sustained process of self-educational and moral training.[13]

This is much closer to the aims of *Jamaat-i Islami Hind*, which is not surprising in that the overt political aims to transform the state which dominate in Pakistan cannot be paramount in Britain. Neither is it surprising, then, that the *UK Islamic Mission* has concentrated its efforts in education. The central aim of Maulana Mawdudi, the establishment of an Islam practised in its entirety and of a pristine purity, is still the central plank of the *UK Islamic Mission's* aims.[14] To this end they are involved in *dawah* work amongst the Muslim community, in distributing literature and in arranging seminars and public meetings. The Mission, however, has responded primarily to the concern of the Muslim population in Britain that their children should not lose their identity in the face of the host nation's predominantly secular culture. Very early on the organisation formed teaching cells in which the children were taught Qur'an classes by Muslim students doing degrees in British universities. Now, these classes are mainly held in the mosques belonging to the *UK Islamic Mission*. Currently they are teaching over four thousand students, and employing over one hundred teachers.[15] Like many Mosque schools, they take place for two hours in the evening after the child returns from regular education. There are some key differences, however; the children are taught by the Mission's members who are qualified teachers rather than by the *imam*. They have studied the Punjab University Matriculation and Intermediate courses of Islamic studies. The quality of the teaching is supervised by the *Central Education Committee*, who advise and maintain standards. At the moment they are recommending that the mosques must provide desks and chairs for the children rather than allowing them to be taught on the floor.[16]

The Mission, like *Jamaat-i Islami* in the subcontinent, is also involved with social welfare activities. These take a different form specific to the needs of the community in Britain. The services provided are the following: visiting Muslim patients in hospitals and assisting in the provision of *Halal* food and the performance of religious obligations; visiting Muslim prisoners in gaol; and visiting Muslims in old people's homes.[17] The organisation also has connections with various other Islamic organisations around the world. Generally, these have a similar ideological viewpoint and link the organisation to that phenomenon known as the Islamic Movement.[18] Part of the Mission's funds has gone towards supporting various Muslim causes throughout the world.[19] This aspect of the Mission's work demonstrates the trend towards identifying with the Islamic causes internationally rather than solely with the activities of *Jamaat-i Islami* in the subcontinent. This is more marked in Britain than in Pakistan, where *Jamaat-i Islami* concentrates its efforts regionally in Afghanistan and Kashmir.

There can be no doubt that the UK Islamic Mission is very closely modelled on the subcontinent *Jamaat-i Islami*. Tanzeem Wasti acknowledges that the majority of the membership is still highly influenced by Maulana Mawdudi's ideas, but suggests that there should now be a rethinking of everything in order to acknowledge the contemporary situation. He says:

> His work is now fifty years old. He is not alive... Maulana Mawdudi's time was basically when it was the colonial era...I think that his early work is more strong which gives the inspiration, and I think from that point of view there is a need for rethinking and reprogramming the Muslim *ummah*...I think that now on his thoughts you have many institutions, you have many organisations working but the times have changed, the factors are changing very fast, and maybe his programmes will not be so relevant for the future.[20]

He sees that the future of the Muslim community in Britain requires a move away from ethnic identities and sectarian loyalties, and that this is beginning to happen.[21] He suggests that since the Rushdie affair there has been much more liaison between the different groups, and that the international situation of Muslims is forcing them to cooperate.[22] Tanzeem Wasti suggests that an important distinction must be made. This is, he argues, that 'the concentration should be on Islam, not on the cultural aspect of Islam.'[23] There is a strong awareness that the common language of the majority of young Muslims is English regardless of place of origin.

In this ambition there is no shift from the aims of Maulana Mawdudi and the work of the *Jamaat-i Islami*, but on the issue of an Islamic state, so central to Mawdudi's thinking, there has been an interesting change. It is acknowledged that this is too far away from actual circumstances to be a practical goal in Britain. The *Constitution* of the *Islami Jami'at-e Talaba* in Pakistan states that one reason for establishing an Islamic state is so that it should be an example for the Western and Muslim worlds.[24] Tanzeem Wasti sees that role as being taken over by a righteous and united minority community in the West.

> The West can create its own creative minority - a Muslim community. Then they can play a very important role in the future development of the Islamic *ummah*. Because the *ummah* concept is not based on territory and nationalism.[25]

He suggests that this is possible not only because of education, but also because Muslims in Britain are from different ethnic backgrounds; they therefore have the possibility of breaking free from cultural diversity and establishing the ideal of the *ummah* consisting of all nationalities and backgrounds united in Islam. He believes that the *UK Islamic Mission* has an important role to play in this process.[26]

These hopes and ideals expressed by the present secretary of the *UK Islamic Mission* will probably not be fulfilled by the organisation at this time without substantial changes. Although there is evidence of change taking place, the organisation remains very close to the *Jamaat-i Islami* model and the teachings of its founder Maulana Mawdudi. Its membership is mainly comprised of first generation migrants who are still too influenced by their connections to the subcontinent. There are, however, two organisations, the *Islamic Foundation* and *Young Muslims UK*, who have moved considerably further towards the ideals expressed by Tanzeem Wasti.

The Islamic Foundation

The Islamic Foundation was founded in 1973 through the inspiration of a group of Muslims led by Khurshid Ahmad and Ahmed Nasiruddin. Khurshid Ahmad is still the Chairman of the Board of Trustees, as well as being Deputy *Amir* of *Jamaat-i Islami* in Pakistan.[27] Khurram Murad, the former Director, has now returned to Pakistan and is very active in *Jamaat-i Islami* there. The Foundation's links to the ideology of Maulana Mawdudi and *Jamaat-i Islami* can also be inferred by the number of books which they publish which are translations of Mawdudi's writings into English. The Foundation is still involved in the major project of translating and publishing Mawdudi's *Tafsir* to the Qur'an. Dr. Ahsan acknowledges that several people working for the Foundation are influenced by the thoughts of Maulana Mawdudi and *Jamaat-i Islami*, and that because of this, these employees align themselves with the work being done by *Young Muslims UK*, the *UK Islamic Mission*, and the *Islamic Society of Britain*. He is adamant, however, that the Foundation is completely independent:

> It is an independent Islamic organisation in which we do, of course, acknowledge the role played by the *Ikhwan Muslimin* in the Arab world and *Jamaat-i Islami* in Pakistan, Bangladesh, the subcontinent, and also similar movements in Turkey and Malaysia [28]

In 1990, *The Islamic Foundation* moved to the current nine acre site, formerly a conference centre, in Markfield, about nine miles outside Leicester. The *Markfield Dawah Centre* now employs about thirty full-time staff who originate from various parts of the Muslim world. Although the majority are of Pakistani background there are also Algerians, Egyptians, Indonesians, Bangladeshis and Indians. This is itself unusual in the context of British Muslim organisations which tend to be identified with one particular ethnic or language grouping. According to a publicity video, the Foundation is first and foremost a training and educational institution. Secondly, it is a research organisation. Thirdly, it serves as a nucleus for the community. Fourthly, it is a publishing house.[29]

The modern and spacious facilities at Markfield provide a unique centre for *dawah* activities directed towards both the Muslim community and the wider British society. Besides the administration of *The Islamic Foundation*, *Young Muslims UK*, and *Islamic Society of Britain* (ISB), and the offices of the specialised units, there are four libraries consisting of a collection of over

20,000 Islamic texts in English, Urdu and Arabic; an international Islamic journals collection; a press cuttings collection of all the articles published in British newspapers concerning Muslims and Islam; and finally a specialised library of works on Islamic Economics. The conference facilities provide accommodation in single rooms for fifty participants, with recreational and relaxation lounges and several meeting and seminar rooms. There is a prayer room, a communal kitchen, and a large dining hall.

The Foundation consists of several specialised units. Education and training is definitely high on the Foundation's priorities. All the staff participate in training courses and programmes, but the Education and Training Unit is specifically charged with designing, organising, and conducting the courses. Some of these courses are used by the *UK Islamic Mission* and the *Young Muslims UK* in their training programmes. Training Muslim youth is paramount, but there are training courses for all age groups and on different aspects of Islam. One day courses for large groups of students from schools and colleges are held at the centre, and the Foundation's staff regularly lecture to both Muslims and non-Muslims in universities, colleges and community centres around the country. Seminars on various academic and topical issues are regularly held to which Islamic scholars of international repute are invited to deliver papers.

There is also a 'cultural awareness' programme which is held once a month for groups of up to fifty people. This programme is designed for such non-Muslim professionals as the police, social workers, teachers, prison officers and health service employees who have day-to-day contact with Muslims, its aim being to enable them to work with more understanding and effectiveness. The participants eat and sleep on campus, the idea being to provide an authentic impression of Islam.

The Education and Training Unit is also very concerned to assist Muslim converts. It offers a series of courses to give them a deeper knowledge of Islam, to perfect their worship rites and to teach them Islamic morals and manners. Dr. Ahsan is concerned that these Muslims, whom he estimates as numbering about ten thousand, are either isolated or find it difficult to adapt to the various ethnic and linguistic divisions in the mosque. He feels that the facilities of the Foundation should be at their disposal to deepen their knowledge of the faith and avoid the errors of 'cultural' Islam.[30]

The conference facilities are available for use by Muslim groups; they have been used by a wide variety of organisations ranging across the full ethnic diversity which constitutes the British Islamic community.[31] Despite the ethnic range, however, there is no doubt that the organisations which predominantly use the facilities share the ideology of the international Islamic Movement.

The remaining units are for specialised areas of research: they consist of the *Islamic Economics Unit*, the *Interfaith Unit*, the *Central Asian Unit*, the *Islamic Resurgence Unit*, and the *Islam in Europe Unit*. Besides the specialised library, which is probably the best in Europe, the *Islamic Economics Unit* receives data from all around the Muslim world, this is used to conduct research and to produce papers and books about contemporary Islamic economics and banking. The Unit's material is used by postgraduate students working in this field who come from universities throughout Britain. Close links have been established with the Economics Department of Loughborough University, which is about to offer its undergraduates an option on Islamic Economics which utilises the Foundation's material. The Unit publishes a quarterly review in English and Arabic entitled *The Review of Islamic Economics*.

The *Interfaith Unit* researches various aspects of Christian/Muslim relations from the

Christian sources. The central project involves monitoring Christian missionary activity in the Muslim world and making Muslims aware of what is occurring. To this effect, the Unit has produced a series of research papers covering developments in Africa, Asia, and the Middle-East. In addition to this work, the Unit is also involved in Christian/Muslim dialogue at local, national and international levels. For example, it is involved at a local level with the Leicester Council of Faiths, and the Foundation was instrumental in beginning interfaith dialogue in this area. At an international level, the Interfaith Unit claims to have represented British Muslims at the World Council of Churches in Geneva.[32] Although members of the Islamic Foundation may have taken part in conferences arranged by the World Council of Churches nevertheless it should be noted that their claim to represent British Muslims must take into account the ethnic and religious divisions in the community. It is highly probable that the majority of British Muslims would contest the Foundation's claim to represent them.

The Unit publishes a monthly review called 'Focus' which covers both aspects its activities. Ataullah Siddiqi of the Interfaith Unit sees two problem areas where the Foundation can contribute. The first necessity is to contextualise Islamic theology within the arena of debate with Western culture so that misconceptions of Islam can be removed. The second necessity is the provision of a voice which represents an Islam that is untainted by cultural accretion.[33] He explains that the *ulema* are not up to this task because 'mentally and spiritually they belong in the village from where they came'.[34] He further argues that the *ulema* have little interest in other faiths, and that even amongst those few that have, there are only a minority that are fluent in English.[35] Ataullah Siddiqi believes that dialogue between religions is not sufficient and that Muslims in Britain must open up a dialogue with the secular humanist strand of Western culture. He believes that the Foundation is in a position to begin to spearhead these two crucial areas of dialogue with the receiving culture.[36]

The *Central Asian Unit* monitors and produces papers on the situation of Muslims in what was once the Soviet Union. The Unit was established in 1981 to obtain information on the circumstances of Muslims under the Soviet regime. Since the collapse of the Soviet Union the Unit has concentrated its efforts on reporting the situation of Muslims in the Central Asian republics, focusing particularly on the political structure which these new Muslim nations will shape. The Unit produces a bi-monthly journal entitled *Central Asian Brief*.

In addition to these Units the Foundation has recently formed the *Islamic Resurgency Unit* whose role is to examine the Islamic Movement and changes taking place in the Muslim world. It will concentrate on Western images of Islam in general, and on the Islamic revival in particular. The *Islam in Europe Unit* is also newly established. All of these activities of the Foundation are assisted by a Computer unit and an Audio-Visual Unit which produces and co-ordinates the vast quantity of slides, video-tapes, audio-cassettes and video-programmes utilised by the Foundation.

The Islamic Foundation is also a publisher. Educational, devotional, inspirational and academic books covering such topics as the Qur'an, *Hadith*, *Seerah*, *Shari'ah* and *Tasawuf* and contemporary Muslim issues are produced and distributed throughout the Muslim world. The Foundation concentrates its publishing activities on the English-speaking parts of the Muslim world, and its catalogue now lists over 160 titles of works written in English. It also publishes many books for children which teach the values of Islam through stories and pictures. In addition to books it offers audio-cassettes, board games, maps and posters and a video-game, all specifically designed to help children to understand the message of Islam. Finally, the Foundation compiles and publishes *The Muslim World Book Review*. This quarterly journal reviews current publications about Islam and the Muslim world. The Review is accompanied by *The Index of Islamic Literature*.

The Islamic Foundation perceives itself as the think-tank of the Islamic Movement in Britain. The major concern here is to create an Islam which is suited to the environment of the West without losing the fundamentals of the faith. Dr. Ahsan sums this up:

> Of course, there is no British Islam but if we can call it British Islam then it will have independent characteristics and features of its own. The Muslims attending universities and those who are born here and believe in religion, they will have a very level view of Islam... for example, the role of women. The girls have been marginalised in most of the Islamic organisations and Muslim countries. In the same room they cannot sit together (with men)... that type of Islam will not be acceptable here.[37]

Jamaat-i Islami is too firmly rooted in the subcontinent milieu to create an Islam suitable for British Muslims whatever their ethnic origin, and is itself regarded as sectarian. The Foundation, however, has taken steps to establish itself as independent of any sectarian organisation. Its multi-national staff ensure that the perspective of the Foundation is not dominated by the concerns of subcontinent Muslims. The international focus of the Foundation is not solely on events taking place in the subcontinent. It is primarily concerned with that struggle of Islamic activists throughout the Muslim and non-Muslim world to fight against oppression and to establish a social system based on the central tenets of Islam.

The new conference facilities provide an excellent forum for debate and dialogue concerning the issues facing British Muslims. The Foundation's pioneering work in making English the language for communicating the message of Islam is very important in this context. The Foundation is now involved with *ISB (Islamic Society of Britain)*, founded in June 1990 [38] as an umbrella organisation for all Islamic groups which are working through the medium of English.[39] The various languages of the original place of origin are divisive in the context of Britain, and they will become decreasingly important for the community here. The Foundation will also be able to take a leading role in these developments for the following reasons: the prestige and status it has earned for the quality of its published material, and the respect which its members have in the community as scholars and academics.

The staff of the Foundation are also highly aware of the needs of young British-born Muslims; they are actively addressing the issues with which the young Muslims are concerned. The magazines and pamphlets produced by various Muslim youth groups indicate their concern with social and political problems, not only in the Muslim world but in the world at large. There are many articles on problems confronting Muslims throughout the world, for example, in Palestine, Bosnia, Central Asia, Iraq, Egypt and Iran; but there are also articles seeking an Islamic perspective on nuclear weapons, disarmament, artificial insemination, genetic engineering, and environmental issues. Farouq Murad, an early leader of *Young Muslims UK*, who now manages the Conference facilities of the Foundation expresses this emphasis on social justice amongst his generation.[40] He argues that Islam will have to tackle these issues if it is going to have any relevance to their lives practically. He insists it will have to look at these wider issues and put an Islamic perspective on them.[41]

This emphasis on the ideological aspects of Islam is as central here as it is to *Jamaat-i Islami* youth in Pakistan. Their struggle for justice, however, focuses on their situation in the social structure of Pakistan. The young activists in Britain seek justice for Muslims throughout the world. Farouq Murad equates justice with Islam itself. 'It is Islam that we want, but Islam itself is not an end in itself. Islam responds to something else which is justice'.[42]

Many young educated British Muslims are led into support for the Islamic Movement orientated groups by this concern for an Islam which involves itself with the kind of social justice/revolutionary approach that is appropriate to the issues which they regard as essential. The Islamic Foundation has placed itself in a unique position to co-ordinate and influence the activities of these groups regardless of whether they originated in the ideas of Maulana Mawdudi or elsewhere in the Muslim world. The ideological position of the Foundation is, however, clear. This can be gathered from the names they have given to the prayer room and the two conference halls on the Markfield complex. The prayer room is *Shah Wali-allah Hall*; the conference rooms are, respectively, *Maulana Mawdudi Hall* and *Hasan al Banna Hall*. Thus the Foundation acknowledges its inspiration and influences from the subcontinent, but indicates clearly its loyalty to the international Islamic Movement. Dr. Ahsan openly acknowledged the latter when directly asked if the Foundation's connections are to the international Islamic Movement rather than to Pakistan and India.[43]

Young Muslims UK

Young Muslims UK is a relatively recent organisation. It was formed in December 1984 on the initiative of twenty-seven young Muslims representing various local youth groups who met together in Spencer Place, Leeds, to form a national organisation.[44] One of the guiding influences from the first generation leadership was Khurram Murad, who was then Director of the Islamic Foundation. He provided the leadership of the new organisation with training programmes both for themselves and their membership, and a meeting-place in the old premises of the Foundation in Leicester. Today, the national administration of the *Young Muslims UK* is run from a portacabin situated on the Markfield complex. In spite of these connections Manozir Ahsan insists that the *Young Muslims UK* are independent from the Foundation.[45]

In the beginning *Young Muslims UK* searched for a group with which to affiliate itself and chose the YMO (*Young Muslims Organisation*), the equivalent organisation of young Bengalis inspired by *Jamaat-i Islami* in Bangladesh. Wasim Yaqub says that although they shared the same vision and ideals, the Bengalis were not very fluent in English, as the process of emigration was not then complete.[46] He explains that the *Young Muslims UK* members were nearly all born in Britain. 'That was one of the unique emphases of the time that we started. We were the only youth group that spoke English. This made it very easy for young people to come to *Young Muslims UK*'.[47]

Many of the founding members were influenced by the *UK Islamic Mission*. Some of the local groups that formed the national organisation were already attached to the Mission, so it was natural to affiliate the organisation with them. The Mission even helped them to write their Constitution, but the *Young Muslims UK* eventually became formally independent of them. There was, however, still a clause in the Constitution stating that should the leadership of *Young Muslims UK* do something seriously against Islam, then the Mission can insist upon calling the membership together and disbanding the leadership. They could also dissolve their centres and deny them access to the Mission *madrasas*.[48] This has enabled the more conservative *UK Islamic Mission* to maintain control over the speed and the type of changes which the more adventurous members of the youth movement may want to introduce. Recently (April 1994) *Young Muslims UK* has become the youth organisation of ISB (*Islamic Society of Britain*).[49]

With reference to the *Young Muslims UK's* connection to the ideas of Maulana Mawdudi or the activities of *Jamaat-i Islami*, Wasim Yaqub acknowledges that he personally believes that Maulana Mawdudi was 'one of the most visionary exponents of Islam, of a pure Islam there has been this century'.[50] He admits, however, that he is one of the most pro-*Jamaat-i Islami* members of the *Young Muslim UK* leadership. He insists that even in the *UK Islamic Mission* they were taught that Mawdudi believed that 'we should give the idea and let the people of any locality pick it up, and develop their own workers for they know best what to do'.[51]

He argues that one of the major changes from the *Islami Jami'at-i Talaba* in Pakistan is in terms of organisation; the *Young Muslims UK* is a much looser structure. The membership, currently around two thousand, is not hierarchical, even though the training schemes are progressively more difficult. The programmes and activities vary considerably from branch to branch. At the present time the *Young Muslims UK* does not even require participants to complete a membership form. This looser organisational structure is intentional. Wasim Yaqub argues that they have been more successful because they adopted a more relaxed approach.[52]

The membership of the *Young Muslims UK* is predominantly of Pakistani origin. This probably represents the statistical make-up of the Muslim community in Britain rather than a specific orientation towards that part of the world. They do, however, have a minority of members from Somalia, the Yemen, and the current leadership is one-third Bengali. There is also a small but significant group of English converts to Islam. The organisation currently stresses *dawah* activity over and above training; consequently, it has always been incidental in bringing 'reverts' from the Muslim community back to Islam. Wasim Yaqub says that this is especially true of the strong female section which is led by 'reverts' to Islam.[53]

The majority of *Young Muslims UK* are university undergraduates and graduates. Wasim Yaqub and Rukhsar Shafiq, the latter a member of the Sheffield branch both spoke of the impact of going to university in Britain. Rukhsar Shafiq comments 'their were ten Muslims in my house from different cultures, and all of them said the same thing, you know, our life has radically changed'.[54] It is this multi-cultural aspect of Britain which excites the members of *Young Muslims UK*. There are Muslims from everywhere in the world in Britain, and this has helped young British Muslims to realise that Islam is not the property of any one particular culture. Wasim Yaqub describes growing up in Britain as a child of migrant parents:

They had lived all their lives in their villages, where Islam was a cultural thing. They would have gone to the elders of the tribe, of the village, and be told this is the way we do it this time. When they came over here, that communal education was cut off, so all they had was the images of cultural life without knowing the reasons for it. So naturally when their children were growing up they wanted to protect them from what they saw in Western society. They said, 'you have to do this because it is religion.' 'Why is it religion?' 'Don't ask questions.' With that approach we would easily leave Islam because it would be of no interest to us, to myself.[55]

The members of *Young Muslims UK* express sentiments which are understood by the Muslim youth of Britain as they seek their identity in a new environment. They are forming close links with others who are trying also to find the direction that Islam should take in the West. Although *Young Muslims UK* was once closely connected to the *UK Islamic Mission* as its youth wing, it is now making alliances with other youth organisations in Britain who share the same ideology. This process will be accelerated by their new connection with ISB (*Islamic Society of Britain*). They are not defensive concerning Western culture or threatened by it, feeling rather that their presence is meant. Wasim Yaqub says 'we think that our existence in the West is a sign for Islam'[56] whilst Rukhsar Shafiq believes 'The West as far as I am concerned is where the purest form of Islam will rise because it is the dirtiest environment'.[57]

The Muslim Educational Trust

The *UK Islamic Mission's* emphasis on education resulted in the establishment of the *Muslim Educational Trust* to oversee the requirements of Muslim children in the British school system. Tanzeem Wasti claims that this organisation was given independence because the issue of education was far too important to be in the hands of any one ideological group; it was felt to be a matter of urgent concern to the whole Muslim community.[58]

The *Muslim Educational Trust* was established in 1966. It is the oldest national Muslim educational organisation in Britain dealing with the concerns of Muslims in regard to the education of their children.[59] The organisation arranges for teachers to give Islamic Studies lessons in English to Muslim children in state schools wherever there are large Muslim communities. It publishes books and posters on Islam for use by teachers and these are used throughout the world. The Trust has also produced the syllabus in Islamic Studies for the GCSE examination of the London East Anglian Group examining board. These efforts in the field of education have resulted in the Trust being regularly consulted by the Department of Education, the National Curriculum Council and several Local Education Authorities.[60] The Trust's work has also placed it in the forefront of the campaign to ensure that the religious needs of Muslim children are met by British schools. They have issued guidelines to that effect on such matters as sex education, diet, dress restrictions, and participation in sports. The Trust actively supports the establishment of full-time and supplementary Muslim schools in Britain.[61]

Conclusion

There is no doubt that there are changes taking place in the development of *Jamaat-i Islami*-influenced groups in Britain which echo wider changes taking place in the community as a whole. These particular groups seem to be equipped to adapt themselves to the new situation, and they even provide the leadership and direction for the changes involved. Despite their relatively small numbers, their influence on Islamic youth is profound. The *Islamic Foundation* and the *UK Islamic Mission* provided the leadership and the direction during the Rushdie affair. They were instrumental in setting up the *UK Action Committee for Islamic Affairs* which brought together

Muslims of all denominations to provide a common voice against the publishing of *The Satanic Verses*. This was an important step on the way to learning to work with each other, it gave status in the community to the *Jamaat-i Islami* influenced groups. This process is likely to continue and intensify through the work and the facilities of the *Islamic Foundation*.

The flexibility of these groups can be traced to Maulana Mawdudi's view that the gates of *ijtihad* cannot be closed. Dr.Chachi of the *Islamic Economics Unit* expresses this viewpoint:'It is open from the time of creation to the Day of Judgement. The only requirement is that the person who does the *ijtihad* should, whatever *ijtihad* he comes up with, not contradict the Qur'an and *Sunna*'.[62] This flexibility provides the ability to respond to the new situation in the West, and is attractive to young Muslims born and educated here in Britain who have been taught to think for themselves and to accept nothing as given.

It is almost certainly not accurate to call these groups *Jamaat-i Islami*. Although there is still strong affection for, and some links with *Jamaat-i Islami* in the subcontinent, together with inspiration from the ideas of Maulana Mawdudi, the '*Jamaat* related' organisations in Britain are beginning to identify themselves not so much with their subcontinent origins, but with their role as representatives of the Islamic Movement in Britain. This enables them to identify with the struggles of various groups throughout the world who are engaged in a struggle to implement radical change in their societies utilising Islam as their ideology. In this way, these organisations in Britain can provide an identity for their members which extends outwards to the wider Muslim world. They consciously promote an Islamic identity over and above ethnic or national identity, and their programmes actively seek to move away from South Asian customs and traditions. This is more evident amongst the younger generation in the organisations, especially in *Young Muslims UK*. The newly-formed link between them and the *Islamic Society of Britain* demonstrates an awareness to promote Islam within the context of wider British society.[63] This aim is also strongly expressed amongst the academics of *The Islamic Foundation*. All the groups openly identify with the ideology and politics of the Islamic Movement throughout the world rather than solely with *Jamaat-i Islami* in the subcontinent. It is this identification worldwide, combined with an emphasis on promoting Islam for British Muslims, which is attractive to some young Muslims attempting to define their identity in Britain.

Endnotes

[1] Nielsen, Jorgen, 1989, 'Islamic Communities in Britain', *Religion, State and Society in Modern Britain*, ed. Badham, Paul, The Edwin Mellin Press, p.232.

[2] Nielsen, Jorgen, 1992, *Muslims in Western Europe*, Islamic Surveys, Edinburgh University Press, Edinburgh, p.136.

[3] UK Islamic Mission, 1992, *Twenty-Ninth Annual Report*, UKIM, London, p.1.

[4] 'The object has not been to quickly gather a large group of people nominally committed to Islam, but rather to develop a core of dedicated workers as a vanguard to spearhead a lifelong struggle in the cause of Allah' (*Twenty-Ninth Annual Report*, p.1).

[5] ibid.

[6] Interview with S.M. Tanzeem Wasti, Secretary-General, UKIM, 1st February 1993, London.

[7] See Appendix H, *The Constitution*, UKIM, London, pp.6-12.

[8] *Twenty-Ninth Annual Report*, op.cit, p.2.

[9] ibid., p.7.

[10] Interview with S.M. Tanzeem Wasti.

[11] *Twenty-Ninth Annual Report*, op.cit., p.7.

[12] Interview with S.M. Tanzeem Wasti.

[13] UK Islamic Mission, N.D., *The U.K. Islamic Mission: An Introduction*, UKIM, London, pp.1-2.

[14] ibid., p.2.

[15] *Twenty-Ninth Annual Report*, op.cit, p.2.

[16] Interview with S.M. Tanzeem Wasti.

[17] *Twenty-Ninth Annual Report*, op.cit., p.5.

[18] Some of the organisations with which the *UK Islamic Mission* maintains contact are: *World Muslim League*, Saudi Arabia; *Islamic National Front Ummah Party*, Sudan; *Jamaat-i Islami* in Pakistan, India, Bangladesh and Kashmir; *Islamic Party*, Tajikistan; *Islamic Salvation Front*, Algeria; *SDA Bosnia*; and the *Islamic Movement of Tunisia* (ibid, p.5).

[19] Some examples of donations that went out to Muslim relief and causes around the world are: £8,000 to Bosnia; £8,155 to Bangladesh; £6,040 to Central Asia; £2,860 to the Sudan; £7,100 to Afghan refugees; £5,023.30 to Kashmiri refugees (ibid. p.6).

[20] Interview with S.M. Tanzeem Wasti.

[21] 'I think that it is a gradual process. Eventually all these national or language groups, Pakistanis, Bengalis, will.... you see, our new generation Muslims are working in English. All these groups will converge eventually' (ibid).

[22] 'Like with the Babri mosque issue. All among the *Barelwis* came, and they invited the Mission, and the Islamic Foundation....and the tendency is this, as I told you, because this is the impact of our younger generation because they know that the younger generation is not going for all this sort of thing....and so they have to come closer. And, of course, the world situation is also demanding their co-operation, and they are realising that the future lies in unity' (ibid).

[23] ibid.

[24] See Appendix G.

[25] ibid.

[26] ibid.

[27] Interview with Dr. Manozir Ahsan, Director of *The Islamic Foundation*, 8th December,1992, Markfield *Dawah* Centre, Leicester.

[28] ibid.

[29] Transcript of a video entitled, *The Islamic Foundation*, 1992, The Islamic Foundation, Leicester.

[30] Interview with Dr. Manozir Ahsan.

[31] Some of the organisations which have used the facilities are: *Young Muslims UK*, the *Islamic Society of Britain*, the *UK Islamic Mission*, Turkish youth groups, Malaysian youth groups, *Dawat ul Islam*, *Islamic Forum Europe*, *Federation of Students and Islamic Societies Great Britain* (Publicity video).

[32] Interview with Ataullah Siddiqi, Interfaith Unit, Islamic Foundation, 14th December, 1992.

[33] Ibid

[34] ibid.

[35] ibid.

[36] ibid.

[37] Interview with Dr. Manozir Ahsan.

[38] Islamic Society of Britain, nd, *Towards a Just Society*, Markfield, Leicester, p.14.

[39] At the time that I began my research the ISB (*Islamic Society of Britain*) was newly formed. They are now operating as a *Dawah* organisation whose emphasis is on promoting Islam in Britain to both Muslims and non-Muslims. The aims of the ISB, as written in their booklet *Towards a Just Society*, confirm my view that the British-born Muslims in the youth movements once associated with the ideals of *Jamaat-i Islami* are moving towards allegiance with the wider Islamic Movement, but specifically in the context of the future of Islam in Britain.

> For ISB, Islamic work is not about campaigning for "our rights" (e.g campaigning for the rights of minorities, for *halal* meat, etc), or merely winning more non-Muslims to Islam. It is about sharing our viewpoint about life, society and the future with everyone. The Islamic message is to be given to all human beings, irrespective of their convictions, religious beliefs, or nationalities (ibid.p.20).

> For non-Muslims, our wish is to make Islamic *Da'wah* relevant to their concerns and experiences, and to relate it to all matters of public policy and morality which affect everyone in one way or another. We will campaign to appeal to those who are affected by unemployment, housing, loneliness, old age, drugs, crime, etc (ibid.p.21).

[40] At the time I interviewed Farooq Murad in 1992 he held this position at the *Islamic Foundation*. In 1994 he was appointed President of ISB (*Islamic Society of Britain*).

[41] Interview with Farooq Murad, *The Islamic Foundation*, December 3rd, 1992, Markfield *Dawah* Centre, Leicester.

[42] ibid.

[43] Interview with Dr. Manozir Ahsan.

[44] Interview with Wasim Yaqub, Founder member of *Young Muslims UK*, 14th December 1992, Markfield *Dawah* Centre.

[45] Interview with Dr. Manozir Ahsan.

[46] Interview with Wasim Yaqub.

[47] ibid.

[48] ibid.

[49] Interview with Amjit Khan, 15th August 1994, *Young Muslims UK*, Bradford.

[50] Interview with Wasim Yaqub.

[51] ibid.

[52] ibid.

[53] ibid.

[54] Interview with Rukhsar Shafiq, member of *Young Muslims UK*, Sheffield Branch, 14th December 1992, Markfield *Dawah* Centre, Leicester.

[55] Interview with Wasim Yaqub.

[56] ibid.

[57] Interview with Rukhsar Shafiq.

[58] Interview with S.M. Tanzeem Wasti.

[59] Interview with Ghulam Sarwar, *Muslim Educational Trust*, 6th April 1993.

[60] Ibid.

[61] Ibid.

[62] Interview with Dr. Chachi, *Islamic Economics Unit*, *The Islamic Foundation*, 14th December 1992, Markfield *Dawah* Centre, Leicester.

[63] *The Constitution of the Islamic Society of Britain* states the organisation's aims to (a) invite British Muslims to adhere to the principles of Islam and to promote unity amongst them. (b) convey the message of Islam, and to establish cordial relations with non-Muslims in general and with the People of the Book in particular in order to promote better understanding of Islam in the multi-cultural society (c) provide social welfare services according to Islamic guidance (pp.2-3). See Appendix I.

12 Conclusion

In order to ascertain the possible direction which could be taken by Islam in Britain and the impact that this will have upon the Muslim communities, this thesis has investigated the key factors likely to be involved. In Chapter II the origins and development of the Muslim concept of *ummah* have been explored. Because minority migrant groups form communities which cannot be explained solely in the light of the Muslim understanding of *ummah*, Chapter III has looked at some sociological analyses of community. This needed to be done before focusing in Chapter IV on the various dilemmas facing Muslims in Britain as they attempt to define themselves as a community in a non-Muslim environment. The remaining chapters explore the various religious organisations and schools of thought most likely to influence the direction of Islam in Britain as they contribute their own attitudes to the dilemmas discussed in Chapter IV. My awareness of the dual influence of the migrants' place of origin and place of present habitation has necessitated the provision of independent chapters in order to examine each religious grouping in both these contexts.

The central concern of the majority of Muslims whom I interviewed was with the transmission of Islam to the younger generation. In this context they felt that it was crucial to establish a community both firmly rooted in Islamic principles and capable of full participation in the resources of the receiving culture. The essential differences of opinion concerning how this could be achieved are often between first-generation migrants and subsequent generations. Both generations affirm the values of religion. The first-generation migrants are more likely to cling onto traditional ideas and customs brought with them from the subcontinental place of origin, and to find their identity within their ethnic community. Their practice of Islam is frequently used to reinforce the lifestyles which they brought with them to Britain. Old customs and traditions are reinforced by sanctifying them as prescribed by religion. A number of British-born Muslims argue that it is necessary to create a community that is integrated into British society but whose locus of identity is Islam. Increasingly, more of them believe that this can be achieved by Muslims separating out the universals of Islam from the accretions added by culture, custom and history. It is already extremely difficult to transfer the values and traditions of the villages of origin to Muslims who were born and educated in Britain and identify themselves as such. This attempt to find an Islamic identity based on the universals of the faith often insists that it is not sufficient to be born a Muslim. Religion has to be more than an accident of birth subservient to culture, it needs to be founded on knowledge and experience. Values which are deeply held by many first-generation migrants as part of their religion and culture are beginning to be criticised by their offspring who are in the process of determining what is intrinsically Islamic. This inter-generational clash of values is central to the various dichotomies (see Chapter IV) that Muslims in Britain need to resolve in order to form a communal self-identity.

I agree with Werner Schiffauer that the process of migration to the advanced industrial and technological societies of the West involves the same changes in religious behaviour that he found often occurred in the movement of rural populations to the cities within Muslim societies.[1] He argues that illiterate villagers are generally dependent upon the ceremonial aspects of religion and daily rites for their apprehension of Islam. The move of the family from the village to the city, whether in the subcontinent or to Britain, usually offers better education for the children and more lucrative employment for the parents. Literacy results in the family having access to the Qur'an and *Hadith* for themselves, and urban *imams* are often better trained in the principles of Islam. Village practices and traditions may well be criticised by 'sophisticated' urban dwellers. All of these factors link the change in class status involved in the move from village to city to a change in religious identity. Gellner argues that rural Muslims who have migrated to an urban environment often become more orthodox and join revivalist and 'fundamentalist' groups not only for enhanced status but in order to replace these close-knit relations of village or tribe which are lost in the more impersonal life of city-dwellers.[2]

Certainly my research indicated that religious identity amongst Muslims is becoming the sharpest focus for establishing a sense of selfhood in an alien environment. In what is often perceived to be a hostile and godless culture, the symbols of Islam take on a new importance when established in Britain. For many they evoke very powerfully the feeling of never-forgotten places of origin, but for numerous British-born Muslims they can enhance a sense of purpose provided by feeling a part of an ideological movement to establish Islam as an alternative to the secular capitalism of the west.

Regardless of these divisions and conflicts, there can be no doubt that belonging to the *ummah* is an integral part of Muslim self-awareness. It has always provided an ideology of unity which should override the variety of ethnic, linguistic and national groupings from which it draws its membership. The ideal of the *ummah*, a community bound together by its belief in Allah and the Prophethood of Muhammad, still supplies striking examples of common unity and fellowship as found within a vast range of ethnic and national groupings. The *salat*, *Ramadan*, the *Hajj*, the respect and status given to the Qur'an, and the principle of *tawhid* bind Muslims together in a common faith which can be drawn upon as a basis for unity and can provide a powerful sense of communal identity. The combination of this basic core of shared religious practices and observation of the *Shari'ah* is central to Muslim life, and creates the bonds that tie together the *ummah*. Because of this unity of Islam's essential ritual and cultic practices, millions of Muslims can look to the wider Islamic community and feel part of it in spite of the fact that it is divided into competing groups. Thus for many Muslims in Britain, the concept of *ummah* becomes of central importance to their religious ideology. In spite of the fact that they live in a non-Muslim state, their membership of the *ummah* is not nullified and may even be strengthened by their isolation. For many first-generation migrants their membership of the *ummah* can be a source of solace and strength, and can be used to legitimise and sanctify time-honoured customs from far-away but intensely remembered places. British-born Muslims can draw upon their membership of the *ummah* in a different way. It links them to an identity which transcends their allegiance to both nationality and the ethnic cultures of their parents. The concept of *ummah* can also be drawn upon to provide an alternative world-view and confront the overriding secular viewpoint that is dominant in the indigenous culture. The need to provide an alternative worldview is reinforced by negativity to the migrants' presence.

This ideal of the *ummah* as a united, indivisible transnational community has been put forward by some modern Islamic thinkers to counteract the pervasive influence of the Western ideologies of nationalism and secularism in Muslim societies. In spite of this attempt to claim unity of the *ummah* in Islam's history, in reality it has not existed since the Prophet's death except as a symbol of cohesion in the minds and hearts of the devout Muslims. McWilliams argues that, if successful, such a close-knit community based on belief contains the seeds of its own destruction. This is because its very success leads to a vast state in which the members can only know each other as abstractions.[3] Furthermore, in a world of constant change and social upheaval, new ideologies and belief system constantly arise to challenge the old ones. This leads to a collapse of intellectual unity[4] which in turn challenges the inherited unity based on Islam. Toynbee suggests that civilisations break down when they are no longer able to respond creatively to new situations. He argues that they rest on their past achievements, idolising their society either at the moment of past success or in terms of some special institution which was instrumental to success.[5]

All of the above analyses of society could be fruitfully applied to counteract the Muslim ideal of the integrity of the *ummah*. The Muslim civilisation has often been guilty of idolising a vision of community which it has not been able historically to maintain. Throughout Islam's history various devout Muslims have tried to restore the unity of the *ummah* by calling for a return to the perceived pristine faith of the Prophet, his companions, and the four *rashidun*. This echoes Toynbee's idea that if the community is a religious one it need not necessarily fall into permanent decline, as breakdown can be followed by renewal.[6] These attempts to restore the *ummah* can be observed in Islam from the *Kharijites* to the organisations which make up the Islamic Movement of the twentieth century.

Impetus has been given to these revivalist movements by the ever-increasing pervasiveness of European ideas and lifestyle throughout the nineteenth and twentieth centuries, and the failure of Muslim societies to respond to the West's technological and military dominance. They raised the ideal of the *ummah* as the banner to fight the European ideologies of secularism and nationalism. These groups declared that the Muslims' real choice was between Islam and *jahiliyya*. There is, however, a paradox in their call for the revival of Muslims' fortunes by restoring the unity of faith implicit in the concept of *ummah*. The revivalist groups' attempts to restore the *ummah* require a more exclusive definition of the concept than that generally held by most Muslims, for whom birth is sufficient qualification. The revivalists have drawn upon the verse of the Qur'an which defines the *ummah* as a righteous group of believers selected from the wider community and charged with the duty to call all Muslims to obedience.[7] It is this narrower definition of *ummah* which has stimulated the development of sectarianism within Islam. The revivalists form organisations and groups which contain the qualities of Poplin's moral communities and Shenkar's intentional communities (see Chapter III).[8] The community becomes relatively self-contained and its members can live most of their lives within it. They have a deep sense of belonging to a morally significant group within the wider Muslim population. A tremendous sense of individual and group identity is achieved by identifying with the first Muslims and the transformation of the Meccan *jahiliyya* into the first city of Islam. Thus it is that self-defined righteous groups within the wider community can claim to be the true '*ummah*'. This inflation of group consciousness results in a strong awareness of distinctiveness, resulting in separation from other Islamic organisations. This makes it very difficult for these religious organisations to resolve their differences and recreate the united *ummah* to which they all aspire.

These historical divisions in the *ummah* have been transported to Britain, but the process of migration further complicates the problem of unity based on faith. Minority communities tend to organise themselves on an ethnic basis which maintains their original languages. They usually stay together in close-knit inner-city enclaves and form different types of community based around kin networks and formed of people from the same regions or even villages of origin. This creates a much smaller locus of group identity than that of common religion or nationality. This urban village which retains its own linguistic, social and ethnic frontiers, interacting on a selective basis with the wider non-Muslim society, can conflict with the Islamic vision of a universal, egalitarian society as based upon the revelation of the Qur'an. Religion is used to reinforce the customs of the smaller ethnic community. This provides a further stimulus to those Islamic revivalist groups which insist that the universal Islamic identity is primary and criticise as unIslamic many traditional customs arising out of the place of origin. Various Islamic groups operating in Britain utilise a revivalist ideology brought with them from the subcontinent in order to oppose ethnic-based urban village communities, whilst other groups are prepared to defend the latter.

Rex suggests that structured interaction begins to take place amongst the migrants in the form of associations whose concern with religion will be based upon maintaining culture in the new environment.[9] These associations tend to be local in organisation, but Joly points out that national religious organisations concerned with the preservation of Islam and the promotion of Islamic identity particularly in regard to British-born generations are increasingly more influential.[10] These groups were formed in the nineteenth and early twentieth centuries in response to the decline of Muslim power and the successful spread of European culture in the subcontinent. Prior to the creation of Pakistan, Muslims had always been a minority in the region and had a long history of regarding themselves as separate and distinct from other social groups and religions. They had developed strategies to deal with living alongside a Hindu majority and later used these to cope with the loss of power to the British. Essential to these strategies was the message of return to the basics of Islam in order to renew the community. This resulted in the Muslims of India becoming inward-looking as some focussed their energies on reform amongst themselves and others defended traditional practices influenced by Hinduism or folk-Sufism criticised by the reformers.

This thesis has focused upon the influence of these groups, namely *Deobandis*, *Tabligh-i Jamaat*, *Barelwis* and *Jamaat-i Islami*, on the development of the Muslim community in Britain. Each has an ideological programme and a specific Islamic outlook which echoes conflicts in the wider Muslim world, but which they specifically inherit from their history in the subcontinent. Each challenges the dominant secular ideology in Britain and promotes Islam as the rallying flag around which the various ethnic and national groups amongst the migrants can unite. It is important to establish whether their ideological programmes can succeed in establishing Islam in Britain to the satisfaction of those later generations for whom the historical controversies of the subcontinent carry far less significance. There is a strong possibility that they are communicating divisions developed in the history of subcontinent Islam which could seriously endanger any efforts towards creating a truly indigenous Islam in Britain. Their history of conflict, if continued in their chosen country of migration, would still further fragment the community.

In order to survive, all religious movements need to satisfy two criteria: they must be sufficiently flexible to adapt to changing circumstances, and at the same time they must be seen as maintaining those essential truths of the faith without which they could not continue to exist as viable carriers of the divine message. The tension created through the process of determining what can be changed, how far it can be changed, to what it can be changed, and finally what is inviolate, will be heightened by the process of migration. The struggle generated by these tensions will create inter-generational stress. It will be particularly acute at the stage of migration, which exists in Britain at present, where the first-generation migrants' belief systems are still dominant but in which the second and third generations are increasingly demanding that their requirements too should be acknowledged.

There are indications that all the Islamic religious movements transported with the migrants from the subcontinent are undergoing change as they adapt to the demands of the new environment. It will be their capacity to change rapidly enough to provide for the new requirements of Muslims born and bred in Britain which will ensure their survival. The majority of the first-generation Muslim migrants were from rural areas of the subcontinent; their religion is the traditional version of Islam practised in their villages of origin. It is this majority and their offspring that have become the targets of *dawah* activity from both the reform groups and *Barelwi* organisations. The relative success of all these groups will depend on their ability to capture the hearts and minds of the young. The *Barelwi* groups need to make the most profound changes.

This is because historically they have defended the kind of Islam which incorporates a wide range of local customs, traditional practices and is usually confined to a particular locale through being focussed around a Sufi shrine. Obviously it will be difficult to replicate this in Britain. The *Barelwi* mosques often function more strongly as a means of reinforcing kinship and ethnic ties than as a means of promoting the awareness of belonging to the wider *ummah*. The *Barelwis* usually focus their activities around personalities, rather than institutions and this can cause problems with unity of purpose. In Britain there has been a history of rivalry between various *pirs*, *Barelwi ulema* and their respective followers. There are indications, however, that the *Barelwis* in Britain are developing a common consciousness and a degree of unity. Various practices and customs have become institutionalised within *Barelwi* worship throughout all their mosques in Britain, these help to provide a common *Barelwi* group identity. Some *Barelwis* are aware of the need to promote a sense of belonging to the wider Muslim *ummah* and thus to bestow legitimacy on themselves. Following in the path of Ahmad Riza Khan, who did much to establish the *Barelwi* beliefs and practices as a coherent and distinct *maslak* in the subcontinent, many *Barelwis* assert that their brand of Islam is *Ahl-i Sunnat wa-jamaat*, or the true *Sunni* path as practised by millions of Muslims throughout the Islamic world. Finally, it is the sometimes vehement critique of popular expressions of Sufism by the better organised, tightly-knit reform groups which has pushed the *Barelwis* towards developing a clearly defined self-identity.

The arrival of Sufi *pirs* in Britain has done much to consolidate *Barelwi* identity and increase their activity. It has enabled *Barelwi* migrants to focus their religious requirements in their new location rather than looking back to the hallowed places in their country of birth. The charisma and message of *pirs* who live in Britain is able to reach out and attract the young who are unfamiliar with the shrines and uneasy with the customs of the rural subcontinent. However, many changes need to occur before the *Barelwi* tradition can fulfil the needs of young British Muslims. Although some *Barelwi* leaders are aware of the need for a wider unity which must include all Muslims in Britain, particularly the young of both sexes, in practice little is being achieved in this direction. In spite of the new-found awareness of the needs of the younger generation, an awareness instigated at least in part by the fear that the better organised reform groups will lure their children away, I saw no indications in the *Barelwi* mosques of English being used or of the problems of British-born Muslims being addressed. The conservatism of the first-generation migrants who control the Barelwi mosques and institutions makes them suspicious of any kind of change in the religion which they have inherited from their forebears and successfully transferred to Britain. The great majority of the British *pirs* are themselves first-generation migrants whose teachings reinforce the beliefs and practices of their own generation. Visiting *pirs* from the subcontinent reinforce the values of these first-generation migrants by reminding them of the traditions still prevalent in the country of origin. In time, however, the mantle of the *pirs* will fall onto their successors born and bred in Britain; they will be more aware of the needs of their own generation and of what is required to establish Islam in Britain. Pir Noor ul-Aqtab Siddiqi in Coventry is the first British-born Muslim to succeed his recently deceased father, Pir Abdul Wahhab Siddiqi. University educated and a qualified barrister, he has inherited an international organisation and personifies his father's belief that the next generation of leaders must be chosen from amongst the educated in the community.

The success of the nineteenth century reform groups in Britain to some extent conforms with Schiffauer's analysis of what takes place when rural Muslims migrate to the cities. They have developed a religion which is generally more systematic, self-conscious and based on abstract principles. Consequently it travels well, since it has escaped the rites and rituals that bind the believer to particular localities in the subcontinent. There are, however, other reasons for the reform groups' success in the new environment. They gain added legitimacy by their strong claim to be perpetuating the teachings of Shah Wali-allah, considered by many to be the foremost Muslim from the subcontinent. Shah Wali-allah had accused the Muslims of India of becoming Indian rather than of identifying with the worldwide *ummah*. He struggled to create an integrated Muslim brotherhood which could call all others Muslims into a united religious social grouping. Throughout the nineteenth and twentieth centuries the reform movements continued and developed his ideas into a successful strategy to cope with the arrival of British colonial power and the subsequent loss of Muslim authority over India. In their efforts to keep Muslim society distinct from both the culture and religion of the invaders and the indigenous Hindu majority, they constructed a wall of isolation maintained by the issue of thousands of *fatwas* concerned with minutiae of daily Muslim life as based on their interpretation of the *Hadith*. The reformers' main strategy was to turn their attentions inwards to the Muslim community and to promote a renewal of Islam that was to be brought about by returning to the universals of the faith. Practically, this involved a propaganda war against rituals and customs regarded by the reformers as *bida*. Their *ulema* intensely disliked anything to do with British culture, language and education. In all these areas they encouraged Muslims to assert their own identity and to perceive the culture of the invaders as *jahiliyya*. The reformers succeeded in making religion a badge of pride which provided a sense of community in the present reinforced by a sense of continuity with the past.

The most successful of these reform groups was the *Deobandis*. They made the *madrasa* or *dar al-Ulum* the centre of their institutional activities in order to create well-educated *ulema* who could preach the reform message effectively. They decided that the teaching within the *dar al-Ulums* would consist only of the traditional religious curriculum taught through the medium of Arabic and Urdu. The *Deobandi* emphasis on observance of correct custom and application of the *Shari'ah* in all areas of life made them deeply conservative. This they held in common with all the nineteenth century reform organisations. They made great use of *fatwas*, but this both established the boundaries of the reform message and also created the boundaries which differentiated those diverse Muslim points of view, from which grew the various reform movements. The *Deobandi* conservatism is combined with a sense of having a special understanding of the reality of God. This gave them a strong sense of uniqueness, of being special. Like the *Barelwis*, they saw themselves as the true *Sunni* Muslims, but the *Deobandis* condemned others as deluded or confused by adding customs derived from local culture to their practice of Islam. This conservatism extended to their attitude towards *ijtihad*. Threaded through these issues is the underlying concept of community. The *Deobandis* felt the need to define the limits of a group of Muslims where unity was secured by maintaining a shared correct perspective on all issues which affected the practice of Islam.

The *Barelwi* fear that their children will be attracted by the reform message is not without foundation. It is not really surprising that the *Deobandis* have achieved a degree of success in establishing themselves in Britain. Their sense of pride resulted in part from their rejection of local Sufi-based customs in favour of regulations drawn from authentic text. The *Deobandis* teach that believers have to be responsible for their own practice rather than relying on the intervention of saints and *pirs*. This shift places more weight on individual initiative and self-understanding. This change of emphasis should ideally be suited to young Muslims born and educated in British cities, and certainly the *Deobandis* appeared to be better placed to provide the religious needs of the migrants within the context of their radically changed situation in Britain. They had already established an esteemed tradition which was able to provide Muslims with self-pride and identity by defining their morality and beliefs favourably against the materialistic culture of the British. To many of the middle-class Muslims who dominate the mosque committees of Britain, the *Deobandi* tradition of scholarship and religious orthodoxy seemed to provide the qualities required to establish and continue Islam amongst the migrants. The central concern of the *Deobandis*, to remove superstitions and folk-belief and to rediscover the pristine faith of Islam through direct study of the *Hadith* and the Qur'an, was ideally suited to the new status of the migrants.

Many Muslims living in Britain feel themselves to be part of a community under threat. The subcontinent Muslim presence in Britain is a direct product of the colonial relationship, and British Muslims still find that they are a relatively powerless minority in the midst of a non-Muslim majority. It is not surprising that Muslims turn to the reform movements for guidance. They have over two hundred years of experience in safeguarding an authentic religious expression and disseminating detailed information in religious matters to a community lacking the security of a Muslim state.

There are, however, problems. Although the *Deobandis* claim to represent an Islam which is universal, in practice they are often closely linked with various class and ethnic groups in the subcontinent. The rivalry between the various reform organisations and the conflict which usually expresses itself as *Deobandi/Barelwi* hostility has little sympathy from the young British-born generations. Many of the latter regard it as part of subcontinent history, having no relevance to their own needs in Britain. As with the *Barelwis*, the concern which the *Deobandi* elders feel for the younger generation is more to do with perpetuating their own traditions than understanding the new requirements of British-born Muslims. Although the *Dar al-Ulums* established in Britain have modified the traditional Deoband curriculum, it will still disadvantage young Muslims who wish to develop skills and careers requiring secular further education. The religious knowledge gained in the *Deobandi dar al-Ulums* will help to preserve the tradition in Britain by providing *ulema* whose framework and life experience is here rather than based in the subcontinent. It will also supply *ulema* who are fluent in English, such *ulema* are, at present, in very short supply. It is reasonable to assume, however, that the present demand for *dar al-Ulum* places is more to do with the *Deobandi* policy of isolation that originates in their fear of the influence of British culture.

This fearful and defensive attitude has been considerably reinforced by the *Deobandis'* close liaison with *Tabligh-i Jamaat*. It must be acknowledged, however, that *Tabligh-i Jamaat's* worldwide activities help the *Deobandis* to widen their frame of reference outwards from the subcontinent to the larger Muslim world. The successful missionary activity of *Tabligh-i Jamaat* revitalises the nineteenth century reform message and carries it forward into the twentieth century. In Britain, Muslims inspired by the *Tabligh-i* missionaries to return to the practice of their faith will do so in the *Deobandi* mosque network. In this way many British-born reverts to their faith may well find themselves joining *Deobandi* congregations without any knowledge of Deoband's history or significance to their parents. In the main, the first-generation migrants are more likely to respond to the orthodox conservatism of the *Deobandi* tradition, because although it frees them from the apparently outmoded folk beliefs of the subcontinent and links them to the wider *ummah* through the teachings of classical Islam, it still does not compromise their identity as a people rooted in the place of origin. For the first-generation migrants, the *Deobandi* reform tradition is familiar and authoritative.

It is the twentieth century revivalist movements based on *Jamaat-i Islami* which seem to have the ability to adapt themselves most readily to the needs of British Muslims. Like the earlier reform movements discussed above they promote Islamic identity over and above ethnic or national identity, and their programmes seek to undermine South Asian customs and traditions which are not essential to the universals of Islam. There are, however, key differences. In the subcontinent they have already proved themselves more adaptable to political and social changes. This can be partly attributed to Mawdudi's insistence that the doors of *ijtihad* were always open and his subsequent critique of the conservative tradition-bound *ulema*. His belief in the use of individual reason to interpret the Qur'an and *Sunna* combined with his acceptance of scientific and technological development won over many middle-class educated young Muslims; they were also attracted by his critique of certain outward forms such as special dress and certain kinds of appearance. In spite of this tolerance, Mawdudi was not prepared to compromise his Islam or be apologetic. He attacked the Western ideologies of nationalism and secularism with intellectual vigour which pleased the newly rising middle-class professionals, who opposed the *ulema* and *pirs* on the ground that they were superstitious but also criticised the West because of colonial and post-colonial exploitation. Mawdudi's Islamic programme was ideological and political and called for a radical overhaul of Muslim society.

The flexibility which *Jamaat-i Islami* has demonstrated in the subcontinent without giving way on fundamentals has intensified on its transposition to Britain. The insistence on the need for a Muslim state has been modified in this country and the focus is on *dawah*. Of greater significance is the fact that the organisations have become less dependent on Maududi's ideas and are prepared to question them when responding to new political, social or economic developments. He is now regarded more as a source of inspiration and it is the Constitutions of the various organisations which dictate purpose and functions. The activists of these organisations are consciously aware of the special needs of British-born Muslims. They are challenging the traditional ideas on the role of women, the use of regional languages to promote Islam, and the identification of ethnicity with religion. In this respect they are beginning to promote the use of English and some of the younger members are challenging marriages on ethnic lines, insisting on the right to choose partners based on their practice of Islam regardless of place of origin. The magazines and pamphlets produced by the various organisations (i.e. *Trends*) address issues with which young British Muslims are concerned, especially in the area of social and political problems, and relate to both Britain and the world at large. In this respect, the *Jamaat-i Islami* influenced organisations are encouraging young British Muslims to identify with the struggle of the Islamic Movement throughout the world rather than with the narrower awareness of issues originating in the subcontinent.

In spite of this awareness of the issues facing young Muslims in Britain, and the need to develop an indigenous Islam without compromising fundamentals, there are still problems to be overcome. The twentieth century revivalist organisations develop into close-knit organisational structures in which members are carefully selected, and trained to ensure ideological conformity and the required level of religious knowledge. A high level of commitment is required. Although recognising a common allegiance with other groups of similiar ideology which they refer to as the Islamic Movement, they distinguish true believers from their fellow Muslims. All too often the distinction is based upon allegiance to their own activities, which invariably opens them to criticism of being sectarian. The *Jamaat-i Islami* organisations in Britain are still too closely connected with the subcontinent organisations to fulfil, as they claim, the needs of all British Muslims regardless of ethnic origin. In Birmingham, for example, a well-established Yemeni community lives alongside the Pakistani migrants, but the *Jamaat-i Islami* organisations' activities are virtually non-existent outside the subcontinent communities. The high degree of qualitative selection for membership limits the numbers able to join as it does in Pakistan and India. Essentially the organisations attract the educated middle-classes, and in Britain the youth organisations' members are almost exclusively university and college graduates. The emphasis on social justice and political issues attracts many young educated Muslims who feel socially downtrodden both in Britain and the subcontinent. There are, however, dangers that the Islamic ideology of the recruits will merely be reactive.

It is difficult to foresee the possible direction which Islam will take in Britain: to some degree this will depend on the attitudes of the receiving culture and events in the wider world. Certainly the demands of British-born Muslims will eventually be met by themselves as they succeed the first-generation migrants. At present the various religious groups are still caught up in conflicts and divisions imported from the subcontinent, and their various activities tend to divide the communities along sectarian and ethnic lines rather than uniting them under the banner of Islam. Several of my informants from both *Barelwi* and *Deobandi* camps were aware of the need to transcend their differences, and recognised that their children would not be concerned with these issues. The *Deobandi* tradition which insists upon a chauvinistic attitude and is isolationist, stressing correct Muslim dress as based on subcontinent styles, length and styles of beards, correct Islamic manners and customs derived from nineteenth century Muslim behaviour, and which is in danger of making Urdu a sacred language used exclusively for worship and the study of sacred texts will need to adapt. Some informants felt that the *Deobandi* tradition was in danger, along with traditional *Barelwis*, of becoming increasingly sectarian and out of touch with modern society along the lines of orthodox Jewish groups, for example the Hassidim.   Maulana Ahmad Shaheed Raza suggested that the main difference between the *Barelwis* and the reform groups lay in their respective attitudes towards Muslim integration with non-Muslim cultures throughout the history of Islam's spread across the globe. He stated that the *Barelwi* attitude was that Islam had always been tolerant of indigenous culture as long as the principles of Islam were observed. Consequently, it had always adapted well. On the other hand, the reform groups attempted to separate out the principles of Islam and to discover the pristine universal faith which can be practised anywhere. If both these courses are pursued in Britain then many young Muslims of *Barelwi* and *Deobandi* parentage may find themselves arriving at a common ground in which they establish a truly British Muslim community for those who wish to continue practising their faith. The danger will be that they will continue to maintain historical conflicts through familial loyalty even though no longer relevant.   In this process of moving towards common ground there is no doubt of the crucial ideological role that will be taken by the activists of the youth movements influenced by *Jamaat-i Islami* and by the Islamic Movement. Their membership may always remain small and elite, but their intellectual vigour and successful publications will pinpoint the issues that the present and future generations of British Muslims will need to tackle. This will be further reinforced by summer camps, conferences and rallies. They can supply the intellectual leadership required providing they can further develop flexibility and moderation. The foundation of the umbrella organisation, *Islamic Society of Britain*, is of key interest in this context.   Despite their assertion, however, to be independent of any sectarian influences, a comparison of their Constitution with those of the *Jamaat-i Islami* organisations in the subcontinent and Britain demonstrates the influence of the latter (see Appendices G-I). The claim of these groups to be moderate will be substantiated as the more reactive elements amongst the Muslim youth are attracted to more extreme organisations such as *Hizb ut Tahrir*. Their focus, however, on the ideological aspect of Islam rather than personal piety may deny them popular support. The richness and variety of the subcontinent Sufi tradition may always be attractive to those seeking a more spiritual personal experience. In this respect, *Tabligh-i Jamaat*, which combines the teachings of the reform movements with the personal piety of the Sufis may prove to be more popular with the less educated as it is in the subcontinent.

There are some interesting lines of research which can be pursued in order to throw more light on this area of study. It would be interesting to know how many young Muslims endorse the ideas put forward by groups such as *Young Muslims UK* without actually becoming members. More work also needs to be done on the direction some *Barelwis* are likely to take under the influence of British *pirs*. In this respect, the views of Pir Noor ul-Aqtab Siddiqi and the direction in which he is intending to take his father's organisation would be revealing. Very soon the first graduates of the *Deobandi dar al-Ulums* in Britain will be taking up their positions as *imams*. Again it would be interesting to discover how their attitudes compared with those of their elders. A substantial piece of work on the ways that *'ummah'* is used as a symbol to promote common Islamic awareness or group identity could be undertaken by someone with the linguistic ability to translate sermons delivered in the mosque by the *imams*. Finally I have not explored the impact of Islamic modernism in Britain on the development of the community because I did not feel that it came under the category of 'sectarian'; nonetheless its influence needs to be assessed.

Endnotes

[1] Schiffauer, Werner, 1988, 'Migration and Religiousness', *The New Islamic Presence in Western Europe*, Ed. Gerholm, Tomas and Lithman,Yngve Georg, Mansell Publishing, London.

[2] Gellner,E., 1968, 'The Pendulum Swing Theory of Islam', *Sociology of Religion*, ed.Robertson,Roland, Penguin,London.

[3] McWilliams, Wilson Carey, 1974, *The Idea of Fraternity in America*, University of California Press, Berkeley.

[4] Mannheim, Karl, 1948, *Ideology and Utopia*, Routledge and Kegan Paul, London, p.57.

[5] Somervell, D.C., *A Study of History -Abridgement of Vol I-VI* by Arnold Toynbee, Issued under the auspices of the Royal Institute of International Affairs, Oxford University Press, London, pp.253-256.

[6] ibid., p.253.

[7] *The Holy Qur'an, Al-Imran* 3.104.

[8] Poplin, Dennis. E., 1972, *Communities - A Study of Theories and Methods of Research*, The MacMillan Company, New York; Shenkar, Barry, 1986, *Intentional Communities - Ideology and Alienation in Communal Societies*, Routledge and Kegan Paul, London.

[9] Rex, John and Josephides, Sasha, 1987, 'Asian and Greek Cypriot Associations and Identity', *Immigrant Associations in Europe*, eds. Rex, John; Joly, Daniele; Wilpert, Czarina, Gower, Aldershot, p.19.

[10] Joly, Daniele, 1987, 'Associations Amongst the Pakistani Population in Britain', *Immigrant Associations in Europe*, eds.Rex, John; Joly, Daniele; Wilpert, Czarina, Gower, Aldershot, p.69.

Appendix A

Usage of Ummah	M2	M3	Medinan
a) oneness of Ummah	43:33;23:52; 21:92	16:92,93;11:118; 42:8;10:19	2:213; 16:120; 5:48
b) Messengers and agents of God connected with Ummah	43:22,23;23:44; 27:83	41:25;16:36,63; 16:84,89;11:48;40:5; 28:75;29:18;10:48; 35:24,42;7:168;46:18; 6:42,108	2:134,141,143,213; 4:41;7:159,160;16:120 22:34;5:48
c) Ummah as appointed term	15:5;23:43;27:83	41:25;16:36,63;16:89; 40:5;29:18;35:24;7:38; 7:164;46:18;6:42;13:30	2:134,141
d) Ummahs which have perished (judgement)	23:44;27:83	41:25;16:36,63,89; 40:5;29:18;35:24;7:38; 7:164;46:18;6:42;13:30	2:134,141;7:160
e) Ummah as religion, connected with a rite	43:22,23;23:52; 21:92	10:19	2:128;3:113;16:120;22:34 22:67
f) Ummah as other godly people	23:52;21:92	16:92;29:18;11:48;7:168 35:42	2:134,141;16:120,121; 3:113;7:159,160;5:66
g) Abraham as Ummah			2:134,141;16:120
h) Muslims as an Ummah	23:52;21:92	45:28;16:89;16:92;29:18 7:181;13:30	2:128,134,141,143;3:104 3:110,113;16:120;22:34; 5:66
g) Ummah as any belief system	43:22,23		
h) Ummah as tribe		28:23;7:164	7:160
i) Ummah as genus		6:38	
j) Ummah as set time		11:8;12:45	

1. Table information taken from Denny, Frederick, Mathewson, 1975, 'The Meaning of Ummah in the Qur'an', *History of Religions* Vol.15, No.1, pp.43,46-47, and the *Holy Qur'an*. The chronology follows Noldeke-Schwally. Where Richard Bell (1936, *The Qur'an: Translated with a Critical Re-arrangement of the Surahs*, T.Clark, Edinburgh) disagrees and places some Meccan verses in the Medinan period, the references are italicised. The *Holy Qur'an* chronology essentially agrees with Noldeke-Schwally concerning Meccan and Medinan *surahs*. There is only a difference concerning the period of the Meccan *surahs*.

Appendix B

THE CONSTITUTION OF MEDINA

The Text of the Document

Ibn Ishaq said: The Messenger of God (God bless and preserve him) wrote a writing (*kitab*) between the Emigrants and the *Ansar*, in which he made a treaty and covenant with the Jews, confirmed them in their religion and possessions, and gave them certain duties and rights:

In the name of God, the Merciful, the Compassionate!

This is the writing of Muhammad the prophet between the believers and Muslims of *Quraysh* and *Yathrib* and those who follow them and are attached to them and who crusade (*jihadu*) along with them.

1. They are a single community (*ummah*) distinct from (other) people.

2. The Emigrants of *Quraysh*, according to their former condition, pay jointly the blood-money between them, and they (as a group) ransom their captive(s), (doing so) with uprightness and justice between the believers.

3. *Banu 'Awf*, according to their former condition, pay jointly the previous blood-wits, and each sub-clan (*ta'ifah*) ransoms its captive(s), (doing so) with uprightness and justice between the believers.

4. *Banu 'l-Harith*, according to their former condition, pay jointly...(as 3).

5. *Banu Sa'idah*...(as 3).

6. *Banu Jusham*...(as 3).

7. *Banu 'n-Najjar*...(as 3).

8. *Banu 'Amr b. 'Awf*...(as 3).

9. *Banu 'n-Nabit*...(as 3).

10. *Banu 'l-Aws*...(as 3).

11. The believers do not forsake a debtor among them, but give him (help), according to what is fair, for ransom or blood-wit.

12. A believer does not take as confederate (*halif*) the client (*mawla*) of a believer without his (the latter's) consent.

13. The God-fearing believers are against whoever of them acts wrongfully or seeks (?plans) an act that is unjust or treacherous or hostile or corrupt among the believers; their hands are all against him, even if he is one of them.

14. A believer does not kill a believer because of an unbeliever, and does not help an unbeliever against a believer.

15. The security (*dhimmah*) of God is one; the granting of 'neighbourly protection' (*yujir*) by the least of them (the believers) is binding on them; the believers are patrons (or *clients-mawali*) of one another to the exclusion of (other) people.

16. Whoever of the Jews follows us has the (same) help and support (*nasr, iswah*) (as the believers), so long as they are not wronged (by him) and he does not help (others) against them.

17. The peace (*silm*) of the believers is one; no believer makes peace apart from another believer, where there is fighting in the way of God, except in so far as equality and justice between them (is maintained).

18. In every expedition made with us the parties take turns with one another.

19. The believers exact vengeance for one another where a man gives his blood in the way of God. The God-fearing believers are under the best and most correct guidance.

20. No idolater (*mushrik*) gives 'neighbourly protection' (*yujir*) for goods or person to *Quraysh*, nor intervenes in his (a *Qurashi's*) favour against a believer.

21. When anyone wrongfully kills a believer, the evidence being clear, then he is liable to be killed in retaliation for him, unless the representative of the murdered man is satisfied (with a payment). The believers are against him (the murderer) entirely; nothing is permissible to them except to oppose him.

22. It is not permissible for a believer who has agreed to what is in this document (*sahifah*) and believed in God and the last day to help a wrong-doer or give him lodging. If anyone helps him or gives him lodging, then upon this man is the curse of God and His wrath on the day of resurrection, and from him nothing will be accepted to make up for it or take its place.

23. Wherever there is anything about which you differ, it is to be referred to God and to Muhammad (peace be upon him).

24. The Jews bear expenses along with the believers so long as they continue at war.

25. The Jews of *Banu 'Awf* are a community (*ummah*) along with the believers. To the Jews their religion (*din*) and to the Muslims their religion. (This applies) both to their clients and to themselves, with the exception of anyone who has done wrong or acted treacherously; he brings evil only on himself and on his household

26. For the Jews of *Banu 'Najjar* the like of what is for the Jews of *Banu 'Awf*.

27. For the Jews of *Banu 'Harith* the like...

28. For the Jews of *Banu Sa'idah* the like...

29. For the Jews of *Banu Jusham* the like...

30. For the Jews of *Banu 'l-Aws* the like...

31. For the Jews of *Banu Tha'labah* the like of what is for the Jews of *Banu 'Awf* with the exception of anyone who has done wrong or acted treacherously; he brings evil only on himself and his household.

32. *Jafnah*, a subdivision (*batn*) of *Tha'labah*, are like them.

33. For *Banu'sh-Sutaybah* the like of what is for the Jews of *Banu 'Awf*; honourable dealing (comes) before treachery.

34. The clients of *Tha'labah* are like them

35. The *bitanah* (obscure) of (particular) Jews are as themselves.

36. Not one of them (? those belonging to the *ummah*) may go out (to war) without the permission of Muhammad (peace be upon him), but he is not restrained from taking vengeance for wounds. Whoever acts rashly (*fataka*), it (involves) only himself and his household, except where a man has been wronged. God is the truest (fulfiller) of this (document).

37. It is for the Jews to bear their expenses and for the Muslims to bear their expenses. Between them (that is, to one another) there is help (*nasr*) against whoever wars against the people of this document. Between them is sincere friendship (*nas'h wa-nasihah*), and honourable dealing, not treachery. A man is not guilty of treachery through (the act of) his confederate. There is help for (or, help is to be given to) the person wronged.

38. The Jews bear expenses along with the believers so long as they continue at war.

39. The valley of Yathrib is sacred for the people of this document.

40. The 'protected neighbour' (*jar*) is as the man himself so long as he does no harm and does not act treacherously.

41. No woman is given 'neighbourly protection' (*tujar*) without the consent of her people.

42. Whenever among the people of this document there occurs an incident (disturbance) or quarrel from which disaster for it (the people) is to be feared, it is to be referred to God and to Muhammad, the Messenger of God (God bless and preserve him) God is the most scrupulous and truest (fulfiller) of what is in this document.

43. No 'neighbourly protection' is given (*la tujar*) to *Quraysh* and those who help them.

44. Between them (? the people of this document) is help against whoever suddenly attacks Yathrib.

45. Whenever they are summoned to conclude and accept a treaty, they conclude and accept it; when they in turn summon to the like of that, it is for them upon the believers, except whoever wars about religion; for (?=incumbent on) each man is his share from their side which is towards them.

46. The Jews of *al-Aws*, both their clients and themselves, are in the same position as belongs to the people of this document while they are thoroughly honourable in their dealings with the people of this document. Honourable dealing (comes) before treachery.

47. A person acquring (? guilt) acquires it only against himself. God is the most upright and truest (fulfiller) of what is in this document. This writing does not intervene to protect a wrongdoer or traitor. He who goes out is safe, and he who sits still is safe in Medina, except whoever does wrong and acts treacherously. God is 'protecting neighbour' (*jar*) of him who acts honourably and fears God, and Muhammad is the Messenger of God (God bless and preserve him).

(Taken from Watt, Montgomery W., 1972, *Muhammad at Medina*, Clarendon Press, Oxford, pp.221-225.

Appendix C

SALAAM

(Translation of *Na't* written by Ahmed Riza Khan Barelwi which is sung by *Barelwis* after Friday Prayers and on special occasions)

One hundred thousand blessings be on Mustafa,
the chosen one,
the essence of Allah's Mercy.
One hundred thousand blessings
be on the lamp of the prophet's company.

Allah's Peace and benedictions
be on the Sun in the Sky of Prophethood
One hundred thousand blessings
be on the Rose in the garden of Messengership.

Eternal peace be on the Bridegroom in the Night of Ascension
who was taken into the presence of God
One hundred thousand blessings
be on the Bridegroom in the company of Paradise.

Countless benedictions be on the Lord of the Poor
One hundred thousand blessings
be on our real wealth.

By the light of whose face, dark hearts began to shine
One hundred thousand blessings
be on his radiant complexion.

His lips are the thin petals of the celestial rose
One hundred thousand blessings
be on their tenderness.

His mouth utters the revelation of God
One hundred thousand blessings
be on this fountain of wisdom.

His tongue is the key to the Divine Command, 'Be!'
One hundred thousand blessings
be on his mighty rule.

Countless benedictions be on his honeyed speech
One hundred thousand blessings
be on his alluring eloquence.

By whose consolation, the suffering laugh
One hundred thousand blessings
be on his manner of smiling.

Given the universe as his possession,
but he eats only barley bread
One hundred thousand blessings
be on the contentment of his heart.

The hour the Moon of Arabia rose and shone
One hundred thousand blessings
be on that brightest hour.

Oh God! Oh God!
the loveliness of his childhood
One hundred thousand blessings
be on his God-loved form

Ask Moses whom he saw
One hundred thousand blessings
be on the boldness of the Prophet's eye.[1]

In short,
One hundred thousand blessings
be on every hair
One hundred thousand blessings
be on all his traits.

Countless benedictions from his Lord be on him
One hundred thousand blessings
be on his companions and family.

[1] This is a reference to the belief that Moses was not able to see God but that Muhammad glimpsed Allah during the *Mi'raj*.

Appendix D

THE SPIRITUAL GENEALOGY OF THE NAQSHBANDI SUFI ORDER OF GHAMKOL
SHARIF, KOHAT, PAKISTAN

Oh Allah

Bless me, for the sake of Your Greatness,
For the sake of Your Chosen Prophet.

Give me most perfect truth and sincerity
For the sake of Hazrat Abu Bakr,
The Truthful and Righteous, Commander of the Faithful.

Give me divine love
For the sake of the sincerity of Hazrat Salman Farsi,
Companion of the Prophet.

Give me steadfastness
For the sake of Imam Qasim, grandson of Imam Jaafar,
The Truthful and Most Pure.

For the sake of the Guides,
The Great Helper (*Ghaus*), the Axis of the world (*Qutb*),
The most elevated of Sufi Masters, Bayazid.

Make my heart beat with God's remembrance (*zikr*)
For the sake of the modesty
Of Abu'l Hasan of Kharqan.

Free me from sin
For the sake of Khajah Abu Qasim of Gargan,
Who is filled with light.

Grant me good deeds
For the sake of Khaja Hazrat 'Bu-Ali of Farmid,
Saint of the World.

Grant me perfection
For the sake of the most wondrous saint, the Leader,
Khaja Abdul Khaliq of Ghadjdawani.

For my faith,
Let the holiness of Hazrat Hoja Muhammad Arif of Regawar
Prevail upon me.

Teach me the lesson of mercy
For the sake of the limitless pearl, the man of truth,
Hazrat Mahmood Al-Khair of Faghna.

May your name be dear
For the sake of the most honest
Hazrat Khaja Azizana Ali of Ramteen.

Fill my heart with love
For the sake of that lover,
Baba Samasee, Lover of God.

Grant me perfect righteousness
For the sake of the Pious Sayyid
Hazrat Shah Kalal Mir, who is filled with generosity.

Imprint Thy Name upon my heart
For the sake of the Saint of Saints, the exalted self,
The King, Naqshband.

Perfume my heart
For the sake of the joyous face of
Hazrat Khaja Ala-Udin of Atar.

Turn me from idleness and neglectfulness
For the sake of Memu Hama,
And of Hazrat Yaqoob Charkhi,
Helper of the destitute.

Make me Your absolute lover
For the sake of Khajah Ubaidullah,
The Noble, the Free, the Beloved.

Grant me abstinence too
For the sake of the wondrous ascetic,
Hazrat Khaja Muhammad Zahid.

Make me special before the saintly ascetics (*darwesh*)
For the sake of the saintly ascetic, Man of Cloak (*aba*),
Khaja Darwesh Muhammad.

Make me a fellow disciple
For the sake of the confidant of God,
King of Saints, Khaja Muhammad Baqi Billah.

Grant me greatness in this world and the hereafter
For the sake of the incomparable Guide of the Truth,
Hazrat Mujaddid-i-Alif Thani.

Give me divine guidance to worship You
And turn me away from evil
For the sake of Muhammad Shah Husain, God's Trusted.

Grant me Your Love, and the love of Mustafa (PBUH),
For the sake of Sayyid Abdul Basit,
Of the auspicious face.

Oh Sustainer

At my death may I die a believer
For the sake of Muhammad Abdul Qadr,
The Leader, may God have mercy on him.

Protect me from the enemies of religion and the world
For the sake of Sayyid Mehmood,
One of the Blessers.

Make my self (hal) in accordance with Thy commands
For the sake of Khaja Abdullah,
Leader of God's Friends.

Fill me with light from head to toe
For the sake of Shah Inayatullah
The Sincere.

Shelter me, Oh God, for I am destitute,
For the sake of Hafiz Ahmed,
The Gracious.

I am no ascetic, no worshipper, only a man of God,
For the sake of Abdul Sabur Sahib,
The Faithful.

I am never separate from you, Oh God,
For the sake of Raja Gul Muhammad,
He who is filled with light.

Cast an eye on my miseries, Oh God,
For the sake of Hazrat Abdul Majid Sahib,
One of the Sufis.

My sins exceed all limits, have mercy,
For the sake of Muhammad Shah Maluk,
One of God's people.

To my friends too, for the sake of Mustafa (PBUH),
For the sake of Shah Nizam Udin,
God's Beloved.

Accept the intercession of these saints in my favour:
Hazrat Muhammad Qasim Mori,
The Great Helper of the World (*ghaus*),
The most noble of Saints,
The Beloved of God.

Have mercy on me, give me blessings
For the sake of Khaja Hazrat Shah of Ghamkol,
God's Beloved, God's Great Helper,
The King of Sufis.

Give me burning love to overcome my selfish self (*nafs*)
For the sake of Khaja Sufi Muhammad Abdullah,
Slave of Mustafa (PBUH).

Appendix E

THE GENEALOGY OF THE REFORM MOVEMENTS TRACING THEIR
ORIGIN TO SHAH WALI ALLAH

Taught *Hadith* ———

Sufi Master/Disciple Relationship - - - - -

SHAH WALI-ALLAH (1702 - 1763)
(Qur'an to Persian)

SHAH ABD AL-AZIZ (1746-1823)
(son and successor to Shah Wali-Allah)

SHAH RAFIUDDIN (1749 -1817)
(Qur'an to Urdu, son of Shah Wali-Allah)

SHAH ABD AL-QADIR (1753 - 1627)
(Qur'an to Urdu, son of Shah Wali-Allah)

SAYYID AHMAD OF RAE BAREILLY (1786 - 1831)

YAQUB

ABD AL-HAYY (d. 1828)
(son-in-law of Abd al-Aziz) Disciple of Sayyid Ahmad

ABD AL-HAYY
(Principal of Farangi Mahal and Nadwah in Lucknow)

MUHAMMAD ISHMAEL (1781 - 1831)
(Author of *Straight Path*;
grandson of Shah Wali-allah,
killed with Sayyid Ahmad in 1831)

RAFIUDDIN DIHLAWI
(Successor to Sayyid Ahmad
in *Jihad* movement)

NASIMIDDIN DIHLAWI
(Grandson of Rafiuddin who
taught Sufism to Imadadullah)

KARAMAT ALI (d.1873)

INAYAT ALI

WILAYAT ALI

(Founders of Bengal
Reform movements)

NOOR MUHAMMAD

MUHAMMAD ISHAQ (1778 - 1846)
(Leadership successor to Delhi
reformists. Grandson of Shah Wali-
allah. He and Yaqub both left for
Hijaz in 1842)

MAULANA RASHIUDDIN KHAN
(First Head of Arabic
at Delhi College)

MAULANA MAMLUK ALI
(succeeded the above as
Head of Arabic at Delhi
College)

ABD AL-GHANI NAQSHBANDI (1819 - 1878)
(successor to Muhammad Ishaq)

SAYYID NAZIR HUSAIN (d.1902)
(Founder of *Ahl-i Hadith*)

SIDDIQ HASAN (d. 1890)
(Founder of Delhi centre
of *Ahl-i Hadith*)

IMADADULLAH (1817 - 1899)
(Famous *Shaikh* of the reformers)

MUHAMMAD QASIM NANAUTAWI (1833 - 1877)
(Co-founder of Deoband and
nephew of Mamluk Ali)

RASHID AHMED GANGOHI (1829 - 1905)
(Co-founder of Deoband;
studied with Mamluk Ali)

MAHMUD AL-HASAN
(First teacher at Deoband)

HUSAIN AHMAD MADANI (1879 -1957)
(Founder of *Jami'a Ulema-i Hind*)

AHMAD ALI SAHARANPUR
(Founder of Saharanpur
Dar al Ulum)

MUHAMMAD ILYAS
(Founder of *Tabligh-i Jamaat*;
studied *Hadith* at Deoband and
taught in Saharanpur)

SAYYID AHMAD KHAN (1817 - 1898)
(Leader of post-1857 modernists
and founder of Aligarh College)

SAMIULLAH KHAN

ZAKAULLAH KHAN
(taught the father of
Maulana Mawdudi)

NAZIR AHMAD
(All associates of Sayyid
Ahmad Khan in Aligarh)

MUHAMMAD ABDULLAH
(Son-in-law of Nanautawi,
supervised religious teaching
of Muslim boys at Aligarh)

Appendix F

The Eight-Year Course of the Arabic Classes

FIRST YEAR

Subject	Books
Conjugation - Grammar (*Sarf*)	Arabic Primer, *Mizan al-Sarf* and *Munsha'ab* (complete), *Panj Ganj* (complete).
Syntax (*Nahv*)	Memorising of *Nahv-e Mir* (complete); *Sharh-e Mi'ata A'mil* (complete).
Arabic Literature	*Rauzat al-Adab* (omitting *Bab al-Makateeb*); *Insha-e Arabi* (Prose); *Arabi ka Mu'allim* (Parts I & II).
Logic	*Taiseer al-Mantiq*.
Chirography (*Khush-navisi*)	Correct writing and dictation.
Cantillation (*Tajvid*)	Exercise in cantillation in the first quarter of the *Para-e Amm* and traditional invocations.

SECOND YEAR

Subject	Books
Jurisprudence (*fiqh*)	*Nur al-Ezah* (complete); *Qaduri* (up to *Kitab al-Hajj*).
Syntax	Hedayat al-Nahv (complete); Al-Nahv al-Wazeh (Elementary Part I).
Conjugation	*'Ilm al-Sigha* (up to *Khasiyat*); *Fusool-e Akbari* (from *Khasiyat*).
Arabic Literature	*Nafahat al-Adab* (complete); *Tamrin-e Arabi*.
Logic	*Mirqat* and *Tehzib*.
Cantillation	Exercise in the last one-third of the *Para-e Amn* with memorising. *Jamal al-Quran* (complete).
Chirography	Correct writing and dictation.

THIRD YEAR

Subject	Books
Quranic Exegesis (*tafsir*)	*Tarjumat al-Quran* (*Sura-e Baqrah*)
Jurisprudence	*Qaduri* (from *Kitab al-Buyu* till the end)
Syntax	*Ibn 'Aqeel* (up to 300 pages); *Sharh-e Jami* (verb and particle).
Arabic Literature	*Nafahat al-Arab* (Prose).
Logic	*Sharh-e-Tehzib* (up to *Zabita*); *Qutbi* (*Tasdiqaat*).
Hadith	*Mishkat al-Athaar*.

FOURTH YEAR

Subject	Books
Quranic Exegesis	*Tarjumat al-Quran* (from *Sura-e Aal-e Imran* up to *Sura-e Mariam*.
Jurisprudence	*Kanz al-Daqa'iq* (up to *Kitab al-Nikah*); *Shah-e Waqaya*, vol ii (up to *Kitab al 'Itaq*).
Principles of Jurisprudence	*Usool al-Shashi* (complete).
Rhetorics	*Mukhtasar al-Ma'ani* (up to the end of the second subject); *Talkhis al-Miftah* (only the third subject).
Logic	*Sallam al-Ulum* (up to the end of *Tasawwurat*).
Philosophy	*Hadya-e Sa'eed* (first half).
Hadith	*Alfiyat al-Hadith*.

FIFTH YEAR

Subject	Books
Jurisprudence	*Hedaya*: First Quarter; Second Quarter.
Arabic Literature	*Maqamat-e Hariri* (10 *Maqalas*).
Logic	*Mulla Hasan* (up to *Jins*).
Principles of Jurisprudence	*Nur al-Anwar* (up to *Qiyas*).
Beliefs ('Aqa'id)	*'Aqidat al-Tahavi* (complete).
Rhetorics	*Al-Balaghat al-Wazeha.*

SIXTH YEAR

Subject	Books
Tafsir	*Jalalayn Sharif* (complete): Two hours daily.
Usool-e Tafsir	*Al-Fawz al-Kabir* (complete).
Usool-e Fiqh	*Husami* (complete).
Philosophy	*Mebazi* (complete).
Arabic Literature	*Divan-e Mutanabbi* (up to the end of the rhyme *Dal*) *Tamrin-e Arabi* (Arabic exercises). *Insha-e Muhadatha* (colloquial prose); Cantillation or Chirography.

SEVENTH YEAR

Subject	Books
Fiqh	*Hedaya* (last portion): two hours daily.
'Aqa'id wa Kalam	*Sharh-e 'Aqa'id-e Nasafi* (complete).
Tafsir	*Baizazi* (one and a quarter portion of *Sura-e Baqrah*).

Hadith	*Mishkat Sharif* (complete).
Usool-e Hadith	*Sharh-e Nakhbat al-Fikr* (complete): two hours daily.
Fara'iz	*Siraji* (complete).

Optional Subjects

Usool-e Tafsir	*Talkhis al-Itqan.*
Usool-e Hadith	*Muqaddama-e Ibn Salah.*
Kalam	*Masamarah.*
Logic	*Hamd Allah.*
Literature	*Divan-e Himasa (Bab al-Adab wal-Himasa); Al-Nathr al-Jadid.*

EIGHTH YEAR
DAURA-E HADITH

Subject **Books**

Hadith

Bukhari Sharif (complete).
Muslim Sharif (complete).
Tirmizi Sharif (complete).
Abu Da'ud Sharif (complete).
Nasa'i Sharif.
Ibn Maja Sharif.
Tahavi Sharif.
Shama'il-e Tirmizi Sharif.
Mu'attaayn (The Two *Mu'attas*).

PRIMARY CLASSES

According to the rules of the *Dar al-Ulum*, the completion of the following primary course is necessary for reaching the above 'Arabic Course':-

The Qur'an Class: (1) First of all it is necessary to be able to read at least the Holy Qur'an. Before the reading of the Qur'an generally the primer which is known as *Qa'ida-e Baghdadi* is taught. The acquiring of the ability to read Qur'an takes more or less two years.

The estimate of this period is for those small children who may have been started to read at the age of five years and may have average intelligence; otherwise intelligent children can complete the reading of the Qur'an in even less time.

The period of committing the Holy Qur'an to memory is more or less three years.

(2) After completing the Qur'an the learning of Urdu and Persian is also necessary, but the Department of Cantillation is also there for those children who wish to be trained in Cantillation and Orthoepy after having memorised the Qur'an.

The Cantillation Class:

In the course of this class, along with the practise of cantillation and orthoepy, the following books are also taught:-

Jamal al Quran, Ma'rifat al-Waqoof, Fawa'id-e Makkia, Shatibia, Rai'yya, Tayyiba.

This is a 2-year course. It has been made compulsory for every student of the Arabic class that, along with other lessons, he should take admission for one period in this department and should practice to read at least the *Para-e Amm* with cantillation.

Urdu Diniyaat (Theology in Urdu):-

(3) Next to the Holy Qur'an class is the Department of *Urdu Diniyaat* in which, besides the teaching of Theology in Urdu language, Arithmetic and other subjects are also taught. The course of this Department is spread over four years.

The Persian Class:-

(4) Next to the *Urdu Diniyaat* Department is the Department of Persian in which primary books of Persian prose and poetry, Arithmetic, Geography, Hindi, and Arabic Grammar are included in the course.

Endnotes

[1] All the information contained in this Appendix is taken from Rizvi, S.M., 1981, *The History of the Dar Al-Ulum, Deoband*, Vol II, Maulana Abdul Haq, Idara-e Ihtemam, Dar al-Ulum, Deoband, pp.202-211. I have not included the Post-Graduate classes or the work of Departments which deal in *Fatwa* writing, *Unani* medicine, or Arabic Calligraphy.

Appendix G

THE CONSTITUTION OF THE ISLAMI JAMIAT-E-TALABA PAKISTAN

Preamble

Whereas we firmly believe

That the creation, continued existence, sustenance and evolution of the universe owes itself to Allah, Alone, Who governs the cosmic order with absolute wisdom, and Who with His Sovereign Will reigns supreme over every atom of the heavens and the earth, Who holds the key to all the resources of sustenance, controls the reigns of life and death and is the fountainhead of all power and strength;

That human life is not confined to this world, rather through the gateway of death man will enter the realm of eternal life wherein he will be required to render an account of every moment and every act of his earthly existence to his Lord Who is aware of the innermost secrets of his heart;

That true success does not lie in securing the ephemeral advantages and transient pleasures of worldly life; it rather lies in achieving success and salvation in the Hereafter and this can be attained only if one orients oneself to living a life in full conformity with the will of the Creator;

That Allah has been raising His prophets (peace be upon them) and revealing His Books for the guidance alone as embodied in His revealed Books and in the life-example of His prophets (peace be upon them) can provide the norms upon which a sound system of human life can be founded; and that the Holy Prophet Muhammad (peace be upon him) is the Last Prophet and Messenger of Allah and that the Qur'an; the Book revealed to him and his inspired life-example shall continue to radiate guidance to all mankind until the end of time;

That the only true course of life for man is to live in total submission to Allah and to follow the directives of the prophets (peace be upon them). In our view the welfare and salvation of man depends upon accepting the principles enshrined in the teachings of the prophets and human history testifies that whenever human life was founded on any other than those principles, man courted his doom. The root cause of all the restlessness found in the present day would also be the large-scale indifference to Divine Guidance, and the only remedy is that man live in obedience to that Guidance;

In view of the above, we, the Islam loving students of Pakistan bring ourselves together under an organisation and hereby resolve:

That our motto shall be to obey Allah and follow in the footsteps of His Messenger (peace and blessings of Allah be upon him). We shall renounce all forms of obedience, worship, and service to false gods and shall devote ourselves exclusively to obeying, worshipping and serving

Allah. We shall look to nothing except the life-example of the Messenger of Allah (peace and blessings of Allah be upon him) as the main source of our guidance and inspiration, and shall do our best to follow the Messenger's life-example in all walks of our life.

That by precept we shall call human beings to obey Allah and worship Him alone and to follow the life-example of His Messenger (peace and blessings of Allah be upon him) and that by our deeds we shall try to bear witness to the fact that obedience to Allah alone is the best course that all men ought to adopt; that the example provided by the prophets (peace be upon them) lead to the true guidance for the entire human race and that the order of life based on obedience to Allah and observance of the life-example of His Messenger (peace and blessings of Allah be upon him) is the best order of life for man;

That all our striving shall be centred around one objective, namely, that the order of life which rests on obedience of Allah and observing the life-example of His Prophet (peace and blessings of Allah be upon him) be established in the world; that the word of Allah be made to prevail; that the way of life prescribed by Allah should govern human life and that mankind abandon every form of servitude except servitude of Allah and follow only the way of His Messenger (peace be upon him);

That as a prelude to the global ISLAMIC REVOLUTION envisioned by us, a full-fledged Islamic system of life should be established in Pakistan. The objective for which Pakistan was established is to build a model Islamic Society and an ideal Islamic State in this part of the world in order that the principles of Islam be presented to the world in an authentic form. We do hereby resolve to bend all our energies so as to bring about a truly ISLAMIC REVOLUTION in Pakistan within the shortest possible time.

We are committed to all this with the aim that our Lord be pleased with us, that we be able to obtain His gracious approbation, and that when we ultimately stand before Him for His final judgement, we might be reckoned as worthy of Success and Salvation.

PART ONE

Chapter 1: NAME, IDEAL AND PROGRAMME

Name:

Article 1.

This organisation of the students of Pakistan shall be called the ISLAMI JAMIAT-E-TALABA PAKISTAN (hereinafter referred to as the '*Jamiat*').

Ideal:

Article 2.

The ideal of the *Islami Jamiat-e-Talaba Pakistan* shall be to seek the pleasure of Allah by ordering human life in accordance with the principles laid down by Allah and His Messenger Muhammad (peace and blessings be upon him).

Programme:

Article 3.

The programme of the *Jamiat* shall be as follows:-

(1) To convey the message of Islam to the students, to induce them to acquire its knowledge, and to awaken them to the task of fulfilling its requirements in practical life.

(2) To organise under the *Jamiat* those students who are prepared to strive for the establishment of Islamic way of life.

(3) To make effective arrangements for the study of Islam and modern thoughts, the building of Islamic character and the development of mental and physical qualities for those students who join the *Jamiat*.

(4) To strive for the implementation of Islamic education system in Pakistan which is the most scientific, comprehensive and easy to establish; to make efforts to solve the problems faced by the students, to get their genuine demands fulfilled and to lead them in their collective problems.

(5) To struggle for the establishment of an Islamic society in Pakistan which ensures human welfare and is free from economic, social and political exploitation.

PART TWO

Chapter 1: MEMBERSHIP

Article 4.

Any Pakistani student who is enrolled in any educational institution or is a private student and who;

(1) affirms the ideals of *Jamiat* as his own ideal of life, after fully understanding it;

(2) fully agrees with the programme and the methodology of the *Jamiat*;

(3) pledges to adhere to the discipline of the *Jamiat* in accordance with its Constitution;

(4) has such minimum knowledge of Islam as to enable him to distinguish between what is Islamic and un-Islamic and is aware of the limits prescribed by Allah;

(5) performs the obligations enjoined upon by Islam in accordance with the *Shari'ah* and refrains from major sins; and

(6) is not associated with any organisation whose principles and methods are in conflict with those of the *Jamiat*;

may be enrolled as a Member of the *Jamiat*.

Article 5.

The procedure to acquire the membership of the *Jamiat*, in accordance with the above Article, shall be as follows:-

(1) Every candidate for membership shall submit the duly filled in membership application form, as per Annexure 1, to the Local President concerned, who shall forward the same, through the Provincial President and along with his own opinion, to the President;

(2) The President shall have power to approve the membership application but, in case of refusal, he shall consult the Central Executive Council;

(3) After approval by the President, the candidate shall make, in a meeting of the members of the *Jamiat*, the oath of membership as provided in Annexure 4;

(4) A candidate shall be entitled to the rights of membership, only from the date of his making the oath of membership.

(note: in places where there is no local unit of the *Jamiat*, the above membership form shall be sent to the Provincial President who shall, along with his recommendation, send it to the President. In such cases, the oath of membership will be made in a manner prescribed by the Provincial President.

Article 6.

Every member shall be required to bring gradually the following changes in his life:-

(1) To mould his thoughts, attitudes and behaviour in accordance with the teachings of the Holy Qur'an and *Sunnah*; to adopt only the pleasure of Allah as the aim of his life, the criterion of his liking and disliking and the centre of his loyalties and become obedient to the commands of Allah by breeding out obstinacy and selfishness;

(2) To give up friendship with those who are disobedient to and forgetful of Allah and establish relations with the righteous;

(3) To develop his academic, mental and physical qualities for the purpose of establishing Islam;

(4) To present the message of the *Jamiat* to the maximum number of students and to invite those who accept it to make a collective struggle by joining the *Jamiat*;

Article 7.

(1) A member may be expelled from the *Jamiat* if:-

(a) he violates (breaks) his oath of membership by deeds or words;

(b) he acts in a manner prejudicial and harmful to the policy, the discipline and the religious or moral position of the *Jamiat*;

(c) his words and deeds show that he has no interest left in the *Jamiat*;

(2) In case the local President finds that any member in that place has committed acts under Clause 1 of this Article to the extent that he ought to be expelled from the membership, he shall report the matter to the Provincial President who shall forward it, along with his opinion, to the President;

(3) In case of a solitary member in any place, the Provincial President shall be competant to make recommendation for expulsion;

(4) The final decision to expel a member shall rest with the President, but he must consult the central Executive Council in this respect.

Article 8.

(1) A member may submit his resignation to the Local President who shall inform the President through the Provincial President;

(2) Deleted)

(3) The membership shall become suspended upon receipt of the above information by the President.

(4) The membership shall cease after the acceptance of the resignation by the President.

Article 9.

(1) A member shall automatically cease to be a member upon the expiry of a period of six months from the termination of his studentship. This period shall be reckoned from the date of declaration of his examination results;

(2) The membership of those members of the *Jamiat*, who go abroad for education shall be no more to exist.

Chapter 2: ASSOCIATESHIP

Article 10.

Any student may become an Associate of the *Jamiat* who:

(1) agrees consciously with the ideal and programme of the *Jamiat*;

(2) is endeavouring to fulfil the preliminary requirements of Islam in practice and;

(3) promises to co-operate in the struggle for the fulfilment of *Jamiat's* programme.

Article 11.

(1) Any student desiring to join as an Associate shall submit the Associateship Form as provided in Annexure 2;

(2) The Local President shall have power to approve Associateship Form within his unit;

(3) In places where there is no Local Unit of the *Jamiat*, power to approve associateship shall vest in the Provincial President.

Article 12.

The Local President and the Provincial President in both the above mentioned cases under Article 11, (2) and (3), shall respectively have the power to expel any associate who does not fulfil the prescribed conditions for Associateship.

Chapter 3: DELETED

Chapter 4: ALUMNI CIRCLE OF THE JAMIAT

Article 14.

(1) This circle shall comprise of those individuals who have been affiliated with the *Jamiat* during their studentship or those who have developed interest in the activities of the *Jamiat*, after their studentship and submit their membership form to the President of the Circle.

(2) (a) The organisation of such individuals shall exist on an all Pakistan basis;

(b) The Central Executive Council shall appoint any member of this Circle to be its President;

(c) The President of the Circle shall, in consultation with the members of the Circle and the President, determine the structure of the Circle.

(3) (a) Two members of the central Executive Council of the *Jamiat* may be from among such members of the Circle who have been members of the *Jamiat*;

(b) Deleted.

(c) The President shall, in consultation with the Central Executive Council, determine the procedure for the inclusion of these members in the Central Executive Council.

PART THREE

Chapter 1: QUALIFICATIONS OF THE OFFICE BEARERS

Article 15.

(1) The following qualifications shall be kept in view while electing a President:

(a) that he is neither a candidate for the office nor is making efforts to secure it.

(b) that the members of the *Jamiat* consider him the best among them in respect of 'taqwa', knowledge, prudence, decision-making, honesty, trustworthiness, and perseverence in the way of Allah;

(c) that he is the best among the members with respect to administrative capability.

(2) While electing members of the Executive Council, the qualifications mentioned in sub-paragraphs (a) and (b) above shall be kept in view.

Article 15.A.

(1) No canvassing shall be permissible in any elections;

(2) No person shall propagate in his own favour nor shall he make others propagate for him, directly or indirectly;

(3) Group formation and group activity shall not be permissible in support of or against a person;

(4) To seek advice or to give advice in respect of an election shall not be deemed to fall under the definition of canvassing;

(5) The elections shall be decided by a simple majority of the votes cast.

Chapter 2: THE CENTRAL ORGANISATION

Article 16.

(1) Deleted;

(2) The Centre shall consist of a President, *Islami Jamiat-e Talaba Pakistan*, a Secretary-General and a Central Executive Council.

Article 17.

(1) The members of the Jamiat shall elect the President through direct voting.

(2) If an annual conference is going to be held, the ballot papers shall be issued to all members at least fifteen days before its commencement. The same shall be received back till an appointment hour on the last day of the annual conference and the name of the President as elected by a majority of the votes cast, shall be announced hereforth;

(3) If no annual conference is going to be held, the procedure for the election shall be determined by the President, in consultation with the Central Executive Council;

(4) The President shall hold office for a term of one year;

(5) The members of the *Jamiat* may elect the same person as the President for more than one term.

Article 18.

(1) If at any time, for any reason, the office of the President falls vacant, the members of the Central Executive Council shall elect the new President with a majority of votes cast, but the same shall have to be ratified by the members of the *Jamiat* within a period of two months;

(2) If the members of the *Jamiat* do not ratify the decision of the Central Executive Council by a majority of votes, then the President so elected by the Central Executive Council shall be deemed to have been removed from office and it shall be necessary to elect a new President within a period of one month.

Article 19.

(1) If at any time it becomes necessary for the President, to relinquish temporarily the functions of his office, he may, in consultation with the Central Executive Office, appoint an Acting President;

(2) Such appointment shall not be extended for more than three months.

Article 20.

(1) Before he enters upon his office, the President shall make the oath in the meeting of the members of the *Jamiat* or in a meeting of the Central Executive Council as provided in Annexure 5;

(2) An Acting President (Article 19) shall make the oath before the President or in a meeting of the Central Executive Council.

Article 21.

The duties of the President shall be as follows:-

(1) To consider as his first and foremost duty to attain the ideal of the *Jamiat* and to fulfil its programme;

(2) To make his best efforts to run, maintain and protect the organisation of the *Jamiat* in the best manner in accordance with the constitution;

(3) To always work in consultation with the Central Executive Council, except in day to day affairs or in discharging general functions of Presidentship or in matters requiring immediate action, unless otherwise provident for in the constitution.

Article 22.

The President shall have the following powers which he shall exercise directly or through persons under him:

(1) All powers as are specified in the constitution vide Articles 5 (2), 7 (4), 14 (3) (c), 19 (1), 22 (1) (a), 24 (1) (a),(b),24 (1) (d), 24 (2), 25, 26 (2), 27 (1), 28, 31 (2), 35, 36 (2), 36 (3), 37, 38 (3), 40 (1) (a), 43 (2), 44, 48 (3), 55 (2), 56 (5), 56 note (d), 57, 59 (3), 61, 62 (3), 62 (5), 63, 64, 66;

(2) All other powers that he feels necessary to exercise in performing duties to attain the ideal of the *Jamiat*, to fulfil its programme and to maintain its discipline in accordance with the constitution, unless any such power is explicitly restricted or made conditional by the constitution or by the *Jamiat*.

Article 22.(A).

(1) There shall be a Secretary in the Centre of the *Jamiat*, to be called as Secretary-General, who shall be appointed by the President, in consultation with the Central Executive Council, and who shall hold office till the President is satisfied with his work;

(2) The Secretary-General shall be appointed from among the members of the *Jamiat*;

(3) The Secretary-General shall be an ex-officio member of the Central Executive Council;

(4) The Secretary-General shall be responsible to satisfactorily run the central departments. His duties shall also include to maintain the discipline of the *Jamiat*, to superintend subordinate *Jamiats* and members and to keep the President fully informed of all affairs.

(5) The Secretary-General shall be responsible to the President in the performance of his duties;

(6) He may be removed from office only in consultation with Central Executive Council.

Article 23.

There shall be a Central Executive Council to assist and advise the President in the performance of his duties.

Article 24.

(1) The Central Executive Council shall consist of members elected both on all Pakistan and electoral units basis and nominated members.

(a) On all Pakistan basis, the members of the *Jamiat* shall directly elect three members to the Council;

(b) On Electoral Unit Basis: The member of each Electoral Unit (Area) shall directly elect from among themselves one member to the Council for every fifty or less than fifty members;

(b-1) The Electoral Units (Areas) shall be delimited by the President, in consultation with the Central Executive Council.

(c) Deleted.

(d) The President may, at his discretion, nominate members to the Council, but their number shall not exceed one half of the members elected under paragraphs (a) and (b) above;

(e) In accordance with Article 14 (3), there shall be two members as representative of the alumni Circle of *Jamiat*;

(f) Deleted.

(2) The President shall be the ex-officio Chairman of the Central Executive Council.

(3) If any seat in the Central Executive Council becomes vacant, it shall be filled within a period of two months;

Article 25.

After being elected, the members of the Central Executive Council shall make the oath as provided in Annexure 6, in a manner to be prescribed by the President;

Article 26.

(1) The Central Executive Council shall hold office for a period of one year;

(2) If the election of a new Central Executive Council is not possible on the expiry of the term of office, the President shall have power to extend its tenure after consultation with the Provincial Presidents;

(3) In case a new President is elected during the term of an Central Executive Council, the existing Council, including the nominated members, shall continue to hold office.

Article 27.

A meeting of the Central Executive Council shall be called whenever:

(1) The President deems it necessary;

(2) One fifth of the members of the *Jamiat* make a written requisition to the President;

(3) One tenth of the members of the *Jamiat* make a written requisition to the President;

(4) in case of written requisition from the members of the Council or those of the *Jamiat*, the meeting of Council shall be held within one month from the date of receipt of such requisition.

Article 28.

The President may, if he deems it necessary, invite persons other than the members of the Council to the meeting of the Council but such invitees shall not have the right to vote.

Article 29.

The Central Executive Council shall frame the rules and regulations for its proceedings;

(1) At least two general sessions of the Council shall be held during a period of one year;

(2) The announcement to hold a general session of the Council shall be made three weeks before the date of the meeting and the agenda shall be sent two weeks before;

(3) If any member of the Council dissents with any decision of the Council and insists upon his opinion, he shall have the right, with the permission of the Council, to raise the issue again in a meeting of the members of the *Jamiat*.

Article 30.

The quorum for any meeting of the Council shall comprise of one-fourth of its members, provided there shall be no quorum for a meeting held after adjournment due to lack of quorum.

Article 31.

(1) The decisions in the Council shall be made by a majority of votes.

(2) The President shall usually accept the decisions of the Council, but he shall have the right to reject them.

Article 32.

If a conflict on any matter arises between the President and the Central Executive Council and none is prepared to accept the opinion of the other, the final decision shall be made by the members of the *Jamiat*.

Article 33.

The duties of the Central Executive Council, acting collectively, and those of its members, as individuals, shall be as follows:

(1) To keep a watch on the President, the *Jamiat* and themselves and ensure that:

(a) the affairs are being conducted in accordance with the correct principles of Islam;

(b) as far as possible, suitable measures are being taken to attain the ideal of the *Jamiat* and to fulfil its programme;

(c) the Constitution of the *Jamiat* is being followed.

(2) To make every effort to rectify any defect they find anywhere in the *Jamiat*;

(3) To consider as their foremost duty to render their advice wherever necessary for the benefit of the *Jamiat*;

(4) To express their opinion without fear or favour;

(5) To attend the meetings of the Council regularly or to send their opinions.

Article 34.

(1) The Central Executive Council shall have all powers as are specified in the Constitution vide Articles: 5 (2), 7 (4), 18 (1), 19 (1), 22a (1), 22a (6), 24 (1), (a & b), 29, 35, 42, 57 (2), 57 (3), 58 (2), 63, 64 (2), 66, 67 (2), 68;

(2) In addition, every member of the Council, in the discharge of his duties under Article 33, shall have the right to raise questions, to discuss, to criticise, to call to account and to freely express his opinion in any meeting of the Council.

Chapter 3: PROVINCIAL ORGANISATION

Article 35.

The President shall, after consultation with the Central Executive Council, determine the organisational limits of the provinces and shall have power to alter these limits after consultation with the Council.

Article 36.

(1) There shall be a President, to be called as "Provincial President" after consultation with the members of the *Jamiat* and while making such an appointment, shall take into consideration the qualifications provided in Article 15(1);

(2) The President shall appoint the Provincial President, after consultation with the members of the *Jamiat* and while making such an appointment, shall take into consideration the qualifications provided in Article 15(1);

(3) The President shall specify the procedure and manner in which the opinion of the members of the *Jamiat* shall be determined;

(4) The appointment of the Provincial President shall be for a period of one year.

Article 37.

Before he enters upon his office, the Provincial President shall make the oath as provided in Annexure 5, in a manner to be prescribed by the President.

Article 38.

(1) The duties of the Provincial President within his province shall be the same as provided in Article 21, for the Central Organisation;

(2) The Provincial President shall have the following powers within his province which he shall exercise directly or through persons under him;

(a) All powers are as specified in the constitution vide Articles 7 (3), 11 (3), 12, 26 (2), 40, 41, 48 (3), 50, 52, 53, 56, Note (b), (d), 57 (1), 57 (2), 62 (3), 62 (5), 65;

(b) All powers required for performing functions required to attain the ideal of the *Jamiat*, to fulfil its programme and to maintain its discipline in accordance with the constitution, unless any such power is explicitly restricted or made conditional by the constitution or the *Jamiat*;

(c) The Provincial President, if he deems necessary, may, in consultation with his Executive Council, appoint a Provincial Secretary who shall have the same status as that of the Secretary-General in the Centre;

(d) The Provincial Secretary shall have such functions and powers as may be entrusted to him by the Provincial President.

Article 39.

The Provincial President if he deems necessary, may, in consultation with the President, constitute a Provincial Executive Council.

Article 40.

(1) The Provincial Executive Council shall consist of:

(a) Elected members whose number shall be determined by the Provincial President after consultation with the President;

(b) Members nominated by the Provincial President whose number shall not exceed one-half of that of members under paragraph (a) above;

(2) The Provincial President shall be the ex-officio Chairman Provincial Executive Council.

Article 41.

The members of the Provincial Executive Council shall make the oath as provided in Annexure 6, in a suitable manner to be prescribed by the Provincial President.

Article 42.

The Provincial Executive Council shall have the same duties and powers within the Province as provided for the Central Executive Council under the Central organisation.

Article 43.

(1) The relation between the Provincial President and the Provincial Executive Council shall be governed by the Provisions of Article 31;

(2) If a conflict on any matter arises between the Provincial President and the Provincial Executive Council, the matter shall be referred to the President.

Article 44.

In all disputes which cannot be resolved within the Province, reference shall be made to the President.

Chapter 4: LOCAL ORGANISATION

Article 45.

(1) A local Unit of *Jamiat* shall be constituted in any place where there are more than two members of the *Jamiat*;

(2) Where there are solitary members, they shall be directly responsible to the Provincial President.

Article 46.

(1) There shall be a President in every 'Local Unit' responsible for its affairs, who shall be called as 'Local President';

(2) The Local President shall be elected directly by the members of the Local Unit, who shall, while electing him, take into consideration the qualification as provided in Article 15 (1);

(3) The election shall be held in the month of October every year and shall be for a period of one year;

(4) Same person can be re-elected more than once;

(5) The members shall have the right to hold an election at any other time during the year if circumstances so warrant.

Article 47.

Before he enters upon his office, the Local President, shall make the oath as provided in Annexure 5, in a meeting of the members of the *Jamiat*.

Article 48.

(1) The Local President shall have the same duties within his Unit as are laid down in Article 21;

(2) The Local President shall have the following powers within his Unit:-

(a) All powers as are specified in the continuation vide Articles 11 (2), 12, 49 (1), 51, 62 (3), 62 (5);

(b) All other powers necessary for performing functions required to attain the ideal of the *Jamiat*, to fulfil its programme and to maintain its discipline in accordance with the Constitution, unless any such power is explicitly restricted or made conditional by the Constitution of the *Jamiat*;

(3) In addition he shall have such duties and powers which the President or the Provincial President may entrust to him.

Article 49.

(1) The Local President may, in consultation with the local members constitute a Local Executive Council and determine its composition.

(2) The relation between the Local President and the Local Executive Council shall be governed by the Provisions of Article 31 and 32.

Article 50.

Any disputes which cannot be resolved locally shall be referred to the Provincial President.

Article 51.

The Local President shall have power to determine the details of the internal structure of the Local Unit.

Chapter 5: ASSOCIATES' CIRCLE

Article 52.

In any place where there are more than one Associate and there is no Local Unit, an Associates' Circle may be constituted with the prior permission of the Provincial President.

Article 53.

The Associates shall elect a person most capable among them as President of the Circle but ratification by the Provincial President shall be required after such an election.

Article 54.

Deleted.

Chapter 6 FINANCE (BAITUL MAL)

Article 55.

(1) There shall be a 'Local *Baitul*' in every province and a 'Central *Baitul Mal*' at the Centre;

(2) All powers pertaining to the administration of the '*Baitul Mal*' shall vest in the President.

Article 56.

The income in the '*Baitul Mal*' shall be under the following heads;

(1) Donations from the members of the *Jamiat* and from other persons who have interest in its work;

(2) Publications and bookstall;

(3) '*Zakat*' and '*Sadaqat*';

(4) Contribution from lower '*Baitul Mals*';

(5) Such other heads for which permission has been obtained from the President.

Note:-

(a) The members shall be required to undertake to give regular subscriptions as donation every month.

(b) Donations from outside the *Jamiat* shall be accepted only from such persons who are not expected to use their donations to influence or exploit the *Jamiat*. The Associates' Circle will obtain permission from the Provincial President before accepting such donations.

(c) Accounts of income from *Zakat* and *Sadaqat* shall be maintained separately.

(d) The 'lower *Baitul Mals*' shall pay such amount into the Provincial and 'Central *Baitul Mal*' as are fixed by the respective Presidents.

Article 57.

(1) Every President from the '*Baitul Mal*' concerned shall have the power to incur expenditures on matters relating to the attainment of the *Jamiat's* ideal, the achievement of its programme and the running of its organisational affairs;

(2) Local Presidents and Provincial Presidents shall be responsible, with respect to their respective Executive Councils and, in cases where no Executive Council exists, to the members, and also to the Presidents above them;

(3) The President shall be responsible to the Central Executive Council in respect to the income and expenditure in the 'Central *Baitul Mal*'.

Chapter 7 REMOVAL FROM OFFICE

Article 58.

(1) The Jamiat shall have power to remove the President from his office in the following cases:

(a) When he insists upon violating any clear injunction of the Qur'an and the *Sunnah*;

(b) When his conduct is likely to cause serious harm to the *Jamiat*.

(2) The Procedure for the removal shall be as follows:

(a) The Central Executive Council may pass a resolution of no confidence against the President by a simple majority of its members, in which case the entire matter shall be placed before the members of the *Jamiat* within a period of one month. If a simple majority of the members of the *Jamiat* ratify the resolution of no confidence, the President shall forthwith cease to hold office. If more than one half of the total number of members vote in support of the President, the Central Executive Council shall be deemed to have been dissolved and fresh elections shall be held;

(b) The members of the *Jamiat* may move a resolution of no confidence against the President provided it is submitted to the Central Executive Council in a written form specifying the grounds and reasons thereof and signed by not less than one-tenth of the total number of members. This resolution shall be placed before the Central Executive Council within a period of one month and shall then be dealt with in accordance with the procedure as contained in sub-clause (a) above.

Article 59.

(1) Deleted.

(2) Deleted.

(3) The President shall have power to remove the Provincial President from his office;

(4) One-fifth of the total number of members of the Provincial *Jamiat* may make a request to the President for the removal of the Provincial President from his office.

Article 60.

If a majority of the total number of members of a Unit pass a resolution of no confidence against a Local President, he shall forthwith cease to hold the office.

Article 61.

If the President is satisfied that circumstances exist which necessitate a change in the Central Executive Council or in its elected members, he shall place the issue before the members of the *Jamiat*. If a majority of the total number of members expresses agreement with the President on this issue, the Central Executive Council shall be deemed to stand dissolved. However, if the majority of the total number of members does not express its agreement with the President, it shall be incumbent upon the President to convene a meeting of the Central Executive Council within a period of one month and place his resignation before it.

Article 62.

A member of the Executive Council shall be liable to be removed from the membership of the Council if:

(1) He ceases to be a member of the *Jamiat*;

(2) He violates Article 33(5) of the Constitution twice in succession without any valid reasons

(3) He resigns from the membership of the Council and his resignation is accepted by the President;

(4) A resolution of no confidence is passed against him by a majority of the members who have elected him;

(5) In case of being a nominated member, he loses the confidence of his President.

Article 63.

The President shall have power to dissolve or suspend a Local Unit after consulting the Central Executive Council.

Chapter 8 MISCELLANEOUS

Article 64.

(1) If in a province, no provincial organisation has been established, it shall be under the direct control of the Centre;

(2) In such province, the President shall, after consultation with the Central Executive Council, establish a suitable organisation for conducting the affairs of the *Jamiat*;

(3) In such province, the President shall exercise all powers of a Provincial   President as provided under the provincial organisation.

Article 65.

The Local units and the Circles of Associates shall obtain permission from the Provincial President for all important publications except ordinary publications, invitations and posters.

Article 66.

To achieve the objectives of this Constitution, President; *Islami Jamiat-e Talaba Pakistan*, shall be the sole authority to frame rules and regulations after consultation with the Central Executive Council.

Article 67.

An Amendment to this Constitution may be:

(1) Passed in a meeting of the members of the *Jamiat* by majority vote, provided that the Notice

for the Amendment is received by the President within a period of two weeks from the date of declaration of the meeting;

(2) Passed by the majority of the total number of members of the Central Executive Council, provided that it is ratified by the majority of the total number of members of the *Jamiat* within a period of two months after its approval.

Article 68.

If a dispute arises with respect to the interpretation of any provision of this Constitution, the matter shall be referred to the Central Executive Council.

Article 69.

This Constitution shall come into force with effect from 1st November, 1952.

'ANNEXURE' 1

Membership Application Form of Islami Jamiat-e Talaba Pakistan

1. Name..

2. Father's Name..

3. Age..

4. Class/Name of Educational Institute....................................

....

5. Present Address..

6. Permanent Address..

7. <u>Educational Resume</u>.

Examination	Year	Marks/Div.	No. of attempts
1.	....	....	....
2.	....	....	....
3.	....	....	....

8. Future Career Planning? or

Your Career Ambitions?

9. Any Hobby? (Past or Present)

10. Your affiliation with the *Jamaat*.

(a) Worker:

(b) Associate (Unit)?

11. Present Office...

12. Your Family Links With The Movement?

13. Your Study of Islam? (Name of Books etc.)

14. Your study of other ideologies?

(eg Democracy, Communism, Socialism, Fascism etc.)

15. Briefly describe your concept of Islam...........

16. How has your study of Islam influenced your practical life?

17. What is your understanding of the purpose of the *Jamiat*?.....................

What inspires you to become a member?..

18. Have you fully understood what you shall have to adopt and to give up in your life after becoming a member of the *Jamiat*?......................................

Signature.....................

Applicant.....................

Date..........................

'ANNEXURE' 2
Islami Jamiat-e Talaba Pakistan
FORM OF THE ASSOCIATESHIP

I do solemnly affirm that I fully agree with the ideal and programme of *Islami Jamiat-e Talaba Pakistan*, and, promise my full co-operation in the endeavours being made by *Islami Jamiat-e Talaba Pakistan* to fulfil its programme. I offer myself for the Associateship.

May Allah help me to fulfil these requirements of Islam. *Ameen*!

Signature...................Date.........................

Signature of President...............Date................

1. Name..

2. Age...

3. Name of Institution and Class...........................

....

4. Home and Postal Address.................................

....

....

Signature of President......................................

Date..

'ANNEXURE' 3

(Deleted)

'ANNEXURE' 4

OATH FOR THE MEMBERSHIP

(I bear witness that there is no God but Allah and that Muhammad (peace be upon him) is His servant and His Messenger

I..........................while taking up the membership of *Islami Jamiat-e-Talaba Pakistan* do solemnly affirm, making the Lord of the Universe as my witness that:

(1) The aim of my life shall be to seek the pleasure of Allah by ordering my life in accordance with the principles laid down by Allah by His messenger (peace and blessings of Allah be upon him) and I am joining *Islami Jamiat-e-Talaba Pakistan* purely for the sake of Allah, in order to strive to achieve this aim.

(2) I fully agree with the methodology and programmes of the *Jamiat* in accordance with this Constitution.

(3) I will observe the discipline of the *Jamiat* in accordance with this Constitution.

I further affirm that to the best of my ability:

(4) I will always be making efforts to mould my thoughts, attitudes, and behaviour in accordance with the teachings of the Holy Qur'an and the *Sunnah* and to adopt the pleasure of Allah as the aim of my life, the criterion of my liking and disliking and the centre of my loyalties.

(5) I will always be endeavouring to gain knowledge of Islam and to develop my mental and physical qualities.

(6) I will always be striving to convey the message of the *Jamiat* to other students and to organise them.

(O Allah! My *Salat*, and my sacrifice, and my living and my dying are all for the Lord of the Universe).

May Allah help me to keep this pledge.

Ameen!

Signature.............................

'ANNEXURE' 5
OATH FOR THE PRESIDENT

I...having been appointed as

President of Islami Jamiat-e-Talaba...............................

making the Lord of the Universe as my witness, do hereby solemnly affirm that:

(1) I will consider as my first and foremost duty to attain the ideal and to fulfil the programme of the Jamiat.

(2) I will follow the Constitution of the Jamiat and will endeavour to run, maintain and protect the organisation of Jamiat in accordance with the Constitution.

May Allah help me to keep my pledge.

Ameen!

Signature...................................

Appendix H

THE CONSTITUTION OF THE UK ISLAMIC MISSION
PART I
CREED-OBJECTIVE-METHOD OF WORK-PROGRAMME

Name

Article 1: The name of this organisation shall be "The United Kingdom Islamic Mission", hereinafter called "The Mission".

Creed

Article 2: The belief in *La Ilaha Ill-Allahu Muhammad-ur-Rasool-ullah* shall be the fundamental creed of the Mission i.e *ILAH* is Allah alone and none else: and *Muhammad-ur-Rasoollah* (peace be upon him) is Allah's Messenger.

Clarification

a) The first part of this creed ie there is no *ILAH* except Allah shall be understood to mean that Allah alone is the Creator, the Sustainer and Master of everything in heavens and earth. He alone is the Fountainhead of all laws - physical and temporal. None else shares with Him in anything and in anyway.

b) The second part of this creed i.e. the prophethood of Muhammad (pbuh) means that, as the last Prophet, he was appointed to set the perfect example for the mankind in accordance with the authentic guidance and code of law which Allah, the Creator of the Universe, revealed through him.

Objective

Article 3: The objective of the Mission shall be to establish the Islamic Order of Life with a view to seeking the blessings of Allah in this life and the life hereafter.

The Method of Work

Article 4: The Qur'an and the *Sunnah* shall form the basis of the Mission's method of work. The Mission shall adopt only peaceful and constructive means to achieve its objective.

Programme

Article 5: The Mission, within its means, will try to carry out the following programme:

a) The establishment of mosques and Islamic centres; provision of facilities for congregational prayers, study of Qur'an and *Hadith* and religious meetings.

b) The making of arrangements for the education and training of Muslim children and youth.

c) The setting up of reading rooms and libraries.

d) The spreading of Islam through literature, lectures, and seminars.

e) The providing of social and welfare services.

f) The providing of help and guidance for students.

PART II

The structure of the mission will consist of Members, Associate Members and sympathisers.

Article 6: Every Muslim irrespective of race and caste may become a member of the Mission provided that he:-

i) affirms and declares his complete agreement with the objectives of the Mission;

ii) pledges, after understanding the Constitution, that he shall abide by it and in conformity therewith, shall abide by the discipline of the Mission;

iii) adheres to *shari'ah* obligations, i.e. regular performance of prayers, fasting, *Zakat*, abstinence from *Kabair* (major sins).

iv) should not have such means of livelihood that may be defined as grossly sinful involving interest, alcohol, adultery, music, dance, perjury, bribery, misappropiation, gambling, etc.

v) should not be a member of any party or organisation whose principles and policies are against the Mission's creed, objective and method of work.

Admission

Article 7: Application for membership shall be submitted through a local Branch or Circle to the Central Office. The President, in consultation with the Central *Shoora*, is empowered to accept or reject such applications.

Membership Responsibilities

Article 8: It is expected of every member of the Mission that he will endeavour to:

i) acquire sufficient knowledge of Islam so that he may be able to differentiate between Islam and *Jahiliyyah* (ignorance of Islam) and become aware of *HUDOODULLAH* i.e. limits imposed by Allah to guide man in his daily life;

ii) recast his thoughts and actions in accordance with the teachings of the Qur'an and *Sunnah*, change the object of his life, his preferences, his criteria of values and the focus of his loyalties and free himself of the idols of arrogance and egoism so that he is in complete obedience to the Will of his Sustainer.

iii) Purge his life of such customs and traditions which are inconsistant with the Qur'an and *Sunnah*, so that his words and actions correspond with the *Shariah*.

iv) purify his heart of those prejudices, interests, pursuits, disputes, and polemics which are based on selfishness and worldliness and which have no importance in Islam;

v) order in, his dealings on the basis of righteousness, justice, and fear of Allah and uphold the truth without fear or favour.

vi) except for the genuine needs of life, concentrate all his efforts on the objective of *Iqamat-e-Deen* and he should disassociate himself from all those activities which may not lead towards this goal.

vii) introduce the Mission, its objectives and programmes to his acquaintances and others wherever and whenever possible according to his ability.

Conditions For Associate Membership

Article 9: Any person who is not prepared to accept the responsibilities of membership, can join as an associate member, provided he fulfils the following minimum conditions:-

i) regular participation in meetings;

ii) regular payment of monthly donations;

iii) sincere efforts in the performance of religious obligations and avoidance of major sins;

iv) sincere efforts to fulfil the aims and objects of the Mission according to his ability.

Admission

Article 10: Application for associate membership shall be submitted through local branch or circle to the Central Office. The President in consultation with the Central *Shoora* is empowered to accept or reject such applications.

Responsibilities

Article 11: Every associate member is expected to try to fulfil the responsibilties as laid down in Article 8.

Sympathisers

Article 12: Anyone can become a sympathiser if he/she agrees with the objectives of the Mission and cooperates to achieve the same in any way. An appropiate form must be completed for this purpose.

PART III
THE STRUCTURE OF THE MISSION

The Organisation

Article 13: The organisation of the Mission shall be *Shura'i* and for the purposes of administration it shall comprise the Central Office, Zones Branches and Circles.

The Central Office

Article 14: The Central Office shall consist of the following constituent parts:
i) The President
ii) Senior Vice President
iii) The Vice President
iv) The Secretary-General
v) The Joint Secretary
vi) The Finance Secretary
vii) Heads of Departments
viii) The Central *Shoora*
ix) The Administrative Committee

Explanation

The Secretary General, the Joint Secretary and the Finance Secretary can be appointed from amongst the members but the Vice-President shall have to be appointed from the members of the Central *Shoora*.

The Congregation of Members

Article 15:

i) The ultimate authority in the Mission rests with the Congregation of Members.

ii) The Congregation of Members shall be convened at least once every year in which members' reports shall be presented and the affairs of the Mission shall be critically assessed and the programme for the next year shall be finalised and approved.

iii) The Quorum for the Congregation shall be 33% of total membership.

The President

Article 16: There shall be a President of the Mission. Members of the Mission shall be bound to obey him in what is *Maaroof* (legitimate).

Requisite Qualifications for the Office of the President

Article 17: The following qualities shall be kept in view in the election of the President:-

i) He should have enough knowledge of Qur'an and *Sunnah* and be God-fearing, far-sighted, honest and sincere. He should possess the highest possible qualities of leadership and be equipped to discharge his duties most ably.

ii) He should neither desire nor seek office in the Mission.

Duties and Offices of the President

Article 18: The duties and power of the President shall be as follows:-

i) The ultimate responsibility with regard to the running of the affairs of the Mission shall be that of the President. The President, in the discharge of his duties, shall be accountable to the Central *Shoora*.

ii) The President shall consult the central *Shoora* in formulating policy before taking important decisions about the Mission.

iii) The President shall nominate an Administrative Committee from amongst the members of the Central *Shoora*.

iv) The President, in the discharge of his duties and in the interest of the Mission, shall, within limitations imposed by the central *Shoora*, use assets of the Mission.

v) The President shall take all decisions with regard to the following:-

a. to accept membership applications;

b. to suspend or expel members;

c. to suspend or remove a President of a Branch or Circle;

d. to appoint or dismiss the central secretaries or other staff;

e. to operate Central Fund for various projects of the Mission;

f. to extend the term of office of the Central *Shoora*.

g. to convene the Congregations of Members.

Election

Article 19:

i) Members shall elect the President of the Mission directly through secret ballot. The election shall be held in two stages.

The first stage will be called 'Primary Election' while the second stage will be called 'Final Election'.

In the event of any member receiving more than fifty percent of votes in the Primary Election he shall be declared elected as President. Failing this, the three members securing most of the votes shall contest the Final Election. The candidate receiving the highest number of votes shall then be declared elected.

ii) The term of Office of the President shall be two years. The same person may be re-elected repeatedly for the office of the President.

iii) The Central *Shoora* shall appoint an Election Commission two months before the expiry of the term of office of the President and shall also frame electoral rules.

iv) In the event of death, resignation, removal or for any other reason when the office of the President falls vacant, a by-election will be held within sixty days. The by-election shall be conducted in the Congregation of Members or through a postal ballot.

v) In the interim period the Senior Vice-President shall be Acting President.

Before assuming the office of President (whether Permanent or Acting) the incumbent shall have to take the oath of office.

Senior Vice-President

Article 21: There shall be a senior Vice-President of the Mission. He shall in the absence of the President exercise the same powers as laid down in Article 18 for the President.

The Central Shoora

Article 22:

i) There shall be a Central *Shoora* to advise the President in formulating the party decisions.

ii) The *Shoora* will consist of ten members elected by direct election on a regional basis by members of the region. In addition all Zonal *Naxzimin* will be ex-office members of the *Shoora*.

iii) The President, in consultation with the Central *Shoora* may co-opt up to three additional members.

iv) The President shall summon a meeting of the *Shoora* within thirty days of its election, when each member of the *Shoora* will be required to take his oath of office.

v) The term of office for members of the *Shoora* shall be two years.

vi) The President will convene at least three meetings of the *Shoora* during a year and preside over these sessions. Decisions will be made by a simple majority. The quorum for the *Shoora* meetings shall be fifty percent of the total membership of the *Shoora*.

vii) In the event of disagreement between the President and the Council, the Congregation of Members shall have the final decisive vote. The losing party shall have to vacate office.

Duties and Powers of the Central Shoora

Article 23: The duties and powers of the *Shoora* are as follows:-

i) to formulate the policy of the Mission;

ii) to appoint auditors for the accounts of the Mission;

iii) to suspend the President of the Mission if two thirds of the Central *Shoora* approve such a move.

iv) to make neccessary changes in the administrative organisation of the Mission;

v) to approve the Central Budget;

vi) to review and critically evaluate the performance of the President and the heads of central departments.

vii) to appoint Boards and Committees and frame their terms of reference for various activities of departments in the Mission, and for the management of its properties.

viii) to interpret the Constitution of the Misssion and this interpretation shall be final.

The Administrative Committee

Article 24:

i) For the day to day administration, the President shall appoint a five-member Administrative Committee. It will consist of the President, Senior Vice President, Vice President, the Secretary-General, the Joint-Secretary and the Finance Secretary.

ii) Meetings of the Committee will be convened by the President and when necessary.

iii) Membership of the Committee will cease with the cessation of membership of the Central *Shoora*.

iv) A quorum for meetings of the Committee shall be three.

v) Decisions taken at the Administrative Committee meeting shall be relayed to the members of the Central *Shoora* every month, and later approved by it.

The Secretary-General

Article 25:

i) The President, in consultation with the Central *Shoora*, shall appoint a Secretary-General.

ii) The Secretary-General will hold office till such time as the President is satisfied with his work. His removal from the office, however, shall be carried out in consultation with the *Shoora*.

iii) The Secretary-General will assist and represent the President in all matters assigned to him. He will hold all powers delegated to him from time to time by the President.

iv) The Secretary-General or the Acting Secretary-General shall take the oaths of office before taking up his responsibilities.

The Joint Secretary

Article 26:

i) The President, in consultation with the Central *Shoora* shall appoint a Joint Secretary.

ii) The Joint Secretary shall undertake such duties as are assigned to him by the Secretary-General.

iii) During the absence of the Secretary-General, the Joint Secretary will be the Acting Secretary-General and shall have the same status.

Heads of Central Departments

Article 27:

i) There shall be a head of every Central Department whose appointment will be made by the President in consultation with the Central *Shoora*.

ii) He will hold this office till such time as the President and the Central *Shoora* are satisfied with his work.

iii) The Central *Shoora* shall define the powers and duties of the heads of the Central Departments and they shall be accountable to the *Shoora*.

Branches and Circles

Article 28:

i) The President may designate any place in the United Kingdom as a Branch of the Mission where there are at least two members of the Mission. Where there is only one member, he may be assigned to the nearest branch or circle.

ii) Each local branch shall comprise a President, a Secretary and a Treasurer. Local members and associate members shall elect the President. Other office bearers will be appointed by the local President in consultation with members and associate members. The Central *Shoora* may, if and when needed, create other posts or appoint a local executive committee.

iii) The President may designate any place in the United Kingdom as the Circle of the Mission where there is more than one associate member.

iv) In places where there is only one member and several associate members the person eligible for the local Presidency shall be the member. However, other offices may be allocated to associate members.

v) Local Presidents and Secretaries shall exercise the same powers and duties as the President and the Secretary-General at the centre, except those which are exclusively reserved for the Centre.

PART IV
WOMEN ' S UNIT

Article 29:

There shall be a separate unit for women members and associate members. The President of the Mission, in consultation with the Central *Shoora*, shall have the power to provide an appropriate structure for this Unit and make changes therein as necessary.

Duties of Women ' s Members and Associate Members

Article 30: All women joining the Mission shall be subject to the same conditions as laid down in Article 6. In addition, their duties will be as follows:-

i) to present the message of the Mission to their family members and acquaintances as far as possible;

ii) to propagate teachings of Islam among their close relations i.e. husbands, parents, brothers and sisters, and other family members;

iii) to kindle the light of faith in the hearts of their children;

iv) to encourage and assist their husbands, sons, fathers, and brothers if they are associated with the Mission;

v) to try to reform with patience and understanding their husbands or guardians if they deviate from Islam.

PART V
DISCIPLINE OF THE MISSION

Removal from the Central Shoora

Article 31:

i) A member of the Central *Shoora* who resigns from the *Shoora* and whose resignation is accepted by the President, will cease to be a member of the Shoora.

ii) A member of the *Shoora* who ceases to remain a member of the Mission shall cease to be a member of the *Shoora*

iii) A member of the *Shoora* who remains absent for two consecutive meetings of the *Shoora* without reasonable excuse may be asked to resign.

iv) A member of the *Shoora* will cease to be so when expelled from it.

Expulsion from the Membership

Article 32: A member of the Mission may be expelled for the following reasons:-

i) deviation, in words or deeds, from his oath of membership;

ii) violation of the discipline of the Mission;

iii) defiance of the declared policy of the Mission;

iv) lack of sincere association with the Mission as may be manifested by his behaviour;

v) lack of interest in the activities of the Mission;

vi) On discovering himself, or after receiving a report from a local President about a member being in contravention of Clause 1 above, the President, having consulted the Central *Shoora*, may expel a member.

Expulsion from the Associate Membership of the Mission

Article 33: An associate member may be expelled for the following reasons:-

i) violation of the discipline of the Mission;

ii) defiance of the declared policy of the Mission;

iii) lack of interest in the activities of the Mission;

vi) On discovering himself, or after receiving a report from a local President about a member being in contravention of Clause 1 above, the President, having consulted the Central *Shoora*, may expel him.

Suspension/Dissolution of Branches and Circles

Article 34:

For the purpose of proper discipline and administration the President may suspend or dissolve any Branch or Circle after consulting the Central *Shoora*.

Limits of Difference of Opinion

Article 35:

A member adhering to the constitution may disagree with the decisions of the Central Shoora or the Congregation of Members regarding practical steps for the achievement of the objectives of the Mission - in such cases, he is required to keep himself within the following limits:-

i) he will have a full right to express his views in member's meetings, but he may not use the mass media or any public platform nor will he have recourse to the legal machinery for this purpose. Furthermore, he shall not have the right to canvass individually among members;

ii) he shall have to accept all majority decisions of the Mission as binding. However, he will have the right to disagree with them and try to have them reversed in the appropriate forums, while remaining within the prescribed limits.

iii) a member or associate member who disagrees with a policy decision of the Mission shall not hold any office which is responsible for implementing that policy decision or act as any spokesman for it.

PART VI
FINANCE

Article 36:

There shall be a local *baitulmal* for every branch/circle and a central *baitulmal* for the headquarters of the Mission. The central *Shoora* may determine a separate *baitulmal* to be unnecessary for a branch/circle or create a single one for more than one branch/circle.

Sources of Income

Article 37: The sources of income for the *baitulmal* are as follows:-

i) Donations

ii) *Zakat*

iii) Alms, welfare money

iv) Contributions from local treasurers

v) Income from the property of the Mission

vi) Income from properties endowed to the Mission

Powers of Expenditure

Article 38:

Baitulmals at the Centre, branches or circles shall be under their respective presidents, who shall have the power to authorise expenditure on the projects of the Mission. The President of the Mission and local presidents are accountable to the Central *Shoora* and local *Shoora* (or members and associate members collectively).

Auditors

Article 39:

i) The Central *Shoora* shall appoint an auditor to audit the central *baitulmal* Accounts and for local branches and circles their local executive committees shall appoint auditors.

ii) Every year accounts of the Mission shall be audited and reports of the auditors shall be presented to their respective appointing bodies. Copies of audit reports of all Branches and Circles shall be sent to the Central Office.

PART VII
ASSESSMENT AND ACCOUNTABILITY (TANQEED 'O' MUHASIBAH)

Right of Assessment

Article 40:

i) Every member of the Mission shall have the right to criticise the Central Administration in the Congregation of Members, provided:

a) he does not exceed the limits laid down in the *Shari'ah* for such criticism:

b) he does not exceed the limits of decency:

c) he does not any other means harmful to the cause of the Mission.

ii) The above rules will also be applicable at the members' meetings at local level.

iii) Every member shall have the right to question the decision of the President or the central *Shoora*. Such questions should be raised at the central *Shoora* meetings through its members or in person at the Congregation of Members.

PART VII
MISCELLANEOUS

Powers of Framing By-Laws

Article 41: To fulfil the intent of this Constitution, the Central *Shoora* shall frame by-laws as necessary.

Amendments to the Constitution

Article 42:

i) Except Article 2, which shall never be subject to alterations or amendments, this Constitution may be amended by a two thirds majority of members present.

ii) Proposed amendments should reach the Secretary General at least thirty days before any Congregation of Members.

iii) Proposed amendments will be circulated to the members before the meeting.

Exemption from Legal Proceedings

Article 43: Except for financial matters, all actions taken in pursuance of the Constitution shall be outside the perview of any judicial adjudication.

Property of the Mission

Article 44:

i) The right of ownership of all properties movable or immovable will be vested in the Mission.

ii) The Central *Shoora* shall have full power to appoint trustees for the properties of the Mission or remove such trustees.

iii) Trustees or administrators of the properties of the Mission shall have no rights of ownership of such properties.

iv) Deeds and other ownership documents of all such properties will remain in the Mission Headquarters.

Article 45: The Mission shall be a member of the Federation of Islamic *Da'awa* Organisations.

Date of Enforcement

Article 46: This Constitution shall come into force on the 3rd Day of February 1980, in place of the previous Constitution which is hereby replaced.

Appendix I

THE CONSTITUTION OF THE ISLAMIC SOCIETY OF BRITAIN

1. Name

The name of the organisation shall be "The Islamic Society of Britain" (ISB), hereinafter called "The Society".

2. Aim

To strive to make the individual and society live in submission to Allah, the Creator, in order to achieve peace and harmony on this earth and salvation in the Hereafter.

3. Objectives

(a) To invite all human beings to the message of the Creator.

(b) To organise those who respond to this invitation into a community (*ummah*) which is disciplined and committed to God-consciousness.

(c) To enjoin good for the benefit of humanity and to campaign against all forms of injustice and oppression in order to create a caring, just and God-conscious society.

4. Programme Guidelines

(a) To invite British Muslims to adhere to the principles of Islam and to promote unity among them.

(b) To convey the message of Islam, and to establish cordial relations with non-Muslims in general and with the people of the Book in particular in order to promote better understanding of Islam in the multi-cultural society.

(c) To provide social welfare services in accordance with the Islamic guidance.

5. Ultimate Sources of Guidance

The Glorious Qur'an and the *Sunnah* of the Prophet (peace and blessings be upon him) shall constitute the ultimate source of reference in all affairs of the society.

6. Membership

Any person residing in Great Britain may apply to become a member of the society provided he/she:

(i) affirms his/her faith in Allah as his/her only Lord and in the Prophet Muhammad (peace and blessings be upon him) as His last Messenger.

(ii) makes sincere efforts to mould his/her life according to the teachings of the Glorious Qur'an and the *Sunnah* of the Prophet (peace and blessings be upon him).

(iii) agrees to strive with his/her abilities and resources as much as possible to achieve the aim and to implement the programmes of the Society.

(iv) agrees to abide by the Constitution and decisions of the Society.

(v) refrains from joining or taking part in any anti-Islamic activity or supporting any such groups.

The membership application will be approved subject to the satisfying of the prescribed regulations as laid down by the *Shura* Council from time to time.

7. The Structure

The structure of the Society shall consist of:

A. A central organisation which will be comprised of:

(i) The *Shura* Council.

(ii) The Executive Committee.

(iii) The Conciliation and Arbitration Committee.

B. Local organisations.

8. The *Shura* Council

(i) *Composition*: The *Shura* Council shall be comprised of:

(a) Ten nationally elected representatives.

(b) Fifteen local representatives.

(c) The consecutive Ex-Presidents as Ex-Officio members.

(ii) *Powers*

(a) The *Shura* will be the supreme policy making body of the Society.

(b) The *Shura* will be responsible for initiating and approving major programmes and plans.

(a) The *Shura* will elect a Chairman from amongst itself, who will organise and conduct *Shura* meetings, which will be held at least twice every year or at such times as the President may deem necessary or upon requisition by one-fourth of the Council members or one-fifth of the members: The Chairman will ensure that agenda and the minutes of the meetings are circulated to all members of the *Shura*. The quorum for *Shura* meetings will be two-thirds of its members. The Council shall take decision by a majority vote.

(b) The *Shura* after deliberation will elect the most suitable person for the office of the President amongst the ten nationally elected representatives.

(c) The *Shura* will oversee the overall running of the Society.

9. The Executive Committee

(a) The Executive Committee shall be comprised of the President, the Vice-President, the General-Secretary, *Bait-ul-Mal* secretary, the other office bearers and up to three nominated members. The President will dominate the rest of the members of the Executive Committee in consultation with and approval of the *Shura* Council for one year.

(b) The Committee will assist the President in the execution and implementation of the work plan approved by the *Shura* Council.

(c) The Committee shall meet regularly and also as and when the President deemed necessary. The Quorum for its meeting shall be two-thirds of its members. It shall take decisions by a majority vote.

10. Power of the President

(a) *The President shall*:

(i) have power to appoint ad hoc committees.

(ii) have power to remove any member from the Executive Committee.

(b) *Duties of the President*:

The President shall:

(i) be responsible for overall conduct and direction of the policies and programmes and all affairs of the Society in accordance with the Constitution and shall be accountable to the Shura Council.

(ii) present to the Shura Council policies and programmes of the Society for approval.

(iii) be responsible for the good conduct of the members of the Executive Committee.

11. Duties of the Vice-President

The Vice President:

(i) will be responsible to the President and will assist him in the performance of his duties.

(ii) will exercise such powers as delegated by the President in the event of his absence.

(iii) shall be Acting President until a new President is elected in the event of the President being incapacitated to perform his duties or suspended or is removed from his office. In these circumstances he will exercise all powers and perform all duties as laid down in Article 10 of the Constitution.

12. Duties of the General Secretary

The General Secretary shall:

(i) be responsible for the co-ordination of the work of the Central Office.

(ii) be responsible for ensuring the taking of minutes of the Executive Committee, and its circulation.

(iii) be responsible for all internal and external communications.

(iv) be responsible to the President for the discharge of his duties.

13. Duties of the *Bait-ul-Mal* Secretary

The Bait-ul-Mal Secretary shall:

(1) formulate financial policies and plans of the Society.

(ii) be in charge of the *Bait-ul-Mal* and maintain its acounts.

(iii) present the annual accounts and the budget.

(iv) monitor and supervise expenditure.

(v) ensure proper collection of contributions and donations

(vi) supervise and provide support towards local *Bait-ul-Mals*.

14. Conciliation and Arbitration Committee

(i) The *Shura* Council shall establish a Committee of three members for conciliation and arbitration for two years. The Committee will resolve differences and arbitrate in conflicts which may arise within the Society and which could not be resolved by the executive Committee or the *Shura* Council. The Committee will have jurisdiction to arbitrate in disputes in which the Executive Committee, the *Shura* Council or any of the office bearers of the Society may be a party.

(ii) The Committee will be the competent body to interpret the Constitution of the Society and its interpretation will be binding.

(iii) The members of the Committee will be ineligible to be members of the *Shura* Council or the Executive Committee.

(iv) The Committee shall elect a convenor to whom all complaints in writing with all relevant documents will be presented.

(v) The Committee will act independently and act as an impartial body and its decisions shall be binding on all members and Constituent bodies of the Society.

(vi) The *Shura* Council will frame the rules of procedure for the Committee.

15. Branches/Circles

The work of the Society will be organised through branches or circles at local level.

(i) The President with the consultation of the Executive Committee may designate any place in Great Britain as a Branch where there are at least ten members of the Society and which fulfils such other requirements as laid down by the *Shura* Council from time to time. A place where a Branch cannot be established may be designated a Circle.

(ii) Each Branch shall have a local President who will be elected in accordance with the provisions laid down in Art.16.

(iii) A Branch will have a local working committee to plan, organise, assign responsibilities and review the work.

(iv) The President with the consultation of the Executive Committee may suspend a Branch or circle for gross violation of the Constitution. The Branch or Circle could be dissolved on the recommendation of the Executive and with the approval of the *Shura* Council.

(v) The President of the Branch or In-charge of the Circle will regularly report on the activities of their localities and send its accounts to the Executive Committee.

16. Elections

(i) Elections to all offices shall be held every two years, according to the procedure laid down by the *Shura* Council. However, due to unavoidable circumstances, if the elections cannot be held, the President may extend the tenure to a maximum of three months. The tenure of the President can only be extended by the *Shura* Council.

(ii) No canvassing in any form shall be carried out in any election nor shall anyone present himself/herself as a candidate for any post.

(iii) The election of local president will be supervised by the Executive Committee.

17. Members' Convention

(i) An Annual Members' Convention shall be held unless prevented by some unavoidable circumstances.

(ii) The quorum for the Convention shall be one-third of the total membership.

(iii) The annual report of work of the Society shall be presented to the Convention. Every member shall have the right, subject to Islamic principles and such rules as may be prescribed by the *Shura* Council, to raise issues, discuss, question, criticise and freely express his/her views in the meeting about the affairs of the Society.

18. Discipline of the Members

Any member shall cease to be a member if he/she

(i) resigns and his/her resignation is accepted by the Executive Committee.

(ii) in the opinion of the Executive Committee fails to fulfil any of the requirements as laid down in Article 6.

(iii) indulges in gross misconduct, disobedience of the Constitution or persistent disregard of the discipine of the Society and his/her expulsion is approved by the Executive Committee.

(iv) before any action is taken under Sub-section (ii) and (v) the member concerned will be given an opportunity to clarify his/her position.

(v) the regulations for suspension and expulsion shall be laid down by the *Shura*.

19. Termination and Removal of Office Bearers

(i) The President or any office bearer shall cease to remain as such if he resigns and his resignation is accepted by the *Shura* Council.

(ii) The President or any other office bearer shall be liable to be removed by a motion of no confidence if:

(a) he consistently fails to fulfil the requirements of discharging the duties and responsibilities laid down for such office in the Constitution.

(b) he deliberately or consistently violates any major explicit injunction of the Qur'an and *Sunnah*.

(iii) A motion of no confidence stating the reason thereof and signed by at least one-third of the members shall be given:

(a) to the General-Secretary in case of a motion against the President.

(b) to the President in case the motion is against a member of the Executive Committee, member of the *Shura* Council or a local President.

(iv) (a) A meeting of the *Shura* Council shall be convened as soon as possible to discuss and decide about the motion of no confidence. The motion against the President will be carried if passed by two-thirds of the *Shura* Council. For others the motion will be passed if carried by a simple majority.

(b) In case of a motion against the local President, the President shall convene a meeting of the local members to discuss the issue and the Executive Committee shall decide about the motion.

(c) The President shall have the power to suspend or remove from office any local President with prior conciliation of the Executive Committee, if he becomes liable for such action.

20. Finance

(i) The President shall be accountable to the *Shura* Council for all incomes and expenditures. The bank account will be operated by such persons as laid down by the *Shura* Council from time to time.

(ii) The funds shall be acquired from the following sources:

(a) regular contributions from members and donations from well-wishers of the Society.

(b) other sources as approved by the *Shura* Council.

(iii) The *Shura* Council shall appoint an auditor to audit the Central *Bait-ul-Mal* accounts. For local branches and circles their local working committees shall appoint auditors.

(iv) Audited accounts for *Bait-ul-Mal* shall be presented to their respective appointing bodies. Copies of all audited accounts of all branches and circles shall be sent to the Executive Committee.

21. Amendments to the Constitution

Except Articles 2,3,5,and 21 which shall never be subject to amendments, this Constitution may be amended by a two-thirds majority of the *Shura* Council members, provided the motion of the amendment is circulated at least two weeks in advance of the *Shura* Council meeting.

Glossary

Abbasid	Dynasty of caliphs that ruled from Baghdad (750-1258CE)
Adab	Ideal behaviour, habit, used by Sufis to describe the practice of *murids* modelling themselves on the behaviour of the *shaikh*. Also used to describe practices unique to the *tariqa*.
Adhan/Azan	Call to prayer.
Ahl al-Kitab	People of the Book; Jews and Christians.
Ahmadiyas	Movement founded by Mirza Ghulam Ahmad (1835-1908) whose members believe him to be the promised messiah. Declared non-Muslims by several Muslim states including Pakistan.
Alim	Singular of *ulema*, a learned man, usually used for a religious scholar or graduate of *madrasa*
Alima	a learned woman, feminine of *alim*
Amir	Title given to a military commander, governor or prince. Used by *Jamaat-i Islami* for its leader.
Ashraf	Claiming ancestry to the Prophet or his companions. Used in the subcontinent by well-born Muslims to claim ancestry to the original Arab/Central Asian invaders. Of high culture.
Ayat	Verse of the Qur'an.
Azad	Free
Azraqites	Sect of *Kharijites*.
Baba	father, old man, term of respect used for both *sadhus* and *faqirs*
Bai'a(t)	oath of allegiance taken to a *shaikh* on becoming a disciple.
Bait al-Mal/ul Mal	lit.'house of wealth'; the public treasury in Muslim lands; used by some Muslim organisations for the post of treasurer.
Baraka(t)	'Blessing'; the power to bless inherent in a saint, his tomb, and his relics. Usually received through physical contact.
Be-pir	(Urdu) 'Without *pir*', cruel, heartless
Bhuta	(Hindi/Urdu) a wandering evil spirit, ghost of a murdered

person; used by both Muslims and Hindus in rural parts of the subcontinent.

Bida	An illegal innovation in religion.
Biradari	(Urdu) 'brotherhood'; extended kinship networks defined through male lineage.
Caliph	see *Khalifa*.
Chela	(Sanskrit) A Hindu disciple of a yogi or guru.
Chishti/Chishtiyya	Sufi order, which in the subcontinent, traces its spiritual ancestry back to Mu'inuddin Chishti of Ajmer (d.1236).
Chutti	(Bengali) Destructive Hindu godling.
Darban	(Urdu) Doorkeeper
Darga(h)	(Urdu) Shrine to a saint and a centre for pilgrimage
Dar al-Amn	Abode of peace; territory not under Islamic law but where Muslims can live peacefully as a minority.
Dar al-Harb	Abode of war; territory not under Islamic law.
Dar al-Islam	Abode of Islam; territory under Islamic law.
Dar al-ulum/Dar ul-uloom	'Abode of Sciences'; higher institution for Islamic religious education.
Dars i Nizami	Curriculum devised by Farangi Mahal, Lucknow, in the eighteenth century
Dawa(h)	The proselytising of Islam to Muslims and non-Muslims.
Dhikr/Zikr	The constant remembrance of God; used by Sufis to describe the continuous and rhythmic repetition of God's names which varies from order to order.
Dhimmi/Zimmi	Protected status given to the followers of revealed religions.
Diwali	Hindu festival of lights held in October/November.
Du'a	Prayer of supplication. Sometimes made through the Prophet
Dussehra	Hindu Festival in September/October; known as *Durga Puja* in Bengal.
Faqir	A mendicant who lives only for God with a vow of poverty.
Fatiha(h)	The first chapter of the Qur'an.

Fatwa	Opinion concerning Islamic law issued by an expert on the *Shari'ah*
Fiqh	Jurisprudence; the science of interpreting *Shari'ah*
Fitna(h)	Disorder.
Giarvin Sharif	Celebration of Sufi teachings often in praise of Abdul Qadir Gilani
Hadhrat/Hazrat	Dignity; nearness; title for Sufi or Companion of the Prophet.
Hadith	Report of the sayings or deeds of the Prophet passed on by the Companions. The *Hadith* collections are second only in authority to the Qur'an.
Hafiz	Muslim who has memorised the Qur'an.
Hajj	Annual pilgrimage to Mecca which every Muslim should undergo at least once in his/her life. One of the five pillars of Islam.
Halal	Permitted
Hanafi	School of Islamic jurisprudence founded by Abu Hanafi (d.767)
Hanbali	School of jurisprudence founded by Ahmad ibn Hanbal (d.855).
Haram	Forbidden
Hidayah	Legal textbook brought to India by Maulana Buhari-uddin from Central Asia in the thirteenth century. It has remained the basis for Muslim law in the subcontinent.
Hifz	Traditional method of learning to recite the Qur'an in Arabic.
Hijab	Headcovering used to maintain modesty by women.
Hijra(h)	The migration from Mecca to Medina in 622CE.
Hookah	Water-pipe or hubble-bubble used for smoking.
Id/Eid	Muslim holy days/festival.
Ijma	Consensus of the Muslim community as a source of law.
Ijtihad	Individual inquiry which goes back to the roots of Islamic jurisprudence in the Qur'an and *Sunna* and thereby circumvents *taqlid*.

Imam	Leader of the community; title given to founders of the four law schools; a leader of the ritual prayers; an honorific for a religious scholar; used by the *Shi'a* as a title for the spiritual descendents of the Prophet through Ali.
Imam Khatib	*Imam* who leads the prayers.
Imam Rhatib	Qualified *Imam* able to preach and instruct.
Iman	Faith
Islah	Reform; the effort to maintain the original purity of the faith.
Istafta	Legal queries
Itikaf	Retreat maintained in the mosque during the last ten days of Ramadan
Izzat	Honour; family pride
Jahiliyya	The time of ignorance first used to describe pre-Islamic Arabia.
Jamaat/Jami'at/Jamiyat	Party of God; Islamic group committed to *Dawah*
Jawaz	(Urdu) Legitimacy
Jihad	Religious obligation to defend Islam if necessary by means of a righteous war; religious effort or striving.
Jinn/djinn	Beings mentioned in the Qur'an made of fire and air, thought to be able to interfere in human affairs.
Jizya	Tax paid by *dhimmis*.
Juba	Cloak given by a *pir* to his successor or *khalifa*.
Julus	(Urdu) Sufi procession usually held on Prophet's birthday.
Juma	Friday; day of assembly in the mosque.
Juma Namaz	Friday prayers.
Kafir	An unbeliever
Kalam	Theology
Kalima	The article of faith: 'There is no god but God; Muhammad is His Prophet'.
Karama(t)	Supernatural power that enables a saint to perform miracles.

Khalifa(h)/Khilifa(t)	Arabic term denoting the notion of deputy or successor. Formerly used by the rulers of the Islamic community. During the rapid growth of the community into an empire, the term came to mean imperial sovereignty combining both political and religious authority. Also used as the title for a representative of a Sufi.
Khanqah	Muslim hospice usually established by Sufi.
Kharaj	Land tax.
Kharijites	Early Islamic sectarian movements.
Khojah	Trading community or caste of Muslim converts found mainly in Sind or Bombay, most of whom are *Ishmailis*.
Khutbah/Qutbah	Address or sermon given during Friday prayers.
Kitab	Book.
Kurta	Long tunic worn by Hindus and Muslims.
Langar	Public kitchen in a *khanqah* or *dargah*.
Madrasa(h)/Madrassa(h)	School for religious study usually attached to a mosque. The graduates are known as '*ulema*'.
Majlis	gathering or assembly
Maktab/Maktub	School for children to study the Qur'an usually attached to a mosque.
Manqulat	Traditional sciences of Qur'an and *Hadith*.
Ma'qulat	Rational sciences of logic, philosophy, etc.
Masjid	mosque
Maslak	School of Islamic thought.
Maulana/Mawlana	Title given to religious scholars.
Maulvi	As above
Mawali	Client or freedman; applied to non-Arab Muslims when Islam first spread from the Arabian peninsula.
Milad an (e) Nabi	Birthday of the Prophet.
Minbar	High seat or chair in the mosque from which the sermon is delivered.
Mi'raj	'ascension'; The Prophet's journey to heaven where he is supposed to have entered the presence of God.

Moharram/Muharram	Festival to mark the tragedy at Kerbala.
Mufti	Specialist in Islamic law able to issue *Fatwas*.
Mughal	Muslim dynasty in India established in 1526CE.
Muhajir	Indian Muslims who migrated to Pakistan on Partition in 1947.
Mujaddid	Person believed to renew the Muslim faith at the beginning of each century.
Mujahiddin	Those engaged in *Jihad*.
Mujawar/Mujawir	Attendants at a shrine.
Mulk	Form of ownership in Islamic law corresponding approximately to modern freehold.
Murid	Follower of a *Pir* or *Shaikh*.
Murji'ite	Early group who believed in 'postponement' - leaving the punishment of sins to God.
Mushriq	Idolater.
Mutakullum	(Urdu) Speaker
Nabi	Prophet.
Nadhir	A warner.
Nafs	Self
Najdites	Sect of Kharijites.
Namaz	(Urdu) Prayers.
Naqshbandi	Sufi order introduced to India by Khwaja Baqi Billah (b.1563).
Na't	(Urdu) Song which praises the Prophet.
Nawwab	Originally used for for the viceroy or governor of a province in the Mughal empire, but later used simply as a title.
Nizam	Governor, particularly the Viveroy of the Deccan.
Nur/Noor	Light; light of God.
Noor e Muhammadi	(Urdu) Sufi doctrine which regards Muhammad as an emanation of God's Light
Paasban	(Urdu) Social work programme.

Pir	(Urdu) Saint, Sufi teacher.
Pirbhai	(Urdu) fellow-follower of a *pir*.
Pirzada	(Urdu) Pl. *pirzade*; descendents of a saint in charge of the shrine.
Purdah	Veiling and seclusion of women.
Qadi	Muslim judge who administers Islamic law.
Qadiani	Another name for the *Ahmadiyya*.
Qadiriyya	Sufi order founded by Abdul Qadir Gilani.
Qawwali	Devotional singing.
Qibla	The direction of Mecca faced during prayer.
Qiyas	The Process of applying *Hadith* and Qur'an to new situations by the use of analogy.
Quraysh	The tribe the Prophet was born into.
Qush	Missionary tours undertaken by *Tabligh-i Jamaat*.
Qutb	The head of an invisible hierarchy of saints upon whom the order of the universe depends.
Rafiq	*Jamaat-i Islami* worker
Rahbar	(Urdu) Guide
Ramadan	Ninth month; the month of fasting; one of the five pillars.
Rashidun	The first four rightly-guided Caliphs.
Rasul	Prophet who comes with a Book of revelation.
Riba	Interest, forbidden in Islam.
Risala(h)	Those who accepted the message.
Sadhu	(Hindi) Hindu wandering holy man.
Sahib	(Urdu) Honorific applied to titles and names.
Sajjada nashin	'He who sits on the mat'; the ancestral successor to a pir.
Salafi	Movement founded by Muhammad Abduh (d.1905). Influenced *Islah* and nationalist groups in North Africa.
Salat	Prayer.

Sama	Listening to music in Sufi circle.
Sanussiyyah	Reform Sufi *tariqa* popular in North Africa. Founded by al-Sanusi (1486).
Sasthi	(Hindi) Hindu deity of children.
Saiyid/Sayyid	Descendant of the Prophet.
Shafi'i	School of jurisprudence named after founder al-Shafi'i (d.820CE).
Shahadah	Witnessing the *kalima* to become a Muslim.
Shahid	Witness; martyr.
Shaikh al Hadith	Senior teacher of *Hadith* in *dar al Ulum*
Shalwar Kamis	Tunic and baggy trousers worn by Muslims in the subcontinent, especially Punjab.
Shari'ah	Islamic law codified into different schools in the middle ages.
Sheikh/Shaikh	Old man, Sufi teacher, saint.
Shi'a	The Party of Ali. Minority tradition which believes the succession came to Ali not Abu Bakr.
Shirk	Associating another with God. The most serious sin in Islam.
Shura	Council.
Silsilah	Sequence of Sufi masters reaching back to the Prophet.
Sirah/Seerah	Corpus of tradition concerning the Prophet.
Sufi	Muslim mystic
Sunna	Custom or tradition associated with Muhammad.
Sunni	'One who follows the beaten path'; the largest group of Muslims.
Sura	Chapter of the Qur'an.
Taffaqa	Legal deduction.
Tafsir	Explanation; commentary on the Qur'an and science of its interpretation.
Tajdid	Renewal
Tajwid	(Urdu) Study of the correct pronunciation of Urdu.

Taqlid	The principle of following the established doctrines of the schools of Islamic law.
Tarbiyah	Islamic training programmes.
Tariqa	The Sufi path; the way; a school of guidance along that path
Tasawuf	Spiritual disciplines of the Sufis
Tawhid	The Divine Unity; the assertion of oneness.
Ta'widh/Ta'wiz	Amulets or bracelets containing verses of the Qur'an given to cure diseases or bring good fortune.
Ta'wil	Allegorical exegesis of the Qur'an.
Tobarrak	(Urdu) Blessed
Ulema	Plural of *Alim*.
Umam	Plural of *Ummah*
Umayyad	First Arab Muslim dynasty founded in 661 CE.
Ummah	The universal Muslim community.
Ummah Wusta	The ideal or model Muslim community.
Umrah	Lesser pilgrimage to Mecca which can be performed at any time.
Unani	Traditional medicine practised by Muslims in subcontinent.
Urs	Anniverary of a saint's death which is regarded as celebrating their union with God.
Wahhabi	Follower of the movement founded by Abdul Wahhab (1703-1787).
Wali	Friend of God; a saint.
Watan	Fatherland.
Wataniyyah	Patriotism.
Wazir	Chief Minister of the Delhi Sultanates; sometimes used to describe an official in charge of finances.
Yathrib	Medina
Zakat	Alms-giving, one of the five pillars of Islam.

Bibliography

Aasi, Ghulam, Haider, 1986, 'The Qur'an and Other Religious Traditions', *Hamdard Islamicus*, Vol. IX, no.2.

Abdullah, H. Kh. A. Hamed, 1988, *Some Aspects of Arabic/Islamic Political Thought in Iraq (4th-8th c. A.H./ 10th-14th centuries AD)*, PhD, University of Manchester.

Adams, Caroline, 1987, *Across Seven Seas and Thirteen Rivers*, London.

Adams, Charles, 1966, 'The Ideology of Maulana Mawdudi', *South Asian Politics and Religion*, ed. D.E. Smith, Princeton University, Princeton.

Adams, Charles, 1983, 'Mawdudi and the Islamic State', *Voices of Resurgent Islam*, ed. Esposito, John, Oxford University Press, New York.

Afshar, Haleh, 1990, 'Sex, Marriage, and the Muslim', *The Correspondent*, 18th November.

Agwani, M.S., 1986, *Islamic Fundamentalism in India*, Twenty-First Century India Society, New Delhi.

Ahmad, Barakat, 1983, 'Mawdudian Concept of Islamic State', *Islam and the Modern Age*, No. 14, November.

Ahmad, Imtiaz, 1985, 'Introduction', *Ritual and Religion among Muslims of the Subcontinent*, Vanguard Books, Lahore.

Ahmad, Khurshid & Ansari, Zafar Ishaq, 1979, 'Mawlana Sayyid Abul A'la Mawdudi: An Introduction to His Vision of Islam and Islamic Revival', *Islamic Perspectives*, ed. Khurshid & Ansari, The Islamic Foundation, Leicester.

Ahmad, Khurshid & Ansari, Zafar Ishaq, 1986, *Mawdudi: An Introduction to His Life and Thought*, The Islamic Foundation, Leicester.

Ahmed, Akbar, 1983, *Religion and Politics in Muslim Society*, Cambridge University Press, New York.

Ahmed, Akbar, 1992, *Postmodernism and Islam*, Routledge, London.

Ahmed, Ishtiaq, 1987, *The Concept of the Islamic State - An Analysis of the Ideological Controversy in Pakistan*, Francis Pinter, London.

Ahmed, Manzooruddin, 1971, 'Ummah - The Idea of Universal Community', *Islamic Studies X*, No.1, March.

Ahmed, Rafiuddin, 1992, 'Muslim-Christian Polemics and Religious Reform in Nineteenth Century Bengal: Munshi Meheru'llah of Jessore', *Religious Controversy in British India: Dialogues in South Asian Languages*, ed. Jones, Kenneth, Suny Series in Religious Studies, New York.

Ahsan, Abdullahil, 1985, *Muslim Society in Crisis: A Case Study of the Organisation of the Islamic Conference*, PhD, The University of Michigan, U.S.A.

Ahsan, M.M. & Kidwai, A.R. (eds), 1991, *Sacrilege Versus Civility - Muslim Perspectives on the Satanic Verses Affair*, The Islamic Foundation, Leicester.

Akram, M., 1974-75, 'Pakistani Migrants in Britain: A Note', *New Community*, 4:1.

Akhtar, Shabbir, 1990, *A Faith for All Seasons: Islam and Western Modernity*, Bellew, London.

Al-Ahsan, Abdullah, 1992, *Ummah or Nation?*, The Islamic Foundation, Leicester.

Al-Braik, Nasser Ahmed M., 1986, *Islam and World Order: Foundations and Values*, PhD, The American University, Washington.

Al-Shafi'i, Muhammad ibn Idris, 1940, *Al-Risala*, Shakir Edition, Cairo.

Alavi, Hamza, 1985, 'Pakistan and Islam: Ethnicity and Ideology', unpublished paper to *the Middle East Discussion Group*, November, Oxford.

Alavi, Hamza, 1988, 'Pakistan and Islam: Ethnicity and Ideology', *State and Ideology in the Middle-East and Pakistan*, ed. Halliday, Frank and Alavi, Hamza, Macmillan Education, London.

Ali, Abdullah Yusef (tr.) The Holy Qur'an, revised and edited by The Presidency of Islamic Researches, IFTA, *Mushaf Al-Madinah An-Nabawiyah*, King Fahd Holy Qur'an Printing Complex, Saudi Arabia.

Ali Yasmin, 1992, 'Muslim Women and the Politics of Ethnicity and Culture in Northern England', Refusing Holy Orders: Women and Fundamentalism, eds. Sahgal, Gita & Yuval-Davis, Nira, Virago, London.

Ally, Mushaq Muhammad Ibn, 1989, 'Stranger Exiled From Home', *The Salman Rushdie Con-*

troversy in Interreligious Perspective, Ed. Cohn-Sherbok, Dan, Symposium Series, Vol.27, The Edwin Mullen Press, Lampeter.

Andrews, A., 1990, 'Muslim Political Elites in the U.K.: A Study of the Jamaat-i Islami', Unpublished, University of Leicester.

Andrews, A., 1993, 'South Asian Sunni Reform Movements in the west: The Lang Scots Mile from Delhi to Dundee', paper presented to the Conference on New Islamic and Related Movements in the West, The Centre for New Religious Movements, 11th December, Kings College, London.

Anwar, Muhammad, 1980, 'Religious Identity in Plural Societies: The Case of Britain', *The Journal of the Institute of Muslim Minority Affairs*, 2:2/3:1, pp.110-121.

Anwar, Muhammad, 1982, *Young Muslims in a Multi-Cultural Society - Their Educational Needs and Policy Implications: The British Case*, The Islamic Foundation, Leicester.

Anwar, Muhammad, 1993, 'Muslims in Britain: 1991 Census and Other Statistical Sources', *CSIC Papers*, No.9, September, Centre for the Study of Islam and Christian/Muslim Relations, Selly Oak, Birmingham.

Anwar, Muhammad & Garaudy, Roger, 1984, 'Social and Cultural Perspectives on Muslims in Western Europe', *Muslims in Europe*, December, Centre for the Study of Islam and Christian/Muslim Relations, Selly Oak, Birmingham.

Arensburg, Conrad & Kimball, Solan, 1965, *Culture and Community*, Harcourt, Brace and World, New York.

Aziz, K.K., 1967, *Islamic Modernism in India and Pakistan 1857-1964*, Oxford University Press, London.

Badawi, Zaki, 1986, 'Religions in Britain: Islam in Britain', *World Religions in Education SHAP Mailing*, SHAP Working Party/CRE, London.

Bagley, F.R.C.,(trs), 1964, *Ghazali's Book of Counsel for Kings*, al-Ghazali, Muhammad ibn Muhammad, Oxford University Press, London.

Ballard, Roger & Ballard, Catherine, 1977, 'The Sikhs: The Development of South Asian Settlements in Britain', *Between Two Cultures*, ed. Watson, James, Basil Blackwell, Oxford.

Banzon, Kenneth Espana, 1981, *Islamic Nationalism in the Phillipines: Reflections in Socio-Political Analysis*, PhD, Duke University, U.S.A.

Barth, Fredrik, 1970, *Ethnic Groups and Boundaries*, George Allen & Unwin, London.

Barton, Stephen, 1986, *The Bengali Muslims of Bradford*, Community Religions Project,

Monograph Series, University of Leeds

Bashier, Zakaria, 1985, *Muslim Women in the Midst of Change*, The Islamic Foundation, Leicester.

Bell, Colin & Newby, Howard, 1971, *Community Studies: An Introduction to the Sociology of the Local Community*, George Allen & Unwin, London.

Bell, Colin & Newby, Howard (eds), 1974, 'Introduction', *The Sociology of Community*, Frank Cass & Co., London.

Bell, Richard, 1936, *The Qur'an: Translated with Critical Rearrangement of the Surahs*, T.Clark, Edinburgh.

Bell, Richard, 1953, *Introduction to the Qur'an*, Edinburgh University Press, Edinburgh.

Bhachu, Parminder, 1985, *Twice Migrants*, Tavistock Publications, London.

Bhardwaj, S.M., 1973, *Hindu Places of Pilgrimage in India*, University of California Press, Berkeley.

Binder, Leonard, 1963, *Religion and Politics in Pakistan*, University of California Press, Berkeley.

Brah, Avtar, 1978, 'South Asian Teenagers in Southall: Their Perceptions of Marriage, Family, and Ethnic Identity', *New Community*, 6:3.

Breton, R., 1964, 'Institutional Completeness of Ethnic Communities and the Personal Relations of Immigrants', *American Journal of Sociology* 70:2.

Brohi, Allahbukhsh, 1980, 'Mawlana Abul A'la Mawdudi: The Man, The Scholar, The Reformer', *Islamic Perspectives*, eds. Ahmad & Ansari, Islamic Foundation, Leicester.

Bunting, Madeleine, 1990, 'A Meeting of Two Worlds', *The Guardian*, 13th June.

Burghart, Richard (ed), 1987, *Hinduism in Great Britain: The Perpetuation of Religion in an Alien Cultural Milieu*, Tavistock Publications, Leicester.

Butterworth, Eric, 1967, 'A Muslim Community in Britain', Church Information Office.

Butterworth, Eric, 1969, 'Muslims in Britain', *A Sociological Yearbook of Religion in Britain 2*, ed. Martin D. & Hill M., London.

Caplan, Lionel (ed), 1987, *Studies in Religious Fundamentalism*, MacMillan, London.

Carey, Sean & Shukur, Abdus, 1985, 'Bangladeshi Community in East London', *New Community*, 12:3.

Chandra, Bipan, 1988, *India's Struggle for Independence*, Penguin, London.

Clarke, Peter, 1985, 'Islam in Britain', *Religion Today*, 2:3.

College de France, 1983, 'Muslim Immigration and Settlement in Britain', Colloquium on *Islam in Europe Today*, October, Association Pour L'Avancement Des Sciences Islamiques, Paris.

Coulson, N.J., 1971, *A History of Islamic Law*, Islamic Surveys 2, University of Edinburgh Press, Edinburgh.

Dabashi, Hamid, 1989, *Authority in Islam*, Transactions Publishers, New Jersey.

Dahya, Badr, 1972-3, 'Pakistanis in England', *New Community*, 2:1.

Dahya, Badr, 1974, 'The Nature of Pakistani Ethnicity in Industrial Cities in Britain', *Urban Ethnicity*, ed. Cohen, Abner, ASA Monographs.

Dalrymple, William, 1989, 'The Arabs of Tyneside', *The Independent Magazine*, 7th October.

Dashefsky, Arnold, 1972, 'And the Search goes on: Religio-ethnic Identity and Identification', *Sociological Analysis* 33:4, pp.239-245.

Dassetto, Felice, 1988, 'The Tabligh Organisation in Belgium', *The New Islamic Presence in Europe, ed.* Gerholm, Tomas & Lithman, Georg Yngve, Mansell, London.

Dawe, Tony, 1987, 'Faith, Hope, & Poverty', *The Times*, 18th August.

Denny, Frederick, 1974, *Community and Salvation: The Meaning of Ummah in the Qur'an*, PhD, The University of Chicago, U.S.A.

Denny, Frederick, 1975, 'The Meaning of Ummah in the Qur'an', *History of Religions*, Vol.15, No.1, pp.34-71.

Donohue, John J., & Esposito, John L. (eds), 1982, *Islam in Transition*, Oxford University Press, Oxford.

Dufferin's 'Minutes of November 1988 in Provincial Councils', enclosed with a letter dated 11th November 1988 to Viscount Cross, Secretary of State for India, *Letters form Dufferin to Cross*, Vol. V., India Office Library.

Elkholy, Abdo A., 1974, 'The Concept of Community in Islam', *Islamic Perspectives*, ed. Ahmad & Ansari, Islamic Foundation, Leicester.

Esposito, John L., 1982, *Islam in Transition*, ed. Donohue, John & Esposito, John L., Oxford University Press, New York.

Esposito, John L., 1984, *Voices of Resurgent Islam,* Syracuse University Press, Syracuse, NY.

Esposito, John L., 1988, *Islam - The Straight Path,* Oxford University Press, New York.

Ferozson's Urdu-English Dictionary, Revised Edition, Ferozsons (Pvt) Ltd., Lahore, Pakistan.

Forbes, A.D.W., ND, Islam in India: The Significance of Shaykh Ahmad Sirhindi and the Naqshbandi Order in the Restoration of Islamic Orthodoxy', Submitted for M.A., University of Leeds, Leeds

Forbes, A.D.W., ND, Islam in India: 'The Influence of Shah Wali-Ullah and Sir Sayyid Ahmad Khan on Indian Islam', Submitted for M.A., University of Leeds, Leeds.

Forbes, A.D.W., ND, Islam in India: 'The Hanbali Response to the decay of Indian Islam and the Challenge of the West; The Wahhabi Movements of Arabia and India', Submitted for M.A., University of Leeds, Leeds.

Forbes, A.D.W., ND, 'Two Concepts of Monism: The *Wahdat Al-Wujud* of Ibn Al-Arabi and *Wahdat Al-Shuhud* of Shaikh Ahmad Sirhindi', Submitted for M.A., University of Leeds, Leeds.

Forbes, A.D.W., ND, 'Mystic Life and organisation in Muslim India: A Comparison Between the Structure of the *Chishti* and *Naqshbandi Silsilahs'*, Submitted for M.A., University of Leeds, Leeds

Francis, E.K., 1976, *Interethnic Relations*, Elsevier, New York.

Freitag, Sandra, 1980, *Religious Rites and Riots: From Community Identity to Communalism in North India 1870-1940*, PhD, Berkeley University.

Fruzzetti, Lina, M., 1985, 'Muslim Rituals; Household Rites vs. the Public Festivals in Rural India', Ahmad, Imtiaz, *Ritual and Religion among Muslims of the Subcontinent*, Vanguard Books, Lahore.

Ganhar, Altaf, 1980, 'Mawlana Abul A'la Mawdudi: A Personal Account', *Islamic Perspectives*, eds. Ahmad & Ansari, The Islamic Foundation, Leicester.

Gans, Herbert J., 1985, 'Urbanism and Suburbanism as Ways of Life', An *Introduction to Sociology*, eds. Bocock R., Hamilton P., Thompson K., Watson A., Open University Press, Milton Keynes.

Geaves, Ronald, 1989, 'An Attempt to Isolate a Uniquely Religious Dimension in the Choices facing the Islamic Minority as it comes to terms with living in Britain', Submitted for Partial Fulfilment of M.A., University of Leeds.

Geaves, Ronald, 1989, 'Maulana Mawdudi: A Pure Islam or Cultural Inheritence', Submitted for Partial Fulfilment of M.A., University of Leeds.

Geaves, Ronald, 1989, 'Muslims in Leeds', Submitted for Partial Fulfilment of M.A., University of Leeds.

Geertz, Clifford, 1963, *Old Societies and New States - the Quest for Modernity in Asia and Africa*, Free Press, Glencoe.

Gellner, E., 1968, 'The Pendulum Swing Theory of Islam', *Sociology of Religion*, ed. Robertson, Roland, Penguin, London.

Gibb, Hamilton, 1963, 'The Community in Islamic History', *The American Philosophical Society Proceedings*, Vol. 107, No.2, April.

Gilani, Syed Asad, 1984, *Mawdudi - Thought and Movement*, Islamic Publications, Lahore.

Goldziher, Ignaz, 1981, *Introduction to Islamic Theology and Law*, Princeton University Press, Princeton.

Gordon, M., 1964, *Assimilation in American Life*, Oxford University Press, New York.

Gordon, Paul, 1992, Senior Research Officer, Runnymede Trust, 'Islam as Europe's Other: Restrictive Immigration Policy as a Response to the Muslim Presence', Conference on *Islam in a Changing Europe*, September 9-11th.

Guillaume, Alfred, 1963, *Islam*, Cassell, London.

Haddad, Yvonne Y., 1983, 'Sayyid Qutb: Ideologue of Islamic Revival', *Voices of Resurgent Islam*, ed. Esposito, John L., Oxford University Press.

Hadden, Jeffery & Shupe, Anson, 1989, *Secularisation and Fundamentalism Reconsidered - Religion and the Political Order, Vol. VIII*, New Era Books, New York.

Hadden, Jeffery & Shupe, Anson, 1989, 'Is there such a thing as Global Fundamentalism?' *Secularisation and Fundamentalism Reconsidered - Religion and the Political Order, Vol. VIII*, New Era Books, New York.

Halliday, Fred, 1989, 'The Struggle for the Migrant Soul', *Times Literary Supplement*, April 14th-20th.

Hamid, Abdul, 1967, *Muslim Separatism in India: A Brief Survey*, Oxford University Press, Karachi.

Haq M. Anwural, 1972, *The Faith Movement of Maulana Muhammad Ilyas*, G. Allen & Unwin, London.

Hardy P., 1972, *The Muslims of British India*, Cambridge University Press, London.

Hasan, Ahmad, 1967, 'Ijma: An Integrating Force in the Muslim Community', *Islamic Studies*, Vol. VI, No.4, December, Islamabad.

Helm, Sarah, 1989, 'Muslims Divided by a Faith Caught in a Period of Change', *The Independent*, 28th January.

Hitti, Philip, 1970, *The History of the Arabs*, Macmillan, London.

Hodgson, Marshall S., 1974, *The Venture of Islam*, Vol. I, University of Chicago Press, Chicago.

Hourani, Albert, 1962, *Arabic Thought in the Liberal Age*, Oxford University Press, London.

Husband, Charles & Waqar Ahmad, 1992, 'Social Welfare', *Conference on Islam in a Changing Europe*, Bradford University, 9-11th September 1992.

Hussein, Ali, 1992, 'Culture, Faith, and Political Ideology: Islam in a Changing Context', *Conference on Islam in a Changing Europe*, Bradford University, 9-11th September 1992.

Ikram, 1964, *Muslim Civilisation in India*, Columbia University Press, New York.

Inkeles, Alex, 1981, 'Convergence and Divergence in Industrial Societies', *Directions of Change*, ed. Attir, Mustafa O., et al, Westview Press, Boulder, Colorado.

Islamic Society of Britain, ND, 'The Constitution of the Islamic Society of Britain', Markfield, Leicester.

Islamic Society of Britain, ND, 'Towards a Just Society', Markfield, Leicester.

James, Brian, 1987, 'Which Path Leads to Paradise', *The Times*, August 16th.

Janson, G.H., 1979, *Militant Islam*, Pan, London.

Jeffery, Patricia, 1972, 'Pakistani Families in Bristol', *New Community*, 1:5.

Jeffery, Patricia, 1985, 'Creating a Scene: The Disruption of Ceremonial in a Sufi Shrine', *Ritual and Religion Among Muslims in the Subcontinent*, Ahmad, Imtiaz, Vanguard Books, Lahore.

Jimenez, M. Ochana, 1985, 'Al-Madina', *First Encyclopaedia of Islam 1913-1936*, 2nd Edition, Vol.V., eds. Houtsma, Wensinck, et al., A.J.Brill, Leiden.

Johnstone, Penelope, 1981, 'Christians and Muslims in Britain', *Islamchristiana*, Roma Pontificio Instituto di Studi Arabi e Islamici, Rome.

Johnstone, Penelope, 1986, 'Millet or Minority: Muslims in Britain', *Identity Issues and World Religions*, Australian Association for the Study of Religions, South Australia.

Joly, Daniele, 1986, 'Making a Place for Islam in British Society: Muslims in Birmingham', *Centre for Research in International Migration and Ethnic Relations*, Warwick.

Joly, Daniele, 1987, 'Associations Amongst Pakistani Population in Britain', *Immigrant Associations in Europe*, eds. Rex, John, Joly, Daniele, Wilpert, Czarina, Gower, Aldershot.

Joly, Daniele, 1988, 'Making a Place for Islam in British Society: Muslims in Birmingham', *The New Islamic Presence in Western Europe*, ed. Gerholm,Tomas & Lithman, Yngve, George, Mansell, London.

Joly, Daniele & Nielsen, Jorgen, 1985, 'Muslims in Britain: An Annotated Bibliography 1960-1984' *Centre for Research in International Migration and Ethnic Relations*, Warwick.

Juynboll, The. W., 1987, 'Hadith', *First Encyclopaedia of Islam 1913-1936*, 2nd Edition, Vol.III., eds. Houtsma, Wensinck, et al., A.J.Brill, Leiden.

Kandhalvi, M., 1931, *Tablighi Nisab*, Vol.I, Book 5, Anjuman-e Islahul Muslimeen, Dewsbury.

Karandikar, M.A., 1968, *Islam in India's Transition to Modernity*, Orient Longmans, Bombay.

Kaufman, Harold, 1959, 'Towards an Interactional Perception of a Community', *Social Forces*, Vol.38, No.1, October.

Khadduri, Majid & Leibesny J. (eds), 1955, *Law in the Middle East*, Vol.I, The Middle East Institute, Washington DC.

Khadduri, Majid (trs), 1966, *The Islamic Law of Nations: Shaybani's Siyar*, John Hopkins Press, Baltimore.

Khan, M.A., 1982, *Pakistan's Long Autumn*, Iqdam Publications, Lahore.

Khan, Verity Saifullah, 1976, 'Pakistanis in Britain: Perceptions of a Population', *New Community*, 5:3.

Khan, Verity Saifullah, 1979, 'Mirpuris in Bradford', *Minority Families in Britain: Support and Stress*, ed. Khan, Verity Saifullah, London.

Khan, Verity Saifullah, 1984, 'The Pakistanis: Mirpuri Villagers at Home and in Bradford', *Between Two Cultures*, ed. Watson, James, Blackwell, Oxford.

Khanum, Saeeda, 1990, 'Finishing School', *New Statesman and Society*, 25th May.

Khanum, Saeeda, 1992, 'Education and the Muslim Girl', *Refusing Holy Orders*, eds. Sahgal & Yugal-Davis, Virago, London.

Khel, Muhammad Nazeer Ka-Ka, 1982, 'The Rise of the Muslim Umma at Mecca and its Integration', *Hamdard Islamicus*, Vol. V, No.3, Autumn.

King, John, 1993, 'Tablighi Jamaat and the Deobandi Mosques in Britain', Paper presented to the Conference on *New Islamic and Related Movements in the West*, 11th December, The Centre for New Religious Movements, Kings College, London.

Knott, Kim, 1986, 'Religion and Identity and the Study of Ethnic Minority Religions in Britain', *Community Religions Project*, Research Papers, University of Leeds.

Knott, Kim, 1987, 'Strategies for Survival among South Asian Religions in Britain: Parallel Developments, Conflict and Co-operation', *Japanese Symposium on Conflict and Co-operation Between Contemporary Religious Groups*, Japan.

Knott, Kim, 1992, 'The Role of Religious Studies in Understanding the Ethnic Experience', *Community Religions Project*, Research Papers, University of Leeds.

Knott, Kim & Khokher, Sajda, 1993, 'Religious and Ethnic Identity Among Young Muslim Women in Bradford', *New Community*, 19:4, July.

Lampton, A.K.S., 1981, *State and Government in Mediaeval Islam: An Introduction to the Study of Islamic Political Theory: The Jurists*, Oxford University Press, Oxford.

Lawrence, Bruce, 1990, *Defenders of God - The Fundamentalist Revolt Against the Modern Age*, I.B. Tauris, London.

Levy, Reuban, 1962, *The Social Structure of Islam*, Cambridge University Press, London.

Lewins, Frank, 1978, 'Religion and Ethnic identity', *Identity and Religion: International Cross-Cultural Approaches*, eds. Mol, Hans, Sage, Los Angeles.

Lewis, Bernard, 1988, *The Political Language of Islam*, The University of Chicago Press, Chicago.

Lewis, Philip, 1985, *Pirs, Shrines, and Pakistani Islam*, Christian Study Centre, Rawalpindi, Lahore.

Lewis, Philip, 1990, 'Being Muslim and British: The Challenge to Bradford Muslims', unpublished paper, Community Religions Library, University of Leeds.

Lewis, Philip, 1993, *Bradford's Muslim Communities and the Reproduction of Islam*, PhD,

Department of Theology and Religious Studies, University of Leeds.

Link International, 1987, 'Muslim Institutions for Muslims in Britain', November.

Linton, Ralph, 1943, 'Nativistic Movements', *American Anthropologist* 45, pp.230-240.

Longley, Clifford, 1987, 'At the Crossroads of Belief', *The Times*, August 17th.

Makdisi, George, 1981, *The Rise of Colleges*, Edinburgh University Press, Edinburgh.

Mannheim, Karl, 1948, *Ideology and Utopia*, Routledge and Kegan Paul, London.

Mawdudi, Sayyid Abul A'la, 1967, *Unity of the Muslim World*, ed. Ahmad, Khurshid, Islamic Publications, Lahore.

Mawdudi, Sayyid Abul A'la, 1984, *The Islamic Movement -Dynamics of Values, Power and Change*, ed. Murad, Khurrum, The Islamic Foundation, Leicester.

Mawdudi, Sayyid Abul A'la, 1985, *Let Us Be Muslims*, The Islamic Foundation, Leicester.

Mawdudi, Sayyid Abul A'la, 1985, *Towards Understanding Islam*, The Islamic Foundation, Leicester.

Mawdudi, Sayyid Abul A'la, 1986, *The Islamic Way of Life*, ed. Ahmed Khurshid, The Islamic Foundation, Leicester.

Mawdudi, Sayyid Abul A'la, 1986, *Witnesses Unto Mankind*, The Islamic Foundation, Leicester.

Mawdudi, Sayyid Abul A'la, 1987, *Capitalism, Socialism, and Islam*, The Islamic Foundation, Leicester.

McIver, R.M., 1970, *Community: A Sociological Study*, Frank cass & Co., London.

McWilliams, Wilson Carey, 1974, *The Idea of Fraternity in America*, University of California Press, Berkeley.

Metcalf, Barbara Daly, 1982, *Islamic Revival in British India: Deoband 1860-1900*, Princeton University Press, New Jersey.

Metcalf, Barbara Daly, 1990, *Perfecting Women: Maulana Ashraf 'Ali Thanawi's Bihishti Zewar*, partial translation and commentary, University of California Press, Berkeley.

Metcalf, Barbara Daly, 1992, 'Imagining Community: Polemical Debates in Colonial India', *Religious Controversies in British India - Dialogues in South Asian Languages*, ed. Jones, Kenneth

W., State University of New York Press, New York.

Minault, Gail, 1992, 'Sayyid Mumtaz 'Ali and Tahzib un-Niswan: Women's Rights and Women's Journalism in Urdu', *Religious Controversies in British India - Dialogues in South Asian Languages*, ed. Jones, Kenneth W., State University of New York Press, New York.

Mines, Mattison, 1973, Towards a New Perspective on Muslim Identity and Integration in Contrasting Social Settings, Typescript, University Of California, Berkeley.

Mines, Mattison, 1985, 'Islamicisation and Muslim Ethnicity in South India', ed. Ahmad, Imtiaz, *Ritual and Religion among Muslims of the Subcontinent*, Vanguard Books, Lahore.

Mi'raj Muhammad, 1980, 'Shah Wali-Allah: Concept of the Shari'ah', *Islamic Perspectives*, eds. Ahmad & Ansari, The Islamic Foundation, Leicester.

Mirza, Kauser, 1989, 'The Silent Cry: Second Generation Bradford Muslim Women Speak', *Muslims in Europe*, No.43, September, ed Nielsen, Jorgen, Centre for the Study of Islam and Christian/Muslim Relations, Selly Oak, Birmingham.

Modood, Tariq, 1990, 'British Asian Muslims and the Rushdie Affair', *Political Quarterly*, 61:2.

Mol, Hans, 1977, *Identity and the Sacred*, Free Press, New York.

Moore, Charles, 1991, 'Time for a More Liberal and "Racist" Immigration Policy', *The Spectator*, 19th October.

Mortimer, Edward, 1982, *Faith and Power: The Politics of Islam*, Faber and Faber, London.

Murad, Khurram, 1986, *Dawah Among Non-Muslims in the West - Some Conceptual and Methodological Aspects*, The Islamic Foundation, Leicester.

Murad, Khurram, 1986, *Muslim Youth in the West - Towards a New Education Strategy*, The Islamic Foundation, Leicester.

Mujeeb, M., 1966, *The Indian Muslims*, George Allen & Unwin, London.

Nadwi, Syed Abdul Hasan Ali, 1983, *Muslims in the West - The Message and Mission*, The Islamic Foundation, Leicester.

Najjar, Fauzi, 1984, 'Islamic Political Philosophy', *Islamic Theology and Philosophy*, ed. Marmura, Midail, State University of the New York Press, Albany.

Newman, K.J., 1956, *Essays on the Constitution of Pakistan*, Pakistan Co-operative Book Society, Dacca.

Nielsen, Jorgen, 1981, 'Muslims in Europe: An Overview', *Muslim in Europe*, No.12, Centre of the Study of Islam and Christian/Muslim Relations, Selly Oak, Birmingham.

Nielsen, Jorgen, 1984, 'Muslim Immigration and Settlement in Britain', *Muslim in Europe*, No.21, Centre of the Study of Islam and Christian/Muslim Relations, Selly Oak, Birmingham.

Nielsen, Jorgen, 1987, 'Muslims in Britain: Searching For an Identity', *New Community*, 13:3.

Nielsen, Jorgen, 1988, 'Muslim in Britain and Local Authority Responses', *The New Islamic Presence in Western Europe*, eds. Gerholm and Lithman, Mansell, London.

Nielsen, Jorgen, 1989, 'Islamic Communities in Britain', *Religion, State and Society in Modern Britain*, ed. Badham, Paul, The Edwin Mellin Press, Lampeter.

Nielsen, Jorgen, 1992, *Muslims in Western Europe*, Islamic Surveys, Edinburgh University Press, Edinburgh.

Nieuwenuijze, C.A. Van, 1959, 'The *Ummah* - An Analytical Approach', *Studia Islamica*, No.10.

Nisbet, Robert, 1953, *The Quest For Community*, Oxford University Press, New York.

North, Neil, 1986, *Mosques and Madrasahs in Birmingham*, M.Phil., Centre for the Study of Islam and Christian-Muslim Relations, Selly Oak, Birmingham.

Othman, Ali Issa, 1960, *The Concept of Man in Islam in the Writings of Al-Ghazali*, Dar al-Maaref, Cairo.

Parekh, Bhikhu, 1989, 'Between Holy Text and Moral Void', *New Statesman and Society*, 24th March.

Paret, R., 1987, 'Umma', *First Encyclopaedia of Islam 1913-1936*, 2nd Edition, Vol.VIII, eds. Houtsma, Wensinck, et al., A.J.Brill, Leiden.

Pasa, Ahmed Cevdet, 1993, *The Sunni Path*, Waqf Ikhlas Publications, Istanbul.

Pfleiderer, Beatrix, 1985, 'Mir Datar Dargah: The Psychiatry of a Muslim Shrine', *Ritual and Religion Among Muslims in the Subcontinent*, ed. Ahmad, Imtiaz, Vanguard Books, Lahore.

Pipes, Daniel, 1989, 'Fundamentalist Muslims in World Politics', *Secularisation and Fundamentalism Reconsidered: Religion and the Political Order*, Vol.VIII, eds. Hadden & Shupe, New Era Books, New York.

Poplin, Dennis E., 1972, *Communities - A Study of Theories and Methods of Research*, The MacMillan Company, New York.

Powers, David, 1986, *Studies in Qur'an and Hadith*, University of California Press, Berkeley.

Rahman, Fazlur, 1958, 'Muslim Modernism in the Indo-Pakistan Sub-Continent', *Bulletin of the School of Oriental and African Studies*, XXI, London.

Rahman, Fazlur, 1966, *Islam*, Holt, Rheinehart and Winston, New York.

Rahman, Fazlur, 1980, *Major Themes in the Qur'an*, Bibliotheca Islamica, Chicago.

Rahman, Tanzil-Ur, 1988, *Essays on Islam*, Islamic Publications, Lahore.

Rashid, S., 1981, 'The Socialisation and Education of Pakistani Teenage Girls in London', M.Phil Thesis, School of Oriental and African Studies, London.

Raza, Muhammad S., 1991, *Islam in Britain - Past, Present and Future*, Volcano Press, Leicester.

Rex, John, 1973, *Race, Colonialism and the City*, Routledge and Kegan Paul, London.

Rex, John, 1986, *Race and Ethnicity*, Open University Press, Milton Keynes.

Rex, John, 1986, 'The Urban Sociology of religion and Islam in Birmingham', *Centre for Research in International Migration and Ethnic Relations*, Stockholm.

Rex, John & Josephides, Sasha, 1987, 'Asian and Greek Cypriot Associations and Identity', *Immigrant Associations in Europe*, eds. Rex, Joly, Czarina, Gower, Aldershot.

Rizvi, Sayyid Mahboob, 1980, *History of the Dar al-Ulum Deoband*, Volume I, Maulana Abdul Haqq, Dar al-Ulum, Deoband.

Rizvi, Sayyid Mahboob, 1980, *History of the Dar al-Ulum Deoband*, Volume II, Maulana Abdul Haqq, Dar al-Ulum, Deoband.

Rizvi, S.S.A., 1970, 'The Breakdown of Traditional Society', *The Cambridge History of Islam*, eds. Holt, Lambton, Lewis, Cambridge University Press, Cambridge.

Robertson, Roland, 1989, 'A New perspective on Religion and Secularisation in the Global Context', *Secularisation and Fundamentalism Reconsidered*, ed. Hadden & Shupe, New Era Books, New York.

Robinson, Francis, 1975, *Separatism Amongst Indian Muslims*, Cambridge University Press, Cambridge.

Robinson, Francis, 1984, 'The *Ulema* of Farangi Mahall and Their *Adab*', Moral Conduct and Authority: *The Place of Adab in South Asian Islam*, University of California, Berkeley.

Robinson, Francis, 1988, 'Varieties of South Asian Islam', *Research Papers in Ethnic Relations*, no.8, Centre for Research in Ethnic Relations, University of Warwick.

Rosenthal, Erwin, 1948, 'Some Aspects of Islamic Political Thought', *Islamic Culture* 22, January.

Rosenthal, Erwin, 1958, *Political Thought in Mediaeval Islam*, Cambridge University Press, Cambridge.

Rosenthal, Erwin, 1965, *Islam in the Modern National State*, Cambridge University Press, Cambridge.

Ruthwen, Malise, 1990, *A Satanic Affair - Salman Rushdie and the Rage of Islam*, Chatto & Windus, London.

Sahgal, G. & Yuval-Davis, N., 1992, 'Introduction: Fundamentalism, Multiculturalism, and Women in Religion', *Refusing Holy Orders*, Virago, London.

Said, Edward, 1985, *Orientalism*, Penguin, London.

Said, Hakim Muhammad, 1982, 'The Islamic Community', *Hamdard Islamicus*, Vol.5, no.2, pp.33-44, Summer.

Sanneh, L.O., ND, 'The Muslim Community in Britain: The Religious Factor in British Immigration', Unpublished Paper.

Sarwar, Ghulam, 1987, *Islam: Belief and Teachings*, The Muslim Educational Trust, London.

Sayeed, Khalid, 1968, *Pakistan, The Formative Phase, 1857-1948*, Oxford University Press, Oxford.

Sayyid, A.R., 1985, 'Ideal and Reality in the Observance of Moharrum: A Behavioural Interpretation', ed. Ahmad, Imtiaz, *Ritual and Religion among Muslims of the Subcontinent*, Vanguard Books, Lahore.

Schiffauer, Werner, 1988, 'Migration and Religiousness', *The New Islamic Presence in Western Europe*, ed. Gerholm,Tomas & Lithman, Yngve, George, Mansell, London.

Sharif, R., 1985, 'Interviews With Young Muslim Women of Pakistani Origin', *Muslims in Europe*, No.27, September, ed. Nielsen, Jurgen, Centre for the Study of Islam and Christian/Muslim Relations, Selly Oak, Birmingham.

Shaw, Alison, 1988, *A Pakistani Community in Oxford*, Blackwell, Oxford.

Shenkar, Barry, 1986, *Intentional Communities - Ideology and Alienation in Communal Societies*, Routledge and Kegan Paul, London.

-317-

Shepherd, D. & Harrison, S., 1975, 'Islam in Preston', 2nd Edition, *Preston Curriculum Development Centre*, Preston.

Silverstone, Daniel, 1978, 'The Bengali Community in Tower Hamlets', Research and Development, *Social Services Departmental Report*, Tower Hamlets.

Smith, Cantwell W., 1946, *Modern Islam in India*, Minerva, Lahore.

Smith, Cantwell W., 1957, *Islam in Modern History*, Penguin, London.

Smith, Donald Eugene, 1963, *India As A Secular State*, Princeton University, Princeton.

Somervell, D.C., 1960, *A Study of History - Abridgement of Vol.I-VI* by Toynbee, Arnold, Issued under the auspices of the Royal Institute of International Affairs, Oxford University Press, Oxford.

Stein, Maurice Robert, 1961, *The Eclipse of Community: An Interpretation of American Studies*, Princeton University Press, Princeton.

Tagavi, Jiman A., 1980, *A Comparative Analysis of Community in Western and Islamic Political Thought*, PhD, The State University of New Jersey, U.S.A.

Tamadonfar, Mehran, 1986, *The Islamic Polity and Political Leadership: A Conceptual and Theoretical Assessment*, PhD, University of Colorado, U.S.A.

Taylor, Monica & Hegarty, Seamus, 1987, *The Best of Both Worlds*, Nfer Nelson, Newcastle-Upon-Tyne.

Titus, Murray, 1979, *Indian Islam - A Religious History of Islam in India*, Munshiram Mandiharial, New Delhi.

Tonnies, Ferdinand, 1963, *Community and Society*, trs. & ed. Loomis, Charles, Harper & Row, New York.

UK Islamic Mission, ND, *The UK Islamic Mission: An Introduction*, UKIM, London.

UK Islamic Mission, 1988, *Twenty-Fifth Annual Report*, UKIM, London.

UK Islamic Mission, 1992, *Twenty-Ninth Annual Report*, UKIM, London.

Vida, G. Levi Della, 1987, 'Umaiyads', *First Encyclopaedia of Islam 1913-1936*, 2nd Edition, Vol.VIII, eds. Houtsma, Wensinck, et al., A.J.Brill, Leiden.

Voll, John, 1983, 'Renewal and Reform in Islamic History', *Voices of Resurgent Islam*, ed. Esposito, John L., Oxford University Press, Oxford.

Von Grunebaum, G.E., 1970, *Classical Islam: A History, 600AD-1258AD*, Aldine, Chicago.

Von Schwerin, Graeffin, 1985, 'Saint Worship in India Islam', *Ritual and Religion Amongst Muslims in the Subcontinent*, Ahmad, Imtiaz, Vanguard Books, Lahore.

Wallman, Sandra, 1986, 'Ethnicity and the Boundary Process in Context', *Theories of Race and Ethnic Relations*, eds. Rex, John & Mason, David, Cambridge University Press, Cambridge.

Ward, David, 1989, 'Girls want in from the Cold', *The Guardian*, 31st January.

Watt, W. Montgomery, 1961, *Islam and the Integration of Society*, Routledge and Kegan Paul, London.

Watt, W. Montgomery, 1968, *Islamic Political Thought*, Islamic Surveys 6, Edinburgh University Press, Edinburgh.

Watt, W. Montgomery, 1968a, *What is Islam?*, Longmans, London.

Watt, W. Montgomery, 1972, *Muhammad at Medina*, Clarendon Press, Oxford.

Watt, W. Montgomery, 1973, *The Formative Period of Islamic Thought*, University of Edinburgh, Edinburgh.

Watt, W. Montgomery, 1988, *Fundamentalism and Modernity*, Routledge, London.

Wentworth, William, 1989, 'A Dialectical Conception of Religion and Religious Movements in Modern Society', *Secularisation and Fundamentalism Reconsidered: Religion and Political Order*, Vol.III, ed. Hadden & Shupe, New Era Books, New York.

Werbner, Pnina, 1981, 'Manchester Pakistanis: Lifestyles, Ritual and the Making of Social Distinctions', *New Community*, 9:2.

Werbner, Pnina, 1987, 'Taking and Giving: Working Women and Female Bonds in a Pakistani Immigrant Neighbourhood', Manchester University.

Werbner, Pnina, 1987, 'The Fiction of Unity in Ethnic Politics: Aspects of Representation and the State among British Pakistanis', *Black and Ethnic Leadership in Britain: The Cultural Dimensions of Political Action*, eds. Werbner, Pnina & Anwar, Muhammad, Routledge, London.

Werbner, Pnina, 1990, 'Stamping the Earth with the Name of Allah: Zikr and the Sacralising of Space Among British Muslims', unpublished paper, University of Manchester.

Whyte, Alison, 1989, 'Flying in the Face of Tradition', *The Guardian*, 25th July.

Williams, John Alden, 1971, *The Themes of Islamic Civilisation*, University of Berkeley Press, California.

Wirth, Louis, 1938, 'Urbanism as a Way of Life', American Journal of Sociology, 44, July, Reprinted in *Cities and Society*, eds. Hatt, Paul & Reiss, Albert, The Free Press, Illinois.

Wilson, Brian, 1969, *Religion in a Secular Society*, Penguin, London.

Yaseen, Moeen, 1992, Islamic Schools Trust, 'Islam and the Educational Systems of Europe', Paper presented at the *Conference on Islam in a Changing Europe*, 9th-11th September, Bradford University.

Zakaria, Rafiq, 1988, *The Struggle Within Islam: The Conflict Between Religion and Politics*, Penguin, London.

Zubaida, Sammi, 1987, 'The Quest for the Islamic State: Islamic Fundamentalism in Egypt and Iran', *Studies in Religious Fundamentalism*, ed. Caplan, Lionel, MacMillan, London.

Department of Theology and Religious Studies
University of Leeds

Community Religions Project Research Papers
(New Series)

1.   'Community Religions' at the University of Leeds.
        Kim Knott, 1984.

2.   A report on Hinduism in Britain.
        Ursula King, 1984.

3.   Religion and identity and the study of ethnic minority religions.
        Kim Knott, 1984.

4.   A report on Afro-Caribbean Christianity in Britain.
        Vanessa Howard, 1987.

5.   The role of the Polish Catholic church in the Polish community of the U.K:
        a study in ethnic identity and religion.
        Joanna Marzec, 1988.

6.   The Greek Orthodox community in Leeds.
        Katherine Kotsoni, 1990.

7.   The role of religious studies in understanding the ethnic experience.
        Kim Knott, 1992.

8.   The religious beliefs and practices of Hindus in Derby.
        Judith Law, 1991.

9.   The religious beliefs and practices of the Vietnamese community in Britain.
        Judith Law, 1991.

10.   Muslims in Leeds.
        Ron Geaves, 1995.

11.   The changing character of the religions of the ethnic minorities of Asian
        origin in Britain: final report of a Leverhulme Project.
        Kim Knott, 1992.

12.   The function, education and influence of the 'Ulama in Bradford's Muslim
        communities.
        Philip Lewis, 1996 (forthcoming)